MW00639145

@Anna-wood-69

When Christians reflect on the gospel, their attention is rightly drawn to the cross and empty tomb. But is this it? Or is there much more to the story? In a ground-breaking work, Fesko reminds us that the great news of this gospel message is rooted in eternity, whereby a covenant was made between the persons of the Trinity in order to redeem sinners like you and me. Though it has sometimes been a forgotten doctrine of the Reformed faith, Fesko breaks the silence, retrieving the covenant of redemption afresh for a new generation. Undoubtedly, no theologian can afford to pass by this historical, exegetical, and theological mosaic.

Matthew Barrett
Tutor of Systematic Theology and Church History,
Oak Hill Theological College, London

The good news of the gospel depends on that word of grace being divine and, thus, eternal news. John Fesko here helps us retrieve the covenant of redemption, a doctrine meant to alert us to the roots of God's mercy in the life of God's inner bliss in eternity past. The volume shows historical care, exegetical soundness, and doctrinal wisdom. I commend it heartily as a wonderful entryway to considering this most profound facet of the Christian confession.

Michael Allen
Associate Professor of Systematic and Historical Theology,
Dean of Students, Reformed Theological Seminary, Orlando, Florida

There are few doctrines of greater importance to the classic Reformed system and of less interest in recent generations than the covenant of redemption. John Fesko remedies that here. Besides demonstrating the exegetical warrant, he displays the vitality and richness of the covenant of redemption for other doctrines – not least, the Trinity. In both method and substance, this is an exemplary work that will edify as well as inform.

Michael Horton
J. Gresham Machen Professor of Systematic Theology and Apologetics,
Westminster Seminary California, Escondido, California

At the height of Reformed theological development, most Reformed authors treated the intra-trinitarian covenant of redemption as the foundation for the historical convent of grace. They argued that this distinction secured the gracious character of the gospel. However, this distinction has virtually disappeared from Reformed literature today. John Fesko pursues "theological retrieval," by engaging in Scripture exegesis, historical reflection, and interaction with modern trends in theology. Fesko admirably puts the covenant of redemption back in its rightful place in Reformed theology.

RYAN M. MCGRAW
Associate Professor of Systematic Theology,
Greenville Presbyterian Theological Seminary, Greenville, South Carolina

Some books today exegete the shining truths of the Holy Scriptures, others mine the treasures of Reformed orthodoxy, and yet others interact with influential theologians of the modern era. This book is one of the few that does all three, and does them well. Dr Fesko's fulsome treatment of the *pactum salutis* between God and the Mediator – a subject seldom explored in depth – is sure to stimulate discussion about a subject that is crucial for a full-orbed faith in Him whom God has sent (John 6:29).

JOEL R. BEEKE
President, Puritan Reformed Theological Seminary,
Grand Rapids, Michigan

THE TRINITY AND THE COVENANT OF REDEMPTION

J. V. FESKO

MENTOR

hardback ISBN 978-1-78191-765-7
epub ISBN 978-1-78191-799-2
Mobi ISBN 978-1-78191-800-5

10 9 8 7 6 5 4 3 2 1

Published in 2016
in the
Mentor Imprint
by
Christian Focus Publications Ltd,
Geanies House, Fearn, Ross-shire,
IV20 1TW, Great Britain.

www.christianfocus.com

Cover design
by
Daniel van Straaten

Printed
by
Bell & Bain, Glasgow

To my good friend,
David Jacks

CONTENTS

PART III
Dogmatic Construction

ABBREVIATIONS

*	Author's translation
AB	Anchor Bible
ANF	Ante-Nicene Fathers
AOTC	Apollos Old Testament Commentary
ATR	*Anglican Theological Review*
BAGD	Bauer Arndt Gingrich and Danker, *Greek-English Lexicon*
BBR	*Bulletin for Biblical Research*
BCOTWS	Baker Commentary on the Old Testament Wisdom Series
BDB	Brown, Driver, Briggs, *Hebrew Lexicon*
BECNT	Baker Exegetical Commentary on the New Testament
Bib	*Biblica*
BNTC	Black's New Testament Commentary
ca.	*circa* ('about')
CBQ	*Catholic Biblical Quarterly*
CD	Karl Barth, *Church Dogmatics*
CH	*Church History*
chp.	Chapter
Cf.	*confer* ('compare')
CNTC	Calvin's New Testament Commentaries
CTJ	*Calvin Theological Journal*
CTS	*Calvin Translation Society*
comm.	exegetical comment on
esp.	Especially
e.g.	*exempli gratia* ('for example')
EBC	Expositor's Bible Commentary
ExpT	*Expository Times*

ff.	Following
fol.	Folio
HALOT	*Hebrew and Aramaic Lexicon of the Old Testament*
ICC	International Critical Commentary
i.e.	*id est* ('that is')
IJST	*International Journal of Systematic Theology*
JBL	*Journal of Biblical Literature*
JETS	*Journal of the Evangelical Theological Society*
JPSTC	Jewish Publication Society Torah Commentary
JSNT	*Journal for the Study of the New Testament*
JSOT	*Journal for the Study of the Old Testament*
JTS	*Journal of Theological Studies*
KJV	King James Version
LCC	Library of Christian Classics
LW	Luther's Works
LXX	Septuagint
MAJT	*Mid-America Journal of Theology*
Misc.	Miscellany
MT	Masoretic Text
NAS	New American Standard Version
NIB	New Interpreter's Bible
NICNT	New International Commentary on the New Testament
NICOT	New International Commentary on the Old Testament
NIGTC	New International Greek Testament Commentary
NIV	New International Version
NIVAC	New International Version Application Commentary
NKJ	New King James Version

NLT	New Living Translation
NLT-SE	New Living Translation – Second Edition
NPNF[1]	Nicene Post-Nicene Fathers, first series
NPNF[2]	Nicene Post-Nicene Fathers, second series
NRSV	New Revised Standard Version
NTS	*New Testament Studies*
OTL	Old Testament Library
passim	'at various places'
PNTC	Pillar New Testament Commentary
PRJ	*Puritan Reformed Journal*
PTR	*Princeton Theological Review*
re.	Regarding
RSV	Revised Standard Version
serm.	Sermon
SJT	*Scottish Journal of Theology*
s.v.	*sub verbo* ('under the word')
TNIV	Today's New International Version
TOTC	Tyndale Old Testament Commentary
TynB	*Tyndale Bulletin*
VT	*Vetus Testamentum*
WBC	Word Biblical Commentary
WCF	Westminster Confession of Faith
WJE	Works of Jonathan Edwards
WLC	Westminster Larger Catechism
WSC	Westminster Shorter Catechism
WTJ	*Westminster Theological Journal*
ZECNT	Zondervan Exegetical Commentary on the New Testament

ACKNOWLEDGEMENTS

WRITING this book has been one of my life's greatest rewards. I have learned so much by immersing myself in the study of the doctrine of the covenant of redemption. In some respects I felt as though I was scaling a grand peak – a technical climb fraught with many challenging obstacles. Were it not for the assistance of many friends and colleagues, I would have undoubtedly plummeted to the bottom. A number of friends and colleagues read through earlier drafts of this project. Thanks are due to Matthew Barrett and Ryan McGraw. I am especially thankful to Mike Allen for taking the time to read through an early draft and offer many helpful comments. My colleagues at Westminster Seminary California (WSC) were also a great source of encouragement. Mike Horton read through several chapters and offered helpful critique. David VanDrunen meticulously worked through my manuscript and offered numerous corrections and posed challenging questions that assisted me in refining and clarifying many points. WSC alumnus, Brian Hecker, has also offered me significant assistance. Not only did he read through the manuscript twice, but he offered many helpful comments and identified some key sources that greatly assisted me in my research. I owe a great deal of thanks to these individuals – thank you for your help and friendship. I'm also grateful to the students in my Fall 2014 elective on the covenant of redemption. You made coming to class a joy. I truly looked forward to coming to class to teach on this sublime doctrine. You also asked many engaging questions, which helped me refine the materials in this book.

My family has also been a great source of encouragement. Thanks to my lads, Val and Rob, and to my wee lass, Carmen. You let me work on this project when I know it would have been a lot more entertaining having me read *The Hobbit* to you. And thank you to my wife, Anneke. Please forgive me for keeping you up at night and for waking you up early in the morning. I still have my doubts, mind you, that you can hear the small wheels turning in my mind. I'll also do a better job ensuring that my alarm isn't set to go off so loudly. If it's any consolation, it also scares me to death. Yikes! I'm just thankful for your love and encouragement, especially when I face obstacles. Anneke, you bring out the best in me, and you challenge me to be a better husband, man, and student of Scripture.

I dedicate this book to my long-time friend, David Jacks. I first met David when we were both in seminary. We immediately hit it off given our mutual appreciation of Reformed theology and the doctrines of grace. We regularly talked about theology on our lunch breaks, started the Dead Theologians Society, much to the displeasure of many of the faculty, and found ourselves in the President's office in a heap of trouble because we wanted to start a Reformed organization on campus. But that's a story for another day. Needless to say, I have always appreciated your friendship, David. You have always been a good friend and extended your hospitality in times of joy and turmoil. You mean what you say, and say what you mean, and that's a rare quality to find in a man. And I know that if I needed someone to charge the gates of hell with a squirt gun, you'd be right beside me. Blessedly, you know that one greater than us both has already conquered sin and death, so there's no need for squirt gun charges. I pray the Lord's blessings upon you and your ministry to Christ's church. And I pray, together, that we would always seek shelter beneath the mighty wings of our faithful covenant surety, Jesus Christ.

PREFACE

THE covenant of redemption, the pre-temporal intra-trinitarian agreement to plan and execute the redemption of the elect, was once a faithful sentry on the ramparts of the Reformed tradition, but in recent years its abilities have been questioned, criticized, and even rejected. I must admit that the first time I read about the doctrine it struck me as a bit arcane and speculative. How can we possibly know what the triune God was doing in eternity before the foundations of the world? I scrutinized the doctrine and was convinced of its validity, but it would be a few years before I would truly appreciate and study the doctrine with great interest. As I was doing research on the doctrine of union with Christ, I was surprised by how often the covenant of redemption was employed in the latter half of the seventeenth century.

The more I researched the more I realized how little literature there was on the doctrine. There have been very few monographs dedicated specifically to the covenant of redemption – only three in the last 325-plus years. I also noted that the doctrine was quite common from the seventeenth century until the twentieth century. But in the twentieth century Reformed theologians rejected it. Theologians once advocated three covenants (redemption, works, and grace) but it is now common to find people only speaking of one, the covenant of grace. As I surveyed this trend, I also discovered how few monographs there are specifically on the covenant of works. Thus far, I have only found one, John Colquhoun's *Treatise on the Covenant of Works* (1821). In my future research, I may uncover other books on the subject. As common as it was in classic Reformed theology, I think numerous theologians have been critical of the doctrine in the contemporary period for a host of reasons. My hope is to remedy this lacuna on these two vital doctrines, the covenants of redemption and works.

My original plan was to write a one-volume comprehensive treatment of the covenant of redemption, but the manuscript grew ungainly and, in a very un-Solomon like manner, I decided to divide it. I offer a detailed history of the doctrine in *The Covenant of Redemption: Origins, Development, and Reception* (Vandenhoeck & Ruprecht, 2016). Readers interested in the history of the doctrine should consult that work. I present a summary of my historical findings in Part I of this study. This book focuses upon a systematic statement of the doctrine.

In my grand scheme, this book constitutes the first of a three-volume covenant theology, with sequel volumes on the covenants of works and grace. I firmly believe that, as suspicious as many people are of it, there are nevertheless tremendous benefits and insights in classic Reformed covenant theology. Even though twentieth-century Reformed theologians such as Murray, Schilder, and Hoeksema either rejected or redefined the covenant of redemption and outright rejected the covenant of works, I remain unpersuaded by their arguments.

Reformed Orthodoxy and classic covenant theology still have much to offer. The threefold covenant scheme (redemption, works, and grace) offers the best explanation of the biblical data. God willing, I aim to continue to defend this claim in forthcoming volumes. For the time being, this is the first installment in proving the viability and orthodoxy of classic Reformed covenant theology. I believe one of the reasons the Reformed church has struggled with matters related to the doctrine of justification is because we have become unfamiliar with key elements in classic covenant theology. Case in point, Christ's identity as covenant surety, a key pillar of the covenant of redemption, provides important data regarding the material cause of justification. The covenant of redemption also delivers important information regarding the priority of the forensic to the transformative benefits in redemption. Or, in more technical terms, the covenant of redemption explains why justification precedes sanctification in the *ordo salutis* (order of salvation). These are not the only issues I address in this book, as the covenant of redemption touches upon many other doctrines. In many respects, I believe that the entire system of doctrine lies in seminal form within the covenant of redemption. This makes explaining and constructing the doctrine very challenging but nevertheless very rewarding.

There are several things to note. First, I use the English Standard Version for Scripture quotations, unless otherwise noted by an asterisk (*). All Scripture quotations with an asterisk are my own translations. Second, all quoted confessions and catechisms, unless otherwise noted, come from Jaroslav Pelikan and Valerie Hotchkiss, eds., *Creeds and Confessions of Faith in the Christian Tradition*, 3 vols. (New Haven: Yale University Press, 2003). All translations are mine unless otherwise noted. Third, I have entered into dialogue with contemporary theology when necessary. One of the Reformed church's failings, I believe, is that she has not engaged recent contemporary theology. Charles Hodge, B. B. Warfield, J. Gresham Machen, Geerhardus Vos, and Herman Bavinck brought classic Reformed theology to the church's public square. It seems to me that in the latter half of the twentieth century, the Reformed church became insular and preoccupied with internecine skirmishes. While people were debating the length of the days of creation, Geneva was burning. The New Perspective on Paul was making deleterious inroads into the Reformed church. Times of small uncivil wars replaced the days of Machen's *Christianity and Liberalism.* The lion of Princeton no longer roared; instead whispers of higher criticism skulked out of Reformed academia. All is not lost and there are, I believe, signs of life. A new generation of Reformed theologians has taken up the cause of bringing Reformed Orthodoxy and covenant theology back to the church's public square. My hope is to contribute in some small way to this ongoing effort – to turn our introspective gaze away from ourselves and once again extraspectively look to the broader church and even the outside world.

My aim is to retrieve and recover classic Reformed covenant theology for the church. My grandfather once said, 'You can't give away what you don't own.' Each generation must appropriate the truth and pass it on to subsequent generations. The moment we believe that we can merely assume key doctrinal truths is the moment that we become vulnerable to forgetting and losing them. My hope and prayer, therefore, is that the church would rediscover the wonder, beauty, and glory of classic Reformed covenant theology. And in this case, I hope that this book on the covenant of redemption is but one small step in having a better understanding of God's covenants. For in them we find life, redemption, and eternal joy – we glorify our triune Lord and enjoy Him forever.

~: PART I :~

Historical Origins and Development

INTRODUCTION

ANY study of doctrine that desires to make a useful contribution to the ongoing discussion, especially one interested in theological retrieval, must begin with a study of the history of the doctrine. Thus, Part I, chapter 1, offers a brief overview of the history of the doctrine of the *pactum salutis* and touches upon the origins of the doctrine and its subsequent reception in the Reformed tradition. From there the overview delves into eight issues that mark the development of the doctrine. First, what are the various exegetical arguments in favor of the doctrine? Second, under what subject should the *pactum* be treated, theology (proper) or christology? Third, how do theologians maintain the unity and plurality of the Godhead, the unity of substance and will, yet the plurality of persons, Father, Son, and Holy Spirit? Does the covenant of redemption compromise the unity of the Trinity? Fourth, in what ways do theologians connect the *pactum* and revelation?

Part I, chapter 2 continues the brief survey of the development of the doctrine by treating four more key issues. First, predestination and the *pactum* lie close at hand. Most advocates of the doctrine locate predestination within the context of the covenant of redemption. If this is so, are contemporary criticisms that predestination is an abstract Christ-less choice accurate?

Second, what is the relationship between justification, imputation, and the *pactum salutis*? In various formulations theologians address the issue of the timing of justification. Third, how does the *ordo salutis* relate to the covenant of redemption? Theologians were keen on preserving the priority of God's grace to human activity in redemption, and did so by means of the *pactum*. And, fourth, how do proponents of the doctrine incorporate the concept of God's love in the *pactum*? A survey of these eight issues will set the stage for recovery of the *pactum salutis*.

~:1:~

Origins, Reception, and Development: Exegesis, Models, Trinity, and Revelation

Introduction

The effort to recover the doctrine of the covenant of redemption must begin with a reconnaissance of its origins, development, and reception. As the doctrine develops, what debates, issues, and formulations arise? This chapter addresses, therefore, the origins and reception of the doctrine, and then succinctly surveys issues that appear in various formulations.[1] First, exegetical arguments deserve consideration. What texts do theologians cite in support of the doctrine? Second, there are two chief models of the doctrine: the christological and trinitarian formulations. These different versions do not represent trinitarian and sub-trinitarian formulations but a difference of opinion regarding placement of the doctrine. Is the doctrine part

1. I present a fuller account and interaction with primary and secondary literature in J. V. Fesko, *The Covenant of Redemption: Origins, Development, and Reception* (Göttingen: Vandenhoeck & Ruprecht, 2016).

of theology (proper) or christology? Third, how do theologians historically explain how the persons of the Godhead enter into an agreement? If the triune God shares a common will, how can individual members of the Trinity enter into a covenant, which implies agreement between two different wills? How do proponents of the doctrine negotiate this potential obstacle? Fourth, in what way does the *pactum* establish the necessity of revelation? Is the *pactum* the illegitimate fruit of gross speculation into the inner workings of the triune God? Or is it the legitimate offspring of revelation and exegesis? Moreover, in what way does the human capacity for revelation find its genesis in the covenant of redemption? Briefly surveying these four issues will provide the initial step in setting the stage for a recovery of the doctrine of the *pactum salutis*.

Origins and reception

Origins of the doctrine

At first glance the *pactum salutis* seems to appear *de novo* on the stage of church history. As a matter of history, the doctrine does not explicitly appear until the middle of the seventeenth century. Does its late birth signal its novelty and hence strike at its veracity? Was it born under a dark star of theological innovation or in the sunlight of scriptural exegesis? There are a host of factors that account for the doctrine's origins, but two noteworthy facts commend attention: refined exegesis and old questions.[2] Ever since Jerome (ca. 347-420) translated the Bible, theologians read and studied the Bible in Latin. To all intents and purposes, the Latin Vulgate was the exegetical and theological standard. The Protestant

2. For a historical survey of the origins of the doctrine, see Richard A. Muller, 'Toward the *Pactum Salutis*: Locating the Origins of a Concept,' *MAJT* 18 (2007): 11-65.

Reformation radically changed the nature of exegesis and theology. Injected with a healthy dose of Renaissance humanism and the desire to recover ancient sources, Protestant theologians engaged the biblical text in its original languages, Hebrew and Greek.

As useful as vernacular translations of the Scriptures are, readers ultimately gaze upon the bride through a veil. The receptor language inevitably conceals some of the original text's finer points. This observation was not lost on Theodore Beza (1519-1605), who expended much of his ministerial labors engaged in textual criticism, translation, and the study of the Greek New Testament. Beza encountered Jerome's translation of Luke 22:29, 'And I appoint unto you a kingdom, as my Father appointed unto me a kingdom.'[3] Beza noted that Jerome used the term *dispono* ('appoint') to translate the Greek term διατίθεμαι ('covenant'), which in his judgment was incorrect. Hence Beza translated the verse: 'Ego igitur paciscor vobis, prout pactus est mihi Pater meus, regnum' ('I therefore covenant to you, just as my Father covenanted to me, a kingdom').[4] Beza dropped this exegetical pebble into the theological pond and it rippled well into the seventeenth century. Theologians who once spoke of Christ's appointment as mediator now believed that Christ was *covenantally* appointed. Exegesis, not speculation, drove the impulse to coordinate the doctrine of the covenant with Christ's appointment.

A second reason that accounts for the *pactum's* origins is that the doctrine was ultimately rooted in ancient theological questions and exegesis. Dutch Reformed theologian Herman Witsius (1636-1708) defended the doctrine's antiquity. Witsius

3. Muller, 'Toward the *Pactum Salutis*,' 39-40.

4. Theodore Beza, *Iesu Christi D. N. Novum Testamentum, Graece & Latine Theodoro Beza Interprete* (n. p.: Henricus Stephanus, 1567), ad loc. Luke 22:29 (fol. 130v); Muller, 'Toward the *Pactum Salutis*,' 40.

exegetically appealed to Zechariah 6:13 as a text that taught the doctrine: 'And there shall be a priest on his throne, and the counsel of peace shall be between them both.' Witsius believed that this text spoke of a covenant between the Father and the Son, and he supported this conclusion by appealing to Jerome's interpretation.[5] Jerome explained that the 'counsel of peace' was between the Father and Son, namely, for the Son to come to do His Father's will.[6] Church fathers such as Jerome, therefore, hinted at the doctrine in their exegesis, but the issue also substantively arose when theologians sought to explain the manner in which the Son submitted to His Father's will.

How could the Son, who was fully God, submit to and obey His Father's will? Seventeenth-century theologians such as Gisbert Voetius (1589-1676) pondered this question and sought answers from antiquity. In his disputation on Christ's merit, Voetius appeals to Augustine (354-430) to explain the nature of the Son's submission. He rejects the opinions of Chrysostom (ca. 349-407), who maintained that Christ never really received a command from His Father. According to Chrysostom, any hint that the Son obeyed His Father's command merely suggested agreement with His Father, not submission.[7] Instead, Voetius mined the insights of Augustine

5. Herman Witsius, *Economy of the Covenants Between God and Man: Comprehending a Complete Body of Divinity*, 2 vols., trans. William Crookshank (1822; Escondido: Den Dulk Foundation, 1990), II.ii.8; idem, *Sacred Dissertations, on What is Commonly Called the Apostles' Creed*, 2 vols., trans. Donald Fraser (1823; Escondido: Den Dulk Foundation, 1993), I:323-24.

6. Jerome, *Commentarii in Zachariam*, in *Patrologia Latina*, ed. J. P. Migne, vol. 25 (Paris: 1845), 1458B-C; cf. Byunghoon Woo, 'The *Pactum Salutis* in the Theologies of Witsius, Owen, Dickson, Goodwin, and Cocceius,' (Ph.D. Diss., Calvin Theological Seminary, 2015), 45, 63-65, 68-70.

7. Gisbert Voetius, 'Problematum De Merito Christi, Pars Tetria,' in *Selectarum Disputationum Theologicarum*, vol. 2 (Ultrajecti: apud Johannem à Waesberge, 1655), 266; cf. John Chrysostom, *Homilies on St. John*, serm. LX.ii, in NPNF 14:218.

and his comments on Christ's statement: 'The Father is greater than I' (John 14:28). Augustine stressed the ontological equality of Father and Son but also underscored the Son's status as a servant. To support his claim, Augustine appealed to Philippians 2:8-9 and Paul's twofold designation of the Son in the form of God and the form of a servant. Augustine does not employ the terms, but he was distinguishing between the ontological and economic aspects of the Son's person and work.[8] Voetius drew upon this insight to explain how Christ was subject to the law as mediator and surety, roles which were established in the covenant between the Father and Son.[9]

In terms of the origins of the doctrine, novelty is the wrong concept to invoke when describing the genesis of the *pactum salutis*. Novelty implies an *ex nihilo* birth – there was nothing and now there is something. The more accurate term to employ is *refine* or *refocus*. Reformed theologians looked upon the Son's appointment as mediator, a scriptural teaching that no one would deny, and refined the exegesis of a number of the texts associated with the idea. They looked through the lens of the original languages and brought the Christ's appointment into sharper focus. Exegesis of the Greek text crystallized the blurry edges of the biblical portrait previously viewed through the veil of Jerome's Vulgate. Moreover, Reformed theologians applied their refined exegesis to ancient questions in order to maintain the full divinity of the Son while also acknowledging His submission and obedience to His Father's will.

Reception

The doctrine of the covenant of redemption began with small exegetical refinements and observations, which eventually flowered into its full articulation and reception. Some of the earliest

8. Augustine, *On the Holy Trinity*, I.vii, in NPNF 3:24.

9. Voetius, 'Problematum De Merito Christi,' 266.

expressions of an intra-trinitarian covenant appear in Caspar Olevianus (1536-87) and even Martin Luther (1483-1546).[10] In the early seventeenth century Jacob Arminius (1560-1609) made explicit reference to a covenant between the Father and the Son.[11] Substantively, the doctrine appears in Reformation confessional documents, which describe the Father's appointment of the Son as mediator.[12] But Scottish theologian David Dickson (1583-1662) offered the first explicit statement and exposition of the doctrine at the General Assembly of the Scottish Kirk in 1638. Dickson outlined his speech and stated that he would first explain the errors of Arminianism and then 'lay out our doctrine.'[13]

Rehearsing the main points of disagreement between Remonstrant and Reformed theology, Dickson identified and engaged the subjects of election, the efficacy of Christ's satisfaction, the nature of free will, and the doctrine of perseverance.[14] But when he sought to identify the chief Remonstrant failing, he argued that they were unfamiliar with the 'Covenant of redemption betwixt God and Christ.' Dickson commented that they should have been familiar with the doctrine, seeing that 'they pointed at it themselves,' which was a likely reference to Arminius and his early statements about it.[15] Dickson explained the difference between the covenant

---

10. Martin Luther, *Galatians – 1519*, comm. Gal. 5:18, LW 27:267-68; Muller 'Toward the *Pactum Salutis*,' 25; Lyle D. Bierma, *German Calvinism in the Confession Ages: The Covenant Theology of Caspar Olevianus* (Grand Rapids: Baker, 1996), 107-12.

11. Jacob Arminius, 'The Priesthood of Christ,' in *The Works of James Arminius*, 3 vols. (1825-75; Grand Rapids: Baker, 1996), I:416.

12. E.g., Belgic Confession, XXVI.

13. David Dickson, 'Arminianism Discussed,' in *Records of the Kirk of Scotland, containing the Acts and Proceedings of the General Assemblies, from the Year 1638 Downwards*, ed. Alexander Peterkin (Edinburgh: Peter Brown, 1845), 156.

14. Dickson, 'Arminianism Discussed,' 156-57.

15. Dickson, 'Arminianism Discussed,' 157.

of redemption, which was a covenant between God and Christ, and the covenant of salvation (or grace), which was between God and man.[16] Dickson invoked the doctrine of the covenant of redemption because he believed that the inviolability of the covenant of grace was secured in it – it was a bulwark against failure.

At the close of his speech Dickson listed five theses to explain how the covenant of redemption undergirds the covenant of grace. First, there is a covenant between God and Christ, which  is the ground of all that God does to redeem fallen man. Second, in the covenant of redemption the elect were designed in terms of their name and number as well as the time in which they would be saved. The election of certain individuals was determined in the covenant of redemption. Third, the price of redemption was established, how Christ would be 'holden captive of death, &tc.' Fourth, the mediator was ensured of His success and the elect were given to Him, and their salvation was placed in His hand. Fifth, no one would truly take God's grace for granted or be robbed of the assurance of salvation given God's wise dispensation of the gospel, the fruit of the covenant of redemption.[17]

Soon after Dickson's speech churches officially codified the doctrine. There are arguably hints of the doctrine in the Westminster Standards, as a number of proponents of the *pactum* were members of the Westminster Assembly including: Samuel Rutherford (1600-61), Thomas Goodwin (1600-80), and Obadiah Sedgwick (ca. 1600-58).[18] The Confession, for example,

16. Dickson, 'Arminianism Discussed,' 157.

17. Dickson, 'Arminianism Discussed,' 158.

18. Samuel Rutherford, *The Covenant of Life Opened, or, a Treatise of the Covenant of Grace* (Edinburgh: Robert Brown, 1654), II.vi (pp. 290-302); Thomas Goodwin, *Christ the Mediator*, in *The Works of Thomas Goodwin*, vol. 5 (1861-66; Eureka: Tanski Publications, 1996), I.vii-viii (pp. 20-27); Obadiah Sedgwick, *The Bowels of Tender Mercy Sealed in the Everlasting Covenant* (London: Adoniram Byfield, 1661), I.i.2 (pp. 3-4).

speaks of Christ's appointment as mediator in terms evocative of the covenant of redemption.[19] Moreover, commentators have noted the tensions between several statements and definitions within the Standards. With whom did God make the covenant of grace? The Standards offer two slightly different answers. Larger Catechism q. 31 states that the covenant of grace is made between Christ and His seed, but the Confession states that it is made only with the elect – there is no mention of Christ.[20] What explains the tension? Perhaps the presence of proponents of the covenant of redemption impacted these statements?

Regardless of the ambiguity, a number of explicit positive statements emerged in the years shortly after the publication of the Westminster Standards. When the Scottish Kirk officially adopted them, they bound a number of brief doctrinal treatises with the Standards. David Dickson and James Durham (1622-58) wrote one of those treatises entitled, *The Sum of Saving Knowledge* (1649). In the *Sum* the authors explicitly affirm and define the doctrine:

> The sum of the Covenant of Redemption is this, God having freely chosen unto life, a certain number of lost mankind, for the glory of his rich Grace did give them before the world began, unto God the Son appointed Redeemer, that upon condition he would humble himself so far as to assume the humane nature of a soul and body, unto personal union with his Divine Nature, and submit himself to the Law as surety for them, and satisfie Justice for them, by giving obedience in their name, even unto the suffering of the cursed death of the Cross, he should ransom and redeem them all from sin and death, and purchase unto them righteousness and eternal life, with all saving graces leading thereunto, to be

19. Westminster Confession, VIII.i.

20. Westminster Confession, VII.iii; cf. Shorter Catechism, q. 20.

> effectually, by means of his own appointment, applied in due time to every one of them.[21]

Even if the Westminster Assembly did not explicitly mention the doctrine, the Church of Scotland believed that it did not contradict the Standards but was entirely compatible with them. In a similar vein, Reformed Congregationalists (1658) and Particular Baptist theologians (1689) adopted modified versions of the Westminster Confession of Faith and explicitly inserted the covenant of redemption.[22] The doctrine also appeared in the Formula Consensus Helvetica (1675), written by Francis Turretin (1623-87) and Johannes Heidegger (1633-98).[23] By the late seventeenth century, the doctrine was a common staple in Reformed theology, officially codified in a number of confessions.

Development and doctrinal issues

Exegesis

Contemporary critics and proponents alike have chided earlier generations of Reformed theologians for erroneous exegesis. They commonly assume that early modern Reformed exegetes mistakenly understood Zechariah 6:13 and deduced the covenant of redemption

---

21. [David Dickson and James Durham], *The Summe of Saving Knoweldge, With the Practical Use Thereof* (Edinburgh: Swintoun and Thomas Brown, n. d.), II.ii; cf. *The Confession of Faith, the Larger and Shorter Catechisms, with the Scripture-proofs at Large: Together with the Sum of Saving Knowledge* (Belfast: James Blow, 1729).

22. *The Savoy Declaration*, VIII.i; and *A Confession of Faith, Put forth by the Elders and Brethren Of Many Congregations of Christians (Baptized upon Profession of their Faith) in London and the Country* (London: John Harris, 1688), VIII.i.

23. Francis Turretin and Johannes Heidegger, 'Formula Consensus Helvetica,' XIII, in A. A. Hodge, *Outlines of Theology* (1860; Edinburgh: Banner of Truth, 1991), Appendix II, 659.

from this one text.[24] But a close engagement with primary sources quickly reveals that the doctrine rests upon a host of different texts. In one sense, there is no one common exegetical path to the doctrine. In what follows, I only touch upon a few of the more frequently cited texts to demonstrate the doctrine's wide exegetical footing.

One of the more regularly cited verses is Luke 22:29, which theologians recognized as a text that reported Christ's covenantal appointment as king.[25] Beside this verse, there were webs of related texts that often appear in support of the doctrine. They rotate around several key themes: David's anointing as king (Pss. 2:7; 110:1; 89:3, 19; 2 Sam. 7:14), Christ's obedience (Ps. 40:8; John 6:38, 57; 10:17-18; Phil. 2:8); imputation (Isa. 53:10-12); Christ's appointment as covenant surety (Heb. 7:22); and predestination (Eph. 1:4; 2 Tim. 1:9). In each of these passages proponents of the doctrine offered careful and at times nuanced exegesis. Second generation reformer, John Calvin (1509-64), argued that Psalm 2:7-8 was proximately about King David's inauguration as Israel's king but that it ultimately pointed forward to Christ's appointment and inauguration.[26] As theologians drilled down into the Hebrew

---

24. See, e.g., Herman Bavinck, *Reformed Dogmatics*, 4 vols. (Grand Rapids: Baker, 2006), III:213; Klaas Schilder, *Heidelbergsche Catechismus*, 3 vols. (Goes: Oosterbaan & Le Cointre, 1947-51), I:383; Herman Hoeksema, *Reformed Dogmatics* (1963; Grand Rapids: Reformed Free Publishing Association, 1985), 286-87; Geerhardus Vos, *Systematiche Theologie: Compendium* (Grand Rapids: 1900), V.8 (p. 76); Louis Berkhof, *Systematic Theology: New Combined Edition* (Grand Rapids: Eerdmans, 1996), 266-67.

25. E.g., Witsius, *Economy of the Covenants*, II.ii.3; Wilhelmus à Brakel, *The Christian's Reasonable Service*, 4 vols., trans. Bartel Elshout (Morgan: Soli Deo Gloria, 1992), I:255; Francis Turretin, *Institutes of Elenctic Theology*, 3 vols., ed. James T. Dennison, Jr., trans. George Musgrave Giger (Phillipsburg: P & R, 1992-97), XII.ii.14; Johannes Cocceius, *Summa Doctrinae de Foedere et Testamento Dei*, in *Opera Omnia*, vol. 7 (Amsterdam: 1701), XIV.xxxiv.2 (p. 238).

26. John Calvin, *Psalms*, Calvin's Commentaries, vol. 4, CTS (rep.; Grand Rapids: Baker, 1993), comm. Ps. 2:7-8 (pp. 17-19).

text, they recognized that there were covenantal elements in Psalm 2:7-8 not previously factored in expositions like Calvin's.

Patrick Gillespie (1617-75), for example, argues that 'today' in Psalm 2:7 does not refer to the eternal generation of the Son, as some commonly argued. Rather, the word 'today' refers to Christ's 'new Sonship for the work of Redemption, whereby he voluntarily became the first born of many brethren, and an obedient Son *even unto death*, Phil. 2:8; and whereby he consented to take a new Covenant-right unto God, *as his Father*, and his God by Covenant, *Heb. 1.5,—I will be to him a father, and he shall be to me a son*.'[27] Gillespie coordinates several texts – he casts a line to the New Testament and exegetically pulls together Christ's appointment, His obedience, and the covenant concept. Gillespie demonstrates that the doctrine of the covenant lies close at hand with the phrase, 'I will tell of the decree.' According to his linguistic analysis, Gillespie argues that term *decree* (חק) comes from a root that originally meant to write, engrave, ordain, appoint, and covenant. He appeals to a number of exegetical authorities to support his conclusion including ancient Targums (paraphrases of the OT) that render the term as *pact* or *covenant*.[28] But Gillespie rests the weight of his argument upon other places in the Old Testament that interchangeably employ the terms *decree* and *covenant* (Jer. 31:35-36; 33:20).[29] Gillespie therefore synchronized these various texts to prove that Psalm 2:7 spoke ultimately of Christ's covenantal appointment as mediator.

A common move for some theologians was to argue that texts that dealt with David's covenantal appointment as king were

27. Patrick Gillespie, *The Ark of the Covenant Opened: Or, a Treatise of the Covenant of Redemption Between God and Christ*, The Second Part (London: Thomas Parkhurst, 1677), 8.

28. Gillespie, *Ark of the Covenant*, 11.

29. Gillespie, *Ark of the Covenant*, 12.

ultimately about Christ. Texts such as 2 Samuel 7:14 had an immediate historical referent and context – God made a promise to David that one of his heirs would reign over Israel. Theologians appealed to the Old Testament's own intra-canonical exegesis of this text to prove that this was a covenantal promise: 'I have made a covenant with my chosen one; I have sworn to David my servant: I will establish your offspring forever, and build your throne for all generations' (Ps. 89:3-4). But they also noted that this covenantal promise ran in two directions: back into eternity and forward into redemptive history. The triune God projected the Father's eternal covenantal activity with the Son into history where it was provisionally revealed in His covenant with David and finally disclosed in its fulfillment in Christ. Edward Fisher (fl. 1627-55), for example, explains: 'The mercies of this Covenant made betwixt Christ and God, under the type of Gods Covenant with *David*, are set forth: *Thou spakest in vision to thy holy one and saidst, I have laid help upon one that is mighty*.'[30] In simpler terms, God's historical covenantal activity has an eternal covenantal source. God reveals the eternal intra-trinitarian covenant in history through His covenant with David and then with Christ.[31]

Another network of cited texts deals with Christ's obedience. Reformed theologians identified the theme of Christ's obedience as numerous others had in previous ages, but they once again coordinated this teaching with the idea of covenant. One commonly cited text is Psalm 40:6-8, 'In sacrifice and offering you have not delighted ... Behold, I have come; in the scroll of the book it is written of me: I delight to do your will, O my

30. Edward Fisher, *The Marrow of Modern Divinity* (London: R. W. for G. Calvert, 1645), 35-36.

31. Similarly Gillespie, *Ark of the Covenant*, 3-8; Charles Hodge, *Romans* (1835; Edinburgh: Banner of Truth, 1989), 162.

God.' Advocates of the *pactum* examined this text from within its original context and its subsequent use in the New Testament (Heb. 10:5). The fact that the New Testament places these words upon Christ's lips means that He spoke them to His Father.[32] Gillespie believed that the counterpart to this statement appeared in Isaiah 53:10, 'Yet it pleased the Lord to bruise him, he hath put him to grief; when thou shalt make his soul an offering for sin.'[33] This collection of texts presents two sides of an intra-trinitarian dialogue: the Father commands the Son (Isa. 53:10) and the Son willingly consents (Ps. 40:6-8; Heb. 10:5).

This brief glimpse at the exegetical strategies that proponents of the doctrine employed reveals that they did not base the doctrine upon one lone text such as Zechariah 6:13. Rather, there were a host of texts and doctrines that constitute the biblical footing for the covenant of redemption. In a sense, no one text serves as the fulcrum for the doctrine. In historic explanations, the *pactum* does not precariously rest upon one passage but lies upon multiple pillars scattered throughout Scripture. Remove one or more pillars and the doctrine never totters because of the other numerous columns bearing its weight.

Chief formulations: theology (proper) or christology?

There are two major formulations of the covenant of redemption: the christological and trinitarian models.[34] Historical analysis reveals that a majority of proponents of the doctrine adhere to the christological model. There are several factors that drive

32. Gillespie, *Ark of the Covenant*, 13-14.

33. Gillespie, *Ark of the Covenant*, 15.

34. Berkouwer employs a similar classification in his historical analysis: *dipleuric* (christological) and *tripleuric* (trinitarian), or christological and pneumatological (G. C. Berkouwer, *Divine Election* [Grand Rapids: Eerdmans, 1960], 170).

this choice. First, proponents recognize that the scriptural data points to interaction exclusively between the Father and Son. All of the scriptural dialogues occur between Father and Son (e.g., Pss. 40:6-8; 22:3; 45:6-7; Isa. 49:4-5; John 20:17).[35] In fact, some proponents argue that the Scriptures never record the Spirit's participation in these dialogues.[36] Second, proponents argue that the *pactum salutis* addresses a very specific issue: the Son's appointment as covenant surety.[37] Third, as mediator and surety, the Father appoints the Son as head of the elect. For these reasons the covenant of redemption pertains specifically to the work of Christ. Gillespie offers a common definition: 'This is an eternal transaction and agreement between *Jehovah* and the Mediator Christ, about the work of our Redemption.'[38] But just because a theologian proposes the christological *pactum* does not mean he has somehow devolved into sub-trinitarianism as some have claimed.[39] Critics fail to notice the broader context of the doctrine of God in christological *pactum* constructions. In this version the *pactum* is the fruit of the trinitarian *consilium Dei* ('council of God'). Within the trinitarian *consilium Dei* the triune God determines to appoint Christ as mediator by means of a covenant between the Father and Son.[40] In this arrangement, the *pactum* falls under the doctrine of Christ, not the doctrine of God.

---

35. Witsius, *Economy of the Covenants*, II.ii.12.

36. Samuel Rutherford, *The Covenant of Life Opened: Or, a Treatise of the Covenant of Grace* (Edinburgh: Robert Brown, 1654), II.vi (pp. 302-05).

37. Fisher, *Marrow*, 37; Gillespie, *Ark of the Covenant*, 57; Witsius, *Economy of the Covenants*, II.ii.4; Berkouwer, *Divine Election*, 165 n. 67.

38. Gillespie, *Ark of the Covenant*, 50.

39. E.g., Robert Letham, 'John Owen's Doctrine of the Trinity in its Catholic Context,' in *The Ashgate Research Companion to John Owen's Theology*, ed. Kelly M. Kapic and Mark Jones (Surrey: Ashgate, 2012), 196.

40. Gillespie, *Ark of the Covenant*, 50; Rutherford, *Covenant of Life*, II.vii

In the second major variant, advocates contend that the *pactum* is part of the doctrine of God and hence articulate a trinitarian model. Rather than distinguish between the trinitarian *consilium Dei* and the *pactum* between the Father and Son, James Durham (1622-58) combines them, which makes the *pactum* fully trinitarian. Durham writes:

> For the Parties, Upon the one side is God essentially considered, or all the three Persons of the glorious God-head, Father, Son, and Holy Ghost, who are all concurring in this Covenant, it being the act of the determinate counsel of God; and in this respect God is the Party to whom the satisfaction for lost Sinners is made, and he is also the Party condescending to accept of the satisfaction.[41]

So on the one side of the covenant is the Trinity, essentially considered. Christ, the God-man, is on the other side of the covenant.[42] According to Durham, the Father acts as the chief representative for the Godhead on the one side; he draws this conclusion from the various dialogues in Scripture between Father and Son (Ps. 40:8; John 6:38). But even though Durham highlights the Father's chief role, he nevertheless stipulates that the covenant involves the triune God: 'For as it was the Father's will that he should lay down his life for his sheep, so it was the will of the Father, Son, and Holy Ghost, that Believers in him

---

(pp. 304-05); John Owen, 'Exercitation XXVII: The Original Priesthood of Christ in the Counsel of God,' in *The Works of John Owen*, vol. 19, ed. William H. Goold (Edinburgh: T & T Clark, 1862), 43; Witsius, *Economy of the Covenants*, II.iii.2; Geerhardus Vos, 'The Doctrine of the Covenant in Reformed Theology,' in *Redemptive History and Biblical Interpretation: The Shorter Writings of Geerhardus Vos*, ed. Richard B. Gaffin, Jr. (Phillipsburg: P & R, 1980), 246.

41. James Durham, *Christ Crucified: or, The Marrow of the Gospel, Evidently Holden Forth in LXXII Sermons, on the Whole 53 Chapter of Isaiah* (Edinburgh: Andrew Anderson, 1683), serm. XXIII (p. 157).

42. Durham, *Christ Crucified*, serm. XXIII (p. 157).

should through his satisfaction have eternal life, *John 6.39, 40*.'[43] Thomas Goodwin (1600-80) and Herman Bavinck (1854-1921) offer similar trinitarian formulations.[44]

These two formulations do not represent the difference between a sub-trinitarian and fully trinitarian construction – the one heretical and the other orthodox. Rather, they represent a divergence of opinion regarding where, precisely, to place the doctrine of the *pactum*. In both formulations the *pactum* originates within the Godhead, but some opt to place the doctrine under christology and others in theology (proper).

One will in threefold execution

In spite of the efforts to connect the doctrines of the Trinity and the *pactum*, critics still label the doctrine as sub-trinitarian or tritheistic. The common argument runs as follows: the church has historically maintained that the works of the triune God are indivisible, *opera trinitatis ad extra indivisa sunt* ('the external work of the trinity is indivisible'). How, then, can the Father and Son enter into an agreement if they share the same undivided will? Moreover, how can only the Father and Son enter into an agreement? Where is the Spirit? Any formulation that excludes the Spirit inherently shatters the indivisible will of the triune God and devolves into sub-trinitarianism.[45] Along similar lines, others have maintained that if the members of the Trinity enter into judicial relations with one another, it fractures the unity of

43. Durham, *Christ Crucified*, serm. XXIII (p. 157).

44. Goodwin, *Of Christ the Mediator*, I.vii, in *Works*, V:23; Herman Bavinck, *Our Reasonable Faith*, trans. Henry Zylstra (Grand Rapids: Eerdmans, 1956), 266-70.

45. Letham,'John Owen,' 196; idem, *The Westminster Assembly: Reading Its Theology in Historical Context* (Phillipsburg: P & R, 2009), 235-37; idem, *The Work of Christ* (Downers Grove: InterVarsity Press, 1993), 52-53, 254 n. 34.

the Godhead and spawns tritheism.[46] According to these critics, introducing a covenant into the doctrine of the Trinity destroys the unity of the godhead.

As common as these criticisms might be, advocates of the *pactum* were keen on preserving the integrity of the doctrine of the Trinity. Important to note is that most of the advocates of the *pactum* labored in the looming shadow of Socinian anti-trinitarianism. It seems that if advocates of the *pactum* had somehow damaged the doctrine of the Trinity, then Socinian theologians would have exploited this weakness to their own advantage. Nevertheless, *pactum* advocates were aware of the need to explain both the unity of God's will and to preserve the distinct work of the individual persons within the Godhead. In short, they sought to preserve both the unity and plurality of persons within the Trinity. John Owen explained that the divine essence unites all three persons of the Godhead, but each person nevertheless subsists distinctly – the Godhead shares the same substance but subsists as Father, Son, and Holy Spirit. And though the Godhead acts in concert, each person has a distinct function in the plan of redemption.

Owen writes: 'The will of God as to the peculiar actings of the Father in this matter is the will of the Father, and the will of God with regard unto the peculiar actings of the Son is the will of the Son; not by a distinction of sundry wills, but by the distinct application of the same will unto its *distinct acts* in the persons of the Father and the Son.'[47] In other words, the triune God determines to save the elect. All three members of

46. Karl Barth, *Church Dogmatics*, 14 vols., ed. G. W. Bromiley and T. F. Torrance (Edinburgh: T & T Clark, 1936-68), IV/1:65.

47. John Owen, 'Exercitation XXVIII: Federal Transactions Between the Father and the Son,' in *The Works of John Owen*, vol. 19, ed. William H. Goold (Edinburgh: T & T Clark, 1862), 87-88.

the Trinity share this will, but each member of the Godhead relates uniquely to it. The Father sends the Son and the Son willingly goes; the Son dies on the cross, the Father does not die on the cross. Just because the Father and Son have unique roles and will actions peculiar to them does not mean that the unity of the Trinity becomes splintered. A number of theologians defended the principles of unity and plurality in the Trinity by distinguishing between the unified will and its personal expression. Wilhelmus à Brakel (1635-1711), for example, writes: 'As far as the Personhood is concerned the Father is not the Son and the Son is not the Father. From this consideration the one divine will can be viewed from a twofold perspective. It is the Father's will to redeem by agency of the second Person as Surety, and it is the will of the Son to redeem by his own agency as Surety.'[48] Once again, à Brakel presents the concept of one will in threefold execution. Similar arguments appear in the works of Johannes Cocceius (1603-69) and Geerhardus Vos (1862-1949).[49]

The immediate reaction to these arguments might be one of suspicion. Perhaps advocates of the *pactum* relied upon novel argumentation to advance their views. The truth of the matter is that such arguments are not peculiar to advocates of the *pactum* but find their origins in medieval theologians such as Thomas Aquinas (1225-74) and Anselm of Canterbury (ca. 1033-1109).[50] Relating the unity of the Trinity to the plurality of persons is not peculiar to

---

48. À Brakel, *Christian's Reasonable Service*, I:252.

49. Cocceius, *Summa Doctrinae*, V.92 (p. 61); Vos, 'Covenant in Reformed Theology,' 245-46.

50. St Anselm, *On the Procession of the Holy Spirit*, §I, in *Anselm of Canterbury: The Major Works*, ed. Brian Davies and G. R. Evans (Oxford: Oxford University Press, 1998), 393; Thomas Aquinas, *Summa Theologica* (rep.; Allen: Christian Classics, 1948), Ia q. 28 art. 4.

the covenant of redemption; the church's greatest theologians have applied their minds to this challenging question. Push unity at the expense of plurality and Unitarianism and modalism result; push plurality at the expense of unity and polytheism is the outcome. Theologians desired neither of these ends and thus employed nuanced arguments and careful distinctions to maintain both unity and plurality. Proponents of the *pactum* were still connected to many of the insights and arguments of the universal church and therefore made use of them to explain the relationship between unity and plurality within the Trinity.

The pactum and revelation

The last issue that warrants consideration is the relationship between the *pactum* and revelation. Exploring this connection is vital for two reasons. First, it demonstrates that proponents of the doctrine believed they were engaged in biblical exegesis, which led to articulation of the doctrine. They were not engaged in illicit speculation about the inner workings of the Trinity. Second, given the relationship between the *pactum* and Christ's appointment as mediator, one of the necessary implications is that the triune God committed to His revelation by means of the incarnation. Humanity can know God because He has become incarnate as man. But God does not immediately appear on the stage of history. Rather, Old Testament divine revelation anticipates the Son's incarnation – God ordains all of history to culminate in the incarnation of His Son.

These two observations substantively appear in a number of formulations, though Gillespie's construction illustrates the point. If the triune God plans redemption and appoints the Son as covenant surety, then by virtue of this plan God has committed to revealing it in history. The Son is 'the word in relation to the revealing all the will of God; he is the *medium revelationis*, as well as *reconciliationis*.'[51] In other words, the Son is both the agent of redemption and revelation. 'Christ is the witness of the covenant,' writes Gillespie, 'who did *declare* and reveal the great secret of the Covenant, even all that he heard, and saw, and acted about it; he doth witness and declare even the whole Counsel of God concerning his Covenant, his purpose and will of grace concerning his people; which things we had never known, had not the witness of the Covenant revealed and declared them.'[52] Gillespie rests revelation, the knowledge of redemption, upon the Son's presence and participation in the *pactum* and upon the recognition that He reveals this plan to His people. The Son is both redeemer and revealer, which means that proponents of the *pactum* did not take off on speculative flights into the theological skies but believed they stood on the *terra firma* of divine revelation. The various exegetical arguments surveyed above confirm this conclusion.

The connection between the *pactum* and revelation is significantly relevant in the theology of Charles Hodge (1797-1878), who some accuse of poisoning the Reformed theological well with rationalism.[53] Yet such criticisms do not account for the role of the *pactum* in Hodge's theology. Hodge specifically maintains, 'Christ's death was *designed* to reveal the love of God, and to secure the reformation of man.'[54] When Hodge invokes the concept of *design*, he ultimately draws upon the covenant of redemption, the 'place'

---

51. Gillespie, *Ark of the Covenant*, 162.

52. Gillespie, *Ark of the Covenant*, 302-03.

53. E.g., Cornelius Van Til, *A Christian Theory of Knowledge* (Phillipsburg: P & R, 1969), 19-20; idem, *Introduction to Systematic Theology* (Phillipsburg: P & R, 1974), 30-42; idem, *The Defense of the Faith* (1955; Phillipsburg: P & R, 1967), 81.

54. Charles Hodge, *Systematic Theology*, 3 vols. (rep.; Grand Rapids: Eerdmans, 1993), I:12, emphasis.

where the triune God designed redemption and revelation. Within the *pactum* God appoints the Son as surety, which entails His incarnation, and hence revelation. Moreover, the *pactum* includes the salvation of the elect, human beings made in the image God, those who have been designed to receive God's revelation in two ways. First, God designs human beings with a capacity for revelation by virtue of their creation in His image.[55] Human beings therefore know God because they bear His image.[56] But Christ is the pinnacle of God's revelation, and His incarnation originates in the *pactum*.

Second, the only way fallen sinners can truly know God is through union with Christ. Hodge explains: 'The divine life can neither be obtained nor continued by any mere efforts of reason or conscience, or by any superstitious observances, but flow from our union with Christ, who causes his Holy Spirit to dwell in all his members.'[57] Only those in union with Christ can ultimately know God. This knowledge never comes by the brute force of natural reason but only by the sovereign work of God's Spirit. And union with Christ begins, not in the application of redemption, but in the *pactum salutis*. Hodge maintains several distinctions to explain the different ways God unites the elect to His Son: the federal and actual unions. The federal union is the covenantal bond initiated in the *pactum salutis* in eternity. The Holy Spirit effects the actual or voluntary union through regeneration of the elect.[58] The federal union originates within

55. Charles Hodge, 'Can God Be Known?' *Biblical Repertory and Princeton Review* 36/1 (1864): 151.

56. Hodge, 'Can God Be Known?' 152.

57. Charles Hodge, *Princeton Sermons: Outlines of Discourses Doctrinal and Practical* (1879; Edinburgh: Banner of Truth, 2011), 232.

58. Charles Hodge, *Ephesians* (1856; Edinburgh: Banner of Truth, 1991), 9.

the *pactum* where the Father appoints the Son as covenant surety. Hence whether through general or special revelation, Hodge locates the genesis of humanity's ability to know God in the covenant of redemption. God designs and gives humanity the capacity for divine revelation, which man knows by virtue of his creation in God's image. But in the wake of the fall, only the elect can ultimately know God because they alone enter into union with Christ, the outworking of the covenant of redemption.

Conclusion

Contrary to contemporary characterizations, the covenant of redemption was not the product of gross speculation or the imposition of a foreign concept upon Scripture. Rather, through the exegesis of the biblical text, theologians coordinated Christ's appointment as mediator with the doctrine of the covenant. These conclusions were not drawn from one or two isolated texts but from a wide array of passages scattered throughout the Scriptures. In the formulation of the doctrine, theologians varied in where they believed the doctrine belonged, whether under theology (proper) or christology. But advocates of the two variants articulated the doctrine within a trinitarian framework, ever mindful to preserve the principles of unity and plurality. In the end, proponents of the doctrine believed that the *pactum* not only rested upon the foundation of divine revelation but was the very source of it. The next chapter deals with four other issues that accompany common explanations of the doctrine: predestination, the timing of justification, the order of salvation, and the love of God.

~:2:~

Development: Predestination, Justification, Order of Salvation, and Love

Introduction

The doctrine of the covenant of redemption lies at a significantly trafficked theological crossroads. Any study of the doctrine must collate numerous concepts to paint an accurate portrait. The previous chapter began a brief historical survey of several issues that pass through the busy intersection: exegesis, the question of placement (christological or trinitarian formulations), how the theologians maintain the unity and plurality of the godhead, and the relationship between the *pactum* and revelation. This chapter succinctly surveys four other issues to set the stage for the recovery of the doctrine: the relationship between predestination and the *pactum,* the timing of justification, connections to the *ordo salutis,* and the theme of God's love.

Unfortunately, many criticisms and half-truths surround these four issues. Is predestination a bald abstract choice devoid of Christ? On the contrary, the *pactum* is the glue that binds together predestination and christology, among other doctrines.

What has the *pactum* to do with the timing of justification? If God appoints the Son as covenant surety and imputes His righteousness to the elect, then in what sense, if any, does God justify the elect in eternity? This question created debate and theologians offered different responses. The *ordo salutis* is another doctrine that has close connections to the *pactum*. Historically, advocates of the doctrine sought to preserve the priority of God's grace over human activity in redemption, and such concerns substantively present the *ordo salutis*. But theologians would later make explicit the connections between the *ordo* and *pactum*. In short, the *ordo salutis* follows the trinitarian processions and covenantally framed missions. The order of salvation reflects the very being and nature of God. And last, but certainly not least, critics have often unfairly characterized the *pactum* as a cold piece of business devoid of love and grace. In truth, love is one of the repeated refrains in numerous expositions of the doctrine. This chapter, therefore, briefly surveys these issues so that we have a better understanding of the historical development of the *pactum salutis*.

Predestination

Contemporary critics of Reformed theology have maintained that theologians historically posited a Christ-less decree of predestination. According to some, the decree of election was a bald abstract choice. Karl Barth (1886-1968), for example, believed that the Reformers foisted a false mythology upon the Scriptures when they argued that Paul spoke of the election and rejection of individuals in Romans 9.[1] For Barth, Christ was the first and last word in revelation, especially in the doctrine of

1. Karl Barth, *The Epistle to the Romans*, 6th ed., trans Edwyn C. Hoskyns (1933; Oxford: Oxford University Press, 1968), 347.

election. Christ is the elected and rejected man.[2] Others followed Barth's lead and criticized Reformed theologians for tinkering with John Calvin's (1509-64) pristine formulations in his *Institutes of the Christian Religion,* where he discussed election under his treatment of soteriology rather than theology (proper). Moving predestination under the doctrine of God distorted Calvin's doctrine and produced a number of negative side-effects, such as supralapsarianism, limited atonement, legalism, and the covenant of works.[3] Barth's observations spawned a historical-theological thesis: Calvin vs. the Calvinists.[4] Calvin was the garden and Reformed Orthodoxy was the fall. A number of historical-theological studies have overturned the now discredited Calvin vs. the Calvinists thesis.[5] Briefly stated, Calvin was never declared or established as the normative theologian for the tradition. Furthermore, seldom do critics carefully examine predestination in the various systems in which it appeared. Reformed theologians never presented predestination as a divine abstract choice. Rather, predestination was always enmeshed within a broader theological

2. Karl Barth, *Church Dogmatics,* 14 vols., eds. T. F. Torrance and G. W. Bromiley (Edinburgh: T & T Clark, 1936-77), II/2:54, 140, 158.

3. See, e.g., J. B. Torrance, 'Strengths and Weaknesses of the Westminster Theology,' in *The Westminster Confession in the Church Today,* ed. Alasdair I. C. Heron (Edinburgh: The Saint Andrew Press, 1982), 46-47; cf. idem, 'The Concept of Federal Theology—Was Calvin a Federal Theologian?' in *Calvinus Sacræ Scripturæ Professor: Calvin as Confessor of Holy Scripture,* ed. Wilhelm H. Neuser (Grand Rapids: Eerdmans, 1994), 18-20.

4. See, e.g., Basil Hall, 'Calvin Against the Calvinists,' in *John Calvin,* Courtenay Studies in Reformation Theology, vol. 1, ed. G. E. Duffield (Appleford: The Sutton Courtenay Press, 1966), 19-37.

5. See, e.g., Richard A. Muller, *Christ and the Decree: Christology and Predestination in Reformed Theology From Calvin to Perkins* (1986; Grand Rapids: Baker, 2008); idem, *After Calvin: Studies in the Development of a Theological Tradition* (Oxford: Oxford University Press, 2003), 63-104.

context. In this case, the covenant of redemption was one of the means by which theologians bound together predestination, christology, and soteriology.

In common formulations of the *pactum*, theologians address the Son's appointment as covenant surety, which also functions as His election as head of the church. The Father chose the elect and united them to Christ in the decree of election. Examples of this arrangement appear, for example, in the Savoy Declaration (1657), the Congregational version of the Westminster Standards. The Declaration states that God predestinated a certain number of individuals unto everlasting life, and they were 'chosen in Christ' (III.iii, v). Christ redeems the elect (III.vi). Read in isolation from the rest of the confession, a person might conclude that predestination is an abstract choice, although he would have to ignore the specific statement that God chose the elect 'in Christ' to reach this conclusion. Nevertheless, the Declaration goes on to state:

> It pleased God, in his eternal purpose, to choose and ordain the Lord Jesus his only begotten Son, according to a covenant made between them both, to be the Mediator between God and man; the Prophet, Priest, and King, the Head and Saviour of his Church, the Heir of all things and Judge of the world; unto whom he did from all eternity give a people to be his seed, and to be by him in time redeemed, called, justified, sanctified, and glorified. (VIII.i)[6]

God both chooses His Son to serve as mediator between God and man and He gives the elect unto Christ, and this occurs within the context of the covenant of redemption.

---

6. *A Declaration of the Faith and Order Owned and Practiced in the Congregational Churches in England* (London: John Field, 1659). All subsequent references and quotations to the Savoy Declaration come from this edition.

Theologians spoke of election in Christ and employed the nomenclature of predestination, choosing, or election, as might be expected.[7] But they also employed other terms to denote the close associations between election and the covenant of redemption. They spoke of union with Christ within the *pactum* by means of terms such as *federal union* or *decretal union*. Herman Witsius (1636-1708), for example, distinguishes between several different aspects of union with Christ: the union of the decree (*in aeterno Dei decreto*), the union of eternal consent (*unione confoederationis aeternae*), by which the Father constitutes Christ as federal head of the elect, and the true and real union (*vera et reali unione*), which occurs through regeneration and faith.[8] Charles Hodge (1797-1878) offers similar distinctions; in his commentary on Ephesians 1 he writes:

> It was in Christ, as their head and representative, they were chosen to holiness and eternal life, and, therefore, in virtue of what he was to do in their behalf. There is a federal union with Christ which is antecedent to all actual union, and is the source of it. God gave a people to his Son in the covenant of redemption. Those included in that covenant, and because they are included in it,—in other words, because they are in Christ as their head and representative,—receive in time the gift of the Holy Spirit, and all other benefits of redemption.[9]

---

7. See, e.g., Francis Turretin and Johannes Heidegger, 'Formula Consensus Helvetica,' XIII, in A. A. Hodge, *Outlines of Theology* (1860; Edinburgh: Banner of Truth, 1991), Appendix II, 659; [David Dickson and James Durham], *The Summe of Saving Knowledge, With the Practical use Thereof* (Edinburgh: George Swintoun and Thomas Brown, n. d.), II.ii; Charles Hodge, *Ephesians* (1856; Edinburgh: Banner of Truth, 1991), 9.

8. Herman Witsius, *Animadversiones Irenicae* (Utrecht, 1696); idem, *Conciliatory or Irenical Animadversions on the Controversies Agitated in Britain, Under the Unhappy Names of Antinomians and Neonomians*, trans. Thomas Bell (Glasgow: W. Lang, 1807), VI.ii-iv (pp. 62, 68).

9. Hodge, *Ephesians*, 9.

God chooses the elect 'in Christ,' who is also their head and representative – He is their federal head, and hence they are in federal union with Christ in the covenant of redemption. The ultimate point of these distinctions was to recognize that theologians considered predestination alongside of several other doctrines, but especially in conjunction with christology. They united these different doctrines through the covenant of redemption.

Justification

The doctrine of justification was one of the issues that was bound with discussions on the *pactum*. Most adherents to the covenant of redemption agreed that God justified the elect the moment they professed faith in Christ. But since Christ was appointed as surety in the *pactum* they also recognized they had to account for the moment when Christ's obedience was imputed to the elect. The moment of imputation played a role in determining the timing of justification. And just because a theologian affirmed the covenant of redemption did not insure that he reached the same conclusions as others. A prime illustration of this point comes from John Gill (1697-1771) and Jonathan Edwards (1703-58). Gill was mildly critical of *pactum* formulations but held a version of the doctrine.[10] He maintained that God justified the elect in eternity. When the elect made a profession of faith they merely became aware of their justified status.[11] There was no sense in which they were not already justified. Conversely, Edwards believed that a person could not conclude his justification until the

---

10. John Gill, *A Complete Body of Doctrinal and Practical Divinity: or A System of Evangelical Truths* (1809; Paris, AR: The Baptist Standard Bearer, Inc., 2007), II.vi-vii (pp. 211-17).

11. Gill, *Complete Body of Divinity*, II.iv-v (pp. 198-209).

final judgment – until he confirmed his justified status through the manifestation of good works.[12] Gill and Edwards represent the polar extremes of the timing of justification, whereas most Reformed theologians were somewhere in between.

One of the more usual ways theologians accounted for the timing of justification and Christ's imputed righteousness was to distinguish between *active* and *passive* justification. Active justification refers to God imputing Christ's righteousness to the elect in the *pactum salutis*. Passive justification refers to the time when the elect lay hold of Christ's righteousness by faith. Witsius, for example, differentiates between *right* to Christ's righteousness and *possession* of it, which parallels the active and passive justification distinction.[13] In other words, when God imputes the Son's righteousness to the elect they have legal right to it but do not yet possess it. The elect can only possess it once they profess faith in Christ. Other seventeenth-century Reformed theologians employed this distinction, and several in the contemporary period also embrace it, such as Geerhardus Vos (1862-1949), Herman Bavinck (1854-1921), and Louis Berkhof (1873-1957).[14] Others

---

12. Jonathan Edwards, 'Miscellany 996: How We Are Justified by Works,' in *The Works of Jonathan Edwards: The 'Miscellanies' (Entry Nos. 833-1152)*, vol. 20, ed. Amy Plantinga Pauw (New Haven: Yale University Press, 2002), 324-25.

13. Herman Witsius, *Economy of the Covenants Between God and Man* (Escondido: Den Dulk Foundation, 1992), II.vii.16.

14. On active and passive justification see Francis Turretin, *Institutes of Elenctic Theology*, ed. James T. Dennison, Jr., trans. George Musgrave Giger (Phillipsburg: P & R, 1992-97), XVI.ix.11; Leonard Rijssen, *Compendium Theologiae Didactico-Elencticae* (Amsterdam: 1695), XIV (pp. 145-46); Johannes Marckius, *Compendium Theologiae Christianae Didactico-Elencticum* (1716; Amsterdam: 1749), XXII.xxiii, XXIV.iii; Bartholomaus Keckerman, *Systema S. S. Theologiae* (Hanau: 1602), III.vii.3; Johannes Heidegger, *Corpus Theologiae Christianae* (Tiguri: ex Officina Heideggeriana, 1732), XXII.lxxviii; cf. Heinrich Heppe, *Reformed Dogmatics: Set Out and Illustrated from the Sources*, trans. G. T. Thomson, ed. Ernst Bizer (London: George Allen & Unwin Ltd., 1950), 555-59; Geerhardus Vos, *Dogmatiek*, 5 vols. (Grand Rapids: 1900), V.12

such as Abraham Kuyper (1837-1920) taught a view similar to Gill, justification from eternity.[15]

A similar issue regarding the nature and timing of justification was the question of whether Christ was a conditional (*fideiussor*) or an absolute (*expromissor*) surety. In other words, did Old Testament believers receive the full and unconditional forgiveness of their sins or merely a provisional forgiveness? The reason this question arose is because theologians recognized that the Father appointed the Son as covenant surety in the *pactum*, but Old Testament believers lived before the incarnation and work of Christ. How could they receive the full forgiveness if Christ had not yet executed His work as covenant surety? Johannes Cocceius (1603-69) argued that Christ was only a conditional surety; he came to this conclusion because of Paul's statement in Romans 3:25, namely, that God 'passed over former sins' rather than forgave them. Cocceius ignited debate and drew criticism from Gisbert Voetius (1589-1676), who contended that Christ was an absolute surety.[16] Cocceians leveled three objections against the Voetians, who believed that Christ was an absolute surety: (1) Christ could not be an absolute surety in the *pactum salutis* because this would make Him a debtor, which suggested that God Himself was guilty of sin; (2) if Christ were an absolute surety, then the incarnation and crucifixion were unnecessary; and (3)

(vol. IV, pp. 22-23); Herman Bavinck, *Reformed Dogmatics*, 4 vols., trans. John Vriend, ed. John Bolt (Grand Rapids: Baker, 2005-09), IV:219-23; Louis Berkhof, *Systematic Theology: New Combined Edition* (Grand Rapids: Eerdmans, 1996), 517.

15. Abraham Kuyper, *The Work of the Holy Spirit*, trans. Henri De Vries (1900; Chattanooga: AMG Publishers, 1995), 322, 389.

16. For an overview of the debate and relevant primary sources, see Willem J. van Asselt, '*Expromissio* or *Fideiussio*? A Seventeenth-Century Theological Debate Between Voetians and Cocceians about the Nature of Christ's Suretyship in Salvation History,' *MAJT* 14 (2003): 37-57.

the view could not account for Colossians 2:14, which states that God forgave sins by nailing them to the cross, an event that took place long after most Old Testament saints lived.[17] The debt of sin, therefore, was not actually canceled until the crucifixion, and not a moment sooner.

This debate largely unfolded in the Netherlands, though other theologians entered the fray. Francis Turretin (1623-87) objected to Cocceius's position and affirmed that Christ was an absolute surety. Turretin was critical of Cocceius on several points. First, he objected to the use of the terms – the distinction between *fideiussio* and *expromissio* originated in Roman law. He believed that Cocceius was unwarranted, therefore, in applying these terms to Christ's role as covenant surety.[18] Second, Turretin delved into the Greek terms that undergirded Cocceius's appeal to Romans 3:25. Yes, Paul stated that God 'passed over' sins (πάρεσιν), but the Septuagint employed this same term to denote the forgiveness of sins, not something less. Moreover, numerous texts affirmed that Old Testament believers received the full forgiveness of sins (Pss. 32:1; 85:2; Isa. 55:7; Exod. 34:7; Pss. 65:3; 130:3; 103:3; Mic. 7:18-19).[19] Turretin presented other reasons but, on the whole, he affirmed that Old Testament believers enjoyed the full forgiveness of their sins.

Turretin explained the relationship between Christ's appointment as surety and the execution of His office in time by use of several distinctions. Turretin writes: 'It is one thing to demand of Christ a debt for present payment; another to lay iniquities upon him, and impute them to him. A debt can be imputed to the

17. Van Asselt, '*Expromissio* or *Fideiussio*,' 49.

18. Turretin, *Institutes*, XII.ix.4.

19. Turretin, *Institutes*, XII.x.15.

surety long before it is demanded for present payment.'[20] Turretin cites Isaiah 53:5, which states that God 'laid on him the iniquity of us all.' Turretin believed that God laid upon Christ the sins of the elect but did not immediately require payment for them. God imputed the debt to Christ but He did not execute payment until His earthly ministry. Turretin appeals to Revelation 13:8 to support his argument, which designates Christ as the lamb that was slain before the foundation of the world. Christ was designated the slain lamb even though His death did not occur for many ages.[21]

With pulling and tugging on both sides of this issue, theologians sought to explain the nexus between Christ's covenantal appointment as surety and its precise relationship to justification and imputation. The tradition largely settled on a mediating position, a view similar to Turretin's. In two different places the Westminster Confession, for example, explains that God's decision to decree to justify the elect is different from their actual justification in history: 'God did, from all eternity, decree to justify all the elect, and Christ did, in the fullness of time, die for their sins, and rise again for their justification: nevertheless, they are not justified, until the Holy Spirit doth, in due time, actually apply Christ unto them.'[22] The Savoy Declaration (1657) added a phrase to make this decree–execution distinction clear: 'God did from all eternity decree to justify all the elect, and Christ did in the fullness of time die for their sins, and rise again for their justification: nevertheless, *they are not justified personally*, until the Holy Spirit doth in due time actually apply Christ unto them.'[23]

20. Turretin, *Institutes*, XII.ix.6.

21. Turretin, *Institutes*, XII.ix.7.

22. Westminster Confession, XI.iv; cf. VIII.i.

23. Savoy Declaration, XI.iv, emphasis.

Even with the confessional codification of the decree–execution principle, theologians still vary how they discuss the timing of justification and imputation. Thomas Goodwin (1600-80), a Westminster divine and one of the chief architects of the Savoy modifications, argued there were three moments of justification: (1) in the covenant of redemption, (2) at the resurrection of Christ, and (3) when the elect profess faith in Christ.[24] In the first moment the Father imputes the sins of the elect to Christ and Christ's righteousness to the elect. In the second moment God justifies the elect in Christ, because He is their federal representative, and His resurrection constitutes His justification. God therefore justifies the elect in the justification of their federal head (1 Tim. 3:16). In the third moment, God personally justifies the elect as they lay hold of the forgiveness of sins and Christ's righteousness by faith. Goodwin summarizes these points:

> From all eternity we were one with Christ by stipulation, he by a secret covenant undertaking for us; and answerably that act of God's justifying us was but as we were considered in his undertaking. When Christ died and rose again, we were in him by representation, as performing it for us, and no otherwise; but as so considered we were justified. But now when we come in our persons, by our own consent, to be made one with him actually, then we come in our persons through him to be *personally* and in ourselves justified, and receive the atonement by faith.[25]

Goodwin therefore located the fount of justification in the *pactum* but carefully explained that the elect were not *personally* justified

24. Thomas Goodwin, *The Objects and Acts of Justifying Faith*, in *The Works of Thomas Goodwin* (1861-64; Eureka: Tanski Publications, 1996), I.xv (pp. 135-38).

25. Goodwin, *Justifying Faith*, I.xv (p. 139).

until they professed their faith in Christ; Goodwin echoes the language of the Savoy Declaration.

Other theologians were not persuaded of such arguments and instead maintained that the elect did not receive Christ's imputed righteousness until they actually professed faith in Christ. Hodge, for example, was likely aware of the earlier formulations regarding active and passive justification given his familiarity with the works of Turretin and Witsius.[26] Moreover, works of the period, such as that of colonial Congregationalist Samuel Willard (1640-1707), embraced something similar to Goodwin's three moments of justification.[27] Hodge's professor and mentor, Archibald Alexander (1772-1851), addressed these different views and argued that the elect cannot obtain the blessing of justification and imputed righteousness until they believe.[28] Hodge seems to have been satisfied with this conclusion and followed Alexander's lead, though he does not specifically address the different views. Hodge was satisfied simply to state that the elect do not receive the saving benefits of Christ until they are united to Him by a voluntary act of faith.[29] Hence, while opinions may vary regarding the nature and precise moment that the elect receive the imputed righteousness of Christ, theologians agree that only faith in Christ truly places the elect in actual possession of His righteousness.

---

26. Cf. Charles Hodge, *Systematic Theology*, 3 vols. (rep.; Grand Rapids: Eerdmans, 1993), II:359; Turretin, *Institutes*, XVI.ix.11; Witsius, *Economy of the Covenants*, II.vii.16.

27. Samuel Willard, *A Brief Discourse of Justification* (Boston: Samuel Phillips, 1686), 69-71

28. Archibald Alexander, *A Treatise on Justification by Faith* (Philadelphia: Presbyterian Tract and Sunday School Society, 1837), 45-46.

29. Hodge, *Systematic Theology*, III:104.

Order of salvation

From the first explicit appearances of the doctrine, theologians were intent on prioritizing the sovereignty of God's grace in redemption. In his speech to the 1638 General Assembly of the Scottish Kirk, David Dickson (1583-1663) brought the *pactum* to bear against the claims of Remonstrant theology. Dickson did not specifically raise the *ordo salutis,* but his remarks substantively addressed the issue. What takes priority in a person's salvation, God's grace or human activity?[30] The same concerns and questions regarding priority appear in the debates over the timing of justification. Theologians were keen to prioritize God's activity over human actions and did so by means of the active–passive justification distinction: the Father's act of imputing the Son's righteousness to the elect in some sense takes priority to the human act of faith. It would take time to develop, but proponents of the *pactum* eventually made explicit connections between the *pactum* and *ordo salutis.*

Vos observed that the *ordo* found its origins in the *pactum*:

> The basis for this order lies in none other than in the covenant of salvation with Christ. In this covenant those chosen by the Father are given to Christ. In it he became the guarantor so that they would be planted into His body in order to live in the thought-world of grace through faith. As the application of salvation by Christ and by Christ's initiative is a fundamental principle of Reformed theology, this theology has correctly viewed this application as a covenantal requirement which fell to the Mediator for the fulfilling of which He became the guarantor.[31]

---

30. David Dickson, 'Arminianism Discussed,' in *Records of the Kirk of Scotland, Containing the Acts and Proceedings of the General Assemblies, from the Year 1638 Downwards*, ed. Alexander Peterkin (Edinburgh: Peter Brown, 1845), 156-58.

31. Geerhardus Vos, 'The Covenant in Reformed Theology,' in *Redemptive History*

Vos maintained that Christ's appointment as mediator took priority over other redemptive considerations, and hence he employed the distinction between active and passive justification.[32] But the *ordo salutis* was not simply a matter of prioritizing imputation over other redemptive benefits. Vos believed that the covenant of redemption was the pattern for the covenant of grace, indeed its effective cause, for later the covenant of grace followed the lines of the *pactum*.[33] Vos's greater point is that the *ordo salutis* ultimately traces the trinitarian processions and missions.[34] Vos argued that the eternal trinitarian relations (processions) were the basis for their respective work of redemption (missions), and the work of the triune God became manifest in the *ordo salutis*. In simpler terms, redemption resembles the triune God who planned and executes it.

The Son's mission as covenant surety, and imputation, takes priority over the Spirit's work, because His mission is logically (in the covenant of redemption) and historically (in the covenant of grace) prior to the Spirit's mission. There is no outpouring of the Spirit apart from the Son's completed work as surety. Hence, Vos prioritizes the forensic aspects of redemption over the transformative aspects. Vos writes: 'The justifying acts serve as the foundation upon which the regenerational acts of God rest. Although (for instance) justification follows the new birth in time, nevertheless, the former is the foundation for the latter.'[35]

---

and Biblical Interpretation: The Shorter Writings of Geerhardus Vos, ed., Richard B. Gaffin, Jr. (Phillipsburg: P & R, 1980), 248.

32. Vos, *Dogmatiek*, V.12 (vol. IV, pp. 22-23).

33. Vos, 'Covenant in Reformed Theology,' 252.

34. See, e.g., Geerhardus Vos, *The Self-Disclosure of Jesus: The Modern Debate About the Messianic Consciousness*, 2nd ed., ed., J. G. Vos (1926; 1953; Phillipsburg: P & R, n. d.), 189-90.

35. Geerhardus Vos, *Systematische Theologie: Compendium* (Grand Rapids: 1900), 133: 'De rechterlijke daden sijn de grond waarop de herscheppende daden berusten. Al

Vos clearly gives priority to the forensic, in this case imputation and justifying acts, over the regenerational acts, or sanctification. Vos elsewhere writes:

> Paul consciously and consistently subordinated the mystical aspect of the relation to Christ to the forensic one. Paul's mind was to such an extent forensically oriented that he regarded the entire complex of subjective spiritual changes that take place in the believer and of the subjective spiritual blessings enjoyed by the believer as the direct outcome of the forensic work of Christ applied in justification. The mystical is based on the forensic, not the forensic on the mystical.[36]

Vos was not alone, as Bavinck affirms something quite similar. Bavinck argues that regeneration, faith, and conversion are not preparatory graces that come apart from Christ, nor are they pre-conditions that a person must meet. They are benefits that flow from the covenant of grace and union with Christ. 'Hence,' writes Bavinck, 'the imputation of Christ precedes the gift of the Spirit, and regeneration, faith, and conversion do not first lead us to Christ but are taken from Christ by the Holy Spirit and imparted to his own.'[37]

Whether in the substantive or explicit connections between the *pactum* and *ordo salutis,* these points open a new window upon the much-criticized *ordo*. Historians and theologians have often criticized proponents of the *ordo* because of its

---

volgt b.v. de Rechtvaardigmaking in tijd op de wadergeboorte, toch is sij de rechtgrond voor den laatste.' I am grateful to my colleague, Derk Bergsma, who translated Vos's section on the *ordo salutis* for me.

36. Geerhardus Vos, 'The Alleged Legalism in Paul's Doctrine of Justification,' in *Redemptive History and Biblical Interpretation: The Shorter Writings of Geerhardus Vos*, ed., Richard B. Gaffin, Jr. (Phillipsburg: P & R, 1980), 384; cf. idem, *Biblical Theology: Old and New Testaments* (1948; Edinburgh: Banner of Truth, 1996), 394.

37. Bavinck, *Reformed Dogmatics*, IV:590.

supposedly thin exegetical basis.[38] According to the contemporary narrative, theologians squeezed the *ordo* from one Pauline text, Romans 8:29-30. As common as this criticism is, the *pactum–ordo* connection reveals that the *ordo* has broader exegetical and theological considerations. The *ordo* was not solely based upon Romans 8:29-30. Critics could remove Romans 8:29-30 from the equation and theologians like Vos would bring other passages and doctrines to bear to contend for the priority of the forensic over the transformative in the *ordo salutis*. For advocates of the *pactum*, placing justification before sanctification in the *ordo* ultimately occurs because of the order of the trinitarian processions and missions.

Love

One of the biggest criticisms against the *pactum* has been the notion that Reformed theologians were too indebted to mercantile imagery. A common line of criticism is that the doctrine of the covenant distorted God's grace and love for fallen sinners. J. B. Torrance, for example, has censured classic Reformed theology because it supposedly confuses the biblical category of covenant with contract. God makes covenants, not contracts. Covenants convey the idea of promises, whereas contracts imply obligations.[39] Others have suggested that the contractualism of the covenant of redemption makes redemption the product of debt and obligation rather than love.[40] The covenant of redemption, therefore,

---

38. For a survey of criticisms and the relevant literature, see J. V. Fesko, 'Romans 8.29-30 and the Question of the *Ordo Salutis*,' *JRT* 8 (2014): 35-60, esp. 38-41.

39. J. B. Torrance, 'Covenant or Contract? A Study of the Theological Background of Worship in Seventeenth-Century Scotland,' *SJT* 23 (1970): 51-76.

40. David Wai-Sing Wong, 'The Covenant Theology of John Owen' (Ph.D. Diss., Westminster Theological Seminary, 1998), 372.

becomes a cold piece of business rather than an outflowing of love for sinners. There are three chief observations regarding these criticisms: (1) mercantile language, (2) the origins of mercantile language, and (3) the underappreciated theme of love in *pactum* formulations.

First, advocates of the covenant of redemption do employ contractual and mercantile language in their formulations. Proponents, for example, define a covenant as an agreement at its most fundamental level. Patrick Gillespie (1617-75) defines a covenant in this manner: 'Concord and agreement is the very foundation of all Contracts, where no agreement is betwixt parties, there is no Covenant, and if there be a Covenant, there is an agreement (Amos 3:3; 2 Cor. 6:14)'.[41] Did Gillespie impose seventeenth-century legal arrangements upon biblical texts? Gillespie does employ the term *contract*, a smoking gun in the eyes of some. Gillespie's repeated term is, however, *agreement*, which is synonymous with *contract*. He did not arrive at this conclusion merely by imposing his cultural experience upon the biblical text but by a careful exegesis of Scripture. In his exposition of Psalm 2:7, for example, Gillespie explains that the Septuagint renders the Hebrew term *decree* as πρόσταγμα, which means *order* or *agreement*. He also consulted other biblical passages, but especially relevant is his citation of Isaiah 28:15: 'We have made a covenant with death, and with hell are we at agreement.' The prophet equates *covenant* and *agreement* by use of a synonymous parallelism.

Second, while proponents of the *pactum* do employ mercantile language, where does it originate? Does it arise from their cultural

---

41. Patrick Gillespie, *Ark of the Covenant Opened: or, A Treatise of the Covenant of Redemption Between God and Christ, as the Foundation of the Covenant of Grace*, The Second Part (London: R. C. 1681), 49-51.

context or from the biblical text? It arguably arises from the biblical text. In numerous places the Bible employs commercial imagery in its discussion of redemption. Christ teaches His disciples to seek the forgiveness of their debts and to forgive their debtors (Matt. 6:12); and Paul speaks of God 'canceling the record of debt' by 'nailing it to the cross' (Col. 2:14). How can these theologians bear guilt for using mercantile language when they merely reflect ideas from the biblical text? If they used such language exclusively, then criticism would be warranted.

Third, there is an abundance of evidence that shows that proponents went far beyond mercantile language to explain the *pactum*. Love is a repeated refrain in expositions of the doctrine. The Son's obedience and voluntary submission to His Father was an expression of love according to Witsius.[42] Gillespie explains that one of the functions of the Spirit in the *pactum* is to spread the love of God in the hearts of the elect.[43] According to Rutherford, the Son's appointment as mediator was a 'vote of love,' which fell upon sinful humanity.[44] Gillespie argued that entire covenant of redemption was shot through with the love of God:

> His Service is commended from the largeness of his design of Love, through which he did drive the serving of this Service; that God, the Son of God, did drive this piece of Service through so deep, and broad, and long a design of transcendent love, from everlasting to everlasting; through so many decrees, which at last could produce nothing in the result, but this price, To have his poor people engaged to him by a Covenant.[45]

---

42. Witsius, *Economy of the Covenants*, II.iii.3, 34.

43. Gillespie, *Ark of the Covenant*, 173.

44. Rutherford, *Covenant of Life*, II.vii (pp. 304-05).

45. Gillespie, *Ark of the Covenant*, 361.

In short, theologians believed that the triune God shared an intra-trinitarian love among Father, Son, and Holy Spirit, which was the ultimate source of the covenant of redemption.[46] This triune manifestation of love overflowed and was poured out upon sinners so that they too might enjoy and know the love of God.[47] 'Love moved the Father,' writes à Brakel, 'and love moved the Lord Jesus. It is a covenant of love between those whose love proceeds within themselves, without there being any loveableness in the object of this love.'[48] Far from a cold piece of business, advocates believed the *pactum* was chiefly an expression of love.

Conclusion

This brief survey reveals that the covenant of redemption was a complex and detailed doctrine. To say that it is an intra-trinitarian agreement barely scratches the surface of the different issues involved. The doctrine's complexity naturally leads theologians to offer slightly different formulations. But in all of these formulations, the details frequently challenge the criticisms often leveled against the *pactum*. Predestination was never a bald choice but always a decision made within the context of Christ's covenantal appointment as mediator. God chose head and body and bound them together in a covenant in eternity that eventually became manifest in history. Christ's appointment as surety,

46. See, e.g., Jonathan Edwards, 'Miscellany 1062: Economy of the Trinity and Covenant of Redemption,' in *The Works of Jonathan Edwards: The 'Miscellanies' (Entry Nos. 833-1152)*, vol. 20, ed. Amy Plantinga Pauw (New Haven: Yale University Press, 2002), 443.

47. See, e.g., Stephen Charnock, *A Discourse Upon the Goodness of God*, in *Works of Stephen Charnock*, vol. 2 (Edinburgh: James Nichol, 1864), 284; Hodge, *Systematic Theology*, I:12, II:362; Vos, 'Covenant in Reformed Theology,' 252.

48. À Brakel, *Christian's Reasonable Service*, I:252.

moreover, meant that His obedience was the sole legal ground for the salvation of the elect. Theologians sometimes disagreed on precisely how to account for Christ's imputed righteousness, and Gill and Edwards's formulations are an exception to the general pattern. Some employed the distinction between active and passive justification while others chose to differentiate between the decree and its execution. Such considerations naturally impacted the nature of the *ordo salutis*, and gave priority to the forensic over the transformative aspects of redemption. But in the end, regardless of technical details, all proponents of the doctrine insisted that the *pactum* was an expression of intra-trinitarian love ultimately shared with the elect. God has first loved us that we might love and know His love.

~: SUMMARY :~

THE survey of the history of the origins and development of the *pactum salutis* reveals a number of interesting twists and turns. Some of the first seminal statements about an intra-trinitarian covenant originated in theologians as diverse as Luther and Arminius, two theologians not ordinarily associated with covenant theology. Nevertheless, whatever inchoate statements about an intra-trinitarian covenant were made in the sixteenth century, the return to the exegesis of the biblical text in the original languages made an impact upon the development of the doctrine. With key texts such as Luke 22:29, theologians began to coordinate the doctrine of the covenant with the Son's appointment as mediator and covenant surety. But the doctrine was not formally born until David Dickson offered his 1638 speech against Arminianism at the General Assembly of the Scottish Kirk. The doctrine had quickly spread and found wide acceptance throughout Europe, both in the British Isles and on the Continent. But the widespread acceptance of the doctrine still manifests a number of significant issues where theologians were in disagreement.

In the effort to retrieve the doctrine of the *pactum salutis*, therefore, the following issues present different questions and debates that should be addressed, and to a certain extent, resolved:

1. There does not appear to be one set exegetical path to establishing the doctrine of the *pactum*. As much as modern critics chide the earlier tradition for its appeal to Zechariah 6:13 as a proof text, many theologians do not appeal to it. There are many texts to which theologians appeal. The exegetically diverse arguments demonstrate that the doctrine has wide attestation throughout the Scriptures and does not rest upon one misread text. The effort to retrieve the doctrine, therefore, need not embrace every text that the earlier tradition sets forth but can instead explore those texts that reveal the doctrine most explicitly.

2. The historical survey revealed two different variants of the *pactum salutis* – the christological and trinitarian models. Is the *pactum* a covenantal agreement between the Father and Son? Or is it an agreement among Father, Son, and Holy Spirit? Retrieval of the doctrine must engage this question.

3. How does the *pactum* relate to the doctrine of the Trinity? A number of theologians (e.g., Owen, à Brakel, Vos) were sensitive to the question of how the Father and the Son, who share a common will, nevertheless enter into an agreement. Some, such as Barth and Letham, leveled the accusation of tritheism against the tradition. Any effort to retrieve the doctrine of the *pactum*, therefore, must address how the Trinity can enter into a covenantal agreement and yet share the same unified will.

4. The 'idea' is implicit in a number of theologians but comes to the fore especially in the thought of Charles Hodge, namely, that the *pactum* is the genesis of divine revelation. Since the *pactum* entails the incarnation, this requires divine revelation to prepare for the advent, incarnation, and subsequent explanation of the significance of the Son's work. The *pactum*, therefore, rests upon divine revelation, not idle speculation. Any construction of the *pactum* should account for the reality and necessity of revelation.

5. What is the precise relationship between the *pactum* and the doctrine of predestination? Is predestination a bald choice, one abstracted from any consideration of Christ's role and place? What other issues arise in determining the connections between these two doctrines?

6. The timing of imputation and justification are significant issues that arise in the various formulations of the *pactum*. Does the imputation of the Son's righteousness occur within the *pactum* (e.g., Witsius, Turretin, Vos, Bavinck, Berkhof) or does it await the elect sinner's profession of faith (e.g., Hodge, WCF)? Related to this is the question of the viability and necessity of the distinction between active and passive justification. Is the distinction warranted, desirable, and the best way to account for the relationship between the covenant surety and His elect bride? Beyond the question of the timing of imputation is the related matter concerning the timing of justification. Is the elect sinner justified in the *pactum* (Gill and Kuyper), does his justification await his profession of faith (Hodge, WCF, Savoy), or does it await the final judgment (Edwards)?

7. The historical survey raises the question regarding the relationship between God and His salvific activity. Generally speaking, advocates such as Dickson and others, raised the *pactum* to safeguard the monergistic nature of salvation. More specifically, Vos and Bavinck raised the point that the *pactum* determines the nature of the *ordo salutis*. To what extent, then, do the trinitarian processions and covenantally framed missions shape and mold the order of salvation?

8. One of the most important things to note is how regularly the theme of love surfaces in discussions of the *pactum salutis*. This is a phenomenon that covers the entire history of the doctrine. Far from being presented as a cold and calculated loveless act, theologians repeatedly appeal to the idea that the *pactum* is a

manifestation of intra-trinitarian love, one that overflows to the elect.

Part III will wrestle with these issues in an effort to recover the doctrine of the *pactum salutis*. But for now, we must first turn to Part II and establish the exegetical warrant for the existence of the doctrine.

PART II

Exegetical Foundations

~: INTRODUCTION :~

ANY effort to recover the doctrine of the *pactum salutis* must establish a firm exegetical footing for it. Doctrinal retrieval is not simply resurrection of old ideas but ultimately recovery of the theological interpretation of Scripture. While there are numerous texts that have been invoked in support of the *pactum*, exploring each and every one cited is beyond the scope of this modest section. Rather, this section aims to explore several key texts: Zechariah 6:13, Psalm 2:7, Psalm 110:1, Ephesians 1, and 2 Timothy 1:9-10. As quickly as some theologians have been to dismiss appeals to these various texts, especially Zechariah 6:13, a careful exploration of each one will reveal that there is indeed covenantal activity in the eternal intra-trinitarian deliberations regarding the salvation of the elect.

Part II, therefore, begins with Zechariah 6:13, a perceived weak link in the exegetical chain of texts that have been amassed in favor of the doctrine. Zechariah 6:13 shares a common bond with a number of texts surrounding the prophecies and fulfillment of Yahweh's covenantal promise to place a Davidic heir upon Israel's throne. Hence, Zechariah 6:13 naturally leads to other texts such as Psalm 2:7 and 110:1. But these three texts only hint at one important element, namely, the time when the events transpired. Yes, Zechariah 6:13, Psalm 2:7, and Psalm 110:1 all have a historical horizon in view, one that originates within redemptive history, but Ephesians 1 and 2 Timothy 1:9-10 reveal that these three texts have an eternal origin within intra-trinitarian covenantal deliberations.

~: 1 :~

Zechariah 6:13

Introduction

The book of Zechariah was written to a people who straddled a life of blessing and covenant curse. Israel had been taken away into exile due to their violation of the Mosaic covenant. From all external appearances the faithful of Israel had reason to doubt the covenant promises of God – the land was in ruins, the temple, the meeting place between God and man, was destroyed, and now Israel, faithful and unfaithful alike, were dwelling in exile under the rule of pagans. But there were glimmering signs of hope that God had not forgotten His covenant promises. Under the reign of Cyrus the Persian, Israelites were allowed to return to the Promised Land to rebuild the temple in 538 BC; the events surrounding the return to the land are captured in the books of Ezra and Nehemiah. However, the prophetic books of Haggai and Zechariah also provide a window into this period, a time when Israel was in the process of returning to the land but while many Israelites still lived abroad. In spite of the many reasons that faithful Israelites might lose heart, Zechariah held out the hope of the coming Messiah, the Davidic heir, who would bring redemption – a hope grounded in a covenant between Yahweh and the Messiah.

The key text that speaks of the covenant between Yahweh and the Messiah is Zechariah 6:13 and it appears within the broader context of verses 9-15. This section falls in the middle of the book and is the fulcrum between the two major sections. Chapters 1:7 through 6:8 recount Zechariah's seven night visions and chapters 9:1 through 14:21 present a series of problems and the future transformation of Jerusalem.[1] At the center of Zechariah's book there is a promised hope, one that points to the future Davidic heir and the redemption He would bring. However, Zechariah's message of hope not only has the Messiah at its center, but also wraps Him in the robe of covenant. How and in what precise manner the covenant manifests itself in this passage remains yet to be seen and requires explanation. But in order to understand and appreciate Zechariah 6:9-15, a summary of Zechariah's visions (1:7-6:8) sets the overall context and establishes the key themes that appear in the crowing of Joshua the high priest.

A summary of Zechariah's night visions

The first vision (1:7-17)

Zechariah sees a vision of the angel of the Lord standing among the myrtle trees and the angel conveys the Lord's jealousy for Jerusalem and Zion (Zech. 1:14).[2] The angel announces the Lord's return to Jerusalem, but not with anger for Israel's breach

---

1. On the unity of Zechariah, see Byron G. Curtis, *Up the Steep and Stony Road: The Book of Zechariah in Social Location Trajectory Analysis* (Atlanta: Society of Biblical Literature, 2006), 231-76.

2. The following summary of Zechariah's seven visions is informed by Meredith G. Kline, *Glory in Our Midst: A Biblical-Theological Reading of Zechariah's Night Visions* (Overland Park: Two Ages Press, 2001).

of the Mosaic covenant but with mercy and with the intention to build His house (Zech. 1:16). Right from the outset of the book, the prophet is keen on the reconstruction of the temple, but given that the chief actor is the Lord, the announcement points to the construction of the eschatological temple, the final dwelling place of God and His covenant people. In Zechariah's day, his vision signals that God would repatriate Israel to the land and that the reconstructed temple would constitute a typological signpost of the coming promise that God would dwell in the midst of His people.

The second vision (1:18-21)

The prophet likens the surrounding Gentile nations to horns and announces the judgment that will fall upon them for their persecution of Judah, Jerusalem, and Israel. In judgment, the Lord would send four craftsmen of war 'to terrify them, to cast down the horns of the nations who lifted up their horns against the land of Judah to scatter it' (Zech. 1:21). If the horns of the nations would be cast down, then the opposite would occur to the righteous: 'All the horns of the wicked I will cut off, but the horns of the righteous shall be lifted up' (Ps. 75:10). And though it may not be explicitly mentioned, the prophet hints of the exaltation of the great priest-king who was to come and redeem God's people. The casting down of the horns of the nations meant the opposite for the anointed, the Messiah, of Israel: 'The adversaries of the LORD shall be broken to pieces; against them he will thunder in heaven. The LORD will judge the ends of the earth; he will give strength to his king and exalt the horn of his anointed' (1 Sam. 2:10).

The third vision (2:2-13)

Elements of the first vision resurface, as Zechariah saw that God would stretch out His measuring line over Jerusalem to begin the process of rebuilding His temple (1:16), and now 'a man with a measuring line' appears 'to measure Jerusalem' (2:2). God's act of measuring Jerusalem is ultimately a verdict that declares what lies under God's domain (cf. Rev. 11:1-2) and, as such, also indicates that God will once again dwell in the midst of His people: 'I will be to her a wall of fire all around, declares the LORD, and I will be the glory in her midst' (Zech. 2:5). God's presence centers upon an idealized, or eschatological, Jerusalem, but His presence will not be a localized phenomenon restricted to the borders of Israel. The vision calls to the exiles to flee Babylon and return to Zion, and the holy city will eventually engulf the nations: 'And many nations shall join themselves to the LORD in that day, and shall be my people. And I will dwell in your midst' (2:11).

Zechariah's language reflects not only the idea of the conversion of the Gentiles but also their inclusion in the 'new covenant', evident in the repetition of the covenantal formula, they 'shall be my people' (cf. Jer. 31:33). But this vision is also replete with covenantal imagery drawn from Israel's desert wanderings, when on the heels of the Mosaic covenant God dwelled in Israel's midst (Exod. 29:45). One last thing to note is that God's conquest of the Gentiles and subsequent dwelling in their midst will confirm that God indeed sent the man with the measuring line: 'You shall know that the LORD of hosts has sent me to you' (Zech. 2:11; cf. John 17:20-23). This statement most likely identifies the man with the measuring line as the Messiah, the Christ.

The vision closes with the announcement that God will inherit Judah as His portion in the holy land and that He will 'choose' Jerusalem (2:12). This language is reminiscent of the covenantal language of Deuteronomy (32:9; Exod. 15:17; cf. 33:3, 15; 34:9). In other words, despite the apparent absence of the covenant in this vision, the covenant is instead like water around a fish – the fish hardly takes notice of his surroundings because they are so common to him, but this does not mean he is not enveloped by water. So too the prophet's vision is shrouded in covenant, whether the Mosaic covenant or the new covenant. Salvation in covenant, which was once the privilege of Israel alone, will now encompass the nations: 'Be silent, all flesh, before the LORD, for he has roused himself from his holy dwelling' (Zech. 2:13).

The fourth vision (3:1-10)

If Zechariah's first three visions dealt with the announcement and plan for God to rebuild His temple, one that would include both Jew and Gentile, then the fourth vision (3:1-10) is the first step in announcing that a priestly retinue would attend this eschatological temple. The message of the restoration of the priesthood rests first in the historical reality of the exile, desecration of the temple, and the need for the restoration of the Levitical line to its priestly duties in a reconstructed temple; however, this earthly restoration is ultimately prophetic of the greater priestly ministry of Christ, a priest according to the order of Melchizedek (Ps. 110). It should be no surprise, then, that this vision rests in the middle of Zechariah's visions and thus functions as a fulcrum or centerpiece that draws the reader's attention to Christ.[3]

In the opening of the scene Joshua the high priest stands before the angel of the LORD and the Accuser, Satan (Zech. 3:1). However, the high priest Joshua was the representative of the people, the nation of Israel.[4] The high priest's ephod was adorned with twelve precious stones representative of the twelve tribes and he carried two stones engraved with the names of the sons

3. Meredith G. Kline, 'The Structure of the Book of Zechariah,' *JETS* 34/2 (1991): 180-81.

4. Anthony R. Petterson, *Behold Your King: The Hope for the House of David in the Book of Zechariah* (New York: T & T Clark, 2009), 50.

of Israel (Exod. 28:9-12, 21-29). But unlike Aaron when he was initially invested with priestly authority and holiness, Joshua stands before the divine bar in soiled garments, reflecting Israel's corporate guilt as covenant-breakers. In the previous vision God reversed the curse that Israel would be *Lo-Ammi*, 'not my people' (Hosea 1:9) and declared that they would be His people (Zech. 2:11). But the Accuser quickly raised the objection that Israel was defiled and unworthy (3:1).

On the one hand, Satan's accusations are true – Joshua, representative of the people, stands before the divine bar soiled by the stains of sin. The angel of the Lord rebukes Satan and proclaims that Jerusalem is 'a brand plucked from the fire' (Zech. 3:2). This rebuke was not merely verbal banter exchanged between enemies who taunt each other like children in a schoolyard. The rebuke constituted a judicial declaration in favor of the defendant, the covenant community of Israel. God's people had been delivered from the fiery wrath of God. But Israel's sins would not be swept away under the carpet. The angel of the Lord instructed the attendants in the courtroom to remove Joshua's filthy garments and to give him clean ones, a symbolic action intended to denote the forgiveness of sin and the imputation of righteousness (Zech. 3:3-4; cf. Exod. 28–29; 39–40; Lev. 8). As the rest of Scripture informs us, this transaction comes at the price of the shed blood of Christ and His perfect obedience to God's law (Rev. 12:10-11). The apostle John writes: 'To him who loves us and has freed us from our sins by his blood and made us a kingdom, priests to his God and Father, to him be glory and dominion forever and ever. Amen' (Rev. 1:5-6).

At first glance there is an apparently ill-fitting element in this vision: 'If you will walk in my ways and keep my charge, then you shall rule my house and have charge of my courts, and I will give you the right of access among those who are standing here' (Zech. 3:7). In what way does the favorable judicial verdict over Joshua, representative of the people, harmonize with the conditional language, 'If you will walk in my ways ... I will give you ... access'? This is covenant-keeping language (Deut. 8:6; 10:12; 26:17; 28:9; 30:16). Does the verdict merely open the possibility of dwelling in God's presence, which must be maintained by covenant faithfulness, or does it actually indefectibly secure it prior to their covenant-keeping? Israel was already in exile because of her covenant faithlessness and the whole point of this series of visions was to announce that God Himself would rebuild His temple and secure Israel's tenure in the land. But the requirements for holiness and obedience had not been abrogated. Hence, if the requirements for obedience still stood, then it means that God Himself would fulfill them on Israel's behalf (cf. Deut. 30:4-8; Ps. 132:9-18).

How would God Himself fulfill the necessary pre-condition of obedience to secure Israel's permanent place in the land and the construction of the temple? The Lord announces to the prophet: 'Behold, I will bring my servant the Branch' (Zech. 3:8). Zechariah's language is immediately identifiable with Isaianic nomenclature of the Servant of the Lord (Isa. 42:1; 52:13), whose ministry is priestly, seeing that he offers himself in sacrifice as the act of satisfaction that would restore Israel to the land (Isa. 52:13-53:12). But Zechariah also identifies the servant as the Branch, which connotes associations with the Davidic kingly heir, the shoot from the stump of Jesse, the branch that would grow and produce fruit (Isa. 11:1; cf. Jer. 33:15; Ps. 132:17). Such connections should not be doubted given Zechariah's knowledge of the former prophets, among whom is included Isaiah (Zech. 1:4).[5] The imagery is still veiled, but in the light

5. Petterson, *Behold Your King*, 87-88.

of the other cited biblical texts the conclusion appears sound – the vision speaks of a priest-king who will bring about Israel's restoration and reconstruction of the temple.

But the timeframe for this restoration was not imminent, especially given Zechariah's language. When might all of this occur? The prophet writes: 'In that day, declares the Lord of hosts, every one of you will invite his neighbor to come under his vine and under his fig tree' (Zech. 3:10). The prophet employs language that described the peace and safety of life in Israel under Solomon's reign, the height of the monarchy (1 Kings 4:25), but Zechariah's gaze was not a retrospective one – a wistful glance at days gone by. Rather, his was a prospective vision to the future – like Micah who prophesied: 'In the latter days ... they shall sit every man under his vine and under his fig tree' (Micah 4:1, 4). Zechariah's vision was a portent into the future when the messianic Branch would restore Israel's fortunes, rebuild the temple, and cleanse the people of their iniquity – He would do this through His sacrifice and obedience to the law.

The fifth vision (4:1-14)

This vision takes us into the holy of holies of Zechariah's visionary temple where the prophet sees two temple Menorah, or lampstands, and two olive trees (Zech. 4:2-3). The lamp stands are a symbol of God's people, the church, which is what we also find in the book of Revelation (1:20); later in John's apocalyptic vision two lampstands are also identified as two olive trees (Rev. 11:4). The likely significance of this imagery, especially in the light of its repetition in Revelation 11, is that the two lampstands and olive trees are representative of the church and the light they diffuse is their prophetic testimony of the gospel. The Spirit of God fuels the covenant community's witness: 'Not by might, nor by power, but by my Spirit, says the Lord of hosts' (Zech. 4:6). By the Spirit of the Lord the 'great mountain,' symbolic of another kingdom (cf. e.g., Ps. 68:15; Isa. 2:2; Jer. 51:25), would become flattened before the Davidic exilic kingly heir, Zerubbabel (Zech. 4:7). Given the earlier visions, the prophet paints a combined portrait of the Messiah rebuilding the temple of God conjointly with the Spirit of the Lord in the last days through the prophetic testimony of the covenant community, the church. This imagery is not new but has precedent, once again, in the prophet Isaiah (Isa. 11:2; 42:1, 6-7; 61:1; Luke 2:32; Acts 26:22-23).

The sixth vision (5:1-11)

This vision consists of three different elements: a flying scroll (vv. 1-4), a woman in a basket (vv. 5-8), and two flying stork-women (vv. 9-11). In the first portion of the vision Zechariah sees a flying scroll that has writing on both sides (v. 3), likely reflective of the stone tablets of the covenant (Exod. 32:15), which were the basis for the covenant arrangement between Israel and the Lord. Moses told the people that if they were obedient, they would be blessed, but if they were disobedient they would be cursed and carried away from the land (Deut. 28:15, 45, 52, 63-64). Confirmation of this connection appears in the visionary description of the scroll: 'This is the curse that goes out over the face of the whole land' (v. 3). For those who have broken the covenant, in this case thieves, deceivers, and those who take the Lord's name in vein, will have God's judgment fall upon them and their homes (vv. 3-4).

The second portion of the vision portrays covenant-breakers as a woman being carried away in a basket, which again echoes the curses of the covenant: 'The Lord uprooted them from their land in anger and fury and great wrath, and cast them into another land' (Deut. 29:28). The vision characterizes this woman as iniquity and wickedness, and as such the woman's head is thrust down into the basket with a lead weight placed on top of it (vv. 6-8).

In the third portion of the vision two winged women, specifically with stork-like characteristics, appear and carry the basket to the land of Shinar. The stork is an unclean animal according to the Levitical code (11:19), and God uses it to carry the woman in the basket into exile, the land of Shinar – to the plains of Babylon (v. 11); the land of Shinar was the location of the disastrous tower of Babel (Gen. 11:2), a monument to the idolatrous exaltation of man. This threefold vision presents the contrasting mirror image to the earlier visions of the restoration of God's presence to Israel and the cleansing and forgiveness of sins they receive. Covenant-breakers will be cast off into exile and covenant-keepers will dwell in the presence of the Lord.

The seventh vision (6:1-8)

The last vision consists of four chariots, which harkens back to the imagery that appears in the first vision (1:7-17). The chariots emerge from between two bronze mountains (Zech. 6:1), which is imagery likely symbolic of the temple and presence of God, since the Solomonic temple had two bronze pillars at its entrance (1 Kings 7:13-22). Despite the fact that there are four chariots, this imagery likely conveys the idea of the throne of God, which the prophet Ezekiel describes as a chariot. In Ezekiel's vision the presence of the Spirit accompanies God's throne (Ezek. 1:12, 20; 2:2; cf. Psa 104:3). The connection between God's throne, the chariot(s), and the Spirit appears in verse 8: 'Behold, those who go toward the north country have set my Spirit at rest in the north country.' Psalm 68 also presents similar imagery – the Lord emerges from His temple through the presence of thousands of chariots: 'O God, when you went out before your people, when you marched through the wilderness, the earth quaked, the heavens poured down rain, before God, the One of Sinai, before God, the God of Israel... The chariots of God are twice ten thousand, thousands upon thousands; the Lord is among them; Sinai is now in the sanctuary' (vv. 7-8, 17).

The chariot-presence of the Lord emerges from the temple and goes 'to the four winds of heaven,' symbolic of the four points on the compass throughout 'all the earth' (Zech. 6:5). And these chariots announce God's judgment; the chariot–judgment connection appears, for example, in Isaiah 66: 'For behold, the LORD will come in fire, and his chariots like the whirlwind, to render his anger in fury, and his rebuke with flames of fire' (v. 15). Another indicator that these chariots bring judgment is the fact that one of them heads to and settles in the north, which was the direction from which the exiles were originally told to flee in Zechariah's third vision: 'Up! Up! Flee from the land of the north, declares the LORD. For I have spread you abroad as the four winds of the heavens, declares the LORD. Up! Escape to Zion, you who dwell with the daughter of Babylon' (Zech. 2:6-7). In the book of Revelation Babylon serves as the antithetical foil for Jerusalem, the city of the faithful versus the city of the wicked (Rev. 14:8; 16:19; 17:5; 18:2, 10, 21). At the conclusion of God's judgment upon Babylon, the north, His Spirit comes to rest (Zech. 6:8) – the long awaited Sabbath-rest arrives, the eschatological rest God first entered at the completion of the creation (Gen. 2:2), the consummation of all things.

Summary

Zechariah's seven visions paint a combined portrait of God returning the exiles to the land, reconstituting His temple, dwelling in Israel's midst, ushering in judgment against the nations and Israel's unrepentant covenant-breakers, and bringing about the consummation. These are all themes that feed into the rest of Zechariah's prophecy but are key to understanding God's instructions for the crowning of Joshua the high priest and how Zechariah 6:13 speaks of a covenant between Yahweh and the Messiah to bring about the events prophesied in these seven visions.

Crowning the priest

The passage begins with instructions to take three of the recently arrived exiles from Babylon – Heldai, Tobijah, and Jedaiah – and to bring them to the house of Josiah, the son of Zephaniah (Zech. 6:9-10). Zechariah was supposed to take their silver and gold, form a crown, and set it upon the head of Joshua, the high priest (Zech. 6:11; cf. Exod. 25:23-28). A likely scenario is that these three returning exiles had prospered in Babylon and brought wealth with them, something in short supply in the recently repatriated Israelite community.[6] For the repatriated Israelites this event was undoubtedly momentous, as it represented part of the reconstitution of the Levitical priesthood, which had not been functioning since the destruction of the temple and Babylonian exile (cf. Zech. 3:1-10). However, one of the discrepancies that immediately surfaces is the impropriety of a high priest wearing a royal crown. In Israel's past King Uzziah tried to assume priestly duties with deadly consequences (2 Chron. 26:16-20). Given that the crowning of the high priest is divinely initiated rather than of human origins, these actions would hint at the fact that they transcend the status quo.[7] It will become quickly evident in the verses that follow that these actions intend to foreshadow the crowning of the Messiah.

---

6. Thomas Edward McComiskey, *Zechariah, in The Minor Prophets: An Exegetical & Expository Commentary*, ed. Thomas Edward McComiskey, vol. 3 (Grand Rapids: Baker, 1998), 1112; Ben C. Ollenburger, *The Book of Zechariah: Introduction, Commentary, and Reflections*, NIB, vol. 7 (Nashville: Abingdon, 1996), 786.

7. McComiskey, *Zechariah*, 1113.

That greater realities are in view is evident in verse 12: 'And say to him, "Thus says the LORD of hosts, 'Behold, the man whose name is the Branch: for he shall branch out from his place, and he shall build the temple of the LORD.'"' The prophet picks up on a theme that appears in other portions of the Old Testament: the Davidic Branch (Isa. 4:2; 11:1; Jer. 23:5-6; 33:14-18; Ezek. 17:11-21).[8] Joshua, the high priest, therefore, serves as a type of Christ. The prophet indicates that the Branch will build the temple of the Lord, an idea repeated and expanded in verse 13a: 'It is he who shall build the temple of the LORD and shall bear royal honor, and shall sit and rule on his throne.' Building the Lord's temple is a function of Israelite royalty, exemplified by Solomon's construction of God's temple. That the Branch is the one who would build the temple is evident in his twofold chiastic structure of verse 12c-d and verse 13a-b:

verse 12c-d
{A} c: for he shall branch out from his place
{B} d: and he shall build the temple of the LORD

verse 13a-b
{B[1]} a: It is he [והוא] who shall build the temple of the LORD
{A[1]} b: and [והוא lit. 'and he'] shall bear royal honor

The 'A' elements (e.g., v. 12c) of the chiasm deal with the Branch's inauguration to the throne, and the A1 clause celebrates the king's investiture with royal authority and honor (cf. Job 40:10; Ps. 104:1c). In particular, the Branch will be robed in the majesty of a king (cf. Pss. 45:4; 21:5; 1 Chron. 29:25).[9] Hence, verses 9-13b

---

8. Petterson, *Behold Your King*, 88-91.

9. Kline, 'Structure of the Book of Zechariah,' 182; Marvin A. Sweeny, *The Twelve Prophets*, vol. 2, Berit Olam (Collegeville: Liturgical Press, 2000), 630; Martin Luther, *Lectures on the Minor Prophets*, LW 20:70.

present the crowned high priest, Joshua, as a type of the Messiah, the one who will eventually build the temple of the Lord.

God's covenant promise

Such a typological prophecy that presents two royal functions, namely, the Davidic heir's right to the throne and his building the temple of the Lord, evokes God's earlier covenant promise to David. In the original context of the Davidic covenant, David's intention was to build a house for the Lord, a project that the Lord gave to a future descendant. God promised David that one of his heirs, a descendant from his own body, would arise and that He would establish his kingdom (2 Sam. 7:5-12). The text specifically states: 'He shall build a house for my name, and I will establish his throne of his kingdom forever' (2 Sam. 7:13). While perhaps not immediately evident in its original context, the psalmist characterizes God's promise as a covenant (Ps. 89:3-4, 39). The immediate horizon for this promise had David's son in view, Solomon, the one who built God's house, but there was also a broader horizon in view that had Christ as its ultimate fulfillment. Zechariah picked up this thread and employed it in his own setting to give hope to the recently returned exiles. But God's plans to send the Messiah did not originate within the hourglass of time but before the foundations of the earth, within the intra-trinitarian plans for the redemption of a sinful people. However, before we consider the timing of God's covenant, further exploration of Zechariah's prophecy is necessary.

Heavenly throne

The rest of verse 13 expounds the enthronement of the priest-king: 'It is he who shall build the temple of the LORD and shall bear royal honor, and shall sit and rule on his throne. And there shall be a priest on his throne, and the counsel of peace shall be between them both.' Question has arisen as to the identity of the priest in the latter portion of verse 13; some have suggested that there are two separate individuals envisioned.[10] However there is good contextual reason to suggest that no one but the Branch is in view; the Branch is the subject of all of the verbs in verses 12 and 13a-b, and he is the subject of verse 13c:

verse 12
Behold, the man whose name is the Branch:
for he [the Branch] shall branch out from his place,
and he [the Branch] shall build the temple of the LORD.

verse 13:
a: It is he [the Branch] who shall build the temple of the LORD
b: and [והוא lit. 'and he,' viz. the Branch] shall bear royal honor,
c: and [he] shall sit and rule on his throne.

The Branch shall sit and rule on his throne. The text presents Joshua, the crowned high priest – he foreshadows the coming priest-king who shall sit and rule.[11] There does not appear to be warrant, therefore, to insert another figure into the scene.

However, some have argued that there are indeed two figures in the text given the fact that Zechariah is instructed to create *crowns* [עטרות] (Zech. 6:11; cf. KJV), though the ESV and other translations render this plural noun in the singular, *crown* (cf. NIV, NKJ, NRSV, RSV, TNIV, NAS, NLT). Some have suggested that the

10. E.g., Hinckley G. Mitchell, John Merlin Powis Smith, and Julius A. Brewer, *Haggai, Zechariah, Malachi, and Jonah*, ICC (Edinburgh: T & T Clark, 1912), 185-86.

11. C. F. Keil and F. Delitzsch, *Commentary on the Old Testament*, vol. 10 (1866-91; Peabody: Hendrickson, 1996), 555.

presence of *crowns*, specifically two crowns (cf. Zech. 4:1-5, 10b-14), presents an exegetical difficulty. Some argue that one of the crowns was placed upon Joshua's head and the other was for Zerubbabel.[12] Others have argued that the reference to *crowns* could mean that there were a number of crowns joined together to form one crown as in Job 31:36 and Revelation 19:12: 'His eyes are like a flame of fire, and on his head are many diadems [διαδήματα πολλά].'[13] Additionally, since there are two precious metals mentioned, gold and silver, a likely scenario is that there was one crown with multiple bands made of the two different metals. Calvin suggests that both priests and kings wore crowns and the fact that both were placed upon the head of Joshua was symbolic of the unification of the priestly and kingly offices in one person.[14] In spite of these various counter-arguments, the mention of *crowns* does not necessitate the insertion of another figure into the narrative.[15] Two grammatical factors confirm this conclusion: (1) the text states, 'And say to him [ואמרת אליו]' (v. 12) – the preposition has the third person singular masculine suffix and indicates that Joshua is the lone recipient; and (2) the verb in v. 14 is in the singular even though the noun, *crowns*, is in the plural: 'And the crown shall be [והעטרת תהיה] in the temple of the Lord.' Therefore, despite the ambiguities in the text,

---

12. David L. Petersen, *Haggai and Zechariah*, OTL (Philadelphia: Westminster, 1984), 275-76; Ralph L. Smith, *Zechariah*, WBC, vol. 32 (Waco: Word, 1984), 218; Carol L. Meyers and Eric M. Meyers, *Haggai, Zechariah 1-8*, AB, vol. 25B (New York: Doubleday, 1987), 349-52.

13. Keil and Delitzsch, *Commentary*, 554; Joyce Baldwin, *Haggai, Zechariah, Malachi: An Introduction and Commentary*, TOTC (London: InterVarsity Press, 1972), 133; Petterson, *Behold Your King*, 106.

14. John Calvin, *Commentaries on the Twelve Minor Prophets: Zechariah and Malachi*, vol. 5 (rep.; Grand Rapids: Baker, 1993), 153-55.

15. Baldwin, *Zechariah*, 134; Walther Eichrodt, *Theology of the Old Testament*, vol. 2, trans. J. A. Baker (Philadelphia: Westminster, 1967), 343 n; Luther, *Minor Prophets*, LW 20:68-69.

the likely scenario is that God only commands the crowning of one person, namely, Joshua the high priest.

There is still a question about the number of participants in this narrative given how the ESV translates v. 13d: 'And there shall be a priest on his throne.' Some, such as Luther, translate it in this manner but interpret it to refer to the one person, Joshua, the one who typifies the future priest-king Messiah.[16] However, given the typological image of the solo figure of the crowned high priest, Joshua, and that the Branch is the subject of verses 12-13c, it appears that the KJV rendering is preferable: 'And he,' the Branch, 'shall be a priest on his throne.'[17] Hence, thus far, we have the following for verses 12-13d: 'Behold, the man whose name is the Branch; for the Branch shall branch out from his place, and the Branch shall build the temple of the LORD. It is the Branch who shall build the temple of the LORD and the Branch shall bear royal honor, and the Branch shall sit and rule on his throne. And the Branch shall be a priest on his throne.' But what about the last phrase of verse 13, namely, 'And the counsel of peace shall be between them both' (v. 13e)?

What is the counsel of peace and who are the two figures that share this peace? We have already ruled out the possibility that Zechariah's prophecy has two individuals in view. We have a portrait of a priest-king, presumably upon his royal throne. There are other passages of Scripture that present this very picture:

> Behold, the days are coming, declares the LORD, when I will fulfill the promise I made to the house of Israel and the house of Judah. In those days and at that time I will cause a righteous Branch to spring up for David, and he shall execute justice and righteousness in the land.... For thus says the LORD: David shall never lack a man

16. Luther, *Minor Prophets*, LW 20:71.

17. Petterson, *Behold Your King*, 108-10.

> to sit on the throne of the house of Israel, and the Levitical priests shall never lack a man in my presence to offer burnt offerings, to burn grain offerings, and to make sacrifices forever (Jer. 33:14-18).

Jeremiah presents the two offices, the priest and the king, residing in one man, the Davidic Branch, ruling upon the throne. So, within context, it is certainly possible that v. 13d, 'And he shall be a priest on his throne,' refers to the Branch's throne. However, we are then left with the question of how v. 13e fits within this picture, as it seems that another mystery figure has been introduced in the last clause of the verse.

If we set aside the idea that the Branch sits upon his throne and recognize that there is a second figure already explicitly introduced in context, not Zerubbabel from the broader context of Zechariah, then we have a fuller picture presented in verses 12-13. In verses 12-13 we have three pairs of clauses with the repetition of a key phrase, which also appears in verses 14-15:

Verses 12-13	And say to him, 'Thus says the LORD of hosts, "Behold, the man whose name is the Branch:
Pair 1	for he shall branch out from his place, and he shall build the temple of the LORD
Pair 2	It is he who shall build the temple of the LORD and shall bear royal honor, and
Pair 3	shall sit and rule on his throne. And [he] shall be a priest on his throne, and
	the counsel of peace shall be between the both."'

Verses 14-15	And the crown shall be in the temple of the LORD as a reminder.... And those who are far off shall come and help to build the temple of the LORD.[18]

Within the context of these three pairs of clauses, the repetition of the phrase 'the temple of the LORD' suggests that the throne belongs to Yahweh.[19] Furthermore, verses 14-15 continue to repeat the phrase 'temple of the LORD,' which adds more weight to the conclusion that 'his throne' is a reference to Yahweh's throne. In other portions of the Old Testament there is a connection between the temple and throne, as both belong to the Lord. The temple, we are told, is 'the place of my throne' (Ezek. 43:7), and the new Jerusalem is the city that is called 'the throne of the LORD' (Jer. 3:17). Hence, the two figures in these verses are the Branch and Yahweh, and together they share the 'counsel of peace ... between them both.'

But like the adjusted aperture ring on a camera lens that brings greater visual clarity to the picture, there is further refinement of the translation of verse 13c-d that brings the

18. Kline, *Glory in our midst*, 222-23.

19. So Johannes Cocceius, *To Dodekapropheton sive Prophfetae Duodecim Minores* (Lugduni Batavorum, 1652), 505; Matthew Henry, *An Exposition of the Old and New Testament*, vol. 4 (Philadelphia: Ed. Barrington & Geo. D. Haswell, 1828), 1121; Adam Clarke, *The Holy Bible with A Commentary and Critical Notes*, vol. 4 (London: Thomas Tegg and Son, 1836), comm. Zech. 6:13; V. M. Jauhiainen, 'Turban and Crown Lost and Regained: Ezekiel 21:29-32 and Zechariah's Zemah,' *JBL* 127 (2008): 501-11, esp. 509; Petterson, *Behold Your King*, 11; David Baron, *The Visions and Prophecies of Zechariah* (1918; Grand Rapids: Kregel, 1972), 201-02; E. B. Pusey, *The Minor Prophets: A Commentary*, vol. 2 (1950; Grand Rapids: Baker, 1976), 376; R. E. Higginson, *Zechariah*, in *The New Bible Commentary: Revised*, ed. D. Guthrie and J. A. Motyer (Grand Rapids: Eerdmans, 1970), 793. Jerome also holds this view (see E. W. Hengstenberg, *Christology of the Old Testament and a Commentary on the Predictions of the Messiah by the Prophets*, vol. 2 [Washington, DC: William M. Morrison, 1839], 59).

picture into sharper focus. In verse 13d we read, 'And he shall be a priest on [על] his throne.' The Hebrew preposition על can certainly be translated by the English prepositions *on* or *upon*, but other prepositions also legitimately reflect the meaning of the Hebrew term. In this case, the term *by* or *beside* helps clarify the translation of verse 13c-d: 'And he shall sit and rule by his throne, and shall be a priest by his throne' (cf. NRSV; LXX).[20] Hence, we have the following presented to us in verses 12-13:

> It is the Branch who shall build the temple of the LORD and shall bear royal honor, and shall sit and rule by Yahweh's throne. And the Branch shall be a priest by Yahweh's throne, and the counsel of peace shall be between them both, Yahweh and the Branch.

At least according to biblical norms, Zechariah's prophecy is not necessarily unique, as he employs Joshua, the priest-king, as the type of Christ, the Messiah, who sits by Yahweh to reign in the midst of His enemies, such as in the psalmist's famous line, 'The LORD says to my Lord: "Sit at my right hand, until I make your enemies your footstool"' (Ps. 110:1; cf. 1 Kings 2:19).

The 'counsel of peace' between Yahweh and the Branch indicates that they have made an agreement to bring about a state of peace for God's people. Other portions of the Old Testament convey this peace in covenantal terminology because to enter into a covenant is to make peace (cf. Deut. 2:26; 20:10-18; Josh. 9:15; 10:1-4; 2 Sam. 10:19 // 1 Chron. 19:19; Job 5:23; 22:21).[21] The psalmist

---

20. For the use of *by* or *beside* to translate the term Hebrew term על cf. Prov. 8:2 and 2 Chron. 26:9; HALOT 1:826; Kline, *Glory in Our Midst*, 223-24; B. A. Mastin, 'A Note on Zechariah VI 13,' *VT* 26/1 (1976): 113-15; cf. Pettersen, *Zechariah*, 277; Baldwin, *Zechariah*, 136; Sweeny, *Twelve Prophets*, 632.

21. Meyers and Meyers, *Zechariah*, 362; cf. Paul Kalluveettil, *Declaration and Covenant: A Comprehensive Review of Covenant Formulae from the Old Testament and the Ancient Near East* (Rome: Biblical Institute Press, 1982), 38-41.

cries out: 'Give the king your justice, O God, and your righteousness to the royal son!... In his days may the righteous flourish, and peace abound, till the moon be no more' (Ps. 72:1-7). The prophet Ezekiel writes of the lifting of the covenant curses from the land in terms of giving God's people peace: 'I will make with them a covenant of peace and banish wild beasts from the land, so that they may dwell securely in the wilderness and sleep in the woods' (Ezek. 34:25). The prophet also writes of peace and does so in terms evocative of the original creation of man (through the use of 'multiply,' reminiscent of the creation mandate, Gen. 1:28) and God dwelling in Israel's midst: 'I will make a covenant of peace with them. It shall be an everlasting covenant with them. And I will set them in their land and multiply them, and will set my sanctuary in their midst forevermore' (Ezek. 37:26). In the three prophetic texts that specifically use the phrase, covenant of peace, ברית שׁלום (Isa. 54:10; Ezek. 34:25; 37:26), all of them speak of this covenant within the context of an announced end of exile and the restoration to the land, themes that appear in Zechariah's visions (1:7-6:8) as well as in this passage, 6:9-15.

The fact that this 'counsel,' or covenant, of peace is 'between them,' reflects an agreement between Yahweh and the Branch.[22] The appearance of these two ideas, covenant and peace, appear in a number of different contexts in the Old Testament, such as in Israel's covenant of peace with the Gibeonites (Josh. 9:15), or Isaiah's promises that God would initiate an eternal covenant of peace with Israel (Isa. 54:10).[23] Within the immediate context of Zechariah's prophecy the two terms appear together when the

22. Ollenburger, *Zechariah*, 787; Bernard F. Batto, *Slaying the Dragon: Mythmaking in the Biblical Tradition* (Louisville: Westminster John Knox, 1992), 157-59.

23. Batto, *Slaying the Dragon*, 154; idem, 'The Covenant of Peace: A Neglected Ancient Near Eastern Motif,' *CBQ* 49 (1987): 187-211.

Messiah 'shall speak peace to the nations,' which comes about through the 'blood of my covenant with you' (Zech. 9:10-11). The agreement in view mirrors a number of Old Testament texts, though Psalm 110 features prominently. In this text the psalmist, like Zechariah, paints a portrait of the priest-king by showing that the Messiah sits in royal session next to Yahweh: 'The LORD says to my Lord: "Sit at my right hand, until I make your enemies your footstool"' (v. 1). But the psalmist also combines this kingly image with the invocation of the priestly order of Melchizedek (Ps. 110:4). Just as in Zechariah, the psalmist speaks of the Davidic heir, the priest-king who sits at the right hand of Yahweh and rules over the nations. Though the terminology does not explicitly appear here, either in Zechariah 6:9-15 or in Psalm 110, the covenant is implicit as other texts identify God's promise to place David's heir upon the throne of Israel as a covenant: 'You have said, "I have made a covenant with my chosen one; I have sworn to David my servant: 'I will establish your offspring forever, and build your throne for all generations'"'(Ps. 89:3-4).

The reign of the Branch

The effects of the covenant of peace between Yahweh and the Branch and His reign appear in v. 15: 'And those who are far off shall come and help to build the temple of the LORD. And you shall know that the LORD of hosts has sent me to you. And this shall come to pass, if you will diligently obey the voice of the LORD your God.' While the Branch would build the temple of the Lord, 'those who are far off,' namely, Gentiles, would also come from afar and assist in the construction of the temple (cf. Isa 46:11; 33:13; 66:19).[24] In fact, the text specifically states

24. Ollenburger, *Zechariah*, 788; Kline, *Glory in Our Midst*, 232; cf. Smith, *Zechariah*, 219.

that the Branch would 'sit and rule' (v. 13c) by Yahweh's throne and employs the term מֹשֵׁל, which means 'to have dominion,' the verb used to denote God's rule over all nations, not simply Israel (Isa. 40:10; Ps. 22:28; 59:13; 1 Chron. 29:12). Zechariah echoes sentiments found in his contemporary, the prophet Haggai, who offers his own vision of the construction of the eschatological temple:

> For thus says the LORD of hosts: Yet once more, in a little while, I will shake the heavens and the earth and the sea and the dry land. And I will shake all nations, so that the treasures of all nations shall come in, and I will fill this house with glory, says the LORD of hosts. The silver is mine, and the gold is mine, declares the LORD of hosts. The latter glory of this house shall be greater than the former, says the LORD of hosts. And in this place I will give peace, declares the LORD of hosts. (Hag. 2:6-9)[25]

That the Gentiles come from the nations also appears in other so-called messianic texts, such as Psalm 2, a passage that we will explore in the next chapter.[26]

One of the key factors about the effect of the Branch's reign that must be factored appears in the latter portion of the verse. The verse states 'this shall come to pass,' which refers to the prophecy of the Branch, but its fulfillment hinges upon the obedience of the people: 'And this shall come to pass, *if you* [pl.] *will diligently obey the voice of the LORD* your God' (emphasis added). In fact, the last part of v. 15 echoes Deuteronomy 28:1: 'And if you faithfully obey the voice of the LORD your God, being careful to do all his commandments that I command you today, the LORD your God

---

25. Meyers and Meyers, *Zechariah*, 360, 372.

26. Petterson, *Behold Your King*, 119; McComiskey, *Zechariah*, 1114; G. K. Beale, *The Temple and the Church's Mission: A Biblical Theology of the Dwelling Place of God* (Downers Grove: InterVarsity Press, 2004), 113.

will set you high above all the nations of the earth.'[27] But how can Israel hope to render acceptable obedience if they are just returning from exile, a punishment for their disobedience? Israel would undoubtedly look at their hands and recognize they were soiled by sin, which would negate their obedience. Hence, one of the constituent elements of the council of peace between Yahweh and the Branch is that the Christ would offer the necessary representative obedience that God required of Israel.[28]

Conclusion

Martin Luther cogently summarizes the overall thrust of this passage:

> Therefore do not be afraid. No one will be able to overcome or hinder you from your building. For because Christ is going to come, all things must be done. When He will have come, He will take up both the kingdom and the priesthood at the same time ... Therefore it becomes clear that we must not apply this text to Joshua the high priest, who is merely a sign and figure of that coming Man about whom he speaks, namely the growing Christ.[29]

God's eternal kingdom and its future ruler were typified in Zechariah's day by the crowning of Joshua the high priest.[30] But Zechariah not only points to the eschatological advent of Christ but also notes that He will sit and rule by Yahweh's throne. He takes up His priest-king role at His right hand and rules over the nations, all of which has been agreed to by Yahweh and Christ

---

27. Smith, *Zechariah*, 219; Meyers and Meyers, *Zechariah*, 365-66; Calvin, *Minor Prophets*, 162-63.

28. Petterson, *Behold Your King*, 113; Kline, *Glory in Our Midst*, 236-38.

29. Luther, *Minor Prophets*, LW 20:69.

30. Eichrodt, *Theology of the Old Testament*, 343.

in a 'counsel,' or covenant, of peace. God covenanted with David that one of his descendants would sit, rule, and build his temple. Zechariah's vision could be restricted to this temporal-historical horizon. Given that Zechariah's vision is not retrospective but prospective (i.e., it does not point back to the reestablishment of the Aaronic priesthood and the David monarchy but to the eschatological establishment of a Davidic king-priest), the more likely scenario is that the prophet has his eschatological vision anchored in eternity. In other words, Yahweh and the Messiah made a covenant in eternity, which was revealed in God's temporal covenant promise to David. And the typological crowning of Joshua the high priest points forward to the ultimate eschatological fulfillment of this intra-trinitarian covenant. But this doctrinal conclusion does not hinge upon Zechariah 6:13 alone. There is considerable evidence in other portions of Scripture that point to a pre-temporal covenant among the members of the triune God. We must therefore turn our attention to another key text, Psalm 2.

~:2:~

Psalm 2:7

Introduction

Psalm 2:7 is a biblical text that features prominently in the history of the exegesis behind the *pactum salutis*. Interpreters have correctly identified this text as a messianic psalm, prophesying the now present reign of the Messiah. But the doctrine of the covenant is an underappreciated dimension of this psalm. At first glance introducing the doctrine of the covenant to this psalm might seem misplaced. After all, the term *covenant* never appears. However, three factors place this psalm in a covenantal context. First, this passage lies within the orbit of Israel's covenantal laws regulating the inauguration of Israel's kings. Second, several key terms in this psalm, such as *decree* and *today*, find explanation in the soil of the Old Testament's doctrine of the covenant. Third, the Messiah was supposed to be an heir of David, the fulfillment of God's covenant promise that one of David's sons would sit upon Israel's throne. Hence, while the word *covenant* does not appear in this psalm, it is unintelligible apart from the doctrine of the covenant.

This chapter will proceed first with a brief survey of Psalm 2 followed by an exposition of Psalm 2:7, the specific verse in question. In the explanation of Psalm 2:7, the chapter divides the verse into its constituent parts: (a) I will tell of the decree; (b) you are my son; (c) today I have begotten you. It then explores the connections of Psalm 2 to its immediate context, and identifies the all-important relationship between the Messiah's obedience and His inauguration and enthronement as God's king on Zion – important elements that eventually figure into the doctrine of the *pactum salutis*. This chapter will also show that though Psalm 2 is a relatively small piece of Scripture, it has a subterranean root system that stretches far throughout the Old Testament and an equally elaborate aboveground series of branches that extend into the New Testament, all of which connect to the concept of covenant.

Background

Psalm 2 is a royal coronation psalm and, as such, should be associated with the monarchy of Israel. All royal psalms share a common term, *king*.[1] The inauguration of Israel's kings involved setting a crown upon the king's head, presenting a formal document to the king, anointing him, and heralding the king's installation.[2] Some suggest that this psalm would have been sung on the occasion of the enthronement of Israel's kings.[3] The psalmist begins the passage with a question as to why the nations rage against the Lord and His anointed, His messiah (Ps. 2:1-2). The kings of the earth take counsel together to break their bonds and cords so they can oppose the Lord's anointed (Ps. 2:3). In the face of such tumult and rebellion, Yahweh's response is not one of fear or concern but of derisive laughter (Ps. 2:4). Beneath His laughter the Lord

1. Hans-Joachim Kraus, *Psalms 1-59* (Minneapolis: Fortress, 1993), 125; idem, *Theology of the Psalms* (1986; Minneapolis: Fortress, 1992), 107-23.

2. Peter C. Craigie, *Psalms 1-50*, WBC (Nashville: Word, 1983), 64.

3. Kraus, *Psalms 1-59*, 126; Walther Eichrodt, *Theology of the Old Testament*, 2 vols. (Philadelphia: Westminster, 1961), I:477.

announces to the nations that He has set His king on Zion, His holy hill (Ps. 2:5-6). In the verses that follow (vv. 7-9) Yahweh then tells of His decree, which identifies the messianic king and the extent and power of His reign – the ends of the earth will be His possession and He will subjugate all opposition. The closing verses of the psalm issue a call to repentance: the kings of the earth should be wise and seek shelter in the Messiah lest He loose His righteous wrath upon them for their rebellion (Ps. 2:10-12).

I will tell of the decree

The establishment of the broader context provides a better position for understanding and appreciating Psalm 2:7: 'I will tell of the decree: The LORD said to me, "You are my Son; today I have begotten you."' The first question that must be answered is, What is the *decree?* The term itself, חק (*decree*) was employed for royal sacral law. It was a document that legitimized and identified the authoritative reign of a king.[4] But there are several other synonymous terms that illuminate the nature of this decree. The term עדות (*testimony*) can also be translated as *law* or *decree*.[5] The inauguration of Joash, king of Judah, is similar to the events described in Psalm 2: 'Then he brought out the king's son and put the crown on him and gave him the testimony [העדות]. And they proclaimed him king and anointed him, and they clapped their hands and said, "Long live the king"' (2 Kings 11:12; 2 Chron. 23:11; cf. 2 Chron. 23:3; Deut. 17:18).[6] Another synonymous term is ברית (*covenant*). The

---

4. Kraus, *Psalms 1-59*, 129.

5. Gerhard Von Rad, 'The Royal Ritual in Judah,' in *From Genesis to Chronicles: Explorations in Old Testament Theology* (Minneapolis: Fortress, 2005), 169; HALOT 1:790-91.

6. T. R. Hobbs, *2 Kings*, WBC (Waco: Word Books, 1985), 141; Raymond B. Dillard, *2 Chronicles*, WBC (Waco: Word Books, 1987), 182; Richard L. Pratt, *1 and*

psalmist writes: 'He remembers his covenant [בריתו] forever, the word that he commanded, for a thousand generations, the covenant that he made with Abraham, his sworn promise to Isaac, which he confirmed to Jacob as a statute [לחק], to Israel as an everlasting covenant [ברית עולם]' (Ps. 105:8-10).[7]

Psalm 105:8-10 reveals an overlap between these three terms: חק (*decree*), עדות (*testimony*), and ברית (*covenant*). The connection between חק and ברית is especially evident in Psalm 105:10, when the author uses the terms in a synonymous parallelism indicating their interchangeability. But how do all of these different ideas relate and inform our understanding of the decree in Psalm 2:7? How do ideas of a decree, testimony, and covenant all converge in the same term? They harmonize because they grow out of fertile covenantal soil and all address the same concept. The psalmist's interchangeable use of חק (*statute* or *decree*) and ברית (*covenant*) reflects the reality that God's laws were virtually synonymous with His covenant; the law at Sinai, for example, was covenantally administered (see, e.g., Exod. 20-24). However, the psalmist also notes that God 'swore a promise to Isaac' (Ps. 105:9), which equates the verbal promises of God with covenantal activity.[8] If we use the covenantal activity at Sinai as a guide, then we can say that God confirms His covenant with a promise and these words are then committed to writing, which constitute God's decrees or laws for His people.[9]

In this particular case, however, the context of Psalm 2:7 is one of royal inauguration, and if the 'decree' can also refer to a covenant, statute, or promise, then this term must indubitably

---

2 Chronicles (Fearn: Mentor, 1998), 367.

7. Hans-Joachim Kraus, *Psalms 60-150* (Minneapolis: Fortress, 1993), 310.

8. Cf. Kraus, *Psalms 60-150*, 310; Derek Kidner, *Psalms 73-150*, TOTC (Downers Grove: InterVarsity Press, 1973), 374-75.

9. Kraus, *Psalms 60-150*, 310.

point to the Davidic covenant. God promised David that one of his heirs would sit upon Israel's throne:

> When your days are fulfilled and you lie down with your fathers, I will raise up your offspring after you, who shall come from your body, and I will establish his kingdom. He shall build a house for my name, and I will establish the throne of his kingdom forever. I will be to him a father, and he shall be to me a son. When he commits iniquity, I will discipline him with the rod of men, with the stripes of the sons of men, but my steadfast love will not depart from him, as I took it from Saul, whom I put away from before you. And your house and your kingdom shall be made sure forever before me. Your throne shall be established forever. (2 Sam. 7:12-16)

Though 'covenant' does not appear in 2 Samuel 7:12-16, later in the narrative David characterizes God's promise as a covenant: 'For does not my house stand so with God? For he has made with me an everlasting covenant, ordered in all things and secure' (2 Sam. 23:5; cf. Gen. 9:16; Isa. 54:9-10; 55:3; Jer. 31:35-37).[10] The psalmist also describes God's promise as a covenant: 'You have said, "I have made a covenant with my chosen one; I have sworn to David my servant: I will establish your offspring forever, and build your throne for all generations"' (Ps. 89:3-4).[11]

In fact, in another passage from the Psalter we find the following: 'If your sons keep my covenant [בריתי] and my testimonies [ועדתי] that I shall teach them, their sons also forever shall sit on your throne' (Ps. 132:12).[12] Here the psalmist echoes the Davidic

---

10. Cf. A. A. Anderson, *2 Samuel*, WBC (Waco: Word Books, 1989), 269; Walter Brueggemann, *First and Second Samuel* (Louisville: John Knox Press, 1990), 346-47.

11. Kraus, *Psalms 60-150*, 204-05.

12. Cf. Kraus, *Psalms 60-150*, 481-82.

covenant with the elements of royal sons, the need for obedience, ruling on Israel's throne, and the close association of *covenant* and *testimonies*. All of this evidence points to the fact that, 'Under certain circumstances "covenant" and "testimony" (*'eduth*) are used as exact synonyms ... We may also refer once again to Psalm 2, for we see from Ps. 105:10 that "decree" (*hoq*) and "covenant" (*berith*) are so closely related as to be interchangeable terms.'[13] These considerations lead to the conclusion that when God announces the decree in Psalm 2:7, the covenant promise made to David that one of his heirs would sit upon Israel's throne to rule is in view. The rest of Psalm 2:7, in effect, confirms this interpretation, which is the substance of the Davidic covenant: 'You are my son.'[14] Recall God's words to David: 'I will be to him a father, and he shall be to me a son' (2 Sam. 7:14a).[15]

Given this information, at this stage we can conclude that the *decree* is a covenantal certificate given to the king during his inauguration ceremony (cf. 2 Kings 11:12). The decree is his personal copy of the document that renews God's covenantal promise to David, in which Yahweh promised to establish David's dynasty forever. This covenant-decree authoritatively establishes the legitimacy and identity of the king as the rightful Davidic heir to Israel's throne.[16]

---

13. Von Rad, 'Royal Ritual in Judah,' 171; idem, *Old Testament Theology*, 2 vols. (Louisville: WJK, 2001), 1.41 n.7; HALOT 1.346-47; cf. Peter Enns, חק, in *New International Dictionary of Old Testament Theology & Exegesis*, vol. 2 (Grand Rapids: Zondervan, 1997), 250-51; Aubrey R. Johnson, *Sacral Kingship in Ancient Israel* (1955; Eugene: Wipf & Stock, 2006), 20-21.

14. Von Rad, 'Royal Ritual in Judah,' 171.

15. Anderson, *2 Samuel*, 122; Bruce K. Waltke, *An Old Testament Theology* (Grand Rapids: Zondervan, 2007), 159; Jon D. Levenson, *Sinai & Zion: An Entry Into the Jewish Bible* (New York: Harper San Francisco, 1985), 201.

16. Craigie, *Psalms 1-50*, 67; Derek Kidner, *Psalms 1-72: An Introduction and*

You are my son

As stated above, at the heart of the covenant promise between God and King David is the father–son relationship: 'I will be to him a father, and he shall be to me a son' (2 Sam. 7:14; cf. Ps. 89:26).[17] But commentators have long argued that these words have greater significance beyond the initial original historical horizon: the Davidic offspring were ultimately prophetic and typological of Christ and His own kingdom.[18] In other words, as we will see below, these words have been applied to Jesus, and as such, 'you are my son,' reveals more when we consider that Yahweh is ultimately saying these words about His son, Jesus, the incarnate second person of the triune God. As the author of Hebrews writes, quoting Psalm 2:7 and 2 Samuel 7:14: 'For to which of the angels did God ever say, "You are my Son, today I have begotten you"? Or again, "I will be to him a father, and he shall be to me a son"' (Heb. 1:5)? The quotations of Psalm 2:7 and 2 Samuel 7:14 confirm that both texts are not only related but also ultimately speak of Jesus.[19] And in this particular case, these words refer to the second person of the Trinity, and His unique ontological relationship

---

Commentary, TOTC (Downers Grove: InterVarsity Press, 1973), 51; Richard P. Belcher, *The Messiah and the Psalms: Preaching Christ from all the Psalms* (Fearn: Mentor, 2006), 123; Mitchell Dahood, S.J., *Psalms I: 1-50*, AB, vol. 16 (New York: Doubleday, 1965), 11; C. A. Briggs, *The Book of Psalms*, ICC (1906; Edinburgh: T & T Clark, 1976), 15.

17. Johnson, *Sacral Kingship*, 25.

18. John Calvin, *The Book of Psalms*, Calvin's Commentaries, CTS, vol. 4 (Grand Rapids: Baker, 1993), 11; Waltke, *Old Testament Theology*, 894.

19. G. K. Beale and D. A. Carson, eds., *Commentary on the New Testament Use of the Old Testament* (Grand Rapids: Baker, 2007), 925-30, esp. 927; William Lane, *Hebrews 1-8*, WBC (Waco: Word Books, 1991), 24-26; Paul Ellingworth, *The Epistle to the Hebrews*, NIGTC (Grand Rapids: Eerdmans, 1993), 112, 114-16.

to God the Father.[20] This is the import of the Hebrews 1:5 citation of Psalm 2:7 – the superiority of Jesus over the angels, and hence a statement concerning His divinity. The incarnation of the eternally begotten Son is manifest in the temporal order through God's covenantal promise to King David.

Today I have begotten you

'Today I have begotten you' might seem to refer to the ontological genesis or alpha-point of the son, Jesus. However, this phrase does not denote the ontology of the son but rather is steeped in the language of the covenantal inauguration of the king, the messiah. The word *today* is related to covenantal renewal ceremonies, evident in several texts: 'You have declared *today* that the LORD is your God, and that you will walk in his ways, and keep his statutes and his commandments and his rules and will obey his voice' (Deut. 26:17; emphasis).[21] Likewise, we read the following: 'I call heaven and earth to witness against you *today*, that I have set before you life and death, blessing and curse. Therefore choose life, that you and your offspring may live' (Deut. 30:19; emphasis). Given that this declaration is the substance of God's covenantal decree, the term *today* emphasizes that this is a covenantal renewal ceremony (cf. Gen. 15:18; 31:48; 47:23; Josh. 14:9; 24:15; Ruth 4:5, 9-10).[22]

---

20. Cf. Ellingworth, *Hebrews*, 113-14; Walter Brueggemann, *Theology of the Old Testament: Testimony, Dispute, Advocacy* (Minneapolis: Fortress, 1997), 620-21; Geerhardus Vos, *The Self-Disclosure of Jesus: The Modern Debate about the Messianic Consciousness* (1926; Phillipsburg: P & R, 2002), 189-94.

21. Peter C. Craigie, *The Book of Deuteronomy*, NICOT (Grand Rapids: Eerdmans, 1976), 325.

22. Paul Kalluveettil, *Declaration and Covenant: A Comprehensive Review of Covenant Formulae from the Old Testament and the Ancient Near East* (Rome: Biblical Institute Press, 1982), 184.

In this case, God declares that His anointed, His Messiah, is the rightful Davidic heir – Yahweh is fulfilling His covenant promise to David.

Hence 'Today I have begotten you' is metaphorical language with legal overtones that convey the legal birth of the king – his inauguration and his coronation, not his ontological genesis.[23] The manner in which the New Testament cites this text confirms that these words apply to Christ's royal inauguration. God's fatherly approbation at His Son's baptism reflect the language of Psalm 2:7, 'This is my beloved Son, with whom I am well pleased' (Matt. 3:17; cf. Mark 1:11; Isa. 42:1).[24] Matthew also echoes these words in his account of Christ's transfiguration: 'This is my beloved Son, with whom I am well pleased; listen to him' (Matt. 17:5; 2 Pet. 1:17).[25] And the apostles cite Psalm 2:7 a number of times in their preaching. For example, Paul connected Christ's resurrection to Psalm 2:7, 'And we bring you the good news that what God promised to the fathers, this he has fulfilled to us their children by raising Jesus, as also it is written in the second Psalm, "You are my Son, today I have begotten you"' (Acts 13:32-33).[26] The author of Hebrews associates this text with Christ's appointment as high priest: 'So also Christ did not

---

23. Craigie, *Psalms 1-50*, 67; Othmar Keel, *The Symbolism of the Biblical World: Ancient Near Eastern Inconography and the Book of Psalms* (Winona: Eisenbrauns, 1997), 248; Beale and Carson, *New Testament Commentary*, 927-28; Joseph Fitzmyer, *The Dead Sea Scrolls and Christian Origins* (Grand Rapids: Eerdmans, 2000), 66; Brueggemann, *Theology of the Old Testament*, 606.

24. Beale and Carson, *New Testament Commentary*, 14; W. D. Davies and D. C. Allison, *Matthew*, ICC, 3 vols. (1988; Edinburgh: T & T Clark, 2006), I:336-40.

25. Beale and Carson, *New Testament Commentary*, 55; Davies and Allison, *Matthew*, 2.701-02.

26. Beale and Carson, *New Testament Commentary*, 584-85; C. K. Barrett, *Acts*, ICC, 2 vols. (Edinburgh: T & T Clark, 1998), 1:648.

exalt himself to be made a high priest, but was appointed by him who said to him, "You are my Son, today I have begotten you"' (Heb. 5:5).[27] The combination of priestly and kingly images evokes Psalm 110.[28]

Romans 1:1-4 combines these same elements and connects them to Christ's resurrection:

> Paul, a servant of Christ Jesus, called to be an apostle, set apart for the gospel of God, which he promised beforehand through his prophets in the holy Scriptures, concerning his Son, who was descended from David according to the flesh and was declared to be the Son of God in power according to the Spirit of holiness by his resurrection from the dead, Jesus Christ our Lord.

In this tightly compact statement Paul identifies the Messiah, as the son of David, promised beforehand in the holy Scriptures through the prophets (such as in Psalm 2). Specifically noteworthy is that Paul says that Christ was 'declared' (ὁρισθέντος), or more properly 'appointed,' the Son of God in power, which echoes Psalm 2:7 and the Lord's decree to appoint the messiah as king.[29] The words, 'Today I have begotten you,' therefore, refer to the inauguration-resurrection of Jesus.

---

27. Patrick Henry Reardon, *Christ in the Psalms* (Chesterton: Conciliar Press, 2000), 4; Kidner, *Psalms 1-72*, 51.

28. Beale and Carson, *New Testament Commentary*, 960; Lane, *Hebrews*, 1.118; David Wallace, 'The Use of Psalms in the Shaping of a Text: Psalm 2:7 and Psalm 110:1 in Hebrews 1,' *Restoration Quarterly* 45/1-2 (2003): 41-50, esp. 48ff.

29. Thomas Schreiner, *Romans*, BECNT (Grand Rapids: Baker, 1998), 39-42; L. C. Allen, 'The Old Testament Background of (προ)Ὀρίζειν in the New Testament,' *NTS* 17 (1970-71): 104-08; Douglas Moo, *The Epistle to the Romans*, NICNT (Grand Rapids: Eerdmans, 1996), 48; Robert Jewett, *Romans*, Hermenia (Minneapolis: Fortress, 2007), 104.

Psalm 2:7 and the Messiah's obedience

The context of Psalm 2 is important for a number of reasons, but chiefly because it draws attention to the necessity of the obedience of the Messiah. Psalm 2 follows Psalm 1, which may seem like an obvious observation until we consider that the two psalms were not randomly placed next to one another. Recent research has persuasively argued that Psalms 1 and 2 were originally viewed as one literary unit; chapters and verses were not added to the Scriptures until the thirteenth century.[30] In fact, certain textual variants of Acts 13:33 cite Psalm 2:7 as appearing in 'the first psalm.'[31] Viewed as an interconnected unit, then, Psalm 1 presents the one man who meditates upon and obeys God's law, and Psalm 2 introduces the covenant promises of the Davidic kingship, the enthroned obedient king. Peter Craigie explains these connections in the following manner:

> The evidence from the early Christian tradition is found in Acts 13:33. The writer, Luke, gives a quotation from Psalm 2:7, but introduces it as coming from the first psalm; the corrections, both in the early Greek text and in modern English versions, to read 'the second psalm,' are appropriate given the change in the conventional system of numbering the Psalms. Nevertheless, the oldest Greek text of Acts provides evidence for the early Christian view that the first two psalms were considered to be a single unit.... It has also been suggested that the two psalms were joined together to form a coronation liturgy, perhaps for one of the last kings of Judah; the

30. G. F. Moore, 'The Vulgate Chapter and Numbered Verses In the Hebrew Bible,' *JBL* 12/1 (1893): 73-78.

31. Gerald Henry Wilson, *The Editing of the Hebrew Psalter* (Atlanta: SBL, 1985), 204-06; Bruce M. Metzger, *A Textual Commentary on the Greek New Testament*, 2nd ed. (1971; Stuttgart: German Bible Society, 2002), 363-65; Kraus, *Psalms 1-59*, 125.

> king, at his coronation, pledged himself to fulfill the Deuteronomic law of kings.[32]

If Craigie's argument is correct, then Psalms 1 and 2 present the picture of the king who is inaugurated and granted his inheritance, to rule over the nations, because of his obedience to the law.[33]

Craigie draws attention to the laws pertaining to the inauguration of kings, which provide greater context for the events described in Psalms 1 and 2. In particular, when an Israelite king was inaugurated, he was supposed to write for himself a personal copy of the book of the law, one approved by the Levitical priests (Deut. 17:18). Against the backdrop of covenant-making practices of the ancient Near East, that Israel's king would keep a duplicate copy of the law makes perfect sense. A duplicate copy of the covenant between a suzerain and his vassal was supposed to be periodically read in public. The suzerain was supposed to keep a copy, which he placed in the temple of his god. In a similar manner, Israel's kings were supposed to maintain a copy of God's covenant law, and the Levites kept this law in the temple.[34] Given that these instructions appear in Deuteronomy, which was a renewal of the Sinai covenant, it appears that the king would have created a copy of the entire Sinai covenant law.[35]

---

32. Craigie, *Psalms 1-50*, 59-60; W. H. Brownlee, 'Psalms 1-2 as Coronation Liturgy,' *Bib* 52 (1971): 321-36.

33. Brevard S. Childs, *Biblical Theology of the Old and New Testaments: Theological Reflection on the Christian Bible* (Minneapolis: Fortress, 1992), 479; Nahum Sarna, *On the Book of Psalms: Exploring the Prayers of Ancient Israel* (New York: Schocken Books, 1993), 27, 31.

34. J. A. Thompson, *Deuteronomy*, TOTC (Downers Grove: InterVarsity Press, 2008), 206; Meredith G. Kline, *Treaty of the Great King* (Grand Rapids: Eerdmans, 1963), 98.

35. Peter C. Craigie, *Deuteronomy*, NICOT (Grand Rapids: Eerdmans, 1976), 256; cf. Meredith G. Kline, *The Structure of Biblical Authority* (Eugene: Wipf & Stock, 1997).

The implication was that the king was responsible to obey the whole law of God, but to what end?

Deuteronomy 17:19-20 helps to answer this question:

> And it shall be with him, and he shall read in it all the days of his life, that he may learn to fear the LORD his God by keeping all the words of this law and these statutes, and doing them, that his heart may not be lifted up above his brothers, and that he may not turn aside from the commandment, either to the right hand or to the left, so that he may continue long in his kingdom, he and his children, in Israel.

The king's obedience was representative on behalf of the people – he was to offer unswerving obedience to God's law and the effect or consequence of this covenant fidelity was long life in the land, for him and his children (cf. Josh. 1:1-8). The king would ensure the perpetuity of his dynasty, a principle that appears in seminal form here in Deuteronomy but is revealed with greater clarity in God's covenant promise to David in 2 Samuel 7:14, and is prophetically anchored in the obedience and eschatological reign of the Messiah in Psalms 1 and 2.[36] Concerning the connections between 2 Samuel 7:14 and Psalm 2, Walter Brueggemann states: 'In one sweeping assurance, the conditional "if" of the Mosaic Torah (Exod. 19:5-6) is overridden, and David is made a vehicle and carrier of Yahweh's unqualified grace in Israel.'[37] In other words, salvation ultimately hinges upon the obedience of the incarnate Messiah and not the people of God.[38]

---

36. J. G. McConville, *Deuteronomy*, AOTC (Downers Grove: InterVarsity Press, 2002), 296; also Johnson, *Sacral Kingship*, 11.

37. Brueggemann, *Theology of the Old Testament*, 604-05; also Patrick D. Miller, 'The Beginning of the Psalter,' in *Shape and Shaping of the Psalter*, ed. J. Clinton McCann, Jr. (Sheffield: JSOT Press, 1993), 91.

38. Johnson, *Sacral Kingship*, 22.

Therefore when Yahweh says to the Messiah, 'Ask of me, and I will make the nations your heritage, and the ends of the earth your possession' (Ps. 2:8), we must not assume God has bequeathed the nations as an inauguration gift. Rather, given the Deuteronomic inauguration backdrop of the requisite kingly obedience, and the immediate context of Psalm 1 and the righteous man, we must view the inheritance of the nations as the Messiah's reward for His faithfulness. Or in the words of the apostle Paul:

> Being found in human form, he humbled himself by becoming obedient to the point of death, even death on a cross. Therefore God has highly exalted him and bestowed on him the name that is above every name, so that at the name of Jesus every knee should bow, in heaven and on earth and under the earth, and every tongue confess that Jesus Christ is Lord, to the glory of God the Father. (Phil. 2:8-11; cf. Isa. 45:18-25)[39]

Paul explains that because Christ was obedient unto death, God *therefore* exalted Him. Paul conveys the move from humiliation to exaltation through the use of an inferential conjunction διὸ together with the conjunction καὶ, which reveals reciprocity between the Father and the Son. In other words, Christ obeys and His Father responds by exalting His Son: obedience ⇨ exaltation. The inference from the preceding verse (v. 8) is plainly manifest, hence Paul's use of *therefore* at the beginning of verse 9.[40] The Messiah's

---

39. Calvin, *Psalms*, 19.

40. Peter T. O'Brien, *The Epistle to the Philippians*, NIGTC (Grand Rapids: Eerdmans, 1991), 232-33; Ralph P. Martin, *A Hymn of Christ: Philippians 2:5-11 in Recent Interpretation & In the Setting of Early Christian Worship* (Downers Grove: InterVarsity Press, 1997), 231-35; Beale and Carson, *New Testament Commentary*, 836-37; cf. Moisés Silva, *Philippians*, 2nd ed., BECNT (Grand Rapids: Baker, 2005), 108-09; Gordon D. Fee, *Paul's Letter to the Philippians*, NICNT (Grand Rapids: Eerdmans, 1995), 220-21; John Calvin, *Galatians, Ephesians, Philippians, & Colossians*, CNTC (Grand Rapids: Eerdmans, 1996), 250.

obedience yields the fruit of His exaltation, kingly inauguration, and rule over the nations.[41]

Conclusion

The overall message of Psalm 2:7 within its immediate context, the broader contexts of Psalms 1 and 2, and the rest of Scripture paints a prophetic portrait of the inauguration of the Messiah's reign. Christ's coronation grows out of the fertile covenantal soil of the Old Testament, whether in the terminology employed in Psalm 2:7, which echoes the Davidic covenant, or in the Deuteronomic backdrop of the covenantal inauguration ceremony for Israel's kings. As Calvin writes:

> Unless, therefore, we suppose this prophecy concerning the vast extent of kingdom to have been uttered in vain and falsely, we must apply it to Christ, who alone has subdued the whole world to himself, and embraced all lands and nations under his dominion. Accordingly, here, as in many other places, the calling of the Gentiles is foretold, to prevent all from imagining that the Redeemer who was to be sent of God was king of one nation only.[42]

Just as with Zechariah's vision of the kingly priest who sits by Yahweh's throne and rules over the nations, Psalm 2 presents a messianic prophecy of Jesus, the Christ, the rightful Davidic heir, the one who is inaugurated as king to rule over the nations. But Christ's inauguration and God's decree is not a bald declaration but rather is enrobed in the covenant.

God's covenantal decree that one of David's heirs would rule over the nations played out on the stage of redemptive history,

41. Belcher, *Messiah and the Psalms*, 123.

42. Calvin, *Psalms*, 19.

yet it was rooted in eternity. While eternity barely raises its head in this psalm, its presence is nonetheless evident with Yahweh's declaration: 'You are my son' (Ps. 2.7a). Some might contend that the original historical horizon exhausts the significance of this statement, namely, that the messiah was legally adopted through God's decree. While this is certainly possible, the more likely answer is the Son's eternal relationship with His Father grounds the redemptive historical outworking of His earthly ministry. This brings two important implications that will be explored in subsequent chapters. First, the Son's eternal procession from the Father undergirds His mission as the Messiah – His life, death, resurrection, and ascension – and is rooted in His identity as the second person of the Trinity. Second, the timeframe of God the Father's covenant with the Son originates in eternity, not in redemptive history. God makes a covenant with David, and the other patriarchs for that matter, because of His covenant with the Son in eternity. The first observation will be explored in Part III, under the dogmatic construction of the doctrine. However, the second observation does not require inference or speculation based merely upon the first half of Psalm 2:7. Rather, the apostle Paul deals with the timing of God's covenantal activity with the Son in Ephesians 1 and 2 Timothy 1:9-10, which will be treated in a subsequent chapter. But first, we must turn to examine briefly another key *pactum* text, namely, Psalm 110.

~:3:~

Psalm 110

Introduction

Thus far in our study we have surveyed two key texts, Zechariah 6:13 and Psalm 2:7. Both of these texts present overlapping themes regarding the Messiah's universal reign over Israel and the Gentile nations. Both texts present images, terms, and ideas associated with the offices of king and priest, and they do so from within a covenantal framework. The covenantal subtext is especially evident in Psalm 2 when Yahweh tells of the covenant-decree, 'You are my son, today I have begotten you.' There is one text in the Old Testament, however, that presents some of the clearest and most powerful priest-king imagery, namely, Psalm 110. This text was not only prominent in the Psalter, but its subsequent use and interpretation by New Testament authors identify it as a crucial passage for a proper christology, one that binds a number of themes across the canon of Scripture. However, as stated in the introduction, christology is not an island unto itself, but straddles and intersects with a number of other doctrines. In this case the doctrine of the covenants is of greatest interest. Christology and covenant find their nexus in Yahweh's oath: 'The LORD says to my Lord: "Sit at my right hand, until I make your enemies your footstool'" (Ps. 110:1). Yahweh's oath is more than a verbal utterance. In common terms, Yahweh's word is His bond, His covenant. Of equal interest and importance is the timeframe of this covenant-oath. When did Yahweh swear a covenant-oath to the Christ? Addressing these two issues, the nature of Yahweh's oath and its timeframe, will occupy the rest of the chapter and provide another chief exegetical mooring for the doctrine of the *pactum salutis*.

Background

Psalm 110 belongs to the category of royal psalms, texts that were sung upon the occasion of the inauguration of Israel's kings. This festival involved the enthronement, the investiture, the declaration that the king was God's son, praise, his ordination as a priest, declared victory over Israel's foes, and a sacramental consumption of holy water, which was likely drawn from the spring of Gihon (Ps. 110:7). As such, the installation ritual indicated that the king was the heir over the old Jebusite city, Jerusalem, as well as the Davidic heir (cf. Gen. 14:18ff; 2 Sam. 7; Ps. 132).[1]

The covenantal inauguration

The psalm begins with the acknowledgement that David is the author, something repeatedly confirmed by the New Testament in a number of places (e.g., Mark 12:36; Acts 2:33-35). David's words constitute the enthronement oracle typically given to Israel's kings, the decree or covenant mentioned, for example, in Psalm 2:7 (cf. 1 Sam. 10:1ff; 2 Kings 11:12). And like Psalm 2:7, where Yahweh utters the decree, 'You are my son, today I have begotten you,' David indicates that this psalm is 'the oracle of

1. Hans-Joachim Kraus, *Theology of the Psalms* (Minneapolis: Fortress, 1992), 110-12.

Yahweh to my lord.'[2] In both texts Yahweh directly addresses the Christ. In fact, Psalm 110 echoes a number of key features present in Psalm 2, such as the declaration of the birth of the king (Ps. 2:7), which has a parallel in Psalm 110's announcement that the priest-king has been born from the 'womb of the morning' (v. 3).[3] Another similar pattern appears with the priest-king ruling over the nations. In Psalm 110 the priest-king shatters the earth's kings on the day of his wrath and executes judgment upon the nations (vv. 5-6). These images correspond to the kings who gather themselves against the Lord and His Anointed and suffer His wrath (Ps. 2:3-5).[4] David, therefore, falls down upon his face and worships the man who stands before him as his descendant, *Adonai*, his lord.[5] David then reveals Yahweh's covenant oracle to his lord: 'Sit at my right hand, until I make your enemies your footstool' (Ps. 110:1). As Samuel announced to David, 'And you shall reign over the people of the LORD and you will save them from the hand of their surrounding enemies' (1 Sam. 10:1), Yahweh announces the Messiah's royal session at His right hand, which entails ruling over both Israel and her enemies.

It may surprise some readers, but Psalm 110 is one of the most cited Old Testament passages in the New Testament, which provides important interpretive data to help us understand its significance. Psalm 110 appears in the New Testament thirty-three times in quotation or allusion (see e.g., Matt. 22:41-45; 26:64;

2. Derek Kidner, *Psalms 73-150*, TOTC (Downers Grove: InterVarsity Press, 1973), 392-93.

3. Hans-Joachim Kraus, *Psalms 60-150* (Minneapolis: Fortress, 1993), 350.

4. G. K. Beale, *A New Testament Biblical Theology: The Unfolding of the Old Testament in the New* (Grand Rapids: Baker, 2011), 286; Aubrey R. Johnson, *Sacral Kingship in Ancient Israel* (Eugene: Wipf & Stock, 1955), 120-22.

5. Kidner, *Psalms 73-150*, 393.

Mark 12:35-37; Luke 20:41-44; 22:69; Acts 2:34-35; 7:55; Rom. 8:34; 1 Cor. 15:25; Eph. 1:20; Col. 3:1; Heb. 1:3, 13; 5:6ff; 7:1ff; 8:1; 10:12; 1 Pet. 3:22).[6] According to the author of Hebrews, Jesus is not only greater than David, as David attests by calling Him, 'my lord,' but Jesus is superior to the angels: 'And to which of the angels has he ever said, "Sit at my right hand until I make your enemies a footstool for your feet"' (Heb. 1:13)?[7] The man that the Jews rejected is the man whom the Father has exalted: 'The God of our fathers raised Jesus, whom you killed by hanging him on a tree. God exalted him at his right hand as Leader and Savior' (Acts 5:30-31). Jesus presently intercedes in royal session 'at the right hand of God' (Rom. 8:34).[8] Unlike the high priests who entered the holy of holies and *stood* to administer the sacrificial rites, Jesus entered the heavenly holy of holies and *sat down* at the Father's right hand, where He awaits the subjugation of His enemies (Heb. 10:11-13; cf. 1 Cor. 15:20-28). David, then, packs this one verse with much grist for the christological mill, as he speaks of the glory of the priest-king and his work.[9] From David's vantage point this priestly king will rule in the future; He will rule both over His enemies as well as over Israel, whose subjects will 'offer themselves freely' (Ps. 110:3-4; cf. Judg. 5:2). Paul employs this very language to characterize believers as 'living sacrifices.' The apostle also describes his own life in a similar manner, as a drink offering (Rom. 12:1; Phil. 2:17).[10]

---

6. Kraus, *Psalms 60-150*, 354; David M. Hay, *Glory at the Right Hand: Psalm 110 in Early Christianity* (Nashville: Abingdon, 1973), 13.

7. G. K. Beale and D. A. Carson, eds., *Commentary on the New Testament Use of the Old Testament* (Grand Rapids: Baker, 2007), 942-44; Hay, *Glory*, 82.

8. Hay, *Glory*, 59-60.

9. Kidner, *Psalms 73-150*, 393.

10. Kidner, *Psalms 73-150*, 394.

The second divine utterance comes in verse 4: 'The LORD has sworn and will not change his mind, "You are a priest forever after the order of Melchizedek."' If there is anything stronger than an oracle, it is God's personal oath, which He swears here to David's lord. The author of Hebrews repeats this point on two different occasions. The first appears in Hebrews 6: 'So when God desired to show more convincingly to the heirs of the promise the unchangeable character of his purpose, he guaranteed it with an oath' (v. 17). The immutability of God's oath is evident from the latter half of Psalm 110:4, which states that God 'will not change his mind.' The second use of the oath-formula occurs later in Hebrews 7: 'And it was not without an oath. For those who formerly became priests were made such without an oath, but this one was made a priest with an oath by the one who said to him: "The LORD has sworn and will not change his mind, You are a priest forever." This makes Jesus the guarantor of a better covenant' (Heb. 7:20-22).[11]

David's revelation of Yahweh's oath is significant for the doctrine of the *pactum salutis* for two chief reasons. First, when God swears an oath, it is not a bald utterance but is robed in the doctrine of the covenant. Within the Old Testament Scriptures swearing an oath is tantamount to invoking a covenantal bond between two or more parties.[12] In fact, some have characterized the covenant as a relationship based on an oath (cf. Gen. 21:22-24, 27, 31; 26:26-30; Josh. 9:15; 14:13; Neh. 6:18).[13] A number of scholars from a diverse representative cross-section

11. Kidner, *Psalms 73-150*, 395; Beale and Carson, *New Testament Commentary*, 960-62.

12. Meredith G. Kline, *By Oath Consigned: A Reinterpretation of the Covenant Signs of Circumcision and Baptism* (Grand Rapids: Eerdmans, 1968), 16.

13. Dennis J. McCarthy, *Treaty and Covenant: A Study in Form in the Ancient Oriental Documents and in the Old Testament* (Rome: Pontifical Biblical Institute, 1981), 43, 185, 253, cf. 143, 182.

draw the same conclusion.[14] In the context of His covenant with Abraham, God swore an oath to confirm the inviolability of His covenantal commitment; this is the point that the author of Hebrews makes in the above-cited passage (Heb. 6:17-18; cf. Gen. 15).[15] The close association between covenant and oath appears in the psalmist's characterization of the Abrahamic covenant reconfirmed to Isaac: 'He remembers his covenant forever, the word that he commanded, for a thousand generations, the covenant that he made with Abraham, his sworn promise [ושׁבועתו] to Isaac' (Ps. 105:9-10).[16] Here in Psalm 105:9 the psalmist employs the noun-form of the verb used in Psalm 110:4, 'The Lord has sworn [נשׁבע].' The correlation between oath and covenant appear in several other texts in the Old Testament: And he made a covenant with them and put them under oath [וישׁבע] in the house of the Lord, and he showed them the king's son' (2 Kings 11:4). A similar pattern appears in the prophet Ezekiel, though the prophet employs a different term: 'And he took one of the royal offspring and made a covenant with him, putting him under oath [באלה]' (17:13; cf. 17:16, 18, 19; 16:59; Ezek. 17:18-20 LXX).[17] A host of other texts also use oath and covenant interchangeably (Deut. 7:12; 8:18; 29:14; Josh. 9:15-20;

---

14. See, e.g., Scott W. Hahn, *Kinship by Covenant: A Canonical Approach to the Fulfillment of God's Saving Purposes* (New Haven: Yale University Press, 2009), 50-59; Jacob Milgrom, *Leviticus 1-16*, AB (New York: Doubleday, 1991), 490; O. Palmer Robertson, *The Christ of the Covenants* (Phillipsburg: P & R, 1980), 7; Gordon P. Hugenburger, *Marriage as Covenant: Biblical Law and Ethics as Developed from Malachi* (Grand Rapids: Baker, 1994), 183; Paul R. Williamson, *Sealed with an Oath: Covenant in God's Unfolding Purpose* (Downers Grove: InterVarsity Press, 2007), 35-36, 39, 42.

15. Kline, *By Oath Consigned*, 16-17.

16. Kline, *By Oath Consigned*, 22.

17. Williamson, *Sealed with an Oath*, 36; Gareth Lee Cockerill, 'The Melchizedek Christology in Hebrews 7:1-28,' (Ph.D. diss., Union Theological Seminary, 1976), 123-24.

Judg. 2:1; 2 Chron. 15:12-15; Hosea 10:4; Wis. 10:22; 12:21; 18:22; Sir. 44:20-21; Luke 1:72-73).[18]

Yahweh's earlier promise to David involves His use of an oath, a sworn promise, to initiate a covenant: 'I will be to him a father, and he shall be to me a son. When he commits iniquity, I will discipline him with the rod of men, with the stripes of the sons of men' (2 Sam. 7:14). This text lies in the background behind Zechariah 6:13 and Psalm 2 and likewise sits beneath the surface here in Psalm 110. Although the term *covenant* does not appear in its original context, Yahweh's oath was later identified as a covenant: 'You have said, "I have made a covenant with my chosen one; I have sworn [נשבעתי] to David my servant: 'I will establish your offspring forever, and build your throne for all generations'"' (Ps. 89:3-4).[19] Hence, when Yahweh swears the oath that David's lord is a priest forever according to the order of Melchizedek, this utterance is a covenant-oath.

Confirmation of Yahweh's covenant-oath appears in the second observation concerning the New Testament interpretation of Psalm 110:4. The author of Hebrews specifically identifies the covenant-oath of Psalm 110:4 as that which establishes Jesus as the 'guarantor of a better covenant' (Heb. 7:22).[20] The guarantor (ἔγγυος) or surety (*sponsio, fideiussor, expromissor*) is the one who certifies that the promises of the covenant will be carried out. In contrast to a mediator, one who merely stands in the gap between two disputants, a guarantor places his own life on the line by his word (cf. Sirach 29:15; 2 Maccabees 10:28).[21] The old covenant

---

18. Hahn, *Kinship by Covenant*, 361 n. 13.

19. Kraus, *Psalms 60-150*, 350-51.

20. Cockerill, 'Melchizedek Christology,' 128.

21. William Lane, *Hebrews 1-8*, WBC (Dallas: Word, 1991), 188; Paul Ellingworth, *The Epistle to the Hebrews*, NIGTC (Grand Rapids: Eerdmans, 1993), 388; Cockerill,

had a mediator, Moses (Gal. 3:19), but not a guarantor.[22] In this particular case, the author of Hebrews contrasts the inferior Levitical priesthood with the superior priesthood of Christ, which is according to the order of Melchizedek.[23]

The Levitical priesthood was predicated upon the law and dependent upon a successive line of genealogical descent, which was constantly hampered by the specter of death. In fact, Josephus (37–ca. 100) claims that from the inauguration of the Aaronide priesthood until the destruction of the temple in AD 70 Israel had eighty-three high priests.[24] If the priestly line were ever cut off, then the sacrificial system would come to a screeching halt because there was no one to offer the requisite daily and yearly sacrifices. In a sense, this breach of the priestly line occurred when Israel was taken into exile – the temple, priests, and sacrificial system ceased to function. The destruction of the temple brought the cessation of all Levitical priestly activity. Christ's priesthood, however, was founded upon the covenant-oath of Yahweh – an everlasting promise, which was fulfilled by Jesus.[25]

However much some interpreters restrict David's psalm to its original horizon and the inauguration of Israel's kings, the reader is irresistibly drawn to view this psalm's fulfillment in Christ. This christological reading is not a foreign imposition upon the text but rather grows out of Christ's own reading of the text along with the subsequent apostolic canonical witness. But from David's vantage point the question arises, At what point did Yahweh say to David's future heir, 'Sit at my right hand until I make your enemies your

---

'Melchizedek Christology,' 125-26.

22. F. F. Bruce, *The Epistle to the Hebrews*, NICNT (Grand Rapids: 1964), 151.

23. Hay, *Glory*, 146-

24. Lane, *Hebrews 1-8*, 188; Josephus, *Antiquities*, 20.227.

25. Cockerill, 'Melchizedek Christology,' 128.

footstool'? When did Yahweh swear a covenant-oath directly to Jesus, 'You are a priest forever after the order of Melchizedek'?[26] Those who correctly identify Jesus as the proper subject of this psalm must acknowledge that Scripture records no historical event when Yahweh uttered this covenantal oath to Jesus.[27] Nothing appears in the Gospels or its subsequent apostolic interpretation, yet Christ nevertheless told His disciples, 'I covenant to you, as my Father covenanted to me, a kingdom' (Luke 22:29*). In fact, within the very context where Christ announces His covenanted kingdom to His disciples, Jesus invokes Psalm 110 before the crowd that has come to arrest Him: 'But from now on the Son of Man shall be seated at the right hand of the power of God' (Luke 22:69).[28] In other words, up until His arrest Jesus had not yet ascended to His royal session at the Father's right hand. Given that we possess no recorded historical event where this covenantal bond was initiated, we are naturally forced to look backward into eternity for the timeframe of this event.

Hebrews confirms this conclusion when the author interprets Psalm 110:3 and identifies Christ as a priest according to the order of Melchizedek. This indicates that the Father made Jesus the surety of a better covenant, the new covenant. The new covenant, which the author of Hebrews identifies as the very same expounded by the prophet Jeremiah (Heb. 8:8-12; cf. Jer. 31:31-34), post-dates Psalm 110.[29] Thus, while David was

26. Lane, *Hebrews*, 187; Cockerill, 'Melchizedek Christology,' 128-29, 186-87.

27. R. Scott Clark and David VanDrunen, 'The Covenant Before the Covenants,' in *Covenant, Justification, and Pastoral Ministry*, ed. R. Scott Clark (Philipsburg: P & R, 2007), 187 n. 57, 193-94.

28. Hay, *Glory*, 69.

29. Beale and Carson, *New Testament Commentary*, 970-72; Ellingworth, *Hebrews*, 414.

perhaps unaware of the specifics, his own prophetic vision of the enthronement of the great priest-king anticipated Jeremiah's vision of the inauguration of the new covenant. From David's vantage point the events he was describing were future, since Jesus had not yet been born. Yet the author of Hebrews argues that this psalm reveals that when Jesus was made the surety of the new covenant, 'this one was made a priest with an oath' (Heb. 7:21). The simplest answer to this apparent dilemma lies in recognizing that the event did not occur in history but in eternity when the Trinity planned and conceived the redemption of the elect.[30]

At this point one might be led to the conclusion that the pre-temporal covenantal activity exists solely between the Father and the Son, given that the former swears a covenant-oath to the latter. Where is the Holy Spirit? While the role of the Spirit in the *pactum salutis* will receive greater attention in the following chapters, suffice it to say that subsequent apostolic interpretation of Psalm 110 connects the work of the Spirit to the Father's covenant-oath to the Son. In particular, Luke links Christ's royal session at the Father's right hand to the outpouring of the Spirit:

> This Jesus God raised up, and of that we all are witnesses. Being therefore exalted at the right hand of God, and having received

---

30. Some might object to this conclusion based upon how some translations render Hebrews 7:28, e.g., 'For the law appoints as high priests men who are weak; but the oath, which came after the law, appointed the Son, who has been made perfect forever' (NIV). The implication of the translation of this verse is that the oath of Hebrews 7:21 (Ps. 110:4) 'came after the law,' which would place it within history rather than eternity. But Hebrews 7:28 specifically states, ὁ λόγος δὲ τῆς ὁρκωμοσας ('but the *word* of the oath,' emphasis). That the author states that the *word* of the oath came after the law indicates that the *revelation* of the oath occurred after the law, i.e., that David revealed the oath in Psalm 110 after the revelation of the law, not that God the Father made the oath to the Son after the administration of the Mosaic covenant (Hay, *Glory*, 148-49). I am grateful to my colleague, Steve Baugh, for making this observation and bringing it to my attention.

> from the Father the promise of the Holy Spirit, he has poured out this that you yourselves are seeing and hearing. For David did not ascend into the heavens, but he himself says, 'The Lord said to my Lord, "Sit at my right hand, until I make your enemies your footstool."' (Acts 2:32-35; cf. Ps. 16:8-11; Joel 2:28-32)[31]

Part of the Father's covenant-oath included sending the Spirit to anoint the Son and equip Him for His work as the Anointed, the Messiah; the Spirit would also apply the Son's work of redemption to the elect.[32] Just as the Father's covenant-oath implies the Son's voluntary willingness to undertake the high-priestly work as covenant surety for the elect, the fact that Peter connects the Spirit's outpouring to the Son's appointment reveals the Spirit's voluntary willingness to assume His role in the *pactum* (cf. John 7:39; 14:26; 15:26; 16:7; Eph. 4:8-10).[33] More broadly, Luke's quotation of Psalm 110 further highlights the trinitarian nature of our redemption as well as the intra-trinitarian deliberation within the *pactum salutis*. Equally noteworthy, and something to be explored in subsequent chapters, is the idea that the *pactum salutis* is the pre-temporal counterpart to all of redemptive history, but especially the eschaton. Or in other terms, the *pactum* is the counterpart to the covenant of grace. Christ's inauguration signals the launch of the last days, and Spirit's outpouring also reveals the dawning of the new creation.[34]

---

31. C. K. Barrett, *Acts*, ICC, vol. 1 (Edinburgh: T & T Clark, 1994), 150.

32. Hay, *Glory*, 92; F. F. Bruce, *The Book of Acts*, NICNT (Grand Rapids: Eerdmans, 1988), 66-67.

33. John Calvin, *Acts 1-13*, CNTC (Grand Rapids: Eerdmans, 1996), 74; Simon J. Kistemaker, *Acts* (Grand Rapids: Baker, 1990), 100-01; Darrell Bock, *Acts*, BECNT (Grand Rapids: Baker, 2007), 132-37.

34. Bock, *Acts*, 137.

Conclusion

Psalm 110 is one of the clearer pieces of evidence for the *pactum salutis*. Yahweh swears a covenant-oath to the Christ in eternity, which establishes His priestly office according to the order of Melchizedek and appoints Him the guarantor or surety of the new covenant. But there are still two other crucial texts that should be considered, Ephesians 1 and 2 Timothy 1:9-10. Themes such as christology, soteriology, covenant, the Messiah, and His kingly rule over the nations have appeared throughout the three surveyed texts, Zechariah 6:13, Psalm 2:7, and Psalm 110. All of these themes and doctrines coalesce in the opening chapters of Paul's letter to the Ephesians and 2 Timothy 1:9-10, two texts to which we now turn.

~:4:~

Ephesians 1 and 2 Timothy 1:9-10

Introduction

The three previous chapters surveyed Zechariah 6:13, Psalm 2:7, and Psalm 110, passages which demonstrate key elements that substantiate the doctrine of the *pactum salutis*. These passages present images of God making a covenant with the Messiah who then rules over the nations. The Davidic covenant (2 Sam. 7:14) permeates all three passages – the priest-king sits by Yahweh's throne and rules over the nations (Zech. 6:13; Ps. 110), the Lord heralds the covenant (the decree), and His anointed rules over the kings of the earth (Ps. 2:7-8). Critics of the *pactum salutis* grant that these verses speak of the covenantal reign of the Messiah, but they contend that these passages deal with the historical unfolding of God's covenant with David, not a pre-temporal covenant made among the members of the Trinity. But the *pactum salutis* does not rest upon one or two isolated texts but rather upon a concatenation of passages spread across the Scriptures. In this case, when we coordinate the themes presented in Zechariah 6:13, Psalm 2:7, and Psalm 110 with those found in Ephesians 1 and 2 Timothy 1:9-10, Scripture itself places the timeframe of elements of these passages within the intra-trinitarian covenantal activity before the foundations of the world.

In order to substantiate this claim, this chapter first reviews the broader issues presented in Zechariah 6:13, Psalm 2:7, and Psalm 110 to demonstrate how they are especially connected to Ephesians 1. Second, the chapter looks specifically at Ephesians 1:4 and 1:11. Third, the chapter examines what Paul has to say about related matters in 2 Timothy 1:9-10. It then concludes with some observations before proceeding to dogmatic construction.

Broader backdrop of Zechariah 6:13 and Psalm 2:7

All three Old Testament texts (Zech. 6:13, Pss. 2:7, and 110) present the Messiah as one who receives the nations as His inheritance. In Zechariah the exiles return with their gold and silver to crown the typical priest-king (Zech. 6:10-11), and 'those who are far off shall come and help to build the temple of the Lord' (Zech. 6:15). In Psalm 2, we read: 'Ask of me, and I will make the nations [גרים] your heritage, and the ends of the earth your possession' (v. 8). In Psalm 110 the Messiah reigns in the midst of His enemies and executes judgment upon the nations (vv. 2, 6). These passages inform the reader that the Messiah will rule over Jew and Gentile – the nations constitute the Messiah's kingdom. These broader themes appear within the early portions of Ephesians, especially in the first two chapters. Paul explains that Jews and Gentiles constitute the people whom Christ has redeemed: 'Remember that you were at that time separated from Christ, alienated from the commonwealth of Israel and strangers to the covenants of promise, having no hope and without God in the world. But now in Christ Jesus you who once were far off have been brought near by the blood of Christ' (Eph. 2:12-13).

Paul continues, 'And he came and preached peace to you who were far off and peace to those who were near' (Eph. 2:17).

Verses 13 and 17 bookend verses 14-16, because verse 13 mentions those who are 'far' and 'near,' and verse 17 speaks of the peace preached to those 'who were far off and peace to those who were near,' which echoes Isaiah 52:7 and 57:18-19. In the former the prophet writes of the one 'who publishes peace,' and the latter states: '"Peace, peace, to the far and to the near," says the LORD.'[1] These Isaianic allusions bookend how the Christ unites both Jew and Gentile through His death on the cross: 'For he himself is our peace, who has made us both one and has broken down in his flesh the dividing wall of hostility by abolishing the law of commandments expressed in ordinances, that he might create in himself one new man in place of the two, so making peace, and might reconcile us both to God in one body through the cross, thereby killing the hostility' (Eph. 2:14-16). Both the Zechariah and the Psalms texts speak of the Messiah's reign over the nations, Jew and Gentile, a theme present also in Ephesians 2.

Temple-building is a second theme in Ephesians 2 that echoes Zechariah 6:13. Zechariah writes that the Messiah will 'build the temple of the LORD' and the nations will come and 'help to build the temple of the LORD' (Zech. 6:13, 15). The end of the second chapter of Ephesians is replete with temple-building imagery. It states that those who have been far off, strangers and aliens to the covenants of God, will be drawn near. They will become fellow citizens of God's household, 'built on the foundation of the apostles and prophets, Christ Jesus himself being the cornerstone, in whom the whole structure, being joined together, grows into a holy temple in the Lord. In him you also

---

1. G. K. Beale and D. A. Carson, *Commentary on the New Testament Use of the Old Testament* (Grand Rapids: Baker, 2007), 817.

are being built together into a dwelling place for God by the Spirit' (Eph. 2:20-22). Hence, ruling over Jews and Gentiles and temple-building appear in Ephesians 2, which have headwaters in Isaiah's prophecies concerning the Messiah's suffering.

Ephesians 1

Chosen in Christ

The key question before us is, When does the triune God deliberate regarding the identity of these redeemed Jews and Gentiles, those who constitute the eschatological dwelling place of God, the final temple? Paul clearly places the trinitarian deliberations over these matters before the creation of the world: 'Even as he chose us in him before the foundation of the world, that we should be holy and blameless before him' (Eph 1:4). Paul states that believers were ἐξελέξατο ('chosen') before the foundation of the world. But God's election is not a bald abstract choice, considered apart from other factors. Particularly noteworthy is that God 'chose us *in him*' (ἐν αὐτῷ), which verse 3 identifies as Christ: 'Blessed be the God and Father of our Lord Jesus Christ, who has blessed us in Christ with every spiritual blessing in the heavenly places.'

Far too often people in the church treat the name *Christ* as an appendix or last name for *Jesus,* much like our own use of first and last names, such as John Smith. But for Paul and every other first-century theologian of Jewish descent *Christ* was a loaded term. Paul therefore identified Jesus of Nazareth as *the* Christ, which meant that He was more than a political messiah (e.g. Acts 21:38). Jesus was the Messiah, the Χριστός, the Anointed – the same individual mentioned in Psalm 2: 'The kings of the earth set themselves, and the rulers take counsel together, against the LORD and against his Anointed [χριστοῦ]' (Ps. 2:2 LXX). When Paul invokes this term, he inevitably connects the full load of all the Old Testament associations and freight with the person and work of Jesus, and hence Psalms 2 and 110 and Zechariah 6 feed into Paul's understanding of the Christ's work. However, Paul clearly places both the election of Jews and Gentiles in Christ before the foundation of the world. In other words, the deliberations regarding the work and circumstances surrounding the redemption of the elect are pre-temporal. We can therefore gloss Ephesians 1:4 in the following manner: 'Even as he chose us in the Messiah before time and history began.'

Before the foundation of the world

To be certain, the phrase πρὸ καταβολῆς κόσμου ('before the foundation of the world') does not occur in the Old Testament.[2] It does occur, however, in a number of places in the New Testament: in Christ's description of the Father's love for Him (John 17:24), in God's purpose for Christ (1 Pet. 1:20), and in John's reference to the names written in the book of the lamb (Rev. 13:8). By placing God's choice of the elect before the foundation of the world, into the realm where only the triune God existed, Paul locates the divine intra-trinitarian deliberations regarding the redemption of the elect completely out of man's reach – the triune God chooses the church, the church does not choose the triune God.[3] But again, God's pre-temporal selection of the elect *in Christ* requires that all that follows must subsequently covenantally unfold in redemptive history. When Zechariah speaks of the council of peace between Yahweh and the Branch, which Paul echoes in Ephesians 2:14, 'he himself is our peace,' this covenanted peace originates before

2. Andrew T. Lincoln, *Ephesians*, WBC (Waco: Word, 1990), 23.

3. Lincoln, *Ephesians*, 23-24; Peter T. O'Brien, *The Letter to the Ephesians*, PNTC (Grand Rapids: Eerdmans, 1999), 100.

the foundations of the world. When the psalmist writes of the covenant, the decree, 'The LORD said to me, "You are my Son; today I have begotten you,"' this covenantal utterance originates before the foundation of the world, as the elect are chosen in the Anointed, the Messiah, the Christ. The second person of the Trinity was identified as the Christ before the foundation of the world, not merely in history. His pre-temporal designation as the Messiah unfolds in history.

Predestined for adoption as sons

A second consideration appears in the fact that God predestined people 'in love' and 'for adoption as sons through Jesus Christ' (Eph 1:5).[4] In its immediate context Paul's readers would likely think of Greco-Roman adoption practices where an adopted child would acquire all of the legal rights of a natural-born child.[5] However, given the Old Testament backdrop for much of what Paul writes, he likely has in mind the adoptive relationship between God and David's offspring, 'I will be to him a father, and he shall be to me a son' (2 Sam. 7:14). In Second Temple Judaism, interpreters expanded this Davidic covenant to encompass all of God's people: 'And I shall be a father to them, and they will be sons to me. And they will all be called "sons of the living God"' (Jubilees 1:24-25). Beyond Second Temple interpretation, Paul certainly drew the connection between union with Christ and sonship in a number of places in his letters (Rom. 8:15, 23; 9:4; Gal. 4:5), which evidences that the believer's sonship originates

---

4. Cf. Frank Thielman, *Ephesians*, BECNT (Grand Rapids: Baker, 2010), 50; Ernest Best, *A Critical and Exegetical Commentary on Ephesians*, ICC (Edinburgh: T & T Clark, 1998), 122-23; Barth, *Ephesians*, 105; O'Brien, *Ephesians*, 101.

5. James M. Scott, *Adoption as Sons of God: An Exegetical Investigation into the Background of υἱοθεσία in the Pauline Corpus* (Tübingen: Mohr Siebeck, 1992), 3-12.

in Christ's sonship.[6] Paul indicates that believers are predestined to adoption διὰ Ἰησοῦ Χριστοῦ ('through Jesus Christ').[7] As we have already seen in Zechariah 6 and Psalm 2, both passages have taproots that reach back to the Davidic covenant and this covenant surfaces here in Paul's reflections upon the pre-temporal source of God's covenantal redemptive activity in Christ.

According to the purpose of his will

But not only are people chosen in Christ before the foundation of the world, they are also predestined to adoption as sons, 'according to the purpose of his will' (κατὰ τὴν εὐδοκίαν τοῦ θελήματος αὐτοῦ). Paul's use of the term εὐδοκία ('purpose' or 'good pleasure') is rare outside of biblical literature, though it occurs throughout the Septuagint in the Old Testament's wisdom literature to denote the satisfaction and joy in a person's heart that forms the ground for deliberation and action (e.g. Ps. 144:16 LXX [145:16 MT]).[8] The precise phrase, κατὰ τὴν εὐδοκίαν, occurs in one instance in extra-biblical literature: 'Like clay in the hand of the potter, to be molded as he pleases, so all are in the hand of their Maker, to be given whatever he decides' (Sir. 33:13 NRSV). Of great interest is the occurrence of the Hebrew parallels for the terms *will* (θελήματος // חפצ) and *good pleasure* (εὐδοκία // רצון), which appear together in a passage from the Dead Sea Scrolls: 'God *established his covenant* with Israel forever, revealing to them hidden matters in which all Israel had gone astray: his holy Sabbaths and his glorious feasts, his

6. Clinton E. Arnold, *Ephesians*, ZECNT (Grand Rapids: Zondervan, 2010), 82; see also Constantine R. Campbell, *Paul and Union with Christ: An Exegetical and Theological Study* (Grand Rapids: Zondervan, 2012), 177, 182, 188, 190.

7. Thielman, *Ephesians*, 52.

8. Thielman, *Ephesians*, 53.

just stipulations and his truthful paths, and *the wishes of his will* which man must do in order to live by them' (CD 3:13-16).[9] This passage from the Dead Sea Scrolls equates God's will and good pleasure with His covenant with Israel. A good case exists, then, to understand God's purpose and will as synonymous with His covenantal activity, and in this case it is a covenant that originates before the foundations of the world (cf. Isa. 53:10).

The inheritance

But there is a third consideration in Ephesians 1 that merits further reflection and substantiates the timing of the intra-trinitarian deliberations regarding the redemption of the elect. Paul writes: 'In him we have obtained an inheritance ['Εν ᾧ καὶ ἐκληρώθημεν], having been predestined according to the purpose of him who works all things according to the counsel of his will' (Eph. 1:11). Once again the theological lexicon of the Old Testament must define Paul's vocabulary. In this case, we must not define the term *inheritance* by some loose association with wealth gained through the reading of a will once a person has died. Rather, the term κληρόω is a cognate of a word used in the Septuagint commonly associated with the tribal inheritance of the land.[10] The following provides an example: 'But the land shall be divided by lot. According to the names of the tribes of their fathers they shall inherit. Their inheritance [κληρονομίαν] shall be divided according to lot between the larger and the smaller' (Num. 26:55-56).[11]

---

9. Arnold, *Ephesians*, 83; Lincoln, *Ephesians*, 26. Damascus Document (CD) cited from Florentino García Martínez, ed. *The Dead Sea Scrolls Translated: The Qumran Texts in English*, 2nd ed. (Grand Rapids: Eerdmans, 1996), 35.

10. Lincoln, *Ephesians*, 36; Barth, *Ephesians*, 92-93.

11. See also Prov. 1:14; Deut. 9:29; 32:8-9; re. last passage cf. O'Brien, *Ephesians*, 115; F. F. Bruce, *The Epistles to the Colossians, to Philemon, and to the Ephesians*, NICNT (Grand Rapids: Eerdmans, 1984), 263.

The inheritance of the land was linked to the representative obedience of the king: 'And when he sits on the throne of his kingdom, he shall write for himself in a book a copy of this law ... it shall be with him, and he shall read in it all the days of his life ... keeping all the words of this law and these statutes, and doing them ... so that he may continue long in his kingdom, he and his children, in Israel' (Deut. 17:18-20). Once again, as with God's election of people in Christ before the foundation of the world, the inheritance comes to believers because they have 'been predestined according to the purpose of him who works all things according to the counsel of his will' (Eph. 1:11). Paul's double use of the preposition κατὰ ('according to') highlights that God's purpose and will take precedence, not the will of human beings.[12]

At God's right hand

A fourth consideration lies with where Paul places the ascended and reigning Christ, 'at his right hand in the heavenly places' (Eph. 1:20). To be sure, Paul connects Christ's ascension to His royal session at the right hand of God the Father to His resurrection from the dead, which means the apostle has temporal events in mind. However, Paul echoes the language of Psalm 110:1, 'The Lord says to my Lord: "Sit at my right hand, until I make your enemies your footstool."'[13] This passage certainly lies in the background of both Zechariah 6:13, which explicates the inauguration of the priest-king, and Psalm 2, which

---

12. Lincoln, *Ephesians*, 36.

13. Arnold, *Ephesians*, 110-11; Thielman, *Ephesians*, 107; Best, *Ephesians*, 172; O'Brien, *Ephesians*, 40-41; David M. Hay, *Glory at the Right Hand: Psalm 110 in Early Christianity* (Nashville: Abingdon, 1973); A. T. Lincoln, 'The Use of the OT in Ephesians,' *JSNT* 14 (1982): 16-57; W. R. G. Loader, 'Christ at the Right Hand—Ps. 110.1 in the New Testament,' *NTS* 24 (1978): 199.

details the enthronement of the Messiah on Zion, Yahweh's holy hill. But in this particular case, Yahweh's pre-temporal oath, His covenant, that the Messiah would be a priest forever according to the order of Melchizedek (Ps. 110:4), occupies the same pre-temporal space as God's predestination of people before the foundation of the world. In other words, God's pre-temporal deliberations regarding the election of people unto salvation in Christ as well as the means by which that redemption will be accomplished, come to fruition on the plain of history. One of the chief highpoints of the triune God's pre-temporal deliberations is the ascension and inauguration of the Messiah to His royal session at the right hand of the Father. Stated simply, the plans for Christ's eschatological reign originate in eternity in the covenantal intra-trinitarian deliberations.

Summary

For all of these reasons, Charles Hodge (1797-1878) rightly reflects upon Paul's words and offers the following theological observation:

> It is best, therefore, to take the words as they stand, and to inquire in what sense our election is in Christ. The purpose of election is very comprehensive. It is the purpose of God to bring his people to holiness, sonship, and eternal glory. He never intended to do this irrespective of Christ. On the contrary, it was his purpose, as revealed in Scripture, to bring his people to these exalted privileges through a Redeemer. It was in Christ, as their head and representative, they were chosen to holiness and eternal life, and, therefore, in virtue of what he was to do in their behalf. There is a federal union with Christ which is antecedent to all actual union, and is the source of it. God gave a people to his Son in the covenant of redemption. Those included in that covenant, and because they are included in it,—in other words, because they

> are in Christ as their head and representative,—receive in time the gift of the Holy Spirit, and all other benefits of redemption. Their voluntary union with Christ by faith is not the ground of their federal union, but, on the contrary, their federal union is the ground of their voluntary union. It is, therefore, in Christ, i.e., as united to him in the covenant of redemption, that the people of God are elected to eternal life, and to all the blessings therewith connected. Much in the same sense the Israelites are said to have been chosen in Abraham. Their relation to Abraham and God's covenant with him, were the ground and reason of all the peculiar blessings they enjoyed. So our covenant union with Christ is the ground of all the benefits which we, as the people of God, possess or hope for.[14]

Hodge invokes several points that will be explained in subsequent chapters, such as the distinction between the church's federal and actual unions with Christ. But his point still stands and, in the light of the previous three chapters, seems more than warranted: the outworking of salvation applied in redemptive history finds its source in a pre-temporal covenant among the members of the Trinity.

2 Timothy 1:9-10

A second chief passage that merits investigation appears in the opening chapter of Paul's second letter to Timothy, when he writes:

> [God] who saved us and called us to a holy calling, not because of our works but because of his own purpose and grace, which he gave us in Christ Jesus before the ages began, and which now has been manifested through the appearing of our Savior Christ Jesus, who

14. Charles Hodge, *Ephesians* (1856; Edinburgh: Banner of Truth, 1991), 9.

> abolished death and brought life and immortality to light through the gospel. (2 Tim. 1:9-10)

The first thing to note is Paul's use of aorist active participles, σώσαντος ἡμᾶς καὶ καλέσαντος κλήσει ἁγίᾳ ('who saved us and called us to a holy calling'). This pair of aorist participles presents God's saving action as complete but Paul places these divine actions in eternity, not in history (cf. Titus 3:5; Eph. 2:5, 8).[15] And though Paul's use of the verb *call* (καλέω) typically denotes the first stage in the process of salvation, in this context it indicates that the believer's prior election is based solely upon God's will and desire and not in any way upon human good works.[16] But as with his elaboration upon election in Ephesians 1, Paul does not present God's selection of individual believers as a bald abstract choice. Rather, Paul links the believer's election, and hence, soteriology, with christology.[17]

Paul highlights the divinely initiated salvation of believers by contrasting what people *do not* contribute and what God brings to the process. Paul indicates that believers are saved οὐ κατὰ τὰ ἔργα ἡμῶν ('not because of our works'). He elsewhere positively uses the phrase κατὰ τὰ ἔργα ('according to works') to indicate the judicial ground for the judgment of the works of the wicked (Rom. 2:6; 2 Cor. 11:15; 2 Tim. 4:14; cf. 1 Pet. 1:17). But with his use of the negative particle we discover that though judgment may be according to works, God

---

15. I. Howard Marshall, *The Pastoral Epistles*, ICC (Edinburgh: T & T Clark, 1999), 704.

16. J. N. D. Kelley, *The Pastoral Epistles*, BNTC (Peabody: Hendrickson, 1998), 162.

17. William D. Mounce, *Pastoral Epistles*, WBC (Nashville: Thomas Nelson, 2000), 481; cf. 482 and literature cited; also George W. Knight, *The Pastoral Epistles: A Commentary on the Greek Text* (Grand Rapids: Eerdmans, 1992), 374.

does not save on this basis.[18] If good works do not form the ground of our salvation, then what does? According to Paul the πρόθεσιν ('purpose') of God is the basis. Paul provides the same rationale in Ephesians 1: 'In him we have obtained an inheritance, having been predestined according to the purpose [πρόθεσιν] of him who works all things according to the counsel of his will' (Eph. 1:11). God's purpose precedes any and all human effort, as it rests in eternity and not within the unfolding tapestry of history.[19] Paul makes it evident that God's purpose stretches back into eternity when he writes that this calling and salvation was given πρὸ χρόνων αἰωνίων ('before the ages began').

Paul further highlights the divine origin of this salvation with his use of an aorist passive verb, δοθεῖσαν ('was given'), which indicates that God is the agent who gives this salvation and that it is a completed action in eternity (cf. John 17:24).[20] Hence Paul's words preclude any notion that this divinely given salvation originates within history. Rather, as with Ephesians 1, God reveals in history through Christ that the triune God in eternity initiated and planned salvation. But we should observe that the gift of salvation is given in *Christ*, the Messiah, the Anointed, which means that all that is associated with Christ, especially the covenantal activity surrounding His incarnation and ministry, was planned and given in eternity.[21] In terms of its timing, Paul's statements here in 2 Timothy 1:9-10 and Ephesians 1:4

18. Marhsall, *Pastoral Epistles*, 705; also Mounce, *Pastoral Epistles*, 482-83; Knight, *Pastoral Epistles*, 374; BAGD, s.v. II.5d; see esp. Titus 3:5; cf. Rom. 3:20; 9:11; Gal. 2:16; and esp. Eph. 2:9.

19. Marshall, *Pastoral Epistles*, 705.

20. Mounce, *Pastoral Epistles*, 483; Kelly, *Pastoral Epistles*, 163.

21. Marshall, *Pastoral Epistles*, 706; Mounce, *Pastoral Epistles*, 483; Knight, *Pastoral Epistles*, 375.

provide vital information about the timeframe of Christ's work as Messiah and His kingdom. When Christ tells His disciples, 'I covenant to you, as my Father covenanted to me, a kingdom' (Luke 22:29*), we know from the *analogia Scripturae* ('analogy of Scripture') that Christ's kingdom, which in part consists of His elected subjects, was covenanted to Him 'before the ages began.' And what was covenanted in eternity '[δὲ νῦν] now has been manifested through the appearing of our Savior Christ Jesus' (2 Tim. 1:10). When Paul uses the phrase δὲ νῦν ('but now'), it is an eschatological νῦν. In other words, Christ's incarnation, ascension, and inauguration signal the dawn of the eschaton and the new creation. This conjunction (νῦν), then, contrasts eternity with the eschatological present – what was decided *then* is *now* manifest.[22] In terms of older dogmatics, Paul excludes the human contribution to salvation by distinguishing between the decree and its execution in time. God's decree, however, must be coordinated with Christ and His covenanted kingdom in eternity. Like Ephesians 1, all of these elements point to the existence of the *pactum salutis*, a covenantal agreement among the triune God to plan and execute the redemption of the elect.

Conclusion

We are likely to read passages such as Ephesians 1 and 2 Timothy 1:9-10 in a thin manner if we fail to account for their Old Testament roots. When Paul invokes the title *Christ*, passages such as Psalms 2 and 110 and Zechariah 6:13, among many others, should immediately come to mind. Without question Paul's catechetical goal was to identify Jesus of Nazareth as *the* long-awaited Christ of the Old Testament. These messianic

22. Mounce, *Pastoral Epistles*, 484; Marshall, *Pastoral Epistles*, 707.

connections between Jesus and the Old Testament Messiah are especially evident in the broader context of the early chapters of Ephesians where the salvation of Jews and Gentiles, temple-building, and the messianic work all appear. And given the timeframe of Ephesians 1 and 2 Timothy 1:9-10, when we coordinate these elements with Christ's statement that God the Father covenanted a kingdom to Him, we cannot restrict this activity to history but are necessarily driven back to eternity and the triune God's pre-temporal purpose in Christ.

This purpose, plan, or covenant, was not an arbitrary choice, disconnected from Christ. Rather it was a choice made in love (Eph. 1:4) among the members of the triune God that the elect would be united to Christ, not only in eternity, but in history. The Christ would take on human flesh, live in obedience to the law, suffer, die, rise, ascend, and sit at the right hand of His Father, from where He would pour out the Holy Spirit to redeem His bride. The Holy Spirit would apply Christ's accomplished work and seal believers with His abiding presence, which would be the down-payment and guarantee of their final redemption (Eph. 1:13-14). In other words, the triune God covenanted to elect and redeem a people in eternity and it has become manifest in history.

But thus far, this exegetical survey has demonstrated the basic elements that prove the existence of a pre-temporal covenant among the members of the Trinity. However, there are still many details that require further exegesis and theological reflection to achieve a clear and cogent presentation of the *pactum salutis*. Hence, Part III turns our attention to dogmatic construction. We must explore what the Scriptures have to say about the intra-trinitarian relationship between Father, Son, and Holy Spirit. In technical terms, we must understand the *opera ad intra* (the internal work) of the Trinity, so we can have a correct understanding of the *opera ad extra* (external work). Or in other words, the processions of the triune God are intimately related to their respective missions, which will help us understand the fundamental nature of the *pactum salutis*.

~: SUMMARY :~

FOR as much as modern critics have chided proponents for advocating the *pactum salutis*, Part II has demonstrated that there is sufficient exegetical warrant to establish the legitimacy of the doctrine. The doctrine does not rest upon one or two isolated proof texts, such as Zechariah 6:13, but upon an interconnected web of passages that course through the Old and New Testaments. Most notably, those passages directly associated with the Messiah, His appointment, work, and royal session at the Father's right hand go hand in hand with the doctrine of the covenant. As much as some have tried to offer alternative interpretations of Zechariah 6:13, claiming that it speaks of the union of the kingly and priestly offices or that there are two individuals in the text (Zerubbabel and Joshua), the simplest explanation is that the prophet saw an eschatological vision of Psalm 110:1 – the inaugurated priest-king sitting in royal session at the right hand of Yahweh. The idea that these covenantal deliberations were planned in eternity is certainly implicit in the three surveyed Old Testament texts (Zech. 6:13; Pss. 2:7; 110:1), but the apostle Paul removes any and all doubt as to when this covenantal appointment of the Son took place. Paul clearly places the Son's appointment before the foundations of the world. This means that the triune God executed an intra-trinitarian covenant to plan and execute the creation and redemption of a chosen people. But there is still much work to be done. We must therefore turn to Part III and dogmatic construction of the covenant of redemption.

PART III

Dogmatic Construction

⁓INTRODUCTION⁓

THE previous section established the exegetical legitimacy of the *pactum salutis*. But to establish the existence of a doctrine is only the first step. One must take the essentials of a doctrine and define it, determine its boundaries, and establish the connections to related issues. In terms of the *loci* of systematic theology, the *pactum* serves as a rubric in which all of the various *loci* intersect. As tempting as it might be to expand upon each and every *locus*, one must stay focused upon the narrower issue of the *pactum salutis*. For example, the *pactum* and election go hand in hand, and election constitutes the foundation of ecclesiology. But discussions about the church are perhaps best postponed for another day. Hence, Part III continues the process of *ressourcement* by engaging the doctrinal issues that were raised in Part I: deciding between the christological and trinitarian *pactum*, the relationship between the *pactum* and the Trinity, the covenant's relationship to the doctrine of predestination, the timing of the imputation, and the connection between the *pactum* and the *ordo salutis*.

Part III therefore begins with a brief statement of the doctrine, offering a definition and outline of the basic contours of the *pactum salutis*. Following this definition and outline are chapters on the *pactum* and the Trinity, predestination, imputation, and the *ordo salutis*. Each of these chapters addresses issues that appeared in

Part I. Part III represents, therefore, the retrieval of the covenant of redemption and its dogmatic construction. But I am not merely interested in parroting earlier formulations and walking in the footprints of my theological forebears. The *pactum* is without doubt unique to the Reformed tradition, but Part I presented evidence to show that its advocates were anything but parochial. The *pactum* deals with the ancient question of how the Son can be subordinate to the Father, which is why many appealed to earlier theological formulations in their construction of their own doctrine, especially to Augustine. The Reformed tradition is not the first to wrestle with these thorny issues. Hence, as important as it is to employ the earlier insights of Reformed theologians, they were not, by any stretch of the imagination, parochial. Rather, they drew upon the riches of the catholic tradition. In this respect, Part III employs the same methodology. I engage a wide range of theologians both to facilitate dialogue and to learn from their insights.

Last but not least, one of the recurring themes that surfaces in Part III is the triune love of God, both among the Father, Son, and Holy Spirit, and His love for fallen sinners. One thing Part III seeks to demonstrate, exegetically, redemptive historically, and theologically, is that the covenant of redemption reveals the eternal love of the triune God.

~: 1 :~

Statement of the Doctrine

Introduction

The historical survey of the *pactum salutis* in Part I demonstrates that despite the fact that the doctrine is well attested in early modern and modern Reformed theology, there are several different variations. For example, one major variant is the christological model (an agreement between the Father and Son), which includes among its advocates David Dickson (1583-1663), Jacob Arminius (1560-1609), Herman Witsius (1636-1708), Franciscus Gomarus (1563-1641), Gisbert Voetius (1589-1676), Patrick Gillespie (1617-75), Samuel Rutherford (1600-61), John Owen (1616-83), Jonathan Edwards (1703-58), Charles Hodge (1797-1878), Geerhardus Vos (1862-1949), and Louis Berkhof (1873-1957).[1] The other model is a trinitarian covenant

1. David Dickson, 'Arminianism Discussed,' in *Records of the Kirk of Scotland, containing the Acts and Proceedings of the General Assemblies, from the Year 1638 Downwards*, ed. Alexander Peterkin (Edinburgh: Peter Brown, 1845), 157; idem, *The Summe of Saving Knowledge, With the Practical Use thereof* (Edinburgh: George Swintoun and Thomas Brown, n. d.), II.ii; Jacob Arminius, 'The Priesthood of Christ,' in *The Works of James Arminius*, 3 vols. (1825-75; Grand Rapids: Baker, 1996), 1:416;

(an agreement among Father, Son, and Holy Spirit), a minority position whose advocates include James Durham (1622-58), Thomas Goodwin (1600-80), Abraham Kuyper (1837-1920), and Herman Bavinck (1854-1921).[2] These differences of opinion do not rise to the level of heterodoxy, that is, if one advocates a christological model of the *pactum* his doctrine does not fall short of trinitarian orthodoxy, as some have maintained.[3] In

---

Herman Witsius, *Economy of the Covenants Between God and Man: Comprehending a Complete Body of Divinity*, trans. William Crookshank (1822; Escondido: Den Dulk Foundation, 1990), II.ii.16; Franciscus Gomarus, *Selectorum, evangelii Lucae locorum illustratio*, in *Opera Theologica Omnia* (Amsterdam: Janssonii, 1644), 252-57; Gisbert Voetius, 'Problematum De Merito Christi, Pars Tertia,' in *Selectarum Disputationum Theologicarum*, vol. 2 (Ultrajecti: apud Johannem a Waesberge, 1655), 265-66; Patrick Gillespie, *The Ark of the Covenant Opened: Or, a Treatise of the Covenant of Redemption Between God and Christ, as the Foundation of the Covenant of Grace*, The Second Part (London: Thomas Parkhurst, 1677), 14; Samuel Rutherford, *The Covenant of Life Opened: Or, A Treatise of the Covenant of Grace* (Edinburgh: Robert Broun, 1654), II.vii (pp. 302-03); John Owen, 'Exercitation XXVII: The Original of the Priesthood of Christ in the Counsel of God,' in *The Works of John Owen*, vol. 19, ed. William H. Goold (Edinburgh: T & T Clark, 1862), 77; John Bunyan, *The Doctrine of the Law and Grace Unfolded; or, A Discourse Touching the Law and Grace*, in *The Works of John Bunyan*, vol. 1, ed. George Offor (Glasgow: Blackie and Son, 1860), 522-23; Jonathan Edwards, Misc. 1062, 'Economy of the Trinity and Covenant of Redemption,' in *WJE* 20:434-35; Charles Hodge, *Ephesians* (1856; Edinburgh: Banner of Truth, 1991), 9; Geerhardus Vos, *Systematische Theologie: Compendium* (Grand Rapids: 1900), III.7 (p. 76); Louis Berkhof, *Systematic Theology: New Combined Edition* (1932, 38: Grand Rapids: Eerdmans, 1996), 271.

2. James Durham, *Christ Crucified: Or, the Marrow of the Gospel* (Edinburgh: 1683), serm. XXIII (p. 157); Thomas Goodwin, *Of Christ the Mediator*, in *The Works of Thomas Goodwin*, 12 vols. (1861-66; Eureka: Tanski Publications, 1996), I.vii (vol. 5, p. 23); idem, *The Work of the Holy Ghost in Our Salvation*, IX.iii, in *Works*, vol. 6, p. 419; Abraham Kuyper, *Dictaten Dogmatiek: collegedictaat van een der studenten*, vol. 3, Locus de Providentia, Peccato, Foedere, Christ, 2nd ed. (Kampen: Stoomdrukkerij van J. H. Kok, n. d.), § V, 90; Herman Bavinck, *Our Reasonable Faith*, trans. Henry Zylstra (Grand Rapids: Eerdmans, 1956), 273; cf. John Gill, *A Complete Body of Doctrine and Practical Divinity: or A System of Evangelical Truths* (1809; Paris: AR: The Baptist Standard Bearer, Inc., 2007), II.vi (pp. 209-14).

3. E.g., Robert Letham, 'John Owen's Doctrine of the Trinity in its Catholic

those instances where theologians have put forth a christological model, they account for the role and function of the Holy Spirit through other doctrines, exemplified by John Owen's use of the *consilium Dei*.[4] Nevertheless, in order to retrieve and employ the doctrine of the *pactum salutis* one must descend from the historical perch of the disinterested observer and argue for a specific set of doctrinal propositions. In Part II I established the exegetical legitimacy of the broad category of the *pactum salutis*, but I have not, as of yet, offered a definition and statement of the doctrine. Hence, this chapter presents a definition of the doctrine and then outlines its essential elements, including scriptural data for the doctrine, parties of the covenant, requirements and promises, the relationship between the *pactum* and the covenants of works and grace, and summary observations in conclusion.[5] This chapter, therefore, presents the basic outline of the doctrine, various elements of which will be explored in subsequent chapters, including the doctrine of the Trinity, predestination, imputation, and the *ordo salutis*.

Definition

At its most fundamental level, the covenant of redemption is the pre-temporal, intra-trinitarian agreement among Father, Son, and Holy Spirit to plan and execute the redemption of the elect. The covenant entails the appointment of the Son as surety

Context,' in *The Ashgate Research Companion to John Owen's Theology*, eds. Kelly M. Kapic and Mark Jones (Farnham: Ashgate, 2012), 196.

4. Laurence O'Donnell, 'The Holy Spirit's Role in John Owen's "Covenant of the Mediator" Formulation: A Case Study in Reformed Orthodox Formulations of the *Pactum Salutis*,' *PRJ* 4/1 (2012): 91-134.

5. I rely upon the outline and elements presented in Berkhof, *Systematic Theology*, 265-71.

of the covenant of grace who accomplishes the redemption of the elect through His incarnation, perfect obedience, suffering, resurrection, and ascension. The covenant of redemption is also the root of the Spirit's role to anoint and equip the Son for His mission as surety and to apply His finished work to the elect.

Scriptural data for the doctrine

The doctrine of the *pactum salutis* rests upon the following scriptural basis:

1. The Scriptures clearly point to the fact that there was from all eternity an eternal decree or counsel among the members of the trinity (Eph. 1:4ff; 3:11; 2 Thess. 2:13; 2 Tim. 1:9; James 2:5; 1 Pet. 1:2). In this economy of redemption the Scriptures present a division of labor: the Father sends the Son, the Son executes the work of mediator and covenant surety, and the Father and the Son both send the Spirit to apply the Son's work. Scripture presents these intra-trinitarian relations in terms of a covenant. At its most basic level, a covenant is an agreement with stipulations between two or more parties.[6] Generally speaking, the Trinity

---

6. Contra John Murray, *The Covenant of Grace: A Biblico-Theological Study* (Phillipsburg: P & R, 1953), 12-15; cf. Meredith G. Kline, *By Oath Consigned: A Reinterpretation of the Covenant Signs of Circumcision and Baptism* (Grand Rapids: Eerdmans, 1968), 16; David VanDrunen, *Divine Covenants and Moral Order: A Biblical Theology of Natural Law* (Grand Rapids: Eerdmans, 2014), 16. Despite the different biblical texts where the term *covenant* (ברית) appears, BDB offers the following terms as potential translations: treaty, alliance, compact, agreement, pledge, alliance (136). HALOT also defines ברית as agreement or contract (Ludwig Koehler and Walter Baumgartner, *The Hebrew and Aramaic Lexicon of the Old Testament*, 2 vols. [Leiden: Brill, 2001], I:157-58). Older literature identifies the nature of a covenant as a promissory oath in a context that would ensure its performance (George E. Mendenhall, *Law and Covenant in Israel and the Ancient Near East* [Pittsburgh: The Biblical Colloquiuum, 1955], 26). Others have similarly concluded that a ברית is an agreement or relationship (Paul Kalluveettil, *Declaration and Covenant* [Rome: Biblical Institute Press, 1982], 15).

is a covenant-making God, a pattern that unfolds in humanity, made in His image.

2. Numerous passages of Scripture point to the fact that the plan of redemption was eternal (Eph. 1:4; 3:9, 11), but they also indicate that it was a plan made in the form of a covenantal agreement. Christ speaks about promises made to Him prior to His incarnation, and repeatedly refers to a commission that He received from His Father (John 5:30, 43; 6:38-40; 17:4-12). Moreover, the apostle Paul clearly presents Christ as the federal head of the elect (Rom. 5:12-21; 1 Cor. 15:22).

3. Wherever the essential elements of a covenant appear, that is, the contracting parties, a promise or promises, requirements, and stipulated rewards, there we have a covenant.[7] As explained in Part II, Psalm 2:7-9 presents the elements of a covenant with Yahweh declaring His decree or covenant. The Son would offer His obedience (Ps. 1), and the Father would give Him the nations as His heritage and the ends of the earth as His possession (cf. Ps. 105:8-10). Psalm 40:7-9 (Heb. 10:5-7) presents a pre-temporal dialogue between the Father and the Son where the latter states that the Father has prepared a body for Him and that He delights to do His will. In this respect Luke 22:29* is significant: 'I covenant to you, even as my Father covenanted to me, a kingdom.' Other texts that speak of Christ's reward for His accomplished work include John 17:6, 9, 24 and Philippians 2:9-11.

4. A number of key Old Testament passages present the Son's work in terms of God making a covenant with Him, such as Psalm 89:3 (cf. 2 Sam. 7:12-14) and Isaiah 42:6. Moreover, the Son refers to Yahweh as 'my God' (Ps. 22:1-2; Ps. 40:8;

---

7. Cf. Gordon P. Hugenberger, *Marriage as a Covenant: Biblical Law and Ethics as Developed from Malachi* (Grand Rapids: Baker, 1994), 168-215.

Matt. 27:46; Mark 15:34; cf. John 20:17), an utterance reserved for those in covenant with Yahweh (Heb. 8:10).

Parties of the covenant

Father

The Father is the one who initiates the *pactum salutis* in concert with the Son and Spirit. The Father appoints the Son to the role of covenant surety. In Ephesians 1, for example, Paul states that the Father 'chose us in him [Christ] before the foundation of the world' (Eph. 1:4). In other words, the Father, not the Son and Spirit, chose the elect in Christ, one of the key elements of the *pactum*. Moreover, Christ repeatedly explains that the Father sent Him (John 6:44, 57; 8:18, 42; 14:24; 17:21, 25; 20:21). In this vein the Son testifies to the fact that the Father 'consecrated and sent [him] into the world' (John 10:36). Notable is Christ's statement in Luke's Gospel that the Father covenanted a kingdom to Him (Luke 22:29). The Father is also the one who promises to give a reward to the Son upon the successful completion of His labors (Ps. 2:7-9; cf. Deut. 17:19-20; 28:1). The Father elects, appoints, sends, consecrates, and promises to reward the Son's labors. Hence, the Father is the one who initiates the *pactum*.

Son

Within the *pactum salutis* the Son functions as covenant surety (ἔγγυος) (Heb. 7:22). A surety, or guarantor, assumes the legal responsibilities on behalf of another. In this respect the Father appoints the Son as surety so that He will offer His perfect obedience to the law as well as intercede on behalf of the covenant people of God and make satisfaction for their sins (Isa. 52:13-53:12; Rom. 4:25; 5:12-21; 2 Cor. 5:17-21). As such, Christ is the last Adam (ὁ ἔσχατος Ἀδὰμ) (1 Cor. 15:45) and is the federal head of the elect. He operates as covenant surety within the covenant of grace, which flows out of the *pactum salutis*. The covenant of works serves as an anticipatory typological precursor of the Son's work in the covenant of grace (Rom. 5:14), as the first Adam (πρῶτος Ἀδὰμ) (1 Cor. 15:45) was a type of the last Adam (τύπος τοῦ μέλλοντος). To be sure, the covenant of works is not merely typological, since there are important anthropological considerations attached to it that will be explored in subsequent chapters. Nevertheless, as covenant surety the Son fulfills the broken covenant of works on behalf of the elect. The elect are first federally united to Christ in the *pactum salutis* and then subsequently, in redemptive history, they are mystically united to Him by the regenerative work of the Holy Spirit.

Holy Spirit

In the formulation of some theologians, the Spirit's work in redemption is placed outside of the *pactum salutis*, either in the logically prior *consilium Dei* or after in the application of the Son's work in the covenant of grace. While such formulations are not sub-trinitarian, as they construe the *pactum* in a christological fashion, a thicker account of the biblical data requires that one coordinate and include the Spirit's role within the *pactum* itself.[8] In this respect, just as the Son acknowledges that the Father sent Him into the world, which implies His willing agreement to be sent, so the fact that the Spirit is sent implies His agreement and consent to the same: 'But the Helper, the Holy Spirit, who the Father will send in my name, he will teach you all things and bring to your remembrance all that I have said to you' (John 14:26; cf. 15:26).

Another element that should be factored is the Spirit's role in the Son's office as covenant surety. The Father appoints the Son to His office but the Son does not execute His work in isolation

8. So, e.g., R. Michael Allen, *The Christ's Faith: A Dogmatic Account* (London: T & T Clark, 2009), 155-56.

from the Spirit. Rather, the Father anoints the Son with the Spirit. Notable in this regard is the title of *Christ* (משיח), which means *anointed one*. This begs the question, With what was the Son anointed? Unlike the Old Testament priests and kings who were anointed with oil (e.g., Exod. 30:30; Lev. 8:12; 1 Sam. 16:12), the Father anointed the Son with the Spirit (Isa. 61:1; Luke 4:18; Acts 10:38). The Son, therefore, carries out His work as covenant surety in the power of the Holy Spirit. The Spirit's involvement with the work of the Son both implies and requires His consent as one of the parties of the covenant of redemption.

Requirements and promises

Requirements

The Father required of the Son as covenant surety, federal head of the elect, and the last Adam, to make amends for the sin of the first Adam and those whom the Father had given to Him to redeem. The Son would accomplish what the first Adam failed to do by keeping the law and therefore securing eternal life for those united to Him. Three requirements are stipulated in the covenant of redemption:

1. That the Son would assume human nature by being born of a woman and would thus enter into history. By the Son's assumption of a human nature He would be subject to human infirmities and weaknesses (hunger, fatigue, etc.) but be without sin. In order to redeem fallen humans it was necessary that the Son become human (Gal. 4:4-5; Heb. 2:10-15; 4:15).
2. Even though the Son is greater than the law, as covenant surety He would place Himself under it, and as such He would have a natural, penal, and federal relation to the law. His natural relationship to the law is by virtue of His incarnation as a man; His penal and federal relationship to the law is due to His status

as federal head of the elect and His willingness to suffer the penal sanction of the law on their behalf (Ps. 40:8; Matt. 5:17-18; John 8:28-29; Gal. 4:4-5; Phil. 2:6-8).

3. After Christ had merited eternal life and the forgiveness of sins through His obedience and satisfaction, the Holy Spirit would apply the fruit of His merit to the elect: pardon of sin, right and title to eternal life, and their transformation into the eschatological image of Christ (John 10:16; 16:14-15; 17:12, 19-22; Heb. 2:10-13; 7:25). In terms of the *ordo salutis*, the Spirit applies the benefits of the *duplex gratia*, the twofold grace of justification and sanctification, which irresistibly lead to the believer's glorification.

Promises

The Father takes a covenantal oath to reward the Son in accordance with the satisfied requirements of the *pactum salutis*. In view of the establishment of the covenant of redemption and in the light of the Son's Spirit-empowered accomplished work as covenant surety, the Father would:

1. Prepare a body for His Son through the agency of the Spirit and uncontaminated by sin (Luke 1:35; Heb. 10:5).
2. Equip the Son with the necessary gifts and graces in order that the Son could carry out His work as covenant surety. The Father, therefore, would anoint the Son with the Spirit without measure, a promise that was fulfilled at His baptism (Isa. 42:1-2; 61:1; John 3:34).
3. Support and undergird Him in His work and deliver Him from the bonds of death and thus enable Him to destroy the kingdom of Satan and establish His covenantal kingdom (Isa. 42:1-7; 49:8; Ps. 16:8-11; Acts 2:25-28).
4. Reward the Son by enabling Him to send out the Holy Spirit for the gathering of His body, the church, and for the

church's instruction, guidance, and protection (John 14:26; 15:26; 16:13-14; Acts 2:33).

5. Give the Son the elect as a reward for His accomplished work, the company of which was so numerous that it would embrace the people of every tribe, tongue, and nation (Ps. 22:27; 72:17; Matt. 28:18-19; Rev. 7:9).

6. Commit all authority and power in heaven and on earth for the government of His church and would finally reward Him as mediator and covenant surety with the glory that He possessed with the Father as the Son of God before the foundation of the world (John 17:5).

Relationship to the covenants of works and grace

The *pactum salutis* is foundational for the covenants of works and grace. The Adamic covenant, or more specifically the covenant of works, is the only analog to the *pactum salutis*. In the covenant of works, God places His son, Adam (Luke 3:38), in the garden-temple of Eden, and gives him the law in the form of two commands – to take dominion over the creation and to refrain from eating from the tree of the knowledge of good and evil. As the federal representative for all humanity, the reward for Adam's obedience would have been eternal life (cf. Lev. 18:5; Gal. 3:12; Rom. 10:5).[9] There was no mediator in the covenant of works. Rather, God dealt directly with Adam. The covenant of works is the mirror image of the *pactum salutis*, as it is a typological portrait of the Son's threefold office (prophet, priest, and king) and work as surety in the covenant of grace.

9. Bryan Estelle, 'Leviticus 18:5 and Deuteronomy 30:1-14 in Biblical Theological Development: Entitlement to Heaven Foreclosed and Proffered,' in *The Law Is Not of Faith: Essays on Works and Grace in the Mosaic Covenant*, eds. Bryan D. Estelle, J. V. Fesko, David VanDrunen (Phillipsburg: P & R, 2009), 109-46.

In terms of the relationship between the *pactum* and the covenant of grace, there are five points to note. The covenant of redemption is:

1. Eternal and the covenant of grace is temporal in the sense that, though it originates in eternity, it is revealed in redemptive history. That is, apart from creation there is no covenant of grace, whereas the *pactum* stands distinct from the creation.
2. Among Father, Son, and Holy Spirit to appoint the Son as surety and the Spirit as the agent of transformation, whereas the covenant of grace is a covenant between the triune God and the elect sinner through the Son as surety.
3. The firm and unassailable eternal foundation of the covenant of grace. If the triune God had not covenanted to plan and execute the redemption of elect sinners, there would be no covenant of grace.
4. The guarantee that the covenant of grace will be efficacious. Only by grace alone through faith alone in Christ alone can the elect sinner partake of the blessings of the covenant of grace, and it is only in the covenant of redemption that the way of faith and salvation is first opened. The Holy Spirit produces faith in the heart of the elect sinner because the triune God covenanted to send the Son to accomplish the work as surety, who would then in turn pour out the Spirit upon the elect.
5. The legal basis for the salvation of the elect. In terms of the *ordo salutis*, there is only one foundation for the sinner's justification, namely, the imputed obedience of the covenant surety. God admits no other legal basis for the sinner's justification because in the *pactum salutis* the Father only appoints one covenant surety and no other, the Son. But the Son's appointment as covenant surety entails the creation of the necessary legal apparatus under which the Son would place Himself to merit the salvation of the elect. The covenant of works clearly establishes

and reveals the merit-reward paradigm, one established in the *pactum salutis*. In other terms, the *pactum* establishes the priority of eschatology to soteriology. That is, the reward of eternal life is present before the need for redemption. The Son was born 'under the law' (Gal. 4:4) and came to fulfill the law and the prophets (Matt. 5:17), which means that the Mosaic covenant was a covenant of works for the Son. Correlatively, the Mosaic covenant is a covenant of works for any who stand outside of Christ. This works element has been historically expressed in the following manner: God gave Adam the moral law, which is summarily comprehended in the Decalogue and subsequently given to Israel at Sinai. Only through union with Christ does the law cease to be a covenant requiring perfect, personal, and perpetual obedience and become a rule for life.[10]

Conclusion

This brief summary outline of the *pactum salutis* presents the broad contours of the doctrine. Each of the statements undoubtedly involves significant exegesis and theological reflection to substantiate the claims. Nevertheless, key in all of these affirmations is the idea that the *pactum* is an agreement of the triune God to elect and redeem fallen sinners, and thus God projects His covenant-making ways into pre-redemptive and redemptive history and reveals His eternal plan to the creation. But lest one think that the *pactum* is a cold piece of business, a blueprint, a plan to be executed with legal precision devoid of love, we must remember that each and every step and element of the *pactum* is bathed in the love of the triune God. 'For God so loved the world that he sent his only begotten Son' (John 3:16),

---

10. See, e.g., WCF, XIX.i-ii.

and Christ loved us and gave Himself for us (Gal. 2:20), and 'God's love has been poured into our hearts through the Holy Spirit' (Rom. 5:5). Even the merit-reward paradigm is couched in terms of love. To love the Lord is to obey the law (Deut. 6:5; John 14:15; 1 John 5:2). Obedience and legal obligation are not antithetical to love but form its very essence. The covenant of redemption, therefore, is a manifestation of the intra-trinitarian love that eternally exists among Father, Son, and Holy Spirit, a love that the triune God decreed to bestow upon sinful and fallen creatures in spite of their rebellion. The *pactum salutis* is the eternal love of the triune God for the elect, the Son's bride. In all of the doctrinal exposition that follows, we must not forget the irrefragable connection between love and the *pactum salutis*.

~:2:~

The Trinity

Introduction

The *pactum salutis* easily and quickly gained wide acceptance in the middle of the seventeenth century, though it certainly had its predecessors in the sixteenth century.[1] The doctrine did not arise *ex nihilo*. But in the twentieth century several different criticisms have arisen about the *pactum salutis* and its connections to the doctrine of the Trinity. Some have criticized the doctrine alleging that even though its proponents have striven to be trinitarian in their formulation, the doctrine introduces the specter of tritheism. How can the persons of the triune God, all of whose external works are the manifestation of the unified singular will, enter into an agreement with one another? The *pactum* introduces three different wills. In this respect, how can one member of the Trinity pledge obedience to another member? Can we speak of the Son's obedience to the Father? The introduction of a covenant between Father and Son sounds more like a business contract

1. Richard A. Muller, 'Toward the *Pactum Salutis*: Locating the Origins of a Concept,' *MAJT* (2007): 11-65.

rather than a manifestation of love. How can proponents of the *pactum* maintain the theological maxim, *opera trinitatis ad extra indivisa sunt* ("The external works of the trinity are indivisible")?

A second criticism within the broader study of the doctrine of the Trinity is that peering into the intra-trinitarian operations exceeds the limits of humanity's abilities to know. Especially with the advent of narrative theology, some have argued that the only thing that one can say about the Trinity is what we find in the narrative of redemptive history. There has been much suspicion of the classic distinction between the economic and ontological Trinity, that is, between God's action in redemptive history and who the triune God is in the intra-trinitarian relations. If one cannot, therefore, truly know the ontological Trinity, who can say whether there was or is a pre-temporal intra-trinitarian covenant among Father, Son, and Holy Spirit? Can we truly claim that the Son willingly agreed to obey the Father in eternity?

This chapter addresses these two different but nevertheless related questions: Does the *pactum salutis* introduce tritheism? And can we know anything about the ontological Trinity and the intra-trinitarian covenant that the Son would obey the Father? This chapter demonstrates that the triune God has revealed the ontology of His being and shares one unified will, but nevertheless executes that will according to the unique economic roles of each person within the Godhead. Stated more succinctly, the trinitarian missions reveal the trinitarian processions and the pre-temporal covenantal context in which they occur. This chapter proves this thesis by first briefly surveying the different contemporary approaches to the doctrine of the Trinity, such as the rationalistic views offered by G. W. F. Hegel (1770-1831), Immanuel Kant (1724-1804), and Ludwig Feuerbach (1804-1872), contemporary reflections offered by Karl Barth (1886-1968) and Karl Rahner (1904-84), and the narrative views of Robert Jenson (1930-), Hans Frei (1922-88), and Catherine LaCugna (1952-97).

Second, the chapter explores the apostolic pattern for the revelation of the ontological and economic Trinity, primarily but not exclusively through the Gospel of John. Contrary to speculative approaches, which either project unscriptural ideas upon the Godhead or maintain God is ultimately unknowable, and in contrast to narrative approaches that demur from saying much about the ontological Trinity, the apostolic witness reveals both who the triune God is and what He has done. Moreover, not only does it reveal God in His being and work, but it also reveals the intra-trinitarian covenantal framework, marked by intra-trinitarian love that overflows to fallen sinners. The *pactum salutis* is not an illicit and unauthorized glance behind the narrative veil of redemptive history, and neither is it a wishful or convenient projection of all-too-human ways and customs upon an unsuspecting God. The *pactum salutis* is the covenantal framework for the intra-trinitarian processions and missions that unveil the unified will of God in a threefold manner to share the love of God with fallen sinners. This love is manifest in the Son's Spirit-anointed covenantal obedience to the Father and the Son's outpouring of the Spirit upon fallen sinners.

Current approaches

When Martin Luther (1483-1546) cast off the authority of the church at the infamous Diet of Worms, his actions constituted yet one more fallen brick in the crumbling walls of medieval culture.[2] What people once took for granted, such as the authority of

2. See, e.g., Scott Swain, 'The Trinity in the Reformers,' in *The Oxford Handbook of the Trinity*, eds. Gilles Emery and Matthew Levering (Oxford: Oxford University Press, 2011), 227-39.

Scripture and the church, was now being questioned on a grand scale. It did not take long for radical elements within the broader reform movement to scuttle long-cherished doctrines such as the Trinity, all in the name of purifying the doctrine of the church. Faustus Socinus (1539-1604), one of the best-known early modern anti-trinitarians, gained a reputation for 'completing' the work of the early Reformers: *Tota licet Babylon destruxit texta Lutherus, muros Calvinus, sed fundamenta Socinus* ('Although Luther destroyed all of the house-tops of Babylon, Calvin the walls, but Socinus destroyed its foundations').[3] Through the translation of the Socinian Racovian Catechism (1605) into English, within a generation there were significant battles over the validity and viability of the doctrine of the Trinity.[4] Coupled with the rise of rationalism and the erosion of biblical authority through higher criticism, this perfect storm toppled the pillars of the Reformation and opened the way to speculative views of the doctrine of the Trinity.[5]

Speculative theology (Hegel, Kant, Feuerbach)

For centuries people never questioned whether they could know God – they simply relied upon the *Deus dixit* of Scripture. But as doubts about the reliability of the Scriptures arose, many questioned the ability to know the historical Christ. Moreover, if people could not access the historical Christ, then they assuredly could not know the transcendent God of eternity. Gotthold

3. Joshua Toulmin, *Memoirs of the Life, Character, Sentiments and Writings of Faustus Socinus* (London: J. Brown, 1777), 12.

4. E.g., Paul C. H. Lim, *Mystery Unveiled: The Crisis of the Trinity in Early Modern England* (Oxford: Oxford University Press, 2012).

5. E.g., Michael C. Legaspi, *The Death of Scripture and the Rise of Biblical Studies* (Oxford: Oxford University Press, 2010).

Ephraim Lessing (1729-81) argued that if the historicity of miracles could not be demonstrated and proven, then how could such history serve as the rational proof for the existence of God: 'That, then, is the ugly great ditch which I cannot cross, however often and however earnestly I have tried to make this leap.'[6] Around the same time Immanuel Kant famously posited the distinction between the noumenal and phenomenal realms and seemingly dropped an epistemic iron curtain between God and man. Since God dwelled in the far country of the noumenal realm, He could not be known. Kant was willing to allow the existence of God, the creator and morally holy legislator, on practical grounds, but dismissed the doctrine of the Trinity as 'a symbol of ecclesiastical faith which is quite incomprehensible to men' and a 'mystery transcending all human concepts, and hence a mystery of revelation, unsuited to man's powers of comprehension.'[7] In the minds of many moderns, Lessing and Kant had diagnosed the problem with theology – the unsuitability of the category of divine revelation – the ditch was too big to leap across and the wall too high to jump over.

This state of affairs left theologians and philosophers with several alternatives. One could jump over the wall through the power of raw reason, assume that religion was entirely false and simply a projection of human desire, take the leap of blind faith across the ditch and hope to arrive safely on the other side, or float across through feeling the need for God. Søren Kierkegaard (1813-55), for example, responded to Lessing's ditch with the idea that a person had to make a

6. Gotthold Ephraim Lessing, *Lessing's Theological Writings*, ed. Henry Chadwick (Stanford: Stanford University Press, 1956), 55.

7. Immanuel Kant, *Religion Within the Limits of Reason Alone*, trans. Theodore M. Greene and Hoyt H. Hudson (1934; New York: Harper Torchbooks, 1960), III. ii (p. 133).

leap of faith.[8] Friedrich Schleiermacher (1768-1834) sought to overcome the impasse through experience and the feeling of absolute dependence upon God. With doctrine no longer directly linked to revelation, it should be no surprise that the doctrine of the Trinity was relegated to an appendix in Schleiermacher's theological system.[9] Schleiermacher doubted whether the distinction between the different members of the Godhead, a unity in essence and trinity of persons, would ever truly emerge in the religious consciousness of humanity.[10] Ludwig Feuerbach (1804-72), on the other hand, was prepared to dispense with religion altogether. In his view, religion was humanity's earliest and indirect form of self-knowledge. Feuerbach contended: 'The historical progress of religion consists in this: that what by an earlier religion was regarded as objective, is now recognized as subjective; that is, what was formerly contemplated and worshipped as God is now perceived to be something *human*.'[11] All so-called knowledge about God was actually wishful human projection.

G. W. F. Hegel sought to overcome the epistemic chasm through his own trinitarian understanding of God, which he saw as an alternative to rationalism and pietism, especially the pietism of Schleiermacher.[12] Hegel's views are complex and

---

8. Søren Kierkegaard, *Concluding Unscientific Postscript*, trans. David F. Swenson and Walter Lowrie (1941; Princeton: Princeton University Press, 1974), 15-16, 61-66, 93-97.

9. Friedrich Schleiermacher, *The Christian Faith*, ed. H. R. Mackintosh and J. S. Stewart (London: T & T Clark, 1999), 739-51.

10. Schleiermacher, *Christian Faith*, 739.

11. Ludwig Feuerbach, *The Essence of Christianity*, trans. George Eliot (1841; New York: Barnes and Noble, 2004), 15.

12. Samuel M. Powell, *The Trinity in German Thought* (Cambridge: Cambridge University Press, 2001), 105-07.

not without competing interpretations.[13] Nevertheless, Hegel believed that the ecclesiastical version of the doctrine of the Trinity was merely a representation, or a placeholder, for the universal truth of the philosophy of 'Spirit' and history.[14] Hegel believed that people needed to move past the representational and embrace comprehension (*Vernunft*) of the true nature of reality.[15] The means by which a person reached comprehension was by recognizing that the true method involves dialectical movement, namely, that all beings, including God, are marked by a unity of opposites. In fact, all reality consists in the unity of opposites, and hence to be real is to participate in this dialectical movement of life: thesis + antithesis = synthesis.[16]

According to Hegel universal truth ultimately produces its own opposite – this self-negation is revelation.[17] As it relates to his doctrine of the trinity, the idea of free universality, or the pure essence of God (kingdom of the Father), produces its opposite in the differentiation of the Son (kingdom of the Son), which is then reconciled through the Spirit (kingdom of the Spirit). This process of self-negation is revelation.[18] In the process of differentiation, the kingdom of the Son becomes externalized in the world and in nature, which is the realm of finite spirits. The unity of humanity with God appears with the revelation of the Son on the stage of nature, which is the beginning of faith.

---

13. Powell, *Trinity in German Thought*, 104.

14. Powell, *Trinity in German Thought*, 110; Michael S. Horton, *The Christian Faith: A Systematic Theology for Pilgrims on the Way* (Grand Rapids: Eerdmans, 2011), 294.

15. Powell, *Trinity in German Thought*, 111.

16. Powell, *Trinity in German Thought*, 112-13.

17. Powell, *Trinity in German Thought*, 117.

18. G. W. F. Hegel, *Lectures on the Philosophy of Religion*, vol. 3, *The Consummate Religion*, ed. Peter C. Hodgson (Berkeley: University of California Press, 1998), 362.

The Son as human has an external nature history and ultimately becomes the divine history – the history of the manifestation of God. This melding of God with history constitutes the evolution from the kingdom of the Son to the kingdom of the Spirit. As human beings become aware of this process they become reconciled with God.[19]

In some respects Hegel's thought sounds orthodox, given his use of trinitarian language and concepts, but he never employs the term *Trinity*, and only refers to Father, Son, and Holy Spirit. Moreover, when he employs the term 'Son,' he refers to the entire created order and all finite spirits.[20] To put Hegel's construct in traditional nomenclature, the ontological God as Spirit is manifest in its economic aspect in creation and history. Additionally, when traditional dogmatics refers, for example, to the Father's eternal begetting of the Son, and the dual procession of the Spirit from the Father and the Son, these are merely representations, or word pictures, that give expression to the dialectics of differentiation and reconciliation, or thesis + antithesis = synthesis.[21] Hence, in order for true being to be actualized, this dialectical process must be completed.[22] Unless one arrives at the synthetic conclusion, being has been shortchanged, and hence, true being must become. Hegel's system, therefore, has been labeled 'Being as becoming.'[23] Once again, to put this into traditional nomenclature, the ontological 'trinity' requires its economic manifestation in order to be God. This means that history and creation, the antithesis of God's existence, the thesis, is part of God. There is no difference

19. Hegel, *Lectures*, 362-63.

20. Powell, *Trinity in German Thought*, 119.

21. Powell, *Trinity in German Thought*, 122.

22. Powell, *Trinity in German Thought*, 128.

23. Horton, *Christian Faith*, 294.

or distinction between God and the creation, though Hegel rejected the charge of pantheism.[24] More recent scholarship identifies Hegel as a panentheist.[25]

Those who think that Hegel was trying to undermine the Christian faith must realize that he thought otherwise: 'The fundamental doctrines of Christianity have for the most part disappeared from dogmatics. Philosophy is preeminently, though not exclusively, what is present essentially orthodox; the propositions that have always been valid, the basic truths of Christianity, are maintained and preserved by it.'[26] So even though Hegel's 'theology' was decidedly anthropocentric, he struck a chord that echoed in the trinitarian theology of Barth and others, such as Wolfhart Pannenberg (1928-).[27]

Trinitarian renaissance (Barth and Rahner)

If the nineteenth century represented the demise of the doctrine of the Trinity, the twentieth century constituted its rebirth, primarily in the theology of Karl Barth. In contrast to Schleiermacher, who placed the doctrine of the Trinity in an appendix, Barth offered a riposte by beginning his massive *Church Dogmatics* with the doctrine.[28] Rather than begin with God's existence, nature, and attributes, as so many historic explanations of the doctrine of God had done, Barth began with the triune God's

---

24. Powell, *Trinity in German Thought*, 129-30.

25. John W. Cooper, *Panentheism: The Other God of the Philosophers: From Plato to the Present* (Grand Rapids: Baker, 2006), 116-17.

26. Hegel, *Lectures*, 261-62.

27. Powell, *Trinity in German Thought*, 141.

28. Karl Barth, *Church Dogmatics*, 14 vols., eds. T. F. Torrance and G. W. Bromiley (Edinburgh: T & T Clark, 1999), I/1:295-490. Hereafter abbreviated as CD followed by the volume and page number(s).

self-disclosure in revelation.[29] Barth writes: 'There is in fact a serious risk, in the doctrine of Scripture as well as the doctrine of God, that we may lose ourselves in considerations and be driven to conclusions which have nothing whatever to do with the supposed concrete theme of the two doctrines, if we begin by discarding the concreteness as it is manifest in the trinitarian form of the Christian doctrine of God.'[30] On this note, Barth positively cites Herman Bavinck (1854-1921): 'In the doctrine of the Trinity beats the heart of the whole revelation of God for the redemption of humanity.'[31]

So Barth marks a renewed interest in the doctrine of the Trinity, but there are two noteworthy elements. First, Barth argues that the root of the doctrine of the Trinity lies in revelation, not that the Trinity is merely an interpretation of revelation. When dealing with revelation we deal with God Himself.[32] And for Barth, revelation chiefly rests upon God's self-disclosure in Christ. Therefore, 'The doctrine of the Trinity is simply a development of the knowledge that Jesus is the Christ or Lord.'[33] Second, this raises the question about the respective priority between the doctrines of the Trinity and christology. In other words, does the Trinity define the nature of Christ's person and work, or does Christ's person and work define the nature of the Trinity? In his effort to explain the trinitarian nature of the crucifixion Barth applies his trinitarian methodological presupposition and argues that obedience marks Christ's work, which is 'the first and inner

29. Barth, CD I/1:300.

30. Barth, CD, I/1:301.

31. Barth, CD I/1:302; Herman Bavinck, *Reformed Dogmatics*, 4 vols., trans. John Vriend, ed. John Bolt (Grand Rapids: Baker, 2003-08), II:260.

32. Barth, CD I/1:311.

33. Barth, CD I/1:334.

moment of the mystery of the deity of Christ.' The mystery of the revelation of Christ shows that it is just as natural for God to be lowly as it is to be high.[34]

This means that Christ reveals who God is because He is the supreme self-disclosure, and in this revelation Christ reveals His divine nature, marked by obedience to the Father. As Barth writes: 'The mirror in which it can be known (and is known) that He is God and of the divine nature, is His becoming flesh and His existence in the flesh.'[35] Consequently, from the vantage point of Christ's obedience, it reveals 'the inner being of God as the being of the Son in relation to the Father.'[36] Obedience marks both Christ's economic and His ontological activity, which means obedience is in the very being of God.[37] This doctrinal chord has resonated in the writings of Hans Urs von Balthasar (1905-88), Jürgen Moltmann (1926-), and Eberhard Jüngel (1934-).[38] This, of course, raises questions regarding the relationship between the ontological and economic Trinity and to what degree economic activity can be carried back into the ontological Trinity. Does the obedience of Christ constitute the core of His divine procession from the Father? This is a question that bears directly upon the doctrine of the *pactum salutis* and will be addressed below.

---

34. Barth, CD IV/1:192.

35. Barth, CD IV/1:177.

36. Barth, CD IV/1:177.

37. Thomas Joseph White, 'Intra-Trinitarian Obedience and Nicene-Chalcedonian Christology,' *Nova et Vera* 6/2 (2008): 382.

38. White, 'Intra-Trinitarian Obedience,' 377; cf. Hans Urs von Balthasar, *The Glory of the Lord*, vol. 1 (San Francisco: Ignatius Press, 1982), 478-80; idem, *Theo-drama*, vol. 5 (San Francisco: Ignatius Press, 1998), 236-39; Eberhard Jüngel, *God's Being Is in Becoming: The Trinitarian Being of God in the Theology of Karl Barth* (Grand Rapids: Eerdmans, 2001), 75-124; Jürgen Moltmann, *The Crucified God* (Philadelphia: Fortress Press, 1993), 200-90.

But Barth was not the only theologian to promote a renewed interest in the doctrine of the Trinity. Despite Barth's trinitarian salvo in the initial volume of his *Dogmatics* in 1932, Karl Rahner lamented some thirty years later that were the doctrine of the Trinity to be proven as false, the lion's share of theological literature would remain virtually unchanged.[39] Hence in the wake of Vatican II's (1962-65) call for a break with Neo-Scholastic theology, which relied heavily upon Aristotelian logic and metaphysics, Rahner leveled the criticism against older treatments of the doctrine of God that first treated God's essence and then later treated the doctrine of the Trinity. Hence, in Rahner's view, theologians separated God's essence from His triune existence.[40]

For Rahner, the Scriptures do not explicitly present the doctrine of the immanent Trinity, or who God is *in se*, not even in John's famous prologue. The only access we have to the immanent Trinity is what has been revealed by the economic Trinity. He succinctly captures this principle in what has been called *Rahner's rule*: 'The "economic" Trinity is the "immanent" Trinity and the "immanent" Trinity is the "economic" Trinity.'[41] This means that the only access we have to the Trinity is through our experience of the triune God in redemptive history.[42] Any declarations about the immanent Trinity must flow exclusively from what we know about the economic Trinity, or God's acts in history.

---

39. Karl Rahner, *The Trinity*, trans. Joseph Donceel (1967; New York: Herder & Herder, 2005), 10-11.

40. Rahner, *The Trinity*, 16. Later scholarship has come to characterize this narrative as a distortion of medieval, Reformation, and post-Reformation doctrines of God (see Richard A. Muller, *Post-Reformation Reformed Dogmatics*, 4 vols. [Grand Rapids: 2003], III:158-59).

41. Rahner, *The Trinity*, 22.

42. Rahner, *The Trinity*, 39.

Narrative theology (Jenson, Frei, LaCugna)

The move away from metaphysics and the focus upon redemptive history influenced a new generation of theologians in their own reflections upon the doctrine of the Trinity. Striking a note from the musical score that Rahner composed, Jenson argues that the function of the biblical narrative is to identify the God who is named therein.[43] 'God's self-identification with the Crucified One,' writes Jenson, 'frees us from having to find God by projection of our own perfections.'[44] Jenson therefore rejects Feuerbach's ideas and embraces a Barthian approach by identifying God by what happens with Jesus.[45] Important to note is that Jenson employs the word *identify* in the theological task of defining who God is. According to Jenson, identification is a pointing operation, and hence it is not exhaustive but merely an indicator. Christian theology, therefore, cannot transcend revelation in time and discover who God is *in se*.[46] It seems that Jenson admits God has bridged Lessing's ditch and Kant's wall, but at the same time all we can say about God is what appears on this side of the wall – we cannot peer over the wall to see exactly who is on the other side.

To illustrate this point we can examine Jenson's criticism of the 'disastrous' Augustinian explanation of the processions and missions of the trinity. According to the Augustinian principle, since the Father sends the Son in the economy of redemption, it must be reflective of His ontological begetting. The same holds true for the Father and the Son sending the

43. Robert W. Jenson, *The Triune Identity: God According to the Gospel* (Philadelphia: Fortress Press, 1982), 7, 139.

44. Jenson, *Triune Identity*, 16.

45. Jenson, *Triune Identity*, 22.

46. Jenson, *Triune Identity*, 24-25.

Spirit, which must be reflective of the Spirit's ontological dual-procession from Father and Son. Jenson argues that such a formulation creates two distinct sets of trinitarian relations, immanent and economic relations. According to Jenson, 'The final consequence of these developments is that the trinitarian language of "persons" and "relations" in God loses its original history-of-salvation meaning, and indeed threatens to lose all meaning of any kind.'[47] Instead of seeking to construct a metaphysical doctrine of God, all we have is redemptive history and the revelation of God in Christ. This is the answer, argues Jenson, to preserving the distinctly trinitarian and therefore Christian nature of theological reflection about God. In Jenson's thought Barth made one of the first big initial steps in the right direction by inverting Hegel's doctrine of the Trinity. Jenson contends, 'Only put *Jesus* in place of Hegel's "world," and you have the doctrine of Barth's *Church Dogmatics*, volume I/1—which observation takes nothing from the extraordinary ingenuity of Barth's move.'[48]

Another contributor to the discussion is Hans Frei, a representative of the Yale postliberal theology and noted for his work on hermeneutics, particularly in *The Eclipse of Biblical Narrative*.[49] Frei's programmatic efforts have been to steer theological reflection away from ontological speculation and focus upon the narrative of Scripture. When a person looks at a sculpture, he does not try to imagine what lies inside of it. Rather, his eyes roam and wander over the surface to grasp its form, proportions, color, and features. Only in this type

47. Jenson, *Triune Identity*, 125.

48. Jenson, *Triune Identity*, 136.

49. Hans Frei, *The Eclipse of Biblical Narrative: A Study in Eighteenth and Nineteenth Century Hermeneutics* (New Haven: Yale University Press, 1974).

of reflection does one gather the 'meaning' of the sculpture.[50] Frei eschews efforts to discuss the ontology of Christ and instead focuses exclusively upon His economic work, or more specifically, His actions. According to Frei, 'A person *is* what he *does* centrally and most significantly.'[51] In this respect, Frei focuses exclusively upon the narrative: 'If the Gospel story is to function religiously in a way that is at once historical and Christological, the central focus will have to be on the history-like narration of the final sequence, rather than on Jesus' sayings in the preaching pericopes.'[52]

Rather than focus upon the 'I am' sayings in the Gospel of John, for example, one must instead focus upon the broad narrative as it culminates in the passion–resurrection. Frei doubts the ability to use the sayings of Jesus to determine ontologically who He is: 'All of this is not to say that we are bound to ignore the story of Jesus' ministry in identifying him. It is simply to affirm that Jesus, in his unique identity, is not available to us directly or unambiguously – either as a character in a story or historically – in the portion of the Gospel accounts describing his ministry.'[53] To illustrate Frei's point, we can turn to the analogy of the theater. Frei wants the readers of Scripture to focus upon the entirety of the play, and in particular, the third and climactic act, not so much upon the specific lines that the lead actor delivers. Moreover, he wants the audience to realize that they know nothing about who the actor truly is because he never steps out of character to reveal himself – we only have the unfolding narrative.

---

50. Hans Frei, *The Identity of Jesus Christ: The Hermeneutical Bases of Dogmatic Theology* (Philadelphia: Fortress Press, 1975), 87.

51. Frei, *Identity of Jesus*, 92.

52. Frei, *Identity of Jesus*, 141.

53. Frei, *Identity of Jesus*, 142-43.

Catherine LaCugna pursues a similar path in her major study on the doctrine of the Trinity, *God For Us*.[54] Writing some twenty years after Rahner, LaCugna laments the decline and absence of trinitarian reflection in the church's theology. To push back in the opposite direction of the trinitarian absence, the thesis of her book is that the doctrine of the Trinity is ultimately practical in nature.[55] That is to say, Scripture does not disclose the ontological Trinity but only the economic Trinity. At a number of points LaCugna echoes Rahner's doctrine of the Trinity, most notably applying his rule – the economic trinity is the immanent trinity – to her own theological project.[56] In particular, LaCugna rejects the traditional distinction between the ontological and economic trinity, or the processions and missions. In her estimation, 'An ontological distinction between God *in se* and God *pro nobis* is, finally, inconsistent with biblical revelation.'[57] The distinction between being and function is invalid.[58]

LaCugna vigorously applies Rahner's rule to her understanding of the Trinity. For her, *theologia* (who God is) is only given in the *oikonomia* (the economy of salvation). LaCugna's desire is to return to a pre-Nicene pattern of thought and abandon the misleading terms of the economic and immanent Trinity. In her view, *theologia* is ultimately a mystery, and *oikonomia* is God's comprehensive plan that stretches from creation to consummation.[59] 'Since our only point of access to *theologia* is through *oikonomia*, then *an*

---

54. Catherine Mowry LaCugna, *God For Us: The Trinity and Christian Life* (San Francisco: Harper San Francisco, 1991).

55. LaCugna, *God For Us*, 1.

56. LaCugna, *God For Us*, 6, 13, 209-42.

57. LaCugna, *God For Us*, 6.

58. LaCugna, *God For Us*, 7.

59. LaCugna, *God For Us*, 223.

"immanent" trinitarian theology of God is nothing more than a theology of the economy of salvation. An immanent theology of the Trinity therefore is not, properly speaking, a theology of an intradivine Trinity of persons unrelated to the world.'[60]

To return to the illustration of the theater, LaCugna wants the audience swept into the drama and to recognize that they cannot know who the actors truly are – it is ultimately a mystery. The lead male role might not even be played by a man, but by a woman, an inversion of the early days of theater when men played the roles of women because women were not allowed to participate. LaCugna avoids using the term *Father* and instead opts for the term *God*.[61] In fact, LaCugna, along similar lines as Jenson's, argues that the doctrine of the Trinity is merely a signpost that points beyond itself to the mystery of God who dwells in inaccessible light.[62] Jenson, Frei, and LaCugna differ on a number of points but nevertheless share something in common. All three allow for the fact that God has tossed a rock with a message tied to it over Kant's epistemic iron curtain. As to what, precisely, the note says, no one is entirely sure. But this much is certain, there is someone on the other side of the wall.

Apostolic pattern

The foregoing brief reconnaissance of the contemporary history of the development of the doctrine of the Trinity places a number of questions before us as we consider them in connection with the *pactum salutis*. First, how can we know God? Is revelation possible

60. LaCugna, *God For Us*, 224.

61. LaCugna, *God For Us*, 356; cf. Thomas Weinandy, *The Father's Spirit of Sonship: Reconceiving the Trinity* (Eugene: Wipf & Stock, 1995), 132.

62. LaCugna, *God For Us*, 321.

in a post-Kantian world? Second, if God can send a note over the Kantian iron curtain, can we read it? Is it possible to leap across Lessing's ugly ditch? Third, assuming that the ditch can be crossed and that knowledge can pass over the Kantian wall, what can we know about God? Are we restricted merely to redemptive history, or the *oikonomia*, to use LaCugna's terms, or can we also know something about *theologia*?[63] Is the distinction between the immanent and economic Trinity valid? In one sense, these questions cannot be answered based upon post-Kantian Enlightenment presuppositions about the (im)possibility of revelation. In this respect, the Barthian and postliberal turn towards the text of Scripture and redemptive history is a positive development. With the onset of the Barthian trinitarian renaissance, the above surveyed theologians are correct to argue that God can only be known on the basis of His divine self-disclosure, or His revelation. But this in turn raises another question: Can one legitimately claim to engage redemptive history and at the same time pick and choose what to accept and what to reject? Whatever professed allegiance there might be towards the economic Trinity, does this not become Feuerbach's projection? Does not *theologia* devolve into anthropology?[64]

In the illustration of the theater the audience does not know very much about the actor playing the lead role. They only know something about the character the actor portrays. But what if the lead actor is in a biographical play where he is playing himself? What if the lead actor is also the play writer, which means that the

63. These terms originate with Thomas Aquinas, though he culled them from Patristic theologians. See, Aquinas, *Summa Theologia* (rep.; Allen: Classic Reprints, 1948), III q. 2 art. 6 ad. 1; cf. Gilles Emery, '*Theologia* and *Dispensatio*: the Centrality of the Divine Missions in St. Thomas's Trinitarian Theology,' *The Thomist* 74 (2010): 515-61.

64. Francesca Aran Murphy, *God Is Not A Story: Realism Revisited* (Oxford: Oxford University Press, 2007), 122-23; Paul Molnar, *Divine Freedom and the Doctrine of the Immanent Trinity* (Edinburgh: T & T Clark, 2005), 7.

lead character's dialogue is genuine and not fictional. And what if after the play, the lead actor sat down for an interview, as many actors do, and was asked about the meaning and significance of the play, as well as the authorial intent behind the dialogue? Such a scenario would reveal much of the mystery about the lead actor. This does not mean that the actor will divulge everything, but just because our knowledge about the actor and his autobiographical role is not comprehensive does not mean that the limited knowledge we do have is not true and that the autobiographical drama does not reveal true knowledge about who the actor is.

In this vein there are two important points to be factored. First, one of the fruits of scholastic theology that post-Reformation theologians developed was the distinction between *archetypal* and *ectypal* theology. According to Francis Junius (1545-1602), archetypal theology deals with matters that pertain to the wisdom of God beyond human investigation.[65] God's own wisdom is something we worship but cannot know because it is God's knowledge *in se*, and as finite creatures, we do not have the capacity for this knowledge.[66] Ectypal knowledge, on the other hand, is the shadow or copy of the archetype, but is nevertheless true, finite, and revealed knowledge of God suited for human capacity for their salvation.[67] Edward Leigh

65. Willem J. Van Asselt, 'The Fundamental Meaning of Theology: Archetypal and Ectypal Theology in Seventeenth-Century Reformed Thought,' *WTJ* 64 (2002): 321.

66. Francis Junius, *De Vera Theologia*, in *Opuscula Theological Selecta*, ed. Abraham Kuyper (Amsterdam: Frederic Muller, 1882), chp. IV (pp. 51-52). See also, Michael Horton, *Covenant and Eschatology: The Divine Drama* (Louisville: Westminster John Knox, 2002), 183; John Webster, '"It was the Will of the Lord to Bruise Him": Soteriology and the Doctrine of God,' in *God of Salvation: Soteriology in Theological Perspective*, eds. Ivor J. Davidson and Murray A. Rae (Aldershot: Ashgate, 2011), 25.

67. Junius, *Vera Theologia*, chp. V (p. 53); also Richard A. Muller, *Dictionary of Latin and Greek Theological Terms: Drawn Principally from Protestant Scholastic Theology* (Grand Rapids: Baker, 1985), s. v. *theologia archetypa, theologia ectypa*.

(1602-71) explains these two terms very succinctly in the following manner: 'Archetypal knowledge, or divinity in God, of God himself,' is that 'by which God by one individual and immutable act knows himself in himself, and all other things out of himself, by himself.' On the other hand, 'Ectypal and communicated' theology is 'expressed in us by divine revelation after the pattern and idea which is in God, and this is called *theologia de Deo*, divinity concerning God.'[68]

Responsible theology should never claim somehow to subvert revelation and explain what has not been revealed, namely, who God is *in se*, His essence.[69] To quote an Old Testament maxim, 'The secret things belong to the LORD our God, but the things that are revealed belong to us and to our children forever, that we may do all the words of this law' (Deut. 29:29). This particular statement comes from a context where Moses revealed to Israel that their venture into the Promised Land would be an utter failure and would end in judgment and exile (Deut. 29:16-28). Rather than try to peer into what has not been revealed, Moses tells the people to embrace what has been revealed to them, namely, the law.[70] Scripture is clear that there are many things that God chooses not to reveal. As with the actor sitting for an interview, some topics are off limits, and there are subjects the actor will not address.

---

68. Edward Leigh, *A System or Body of Divinity: Consisting of Ten Books. Wherein the Fundamentals of the main Grounds of Religion Are Opened* (London: William Lee, 1654), I.i (p. 2).

69. So, e.g., Aquinas, *Summa Theologica*, Ia q. 32 art. 1; Hilary of Poitiers, *De Trinitate*, I.vii, in NPNF[2] 9:42; cf. Muller, *Post-Reformation Reformed Dogmatics*, IV:257-60.

70. J. A. Thompson, *Deuteronomy*, TOTC (Downers Grove: InterVarsity Press, 1974), 283-84; J. G. McConville, *Deuteronomy*, AOTC (Downers Grove: InterVarsity Press, 2002), 419.

So, then, this leads to a second question: What is the nature of revelation? Narrative theologians marginalize portions of the text, privileging the crucifixion–resurrection over the earlier portions of the gospel. Such a move fails to recognize and accept the structure and content of the narrative. Geerhardus Vos (1862-1949) summarizes the structural form of narrative revelation in the following manner: 'First word, then the fact, then again the interpretive word. The Old Testament brings the predictive preparatory word, the Gospel records the redemptive-revelatory fact, the Epistles supply the subsequent, final interpretation.'[71] In other words, we can certainly agree that the crucifixion–resurrection is a chief focal point in the redemptive narrative and that it reveals, in some sense, who God is. But the Scriptures do not present a bald narrative. The drama of redemptive history is not a silent movie with no dialogue, nor is it a mime standing mute on stage acting silently before the audience. Rather, the unfolding drama has dialogue written by the chief protagonist, who narrates the drama to explain what will occur in each act of the play, explains the significance of each event as it occurs within each act, and offers a subsequent interpretation of what just occurred. This word–act–word revelatory pattern is crucial for comprehending the chief purpose of the Scriptures: to reveal the triune God in Christ.

Case in point, word-revelation preceded Christ's crucifixion; Jesus was Isaiah's suffering servant, who would be 'pierced for our transgressions' and 'crushed for our iniquities' (Isa. 53:5). As Christ hung on the cross and took His last breath the narrative is not silent. It records the words of the Roman centurion, 'Truly

71. Geerhardus Vos, *Biblical Theology: Old and New Testaments* (1948; Edinburgh: Banner of Truth, 1996), 7; Boris Bobrinskoy, *The Mystery of the Trinity: Trinitarian Experience and Vision in the Biblical and Patristic Tradition* (Crestwood: St. Vladimir's Seminary Press, 1999), 28.

this man was the Son of God!' (Mark 15:39). Within the context of Mark's Gospel, this is no idle claim – to rend the earlier Gospel narrative from the crucifixion–resurrection radically alters the script. Mark begins his Gospel with the claim that Jesus Christ is the Son of God (1:1) and the demons shudder in utter fear before Christ because they knew He was the Son of God (3:11; 5:7).[72] The pre- and post- word-revelation bookends the act of Christ's crucifixion – they cannot be separated without significantly destroying the drama. Thus we should ask: What does Scripture specifically reveal about the triune God?

The Gospel of John gives evidence that revelation provides information about the immanent and economic Trinity. The opening chapter of John gives us a glimpse behind the Kantian wall when he invokes the opening words of Genesis 1:1, but with more revelatory light: 'In the beginning was the Word, and the Word was with God, and the Word was God' (John 1:1). To invoke the name of God with the words 'Εν ἀρχῆ, the same words that open the Septuagint, undoubtedly places Yahweh front and center on the stage of redemptive history. But John introduces a twist, not by adding new information but by shedding more light upon the stage. Where people originally thought that there was only one person on the stage, the spotlight reveals a second person, the Word. The Word, moreover, 'was God.' 'All things were made through him,' writes John, 'and without him was not any thing made that was made' (John 1:3).

What most first-century Jews would have attributed to Yahweh, the creation of the heavens and the earth, John assigns to the agency of the Word. How does John remain within the revelatory guardrails of Israel's *shema*, 'Hear, O Israel: The LORD our God, the LORD is one' (Deut. 6:4)? How can he maintain that

72. C. S. Mann, *Mark*, AB, vol. 27 (New York: Doubleday, 1986), 654.

God is one and at the same time maintain that the Word is also God?[73] John distinguishes between God and the Word, and God the Father did not became flesh and 'tabernacle' in Israel's midst but the Word did (John 1:14*). John's movement from 'in the beginning' to 'the Word became flesh and tabernacled among us' takes us from eternity into the middle of redemptive history. As much as some think that talking about the immanent Trinity is speculative, John has opened a revelatory window disclosing who God is. John, however, does not provide us with an archetypal knowledge of God, concerning what God is *in se*. Our knowledge is finite and designed for human capacity – to use John Calvin's (1509-64) phrase, He lisps to us like a nursemaid to an infant – but it is nevertheless true.[74] For example, we do not know the specific nature of the quiddity of God's essence – John does not reveal this. But we do know that in some sense the Father and the Son are both one God, yet they are distinct from one another.

The same pattern unfolds with respect to the Holy Spirit and His connection to the Father and the Son in John's Gospel. When Christ receives John's baptism, the Spirit descends upon Him like a dove (1:33), and in His conversation with Nicodemus, Jesus states that in order to enter the kingdom of God, one must be born of the Spirit (3:5). In this respect, the Spirit gives life (John 6:63), which according to the Old Testament was exclusively the prerogative of God (Gen. 2:7; Job 24:22; 33:4; Ps. 54:4; Isa. 38:5). And when Jesus was preparing His disciples for His imminent crucifixion, resurrection, and ascension, He told them that the Father and the Son would send the Spirit to bear

---

73. McConville, *Deuteronomy*, 140-42; R. W. L. Moberly, *Old Testament Theology: Reading the Hebrew Bible as Christian Scripture* (Grand Rapids: Baker, 2013), 7-40.

74. John Calvin, *Institutes of the Christian Religion*, trans. John Allen (Grand Rapids: Eerdmans, 1949), I.xiii.1.

witness about Christ and cause them to remember His teaching (John 14:26; 15:26; 16:13). But the absence of Christ and the presence of the Spirit, a presence that makes Christ somehow present, signals that the Spirit is somehow part of this one God, but nevertheless distinct from the Father and the Son. That the Father and Son send the Spirit means that He is not the Father and the Son, yet He is also God (John 14:18).

The Old Testament backdrop to John's Gospel also informs the reader that the Spirit has the same origin as the Son. Just as John's words 'in the beginning' draw the reader's mind back to Genesis 1, the life-giving work of the Spirit and the birth that comes through water and Spirit draws us back to the same text, as the 'Spirit of God was hovering over the face of the waters' (Gen. 1:2). John's Gospel and the broader witness of Scripture continually point back to the eternal origin of the economic work of the Father, Son, and Holy Spirit. Once again the spotlight shines upon the stage and reveals a third character that has always been present, standing in the shadows. But we should not miss the fact that before the play began the actors had to come from somewhere – they moved from backstage to center stage (assuming that the stage is the earth) as the curtain was drawn and the drama began. Not only is this truth evident in the sending of the Son and the Spirit (whence did they come?), but it is also apparent in Christ's departure (where did He go?). In theater terms – He has stepped off stage and is waiting to reappear at the end of the third and final act. In other words, the biblical witness itself testifies to the eternal origins of the economic work of the triune God. This information has been revealed; it is not, therefore, speculative to speak about the eternal origins of the triune God.[75]

---

75. Molnar, *Divine Freedom*, 21.

Processions and missions

But how do we synthesize the biblical data? How do we have Father, Son, and Holy Spirit as one God, yet with three distinct persons? Moreover, what precisely is the relationship between the so-called immanent (or ontological) and economic trinity? And what place does the doctrine of the *pactum salutis* serve in explaining the biblical data? And how does this relate to the intra-trinitarian love and its outpouring upon fallen sinners? We must begin with the distinction between the immanent and economic Trinity.[76] In the broad picture, Rahner's rule offers a helpful way to distinguish God from His activity in creation and redemption: 'The "economic" Trinity is the "immanent" Trinity and the "immanent" Trinity is the "economic" Trinity.'[77] At its most fundamental level, Rahner's rule affirms that the God of eternity is the same God who acts in history, and that His revelation in the economy of creation and salvation is the only access we have to Him. But as important as Rahner's rule is, there are a number of desirable qualifications.[78]

First, the economy of redemption does not establish the Trinity. The Father does not become the Father only within the economy of redemption. The Father, Son, and Holy Spirit are eternally Father, Son and Spirit. Second, God's eternal triune existence is

---

76. For what follows, see Gilles Emery, *The Trinity: An Introduction to Catholic Doctrine on the Triune God*, trans. Matthew Levering (Washington, DC: Catholic University of America Press, 2011), 175-78.

77. Rahner, *Trinity*, 22.

78. For contemporary treatments of the processions and missions, see Bernard Lonergan, *The Triune God: Systematics*, Collected Works of Bernard Lonergan, vol. 12, trans. Michael Shields, eds. Robert M. Doran and H. Daniel Monsour (Toronto: University of Toronto Press, 2007), 125-232, 437-522; Robert M. Doran, *The Trinity In History: A Theology of the Divine Missions*, vol. 1, *Missions and Processions* (Toronto: University of Toronto Press, n. d.).

necessary, whereas the economy is contingent. The term *contingent* simply means that something could be otherwise. God could have decided to create or not to create, whereas His existence is not contingent because God exists necessarily. If we do not distinguish between God's necessary existence and the contingent economy, then Hegel is correct. God's existence would be truly marked by becoming and process, and the creation would be part of God. Hence, pantheism is unavoidable. Third, as stated above, we must maintain the epistemological distinction between archetypal and ectypal theology. In all exposition of the immanent Trinity, we are not able to penetrate the quiddity of God, we cannot know His essence, only what He has revealed.[79] Given these points, it seems preferable to use a different set of terms to ensure that we maintain these three principles. It is better to speak of the *processions* and the *missions*, which help us distinguish between immanent and economic Trinity, for such terms do not seem to be as liable to misunderstanding as Rahner's rule.[80]

Aquinas explains that *missions* only have a temporal significance for God, whereas generation and spiration (*opera ad intra*) are exclusively eternal. But the processions are both eternal and temporal: 'For the Son may proceed eternally as God; but temporally, by becoming man, according to his visible mission, or likewise by dwelling in man according to his invisible mission.'[81] In other words, the terms *economic* and *ontological Trinity* can be misleading because they might imply a separation from history – it might imply there is an unknown and hidden God who stands

79. For similar observations, see Peter C. Phan, 'Systematic Issues in Trinitarian Theology,' in *The Cambridge Companion to the Trinity*, ed. Peter C. Phan (Cambridge: Cambridge University Press, 2011), 16-17.

80. Aquinas, *Summa Theologica*, Ia q. 43 arts. 1-8.

81. Aquinas, *Summa Theologica*, Ia q. 43 art. 2.

behind the economic Trinity as some narrative theologians have claimed (e.g., Jenson, Frei, and LaCugna). The economic Trinity might not truly reveal the ontological Trinity. In contrast, Thomas's point is that the triune God reveals the eternal processions in their covenantal missions. The trinitarian processions become manifest in time through creation and especially redemption.[82]

Hence, as we examine the relationship between the processions and missions, we must start with the missions. As Vos has rightly noted, there is a difference between the sequences in the spheres of being and revelation. In other words, our only starting point is revelation: 'That which is the *outcome* of the higher naturally appears in history as the medium for the disclosure of that higher thing, and consequently appears earlier in time.'[83] Our knowledge of the triune God begins with Christ's incarnation in redemptive history. This does not mean that we can only construct the doctrine of the Trinity from below, which would essentially follow the methodology of narrative theologians (LaCugna, Frei, and Jenson). Rather, we construct our doctrine of the Trinity, their processions and missions, from divine revelation. Scripture presents both the Trinity's processions and missions. Given the presupposition of divine revelation, we do not face the false dichotomy between choosing a starting point. We do not have to start below with the Christ of history, nor do we have to try to start from above with the transcendent Trinity. Revelation gives us both. Nevertheless, by starting with the missions of Christ and the Spirit, we can look back to the revealed eternal origins in their intra-trinitarian processions.

---

82. Gilles Emery, 'Essentialism or Personalism in the Treatise on God in St. Thomas Aquinas,' *The Thomist* 64 (2000): 527-28; idem, '*Theologia* and *Dispensatio*,' 527-28; cf. Molnar, *Divine Freedom*, 69; Webster, 'It Was His Will to Crush Him,' 25-28.

83. Geerhardus Vos, *The Self-Disclosure Jesus: The Modern Debate about the Messianic Consciousness* (1926, 1953; Phillipsburg: P & R, n. d.), 189-90.

Throughout John's Gospel Christ repeatedly states that He was sent: 'Truly, truly, I say to you, whoever hears my word and believes him who sent me has eternal life' (John 5:23). In fact, Christ mentions His sent status thirty-one times in John's Gospel (5:30, 38; 6:29, 38-39, 44; 7:16, 18, 28-29, 33; 8:16, 18, 26, 29, 42; 9:4; 10:36; 12:44-45, 49; 13:16; 14:24; 15:21; 16:5; 17:3, 18, 23, 25; 20:21).[84] John's Gospel also speaks of the Spirit being sent by the Father and the Son, though more infrequently (14:26; 15:26). Do these sending texts reflect the intra-trinitarian processions? Do these passages suggest that because the Father sends the Son, and the Father and the Son send the Spirit, that the Son eternally proceeds from the Father (filiation) and the Spirit eternally proceeds from the Father and Son (spiration)?

Theologians from both the East and West have spilled an ocean of ink over this question. There are scriptural indicators, however, that suggest that the trinitarian missions reveal the eternal processions. Concerning the Son, Christ states the following during one of His debates with the religious leaders: 'Do you say of him whom the Father consecrated and sent into the world ...' (John 10:36). Christ's statement cannot refer to His consecration at His baptism, otherwise Christ would have spoken, first, of being sent into the world and then His subsequent consecration. Hence, Christ speaks of a pre-temporal, or eternal, consecration.[85] But important to note is that Christ identifies His eternal sender as His Father. We find a counterpart to this statement in John 3:16*, which states that God so loved the world

---

84. Francis J. Moloney, *Love in the Gospel of John: An Exegetical, Theological, and Literary Study* (Grand Rapids: Baker, 2013), 57.

85. John Calvin, *John 1-10*, CNTC (Grand Rapids: Eerdmans, 1996), 276; Thomas Aquinas, *Commentary on the Gospel of John*, 3 vols. (Washington, DC: Catholic University Press of America, 2010), 2.216.

that He sent His 'only begotten Son' (υἱὸν τὸν μονογενῆ).[86] Christ once again identifies His Father as the one who sends the Son into the world.[87]

Some may object to translating the term μονογενής as 'only begotten,' thereby suggesting the Son's eternal generation from the Father. Critics instead claim that this term only indicates the Son's uniqueness and does not reveal anything about His ontology.[88] But critics fail to see that the eternal generation of the Son does not hinge solely upon this one term. Other scriptural terms suggest the Son's eternal procession from the Father. Fathers beget sons, images reflected in a mirror have an image-source, and spoken words have mouths that utter them.[89] Christ is the eternal Son of God, the eternal uncreated image, and the eternal Word of God. For the sake of discussion, we can eliminate any reference to John 3:16 and the question of how to translate μονογενής. The doctrine of the eternal generation of the Son does not rest upon this one text. The relationship between image-source and image presents the same truth. Is the Son eternally the uncreated image of God? Correlatively, is the Son eternally the Word? The eternal Son is also eternally the uncreated image of God and the eternal Word. These three images reveal the eternal nature of the relationship between Father and Son. Hence, the fact that the Father has sent the

---

86. On the translation of μονογενής, see Robert Letham, *The Holy Trinity: In Scripture, History, Theology, and Worship* (Phillipsburg: P & R, 2004), 383-89; J. M. Buchanan, 'The Only Begotten Son,' *CTJ* 16/1 (1981): 56-79.

87. Moloney, *Love*, 59.

88. See, e.g., Dale Moody, 'The Translation of John 3:16 in the Revised Standard Version,' *JBL* 72 (1952): 213-19; M. Peppard, 'Adopted and Begotten Sons of God: Paul and John on Divine Sonship,' *CBQ* 73/1 (2011): 92-110.

89. Aquinas, *Summa Theologica*, Ia q. 34; q. 35 art. 1; Augustine, *On the Holy Trinity*, VII.i, in NPNF III:104-06.

Son reflects the eternal relationship that they have – the Father is eternally the Father and the Son is eternally the Son.[90]

As we explored in Part II, the sending of the Son has its basis in the eternal processions and its context within the intra-trinitarian covenant. Psalm 2:7 reveals both sides of the procession–mission equation. As debated as this text is, with some exegetes choosing to associate it with the eternal generation of the Son and others exclusively with His resurrection from the dead, we do not have to choose between the two.[91] The begetting of the Son in redemptive history, 'today I have begotten you,' what Paul identifies as Christ's resurrection and the fulfillment of this text (Acts 13:33), is rooted in the first part of the statement, 'You are my Son.' In fact, Yahweh's declaration of the Messiah's sonship, 'You are my son,' is a nominal clause that expresses a condition or state. In contrast, the phrase, 'Today I have begotten you,' is a verbal clause, which expresses an action. The Messiah was God's Son before He was inaugurated as Zion's king.[92]

Some might counter-argue that the text refers exclusively to David and his original historical horizon, as it echoes the Davidic

---

90. See John Webster, 'Eternal Generation,' in John Webster, *God Without Measure* (London: Bloomsbury T & T Clark, forthcoming).

91. E.g., Walter Brueggemann, *Theology of the Old Testament: Testimony, Dispute, Advocacy* (Minneapolis: Fortress, 1997), 620-21; cf. Aquinas, *Summa Theologica*, Ia q. 27 art. 2.

92. Robert L. Cole, *Psalms 1-2: Gateway to the Psalter* (Sheffield: Sheffield Phoenix Press, 2013), 114; Wilhelm Gesenius, *Gesenius's Hebrew Grammar*, ed. Emil Kautzsch, trans. Arthur Ernest Cowley (1909; Mineola: Dover Publications, 2006), §140.4; Bill T. Arnold and John H. Choi, *A Guide to Biblical Hebrew Syntax* (Cambridge: Cambridge University Press, 2003), 164-70. Some, however, contend that the phrase, 'You are my son,' is not a nominal clause but a performative phrase that is parallel to the, 'Today I have begotten you.' In other words, both clauses mean exactly the same thing – the inauguration of the Messiah's kingship (John Goldingay, *Psalms*, 3 vols. [Grand Rapids: Baker, 2008], I:100).

covenant (2 Sam. 7:14; Ps. 89:3-4).[93] We should indeed account for the original historical horizon, but New Testament authors did not believe that this horizon exhausted the significance of the text and therefore connected the text to Christ, David's greater son. The text, therefore, reveals Christ's mission. What occurred in eternity within the intra-trinitarian covenant is typified in God's covenant with David, which finds its antitypical fulfillment in Christ's mission.

Based upon the two halves of the text, the Son's eternal procession from the Father ('You are my Son') uniquely qualifies Him to assume His mediatorial mission ('Today I have begotten you'). But, the text also states, 'I will tell of the decree.' As I have previously argued, *decree* is a synonym for *covenant*. The eternal Father covenants with the eternal Son to create His mediatorial mission. This intra-trinitarian covenantal activity constitutes the foundation for the Son's mission. Moreover, part of the covenantal agreement includes the Spirit's consent and participation in the Son's mission, whether in His anointing with the Spirit at His baptism (Matt. 3:15-17), or Christ's subsequent outpouring of the Spirit at Pentecost (Acts 2:30-35). To be sent implies that there is a sender. In this case, the Father and the Son send the Spirit to apply the Son's role as covenant surety. And if the Spirit is sent, then, like Christ, He is sent to do the will of the ones who sent Him. The Spirit's mission reflects His ontological procession from the Father and the Son. When we look in the mirror of redemptive history, it reflects who God is in eternity.

One will in threefold execution

The question, then, naturally arises: Does the introduction of a covenant (an agreement) within the Godhead necessitate the

---

93. E.g., Goldingay, *Psalms*, I:103-06; Herman Hoeksema, *Reformed Dogmatics* (Grand Rapids: Reformed Free Publishing Association, 1966), 307-09.

postulate of three separate wills? Does this introduce the specter of tritheism and compromise the unitary will of the triune God? Robert Letham has made this claim in a number of places and has suggested that certain formulations eliminate the role of the Holy Spirit, or that if the Trinity requires federal relations to unite them, then it brings into question their indivisible divine will.[94] Barth levels a similar claim. According to Barth there is only one subject, God, and He is one. If there are various parties to a covenant, then they are the one triune God and man. How can the one God, for example, have different wills? How can the will of the Father be different from the will of the Son?[95] Barth does not level the specific criticism, but his language is clear enough: the *pactum* introduces tritheism.

These criticisms seem to miss the mark because they fail to account for the fact that the church has long wrestled with the question of how the Father, Son, and Spirit relate to one another apart from the question of the *pactum*. In other words, this issue is not restricted to the *pactum* but challenges any doctrine of the

---

94. Robert Letham, 'John Owen's Doctrine of the Trinity in its Catholic Context,' in *The Ashgate Research Companion to John Owen's Theology*, eds. Kelly M. Kapic and Mark Jones (Farnham: Ashgate, 2012), 196. Letham makes similar claims elsewhere and, without supporting documentation, argues that the *pactum salutis* opened the door to heresy (Robert Letham, *The Westminster Assembly: Reading Its Theology in Historical Context* [Phillipsburg: P & R, 2009], 235-37; cf. idem, *The Work of Christ* [Downers Grove: InterVarsity Press, 1993], 52-53, 254 n. 34). He offers no proof that the *pactum salutis* was the direct cause of tritheism, nor does he specifically name those who embraced heresy as a result of the *pactum*. In fact, recent research on the devolution of trinitarian theology in early modern England has turned up no purported connections between the *pactum* and trinitarian heresy, but instead identifies the heretical roots in Socinianism and the labors of the anti-trinitarian John Biddle (1615-62) (Paul C. H. Lim, *Mystery Unveiled: The Crisis of the Trinity Early Modern England* [Oxford: Oxford University Press, 2012], 16-68). Owen employed the *pactum* as a counter-argument against Socinian claims (Lim, *Mystery Unveiled*, 190).

95. Barth, CD, IV/1:65.

Trinity. In the history of the church few have questioned the indivisibility of the divine will.[96] But numerous theologians have sought to explain several elements that appear prominently in John's Gospel, such as how the Father can send the Son, which implies that the Father did the sending, not the Son, and the Son went but the Father was not sent (John 3:17; 5:23; 10:36). Moreover, Christ states, 'For the works that the Father has given me to accomplish, the very works that I am doing, bear witness about me that the Father has sent me' (John 5:36; cf. 6:29). How does Christ accomplish something that the Father does not Himself do if the theological maxim must be preserved, namely, *opera trinitatis ad extra sunt indivisa* ('the external works of the Trinity are undivided')? The Father, for example, does not die on the cross, the Son does. How does one account for this trinitarian division of labor while at the same time maintaining the unity of the divine will and external works?

We should note from the outset that introducing federal or judicial relations among the persons of the Trinity does not

---

96. Though social trinitarianism, which posits three separate centers of consciousness within the Trinity and has therefore opened itself to the criticism of tritheism, may be popular in our own day, in the bigger picture of the church's nearly 2,000 years of reflection upon the doctrine it is a small and arguably insignificant trend. See, e.g., J. Scott Horrell, 'Toward a Biblical Model of the Social Trinity: Avoiding Equivocation of Nature and Order,' *JETS* 47/3 (2004): 399-421; Cornelius Plantinga, Jr., 'Social Trinity and Tritheism,' in *Trinity, Incarnation, and Atonement: Philosophical and Theological Essays*, eds. Ronald J. Feenstra, Cornelius Plantinga, Jr. (Notre Dame: University of Notre Dame Press, 1989), 21-47; Jürgen Moltmann, *The Trinity and Kingdom: The Doctrine of God* (Minneapolis: Fortress, 1993), 154-58; cf. Brian Leftow, 'Anti Social Trinitarianism,' in *The Trinity: An Interdisciplinary Symposium on the Trinity*, eds. Stephen T. Davis, Daniel Kendall, Gerald O'Collins (Oxford: Oxford University Press, 1999), 203-49; Kevin Vanhoozer, *Remythologizing Theology: Divine Action, Passion, and Authorship* (Cambridge: Cambridge University Press, 2010), 139-77; Karen Kilby, 'Perichoresis and Projection: Problems with Social Doctrines of the Trinity,' *New Blackfriars* 81 (2000): 432-45.

alter the nature of accounting for the intra-trinitarian relations. Take away the *pactum salutis* and these questions still persist. Some might take this admission and apply Ockham's razor: 'If the question of relating the indivisible will and external work of the Trinity still remains apart from the *pactum salutis*, then is the doctrine therefore not extraneous? Should it not be eliminated? How does it solve this particular question?' True, theologians have answered this question apart from the *pactum salutis*, as we will see below in the exegetical-theological formulations of Thomas Aquinas (1225-74). Nevertheless, as I have demonstrated in Part II, the interaction between the members of the Trinity, particularly the Father and the Son in the *constitutio mediatoris* ('appointment of the mediator'), bear all of the markings of a federal, or covenantal, relationship. Hence, my overall contention is that, yes, theologians can account for the intra-trinitarian interaction apart from the *pactum*, but such explanations are thin and do not factor the relevant covenantal elements that appear in the various scriptural texts. The *pactum salutis*, therefore, offers a thicker explanation of the intra-trinitarian interactions. We can explore the intra-trinitarian deliberations by reflecting upon a number of texts from John's Gospel in the effort to understand how the unified will and work of the triune God unfold in a threefold manner.

First, we must account for the broader canonical context concerning the mission of the Son, particularly texts such as Psalm 2:7, 'I will tell of the decree,' or 'covenant,' 'The LORD said to me, "You are my Son; today I have begotten you,"' or Luke 22:29*, 'I covenant to you, as my Father covenanted to me, a kingdom.' These passages provide the broader context of covenant – the arena in which Christ executes His mediatory work. Moreover, recent scholarship has identified the overall covenantal backdrop for John's Gospel, a portion of Scripture that deals with the work of Christ.[97] In other words, when we read of Christ's work and His interaction with the Father, it takes place within a covenantal context. One such text is John 5:30, 'I can do nothing on my own. As I hear, I judge, and my judgment is just, because I seek not my own will but the will of him who sent me.' Within the immediate context Jesus engaged the religious leaders on the question of Sabbath observance and whether it was permissible to heal on the holy day (John 5:1ff). Christ therefore appealed to the authority of His Father as the one who sent Him to accomplish His, the Father's, will.

Does not Christ's statement reveal that there is more than one will within the Godhead? Social trinitarians might come to such a conclusion, but Aquinas offers a helpful explanation that does not require two independent wills:

> The Father and the Son do have the same will, but the Father does not have his will from another, whereas the Son does have his will from another, i.e., from the Father. Thus the Son accomplishes his own will as from another, i.e., as having it from another; the Father accomplishes his will as his own, i.e., not having it from another. Thus he says: *I am not seeking my own will,* that is, such as would be mine if it originated from myself, but my will, as being from another, that is from the Father.[98]

Thomas's point rests upon the following distinction: there is one trinitarian will – e.g., to save sinners. And all three members of the Godhead share this same will and execute it. But in the execution of the unified trinitarian will, each member of the

---

97. E.g., Sherri Brown, *God's Promise: Covenant Relationship in John* (New York: Paulist Press, 2014).

98. Aquinas, *Gospel of John,* 1:294-95.

Godhead acts in a manner suited to His person and mission.[99] The Father sends the Son and the Spirit, and the Son and the Spirit are sent. The Son and the Spirit perform their economic missions as a part of the shared trinitarian will, but they do not all execute this will in the same manner. Likewise, the Father is neither sent nor dies on the cross – this is properly the work of Christ. To say, therefore, that Christ executes His Father's will does not posit two separate wills within the godhead but merely recognizes the different ontological and economic differentiations among the three members of the trinity.

Some might object that Christ's execution of His Father's will is purely an economic phenomenon, something restricted to His mission and not reflective of His eternal procession from the Father.[100] But such objections seem to be held captive by Kant's supposedly insuperable epistemic iron curtain – they also, to a certain degree, loiter on the other side of Lessing's ugly ditch because they fail to take Christ's statements at face value. But in the *pactum* Christ willingly agrees to take upon Himself human nature in the incarnation, thus revealing who God is, and He breaches Kant's iron curtain. Moreover, according to the terms of the *pactum* the Holy Spirit applies the word-revelation that testifies to the work of the covenant surety, which means that the triune God bridges Lessing's ugly ditch. And in this case, whether in the act-revelation of Christ's mission or in its antecedent-preparatory or subsequent-interpretive word-revelation, Scripture reveals both the trinitarian processions and covenantal missions.

The interplay between the processions and missions occurs prominently in Christ's high priestly prayer. The fact that Christ

---

99. Scott Swain and Michael Allen, 'The Obedience of the Eternal Son,' *IJST* 15/2 (2013): 117, 127.

100. So, e.g., Robert Jenson, 'Once More the *Logos asarkos*,' *IJST* 13 (2011): 130-33.

prays to His Father means that, once again, even though the Trinity shares one will it finds expression in a pluriform manner. In this case, the Son prays to the Father – this is a genuine dialogue between Father and Son in the power of the Spirit, not merely a modalistic monologue. Moreover, Christ repeatedly crosses the boundaries between eternity and time as He oscillates between the work He has accomplished and His pre-incarnate fellowship with the Father: 'I glorified you on earth, having accomplished the work that you gave me to do. And now, Father, glorify me in your own presence with the glory that I had with you before the world existed' (John 17:4-5).[101] Christ states to His Father, 'You sent me into the world' (John 17:18), which means that prior to the creation of the world the Father decided to send the Son and the Son willingly consented to go. The unified will of the triune God was manifest in terms of the agreement to send and be sent – they are different sides of the same coin, not two different coins.

Some might try to eliminate the dialogue between the Father and Son by arguing that this is purely an economic event and not necessarily reflective of an ontological reality.[102] Or in the desire to preserve the unity of the divine will they eliminate the idea of Father–Son agreement.[103] First, we must remember that Christ dialogues with the Father as the God-man. To say that only the human nature participates in these dialogues invites the Nestorian heresy, the postulation of two separate persons. Second, if we eliminate the idea of covenant (in a thicker account), in the effort to preserve the unity of the triune will, we invite hints

101. Herman Ridderbos, *The Gospel of John* (Grand Rapids: Eerdmans, 1997), 549-50; D. A. Carson, *The Gospel According to John* (Grand Rapids: Eerdmans, 1991), 557.

102. E.g., Hoeksema, *Reformed Dogmatics*, 312.

103. Cf., e.g., Kathryn Tanner, *Jesus, Humanity and the Trinity: A Brief Systematic Theology* (Minneapolis: Fortress Press, 2001), 40-41.

of modalism. The dialogue between Father and Son becomes an elaborate monologue. The Son does not truly engage the Father in prayer but merely talks to Himself under the guise of a dialogue. To admit a dialogue between Father and Son, or more broadly among the members of the Godhead, does not divide the unity of the Trinity. As St Anselm (ca. 1033-1109) long ago observed, given the divine simplicity and unity of the God's essence, whatever God is, we say about the whole Trinity. However, 'The unity should never lose its consequences except when a relational opposition stands in the way.'[104] In other words, we must not allow the triune unity to compromise the 'relational opposition' of the persons of the Godhead.[105] The triune unity does not eliminate dialogue and interaction, indeed communion, among Father, Son, and Holy Spirit. To recognize the category of agreement (or covenant) simply entails acknowledging the unity of the triune will as it is manifest in the three unique persons of the trinity.

The fact that this sending–sent agreement is rooted and grounded in the unity of the triune God is evident from Christ's testimony of the perichoresis between the Father and the Son. The whole point of Christ's mission is for redeemed sinners to reflect this covenantal relationship between Father and Son, 'As you sent me into the world, so I have sent them into the world ... that they may all be one, just as you, Father, are in me, and I in you, that they also may be in us, so that the world may believe that you have sent me. The glory that you have given me I have given to them, that they may be one even as we are one, I in them and you in me, that they may become perfectly one, so that the

---

104. St. Anselm, *On the Procession of the Holy Spirit*, § I, in *Anselm of Canterbury: The Major Works*, eds. Brian Davies and G. R. Evans (Oxford: Oxford University Press, 1998), 393; cf. Aquinas, *Summa Theologica*, Ia q. 34 art. 1.

105. Cf. Aquinas, *Summa Theologica*, Ia q. 28 art. 4.

world may know that you sent me and love them even as you loved me' (John 17:18-23).

At this point several observations are in order. First, the triune perichoretic unity does not preclude differentiation within the Trinity. If, for example, the Son's mission was necessary rather than contingent, then God would resemble something of Hegel's understanding of being as becoming. That is, the incarnation and creation would be a necessary part of the Trinity. The Son's mission is contingent and therefore cannot be collapsed into His divine procession. Second, the Son's mission reveals His divine procession because the missions are in accordance with the divine processions. But the movement from ontological processions to divine missions is, as noted, a contingent act of the Trinity. This means that the Trinity deliberated regarding the divine missions. Christ's dialogue with the Father in His high priestly prayer reflects something of this intra-trinitarian dialogue. But to posit an intra-trinitarian dialogue does not require tritheism or social trinitarianism. Third, though our attention has focused primarily upon the dialogue between the Father and Son, especially in the high priestly prayer, we must factor the Spirit's role in the intra-trinitarian deliberations, as one who applies the work of the covenant surety (John 14:26; 15:26; 16:13). Fourth, and finally, the high priestly prayer is bathed in the doctrine of the covenant, even though John never employs the term.[106]

Love and obedience

This brings us to the last of our considerations, the question of the nature and viability of intra-trinitarian obedience. Can the second person of the Trinity obey the first? Is this

---

106. Rekha M. Chennattu, *Johannine Discipleship as a Covenant Relationship* (Peabody: Hendrickson, 2006), 130-37.

a viable construction? There are two issues for consideration. The first is whether identification of a covenant within the intra-trinitarian life introduces a foreign legal and contractual element. J. B. Torrance (1923-2003) has famously criticized the classic Reformed understanding of covenant because it supposedly confuses the biblical category with the idea of a contract. God is a covenant-making God, not a contract-making God. Covenants are associated with promises, and there are obligations, but these requirements are never conditions of grace.[107] Even though Torrance offered his critique more than forty years ago, his arguments still resonate with some despite trenchant historical-theological criticism of his reading of the primary sources.[108]

Torrance's brother, T. F. Torrance (1913-2007), has made similar claims regarding the nature of covenant and with his critique of the *pactum salutis*. In his mind, having a 'forensically predetermined covenant-structure' precluded God's ability to make the covenant of grace universally applicable to all humanity.[109] The spirit of these criticisms appears to originate with Barth's critique of the *pactum salutis*.[110] One of the clearest criticisms on this point comes from David Wong's doctoral thesis in which he critiques John Owen's formulation of the *pactum*:

---

107. J. B. Torrance, 'Covenant or Contract?: A Study of the Theological Background of Worship in Seventeenth-Century Scotland,' *SJT* 23 (1970): 51-76.

108. E.g., Douglas A. Campbell, *The Deliverance of God: An Apocalyptic Rereading of Justification in Paul* (Grand Rapids: Eerdmans, 2009), 14-15, 985 n. 82; cf. Richard A. Muller, *After Calvin: Studies in the Development of a Theological Tradition* (Oxford: Oxford University Press, 2003), 175-90.

109. T. F. Torrance, *Scottish Theology: From John Knox to John McLeod Campbell* (Edinburgh: T & T Clark, 1996), 104-05, 107.

110. Barth, CD, IV/1:65.

> This strong contractualism in the covenant of redemption makes the salvation of man not as a [*sic*] outcome of the 'love' of the Father, but as a 'debt' to be paid to the Son. The faithfulness and righteousness of the Father, rather than His pure *agape* love, is manifested in giving His Son the delivery and salvation of the elect. With such a contractual covenant of redemption as the source of man's salvation, it seems that the classical truth about the Father that 'God so loved the *world* that he gave his only begotten *son*' is transformed to 'God so loved his Son (for his obedience) that he gave him the *world* (for his reward).' The pure, *immediate* love of the Father for the salvation of man is replaced by a mediate transaction between the Father and the Son. The picture of a loving and merciful Father is replaced by a commercial merchant God, who primarily honors the contract with His son. The primal relation of love between the Father and man is eclipsed and surpassed by a contractual relation between the Father and Son. The salvation of man is only a 'profit' gained by the Son in this bargain or contract.[111]

The *pactum*, therefore, supposedly turns love into a transaction where the Father and Son haggle and negotiate a price, and the Son then pays the price – a cold piece of business but hardly an expression of love.

The second related issue concerns Barth's understanding of the place of Christ's obedience in relation to the ontological Trinity. Like most theologians, Barth recognizes that Christ's obedience is a major component of His incarnate mission. Theologians typically associate the obedience of Christ with His economic mission, but Barth takes a different tack and locates it within the Son's ontological procession. According to Barth, the incarnate God is a mirror in which He reveals His divine nature. As such,

---

111. David Wai-Sing Wong, 'The Covenant Theology of John Owen' (Ph.D Dissertation, Westminster Theological Seminary, 1998), 372.

the Son's mission into the far country where He offered His obedience to the Father and His death on the cross reveals the very mystery of God's divine nature. Barth writes:

> From the point of view of the obedience of Jesus Christ as such, fulfilled in that astonishing form, it is a matter of the mystery of the inner being of God as the being of the Son in relation to the Father. From the point of view of that form, of the character of that obedience as an obedience of suffering, of the self-humiliation of Jesus Christ, of the way of the Son into the far country, it is a matter of the mystery of His deity in His work *ad extra*, in His presence in the world.[112]

The Son's obedience, according to Barth, is the 'inner moment of the mystery of the deity of Christ.' This mystery reveals that it is just as natural for God to be high as it is to be low. Christ's lowly estate, therefore, is not alien but proper to Him. Barth concludes, 'We have to see here the other and inner side of the mystery of the divine nature of Christ and therefore of the nature of the one true God – that He Himself is also able and free to render obedience.'[113]

Hence these two issues, the relationship of Christ's obedience to His ontological procession and the nature of the intra-trinitarian covenant, require brief exploration. The ideas of love and the intra-trinitarian covenant provide answers to both of these issues. The connections between these two concepts surface quite prominently in the Old Testament's covenantal *magna carta*, the book of Deuteronomy. While the covenant concept appears in earlier portions of the Pentateuch, the fullest exposition of Israel's covenant with Yahweh appears in

112. Barth, CD, IV/1:177.

113. Barth, CD, IV/1:192-93, 199.

Deuteronomy. But Deuteronomy is also the biblical document *par excellence* of love, not only in God's love for Israel but in Israel's required love for God (Deut. 4:37; 5:10; 7:7-9, 12; 10:12, 15, 18; 11:1, 13, 22; 13:3; 19:9; 23:5; 30:6, 16, 20; 33:3).[114] This love within the context of Israel's covenant is something that God commanded.

Above all else, Israel was supposed to express its love for Yahweh in terms of service, loyalty, and absolute obedience to His law. They were supposed to:

- Love Him (6:4)
- Be loyal to Him (11:1-22; 30:20)
- Walk in His ways (10:12; 11:22; 19:9; 30:16)
- Keep His commandments (10:12; 11:1-22)
- Serve Him (10:12; 11:1-13)
- Heed His voice (11:13; 30:16).[115]

Israel's love, moreover, was not merely a cognitive or mechanical response to their covenant Lord but was supposed to involve affective categories.[116] The compatibility between love and obedience later appears quite succinctly in several different New Testament axioms. The summary of the law, Christ tells us, is to love God with heart, soul, mind, and strength (Matt. 22:36-37; Luke 10:27; Mark 12:30; cf. Deut. 6:4). Or there is also Christ's statement, 'If you love me, you will keep my commandments' (John 14:15).

---

114. William L. Moran, 'The Ancient Near Eastern Background of the Love of God in Deuteronomy,' *CBQ* 25 (1963): 82; Geerhardus Vos, 'The Scriptural Doctrine of the Love of God,' in *Redemptive History and Biblical Interpretation: The Shorter Writings of Geerhardus Vos*, ed. Richard B. Gaffin, Jr. (Phillipsburg: P & R, 1980), 430-35.

115. Moran, 'Love of God in Deuteronomy,' 78.

116. Bill T. Arnold, 'The Love-Fear Antinomy in Deuteronomy 5-11,' *VT* 61 (2011): 551-69, esp. 552-62.

In addition to the covenant-love connection, there are important links to the father–son relationship within the context of the covenant, which is another key theme within the book of Deuteronomy. Dennis McCarthy notes: 'The father-son relationship of Israel to Yahweh was conceived in terms which correspond to the definition of covenantal love as found in Deuteronomy.'[117] Deuteronomy casts Israel's relationship as one between father and son, which inextricably weds the themes of sonship, obedience, covenant, and love.[118] Israel's sonship first appears in Exodus 4:22 where Yahweh declares, 'Israel is my firstborn son.' Israel's filial identity is one that entails, among other things, covenantal obedience.[119] In fact, Walter Brueggemann notes: 'Yahweh designates Israel as Yahweh's covenant partner, so that Israel is, from the outset, obligated to respond to and meet Yahweh's expectations. As covenant partner of Yahweh, Israel is a people defined by obedience.'[120]

A number of texts characterize Israel's father–son relationship with Yahweh:

> In the wilderness ... the Lord your God carried you, as a man carries his son (Deut. 1:31).

> Know then in your heart that, as a man disciplines his son, the Lord your God disciplines you. So you shall keep the commandments

117. Dennis J. McCarthy, 'Notes on the Love of God in Deuteronomy and the Father-Son Relationship Between Yahweh and Israel,' *CBQ* 27 (1965): 145.

118. Brandon C. Crowe, *The Obedient Son: Deuteronomy and Christology in the Gospel of Matthew* (Berlin: De Gruyter, 2012), 89; also John L. McKenzie, 'The Divine Sonship of Israel and the Covenant,' *CBQ* 8 (1946): 320-31; Scott W. Hahn, *Kinship by Covenant: A Canonical Approach to the Fulfillment of God's Saving Promises* (New Haven: Yale University Press, 2009), 91-92.

119. Crowe, *Obedient Son*, 95.

120. Walter Brueggemann, *Theology of the Old Testament: Testimony, Dispute, Advocacy* (Minneapolis: Fortress Press, 1997), 417.

> of the LORD your God by walking in his ways and by fearing him (Deut. 8:5-6).
>
> Do you thus repay the LORD, you foolish and senseless people? Is not he your father, who created you, who made you and established you? ... You were unmindful of the Rock that bore you, and you forgot the God who gave you birth. The LORD saw it and spurned them, because of the provocation of his sons and daughters. And he said, 'I will hide my face from them; I will see what their end will be, for they are a perverse generation, children in whom there is no faithfulness.' (Deut. 32:6, 18-20) [121]

In these passages, and others from the Old Testament, the covenant provides the context for the father–son relationship between Yahweh and Israel, in which the father expects covenant loyalty (*hesed*), love, and obedience, from his son.[122]

But these themes also relate to inheritance, another prominent motif in Deuteronomy. Deuteronomy often links obedience and inheritance: 'And you shall do what is right and good in the sight of the LORD, that it may go well with you, and that you may go in and take possession of the good land that the LORD swore to give to your fathers' (Deut. 6:18; cf. 8:1; 11:8-9).[123] And while God gives the land to Israel, nevertheless covenant fidelity (*hesed*),

---

121. Hahn, *Kinship by Covenant*, 91.

122. On these and other texts, see Crowe, *Obedient Son*, 98-113; cf. Nelson Glueck, *Hesed in the Bible* (New York: Ktav Publishing House, 1975), 35-37; 39, 51-52, 86-87; Gordon R. Clark, *The Word Hesed in the Hebrew Bible* (Sheffield: JSOT Press, 1993), 259-61, 267-68; Katherine Doob Sakenfeld, *The Meaning of Hesed in the Hebrew Bible* (Missoula: Scholars Press, 1978), 233-39.

123. Crowe, *Obedient Son*, 116. Also, Bryan D. Estelle, 'Leviticus 18:5 and Deuteronomy 30:1-14 in Biblical Theological Development: Entitlement to Heaven Foreclosed and Proffered,' in *The Law is Not of Faith: Essays on Works and Grace in the Mosaic Covenant*, eds. Bryan D. Estelle, J. V. Fesko, David VanDrunen (Phillipsburg: P & R, 2009), 109-46.

obedience, is necessary for conquering (Josh. 1–12), possessing (Josh. 13–21; cf. Deut. 9:26; 18:1; Josh. 24:1-27; 2 Sam. 20:19; 21:3; Jer. 2:7; 16:18), and keeping the land (Josh. 22–24).[124] All of this evidence points to the idea that Israel is God's son and is in covenant with his father and must demonstrate his love, his covenant loyalty, by obeying his father to the end of obtaining the inheritance. These categories bring us full-circle to other texts examined earlier in Part II, especially Psalm 2:7, that unite the same themes but center them upon the Messiah. Psalms 1 and 2 present the Father who grants the nations as His Son's inheritance because of His covenant loyalty, His obedience, His love for His heavenly Father.[125]

Christ as the obedient son is the major theme of many New Testament texts that draw upon Deuteronomy in a significant way.[126] The same can be said for other key texts that breathe the typological atmosphere of Israel's father–son relationship to Yahweh. One of the prominent texts in this respect is Matthew's quotation of Hosea 11:1, 'Out of Egypt I called my son' (2:15). Although frequently debated, recent scholarship classifies the intended point of this Old Testament quotation as identifying Jesus as the obedient and faithful son in contrast to Israel, the disobedient son.[127] This matrix of texts and concepts from Deuteronomy forms the subterranean spring from which John relates much of the information presented in John 13–17, the core

---

124. Bruce Waltke, *An Old Testament Theology: An Exegetical, Canonical, and Thematic Approach* (Grand Rapids: Zondervan, 2007), 544.

125. E.g., Cole, *Psalms 1-2, passim.*

126. See, e.g., Joel Kenney, *The Recapitulation of Israel: Use of Israel's History in Matthew 1:1-4:11* (Tübingen: Mohr Siebeck, 2008); cf. Vos, *Self-Disclosure*, 206.

127. See, e.g., G. K. Beale, 'The Use of Hosea 11:1 in Matthew 2:15: One More Time,' *JETS* 55/4 (2012): 697-716.

source of many of the sending–sent texts. One such sending–sent passage is Christ's vine and the branches parable (John 15:1-17). This parable weaves a number of the Deuteronomic covenant themes together, though Christ never invokes the term *covenant*. For example, Christ states: 'If you keep my commandments, you will abide in my love, just as I have kept my Father's commandments and abide in his love' (John 15:10). Jesus has been covenantally faithful in obeying the Father's commandments, and hence, He calls His disciples to do the same.[128] Moreover, even the language of *abiding* (μένω), is covenantal in nature, invoking Old Testament covenantal promises of God's indwelling and abiding presence (Ezek. 36:36), but also reminiscent of curses for those who do not abide in words of the law (Deut. 27:26; Isa. 30:18 LXX).[129]

All of this data confirms that love and obedience are not incompatible. This is especially evident when we factor the word–act–word pattern of revelation. The Old Testament preparatory and typological revelation of Israel's covenantal sonship was anticipatory of the antitypical revelation of Christ. But as I demonstrated in Part II, this father–son covenantal pattern did not emerge within redemptive history, but in eternity within the intra-trinitarian covenant. In other words, this is not a retrogressive Feuerbachian projection upon the processions of the triune God. Rather, the intra-trinitarian covenant stands at the front and projects into pre-redemptive and redemptive

---

128. Rekha M. Chennattu, 'The Covenant Motif: A Key to the Interpretation of John 15-16,' in *Transcending Boundaries: Contemporary Readings of the New Testament. Essays In Honor of Francis J. Moloney*, eds. Rekha M. Chennattu and Mary L. Coloe (Rome: Libreria Ateneo Salesiano, 2005), 148; idem, *Johannine Discipleship*, 67, 76, 83, 85, 87; Moloney, *Love*, 120.

129. Edward Malatesta, *Interiority and Covenant: A Study of* εἶναι ἐν *and* μένειν ἐν *In the First Letter of Saint John* (Rome: Biblical Institute Press, 1978), 58-64; Sherri Brown, *Gift Upon Gift: Covenant Through Word in the Gospel of John* (Eugene: Pickwick, 2010), 3.

history. That is, the Trinity projects its covenantal activity into the world in both creation and redemption; this is what some have called 'world projection.'[130] Israel's existence and placement in the land was, therefore, among other things, a play within the play, a shadowy sketch of God's only begotten Son and His covenantal love for His Father, manifest through His obedience.

But this then raises a question surrounding Barth's theory that the origin of Christ's obedience rests in His nature, within the divine essence. Is it proper to locate Christ's obedience within His ontological procession? In one sense, Barth is correct to seek the origins of Christ's obedience in His deity in the nature of God Himself. But one has to wonder whether moving obedience into the processions of the trinity produces two negative consequences. First, it has the same weaknesses as the unqualified version of Rahner's rule (i.e., that the economic Trinity is the ontological Trinity): it runs the risk of placing economic categories within the ontological processions. Along these lines, why not argue that since Christ is incarnate in His economic mission, the incarnation is part of His ontological procession? The formulation leans heavily, it seems, towards pantheism. Second, to push Christ's obedience into His ontological procession and argue that it is part of the divine nature seems to run the risk of christology swallowing the doctrine of the Trinity. Christ's mission ends up defining the Trinity rather than revealing it. Third, if Christ's obedience is part of His procession or nature, then can we say that Christ willingly and voluntarily came to do the work the Father gave Him (John 17:4)? Christ's work would no longer be contingent and voluntary but necessary and involuntary – simply the necessary outworking of His procession.[131]

---

130. Vanhoozer, *Remythologizing Theology*, 7; cf. Nicholas Wolterstorff, *Art in Action: Toward a Christian Aesthetic* (Grand Rapids: Eerdmans, 1980), 122-25.

131. White, 'Intra-Trinitarian Obedience,' 390-91.

On the one hand, Barth touches upon a necessary and important element of trinitarian doctrine, namely, how to account for the obedience of Christ in relation to the Trinity. On the other hand, his proposed solution seems to create unintended problems.

A better way forward, which preserves the distinction between the processions and missions, is to recognize that obedience is the hyponym of love within the covenantal framework of Deuteronomy. And Deuteronomy ultimately finds its origins in the intra-trinitarian covenant. Barth is correct to seek the ontological basis for the economic trinitarian activity, but he seems to invert the relationship between obedience and procession. I contend that obedience is economic and part of the Son's mission, not part of His eternal procession from the Father.[132] Instead, it is preferable to argue that the Son proceeds eternally from the Father, which means He eternally shares in the trinitarian will to redeem fallen humanity, but more specifically voluntarily pledges His obedience to the Father's covenantal command to be sent into the far country.[133] This is first and foremost an action of love. As Boris Bobrinskoy explains:

> The obedience of Jesus is the hinge of His double relation to the Father: as eternal Son and Suffering Servant. It represents the human and 'terrestrial' aspect of the love of the Son, who came to do the will of the Father (John 6:38), 'he learnt obedience, Son though he was, through his sufferings' (Heb. 5:8). This obedience of Jesus who 'in the days of his flesh ... offered up prayers and supplications, with loud cries and tears, to him who was able to save him from death' (Heb. 5:7) derives therefore from His eternal condition of Son; it is rooted, with the Cross and the death of the Lamb, in the divine love itself (see Rev. 13:8; 1 Pet. 1:19-20).[134]

---

132. White, 'Intra-Trinitarian Obedience,' 398.

133. White, 'Intra-Trinitarian Obedience,' 402.

134. Bobrinskoy, *Trinity*, 118.

The Son's love becomes manifest in His obedience when He enters the far country and is born of a woman 'under the law' to fulfill and obey it (Gal. 4:4; Matt. 5:17; 3:15).

Such a construction aligns more closely with key affirmations about the triune God. God is not obedience; rather, 'God is love' (1 John 4:8).[135] The love of God as the source of Christ's mission appears quite prominently: 'In this the love of God was made manifest among us, that God sent his only Son into the world, so that we might live through him. In this is love, not that we have loved God but that he loved us and sent his Son to be the propitiation for our sins' (1 John 4:9-10). And when the Father and the Son send the Holy Spirit, it is a gift of love: 'God's love has been poured into our hearts through the Holy Spirit who has been given to us' (Rom. 5:5; cf. Acts 2:38; 10:45; Heb. 6:4).[136] The love of the immanent Trinity becomes manifest in the covenantal economic missions of both the Son and Spirit, namely, the Son's obedience and the outpouring of the Spirit. The execution of the *pactum*, therefore, is rooted and grounded in intra-trinitarian love, which becomes manifest in creation and ultimately redemption (John 3:35; 10:17; 17:23-26; Eph. 1:6; Col. 1:13).[137] The categories of covenant, love, and obedience find their origins in the *pactum salutis* in the Father's command, the

---

135. Maloney, *Love*, 194-95.

136. Aquinas, *Summa Theologica*, Ia q. 36 art. 2.

137. Xavier Zubiri, *Nature, History, God*, trans. Thomas B. Fowler, Jr. (Washington, DC: University Press of America, 1981), 358, 374, 419; Bobrinskoy, *Trinity*, 4; Aquinas, *Summa Theologica*, Ia q. 32 art. 1; John Owen, ΧΡΙΣΤΟΛΟΓΙΑ: or, *A Declaration of the Glorious Mystery of the Person of Christ*, XII, in *The Works of John Owen*, 24 vols., ed. William H. Goold (Edinburgh: Banner of Truth, 1862), I:145; idem, ΠΝΕΥΜΑΤΟΛΟΓΙΑ: *A Discourse Concerning the Holy Spirit*, III.i, in *The Works of John Owen*, 24 vols., ed. William H. Goold (Edinburgh: Banner of Truth, 1862), III:209.

Son's obedience, and the outpouring of the Spirit to redeem fallen sinners. Far from a cold piece of business, moving numbers from one side of the ledger to the other, the Father sends the Son in love, and the Son obeys the Father in love, and the Spirit applies the Son's work in love.[138]

Conclusion

In one sense Lessing's ditch and Kant's epistemic iron curtain are genuine realities. Under its own rational power fallen humanity cannot leap the ugly ditch and scale the wall. But humanity's saving grace is that the triune God has covenanted to scale the wall and bridge the ditch. Christ has come because He willingly entered into a covenant with His heavenly Father to be the surety for the elect – to love and obey His Father. And the Holy Spirit agreed in this covenant to bridge Lessing's ugly ditch by teaching Christ's body, the church, what Christ has done and applying His work in a saving manner. The triune missions reveal their eternal processions and in particular, their covenant-making, world-projecting, work of salvation. Such is not the fruit of rational speculation but the result of divine revelation – the divine covenantal drama where the chief protagonist stands upon the stage of redemptive history and narrates the grand play, in which He invites the audience to participate in the drama. I take up the invitation to the divine drama in the next chapter – predestination and its relationship to the covenant of redemption.

---

138. Cf. Aquinas, *Summa Theologica*, Ia q. 36 art. 2; Vanhoozer, *Remythologizing Theology*, 258.

~:3:~

Predestination

Introduction

The *pactum salutis* deals with matters pertaining to the plan of redemption and the Son's election. The Son's election means that any exposition of the *pactum salutis* must explain the relationship between the intra-trinitarian covenant and the doctrine of predestination. In the history of the church two major predestinarian paradigms have dominated the theological scene, the Augustinian and semi-Pelagian views.[1] Stated simply, theologians have argued that the triune God's election of sinners is a sovereign choice that is not based upon the human will or actions (Augustine) or is a divine ratification of foreseen faith and perseverance (semi-Pelagianism). But in the twentieth century Karl Barth (1886-1968) challenged the two dominant paradigms by reconceiving the doctrine of election.

In brief, Barth believed that the prevailing Reformed paradigm was too reliant upon a metaphysics of being that foisted artificial

1. Jaroslav Pelikan, *The Christian Tradition*, vol. 1 (Chicago: University of Chicago Press, 1971), 296-304, 319-31.

Greek ontology upon the God of the Scriptures. In Barth's judgment, the common Reformed doctrine was insufficiently christological. To say the least, Barth's reconfigured doctrine of election was an artillery shell that left a significant crater in twentieth- and twenty-first-century theology. Any attempt to explain the doctrine of predestination (or election and reprobation) must deal with Barth's critique of the tradition and his alternative paradigm. In addition to Barth's view, in recent years a significant debate has erupted among Barth scholars regarding the proper relationship between election and the doctrine of the Trinity. Any serious treatment of Barth's doctrine of election must also take these recent developments into account, as they deal with many of the issues raised in the previous chapter on the Trinity and intersect with matters related to the doctrine of election.

By engaging Barth's doctrine of predestination as a conversation partner, this chapter demonstrates that the *pactum salutis* is the covenantal context in which the triune God coordinately predestines the Son as covenant surety and His body, the particular group of individuals designated as the elect. The Father chooses and appoints the Son to His mission as covenant surety, which establishes the foundational nature of His imputed obedience (active and passive), the foreordination of all antecedent history leading to His incarnation and subsequent post-resurrection history. This decree also contains the blueprints for the new heavens and earth, the seeds of the eschatological age. The triune God writes the script for the divine play, one that establishes Him as the chief player and His image-bearers as participants in the grand drama of redemptive history. Apart from the context of the *pactum salutis*, election, christology, soteriology, providence, and eschatology can potentially become disparate, disconnected, and unglued. The *pactum* is the string that holds all of the pearls together to form a beautiful necklace.

First, this chapter examines Barth's doctrine of election in its four chief principal parts: it is post-metaphysical, supralapsarian, christological (Christ as subject and object of election), and universal. The chapter also interacts with the recent debate within Barthian circles about the correct interpretation of Barth's doctrine. Second, the chapter critiques Barth's doctrine by setting forth a case for the traditional Reformed confessional understanding of predestination. In this understanding, predestination is the sovereign will of the triune God to elect fallen sinners unto salvation, which is a manifestation of the triune covenantal love of God. Contrary to popular caricatures, the traditional Reformed view is not speculative or based upon Greek ontology. All theology employs metaphysics to explain it. The question is not whether a doctrine is too metaphysical or not but whether biblical exegesis regulates metaphysical claims. To borrow a turn of phrase, we should not engage in much-criticized onto-theology, but rather in theo-ontology.[2] In other words, Scripture must always be supreme and metaphysics and philosophy must always serve in a heuristic, never a magisterial, role. As influential as Barth's views have been in the effort to purge theology of metaphysics and speculation, one must ask whether he has been successful or whether he has simply substituted modern metaphysics for pre-modern metaphysics, and German philosophy replaces Greek philosophy.[3] To employ modern metaphysics is not necessarily a bad thing, but one must ask whether such a move elucidates or obfuscates the theological enterprise.[4] This question

2. Kevin J. Vanhoozer, *Remytheologizing Theology: Divine Action, Passion, and Authorship* (Cambridge: Cambridge University Press, 2010), 104-05.

3. E.g., Merold Westphal, *Overcoming Onto-Theology: Toward a Postmodern Christian Faith* (New York: Fordham University Press, 2001), 1-28.

4. G. C. Berkouwer, *The Triumph of Grace in the Theology of Karl Barth: An Introduction and Critical Appraisal* (Grand Rapids: Eerdmans, 1956), 21.

can only be answered by placing such claims alongside the ultimate standard of all things theological, the canon of Scripture.[5] Third, the chapter will explore the theological implications of the relationship between predestination and the *pactum*, chiefly as they relate to the incarnation, the imputed obedience of Christ, and eschatology.

The Barthian reformulation of predestination

A quick survey of several of the major confessions reveals that the Reformation was truly a renaissance of the Augustinian doctrine of grace.[6] The Scots Confession (1560) states: 'The same eternal God and Father, who by grace alone chose us in his Son Christ Jesus before the foundation of the world was laid, appointed him to be our head, our brother, our pastor, and great bishop of our souls ... giving power to as many as believe in him to be the sons of God' (§ VIII). The Belgic Confession (1561) similarly states that God, who is merciful and just, withdrew and saved from fallen humanity 'those whom he, in his eternal and unchangeable counsel, has elected and chosen in Jesus Christ our Lord by his pure goodness, without any consideration of their works' (§ XVI). Comparable statements appear in other confessional documents of the period, including the Second Helvetic Confession (1566), the Canons of Dort (1618-19), and the Westminster Standards (1647). In brief, the confessional Reformed tradition holds that election is particular, that the elect have been chosen according to the *beneplacitum Dei* without reference to foreseen faith or works, and that election is entirely monergistic.

---

5. Contra Mark C. Taylor, *Erring: A Postmodern A/Theology* (Chicago: University of Chicago Press, 1981), 3-8, 74-120.

6. Cf. Arnoud S. Q. Visser, *Reading Augustine in the Reformation: The Flexibility of Intellectual Authority in Europe, 1500-1620* (Oxford: Oxford University Press, 2011).

Barth's doctrine of election

Barth was familiar with both the Reformed catechisms and confessions and the theological tradition that underlies them. Early in his theological career Barth quickly acquainted himself with traditional Reformed theology for his lectures on the Reformed Confessions through mining the dusty logarithmic pages of Heinrich Heppe's (1820-79) *Reformed Dogmatics*.[7] As appreciative as Barth was for what he excavated from Heppe's work, he refused to repristinate what he found. He believed a return to Reformed Orthodoxy, sixteenth- and seventeenth-century Reformed theology, was unacceptable:

> The dogmatics of these centuries had already been too closely bound up with a form not taken from the thing itself but from contemporary philosophies, for the substance itself not to have suffered thereby as a whole as well as in detail. All too confidently the heroes of orthodoxy, in their justifiable attempt to adopt the Early and Medieval Church tradition, overloaded it with presuppositions which were bound sooner or later to jeopardize Reformed knowledge of God and of salvation.[8]

Barth rejected many tenets of Reformed Orthodoxy, chief among them was its doctrine of predestination. He rejected its doctrine of predestination not because it posited the salvation of some and the rejection of others, but because it was built upon a faulty ontology.[9]

---

7. Karl Barth, *The Theology of the Reformed Confessions*, trans. Darrell L. Guder and Judith J. Guder (Louisville: Westminster John Knox, 2002); Eberhard Busch, *Karl Barth: His Life from Letters and Autobiographical Texts* (Philadelphia: Fortress, 1975), 153-54; Heinrich Heppe, *Reformed Dogmatics: Set Out and Illustrated from the Sources*, trans. G. W. Thomson, ed. Ernst Bizer (London: George Allen & Unwin Ltd., 1950).

8. Karl Barth, 'Foreword,' in Heppe, *Reformed Dogmatics*, vi.

9. Bruce McCormack, 'Grace and Being: The Role of God's Gracious Election in Karl Barth's Theological Ontology,' in *The Cambridge Companion to Karl Barth*, ed. John Webster (Cambridge: Cambridge University Press, 2007), 97-98.

In Barth's understanding there is no knowledge of God apart from Christ. In contrast to the earlier tradition, Barth was leery of any concept of the *logos asarkos* ('the word without the flesh'). In other words, he thought that there is no knowledge of God apart from the supreme self-disclosure in Christ. This means that, in one respect, there is no *logos asarkos* but only a *logos incarnandus* ('word to be incarnate'). The only God we know is the one revealed in Jesus Christ, and this means that Christ is the key presupposition of election and reprobation. Hence, one cannot go behind what God has revealed and posit who God is or who He has elected prior to consideration of the election and incarnation of Christ. Rather, the triune God, not merely the Father, has established the covenant of grace with the election and reprobation of Jesus Christ, the one elected and rejected man. Richard Muller has characterized the differences between classical and Barthian position as soteriological christocentrism versus principal christocentrism. That is, in the former Christ stands at the center of soteriology, whereas in the latter Christ is at the center of the theological system in terms of the ontology of the Trinity, revelation, creation, and redemption.[10]

Christ is, consequently, both the object and the subject of election for Barth. In his exegesis of Romans 9 Barth explains the tradition's error regarding Paul's infamous statement, 'Jacob I love, but Esau I hated':

> When the Reformers applied the doctrine of election and rejection (Predestination) to the psychological unity of this or that individual, and when they referred quantitatively to the 'elect' and the 'damned',

---

10. Richard A. Muller, 'The Barth Legacy: New Athanasius or Origen Redivivus? A Response to T. F. Torrance,' *The Thomist* 54 (1990): 685-86; idem, 'A Note on "Christocentrism' and the Imprudent Use of Such Terminology,' *WTJ* 68 (2006): 255-56; cf. Berkouwer, *Triumph of Grace*, 18, 53.

> they were, as we can now see, speaking mythologically. Paul did not think either quantitatively or psychologically, nor could he have done so, since his emphasis is set altogether upon God's concern with the individual, and not upon the individual's concern with God. And how indeed can the temporal, observable, psychologically visible individual be at all capable of eternal election or rejection?

Rather than dividing humanity into two separate groups, which Barth calls a 'mythology,' he believed that '[God] makes Himself known in the parable and riddle of the beloved Jacob and the hated Esau, that is to say, in the secret of eternal, twofold predestination. Now, this secret concerns not this or that man, but all men. By it men are not divided, but united.'[11] Barth contends that predestination unites humanity because Christ is both subject (the electing God) and object (the elect and reprobate man). This means that Barth configures his doctrine of election in the highest supralapsarian form.

Infra- and supralapsarianism were the two major forms of the doctrine of predestination in Reformed Orthodoxy.[12] Barth was familiar with the basics of both positions, namely, that the object of predestination was either *homo creatus et lapsus* or *creabilis et labilis*, man as created and fallen or man as creatable and liable to fall. In other words, the theologians who held these views were concerned with the question of whether God takes sin into account in His decision to elect some to salvation. Barth believed that the traditional Reformed account of predestination in both lapsarian variants suffered from the fatal flaw of presupposing a

---

11. Karl Barth, *The Epistle to the Romans*, 6th ed., trans. Edwyn C. Hoskyns (1933; Oxford: Oxford University Press, 1968), 347.

12. E.g., J. V. Fesko, 'Lapsarian Diversity at the Synod of Dort,' in *Drawn Into Controversie: Reformed Theological Diversity and Debates Within Seventeenth-Century British Puritanism*, eds. Michael A. G. Haykin and Mark Jones (Göttingen: Vandenhoeck & Ruprecht, 2011): 99-123.

metaphysical notion of God's being. This 'God' predestined and reprobated individuals to salvation and condemnation and did so apart from any connection to Christ. In spite of this shortcoming, Barth believed that the supralapsarian position was commendable because it sought to place God's soteriological action first above all other considerations. Barth adopted this stance and modified the view to offer what he termed a 'purified supralapsarianism.'[13]

Barth believed that the decree of predestination had the first consideration, and that the decree had to begin, not with the selection and rejection of individuals, but with the election and reprobation of the elect man, Jesus Christ.[14] At this point Barth's doctrine of predestination intersects with his christology. Rather than assume an essentialist ontology, which begins with God's being in the abstract, and hence an abstract election of individuals, Barth articulates an actualist ontology.[15] Barth's actualist ontology supposes a christological foundation. The only God we know is God's action in Christ – we cannot somehow pull back the veil and know God in the abstract. We only know Him in the concrete revelation of Christ, and hence in God's act, or event, in Christ. Christ, therefore, is predestination. He is

---

13. Karl Barth, *Church Dogmatics*, 14 vols., eds. T. F. Torrance and G. W. Bromiley (Edinburgh: T & T Clark, 1936-77), II/2:127-45. Recent research has brought into question Barth's identity as a supralapsarian. Even though Barth places the election of Christ first, this move does not automatically qualify him as a supralapsarian. The chief consideration is not the placement of Christ in the order of decrees but whether God elects *homo creatus et lapsus* or *creabilis et labilis*. The issue is the object of election. Barth's view regarding the object of election appears to be *homo creatus et lapsus*, which would make him an infralapsarian according to the terms of the historic debate (see Shao Kai Tseng, 'God's Non-Capricious No: Karl Barth's "Purified Infralapsarianism" in Development 1920-23,' [D. Phil. Diss., Wycliffe Hall, Oxford University, 2013], esp. chp. 6).

14. Barth, CD, II/2: 6-7, 60, 103-04, 145, 157, 174.

15. Barth, CD, II/2: 155, 158, 187-88.

the covenant of grace, the electing God and the universally elect and reprobate man.[16] The election of Christ supersedes all other considerations. We do not know of the *logos asarkos* but only of the *logos incarnandus* and eventually of the *logos incarnatus* ('the incarnated word'). We do not know of God's being, only Christ. And for this reason Barth says the only name we know of for the second person of the Trinity is Jesus Christ.[17]

The debate over Barth's doctrine

Barth's doctrine of predestination has certainly had its critics, but others have warmly received and promoted his views, especially Bruce McCormack. McCormack, however, advances the thesis that Barth's theology underwent significant development between volumes I and II of his massive *Church Dogmatics*. In the wake of Pierre Maury's (1890-1956) 1936 lecture on predestination at the Calvin Congress in Geneva, Barth's understanding of the doctrine was revolutionized.[18] McCormack contends that Barth's revolutionary, or perhaps evolutionary, awakening to his actualist christological doctrine of predestination was far more radical than most realize.[19] Most Barth scholars contend that, for Barth, ontology precedes election – God is before He acts.[20]

---

16. Barth, CD, II/2: 54, 140, 158.

17. Barth, CD, II/2: 175.

18. Karl Barth, 'Foreword,' in Pierre Maury, *Predestination and Other papers by Pierre Maury*, trans. Edwin Hudson (Richmond: John Knox, 1960), 15-16; idem, 'Grace and Being,' 101.

19. Bruce McCormack, *Karl Barth's Critically Realistic Dialectical Theology: Its Genesis and Development 1909-1936* (Oxford: Clarendon Press, 1995), 462-63.

20. There are a number of key rebuttals to McCormack's proposals. See, e.g., Edwin Christian van Driel, 'Karl Barth on the Eternal Existence of Jesus Christ,' *SJT* 60/1 (2007): 45-61; Paul Molnar, *Divine Freedom and the Doctrine of the Immanent Trinity: In Dialogue with Karl Barth and Contemporary Theology* (London: T & T Clark, 2002), 62-64, 81. See also the contributions by Paul Molnar, 'Can the Electing God Be

McCormack, on the other hand, claims the opposite – for Barth, God acts before He is.

Taking his cue from Barth's uneasiness about the *logos asarkos*, McCormack believes that Barth held that God's triunity is a logical function of divine election.[21] McCormack presents his thesis in the title of his essay on Barth's doctrine of election, 'Grace and Being.' McCormack writes:

> The *decision* for the covenant of grace is the ground of God's triunity and, therefore, of the eternal generation of the Son and of the eternal procession of the Holy Spirit from the Father and the Son. In other words, the works of God *ad intra* (the trinitarian processions) find their ground in the *first* of the works of God *ad extra* (viz. election). And that also means that eternal generation and eternal procession are willed by God; they are not natural to him if 'natural' is taken to mean a determination of being fixed in advance of all actions and relations.[22]

The accuracy of McCormack's exegesis of Barth is beyond the scope of this chapter and better left to Barth scholars. Some

---

Without Us? Some Implications of Bruce McCormack's Doctrine of Election for the Doctrine of the Trinity,' and George Husinger,'Election and the Trinity: Twenty-Five Theses on the Theology of Karl Barth,' in *Trinity and Election in Contemporary Theology*, ed. Michael T. Dempsey (Grand Rapids: Eerdmans, 2011), 63-90, 91-114. Also note Michael S. Horton,'Covenant, Election, and Incarnation: Evaluating Barth's Actualist Christology,' in *Karl Barth and American Evangelicalism*, eds. Bruce McCormack and Clifford B. Anderson (Grand Rapids: Eerdmans, 2011), 112-47.

21. McCormack,'Grace and Being,' 103; cf. Paul Dafydd Jones, *The Humanity of Christ: Christology in Karl Barth's Church Dogmatics* (London: T & T Clark, 2008), 41, 61, 66-76, 92-95. In fact, in later years Barth believed that any talk of the *logos asarkos* was illegitimate: 'Do not ever think of the second Person of the Trinity as only *Logos*. That is the mistake of Emil Brunner. There is no *Logos asarkos*, but only *ensarkos*. Brunner thinks of a *Logos asarkos*, and I think this is the reason for his natural theology. The *Logos* becomes an abstract principle' (Karl Barth, *Karl Barth's Table Talk*, ed. John D. Godsey [Edinburgh: Oliver and Boyd, 1963], 49).

22. McCormack,'Grace and Being,' 103.

have embraced McCormack's interpretation of Barth, but he has also had vigorous opposition.[23] The issues that McCormack raises, however, are not merely a parochial Barthian question. As a matter of dogmatics, one should engage the issue of whether an actualist christological doctrine of election is superior to an essentialist understanding. Simply stated, does God's will determine His being or does His being determine His will? This brings us to the question of the relationship between the *pactum* and predestination.

Predestination and the pactum salutis

Clearing false presuppositions

One of the first steps in establishing the validity and superiority of an essentialist approach to theology is to recognize the faulty presuppositions that Barth and McCormack bring to the discussion. In many respects Barth's rejection of the tradition is based upon a caricature. Barth employs the distinction between God in the abstract (being) and in the concrete (Jesus Christ).[24] His assumption at this point is that Reformed Orthodoxy embraced the former, and hence produced a mythological doctrine of predestination. McCormack follows Barth's assessment and therefore characterizes Barth's approach as post-metaphysical. That is, Barth does not approach the question of predestination from a speculative ontology and a consideration of abstract divine attributes, but rather from the only epistemological access point we have, Christ.[25] There are two likely reasons for Barth's erroneous

23. For one who follows McCormack's thesis, see, e.g., Matthias Gockel, *Barth and Schleiermacher on the Doctrine of Election: A Systematic-Theological Comparison* (Oxford: Oxford University Press, 2006).

24. Barth, CD, II/2: 36, 54, 139-40, 166, 182, 184-85, 187, 192-93.

25. Barth, CD, II/2: 37-39, 54.

assessment: (1) he largely accessed Reformed Orthodoxy through the filter of Heinrich Heppe's *Reformed Dogmatics*; and (2) Barth misunderstood the nature of the Reformed Orthodox doctrine of the decree.

First, Heppe's presentation has distorted the arrangement of topics as they originally appeared in the various doctrinal works from which they were gathered.[26] Recent research has demonstrated that Barth relied upon Heppe's work rather than direct access to primary sources.[27] Reading primary sources through Heppe distorted Barth's understanding. What some theologians connected in their own systems, such as predestination and the *pactum*, was separated in Heppe's presentation. One of the glaring effects of Barth's mediated access to the primary sources is his claim that Reformed Orthodoxy posited an abstract doctrine of predestination devoid of Christ. Yet nothing could be further from the truth. Those Reformed theologians who did not yet advocate the *pactum salutis* nevertheless intimately coordinated predestination and christology. For example, Girolamo Zanchi (1516-90) writes: 'Wherefore we also doubt not that God, when he created all men (to speake nothing of angells) in Adam righteous, he foresawe that in him all should sinne and elected some in Christ.'[28] Early modern Reformed theologians did not divorce christology from predestination. Richard Muller's *Christ*

26. Richard A. Muller, *After Calvin: Studies in the Development of a Theological Tradition* (Oxford: Oxford University Press, 2003), 63-65, 92.

27. Ryan D. Glomsrud, 'Engaging the Tradition: Karl Barth's Use of Reformed Orthodox Sources in *The Göttingen Dogmatics* (1924/25)' (M. A. Thesis, Westminster Seminary California, 2004), esp. 131-63; idem, 'Karl Barth: Between Pietism and Orthodoxy: A Post-Enlightenment Resourcement of Classical Protestantism' (D. Phil. Diss., Pembroke College, University of Oxford, 2009), esp. 201-46.

28. Girolamo Zanchi, *De Religione Fides – Confession of Christian Religion*, 2 vols., eds. Luca Baschera and Christian Moser (Leiden: Brill, 2007), III.iii (1:139).

and the Decree ably proves this point.[29] But in particular, the explicit coordination of christology and predestination is the specific function of the covenant of redemption. The *pactum* inseparably joins predestination and christology.

The second issue relates to Barth's misunderstanding of the nature of the decree according to Reformed Orthodoxy. One of the likely reasons Barth concludes that Reformed Orthodoxy advocated abstract doctrines of predestination and God is because of his reading of the seventeenth-century lapsarian controversy. He identifies the key difference between infra- and supralapsarianism as a disagreement over the object of predestination. Is the object fallen or un-fallen man? Does God choose to elect, create, permit the fall, and redeem, or does He create, permit the fall, elect, and then redeem? The impression that one might get from this order of the decrees is that election, especially in the supralapsarian understanding, is an abstract choice. Yet: (1) even for the supralapsarian election is *in Christ*; (2) there are not multiple decrees, but only one decree given divine simplicity; and (3) Barth's analysis of the two lapsarian positions fails to account for their complexity. As stated above, few, if any, Reformed theologians posit election apart from Christ. Moreover, because of divine simplicity, Reformed theologians recognized that there were not multiple decrees, but only one decree. The distinction among multiple decrees is the only way that finite creatures can reflect upon God's ectypal revelation. So even though a theologian might posit various decrees, he did not mean to divorce one from the others.

For example, Johannes Maccovius (1588-1644), a notoriously bold supralapsarian who was brought up on charges at the Synod

29. Richard A. Muller, *Christ and the Decree: Christology and Predestination in Reformed Theology from Calvin to Perkins* (Grand Rapids: Baker, 1986).

of Dort (1618-19) for his supposed incautious doctrine of predestination, held that election as a decree is 'in Christ' (Eph. 1:4).[30] Maccovius writes: 'He has chosen us not because we were in Christ, but He has chosen us so that we should be in Christ.'[31] Maccovius was a supralapsarian and therefore believed that the object of election was *homo creabilis et labilis* ('man as creatable and liable to fall'). But Maccovius could look at the object of election from several different angles:

> In respect to its goal it is one thing to consider the object of predestination in so far as it exists in intention, but it is another thing to consider the object of predestination in so far as it exists in execution. Regarding the goal, with respect to the intention, the human object of predestination is creatable man [*homo creabilis*]. Regarding the goal with respect to execution, the human object of predestination is man to be created and created, man being permitted to fall and fallen [*homo condendus, conditus, permittendus in lapsum, lapsus*].[32]

Yes, Maccovius identifies the object of predestination as *creabilis,* but from other vantage points he identifies it as *homo condendus* or *conditus,* man as to be created and already created. In other words, even for a supralapsarian like Maccovius, there is no sense in which election is abstract, in light of divine simplicity and the unity of the decree, and the numerous vantage points from which one might consider the object of predestination. God never makes a bald abstract choice – election, christology, redemption, all cohere

30. Johannes Maccovius, *Scholastic Discourse: Johannes Maccovius (1588-1644) on Theological and Philosophical Distinctions,* trans. Willem J. van Asselt, et al. (Apeldoorn: Instituut voor Reformatieonderzoek, 2009), VII.x (p. 161).

31. Maccovius, *Scholastic Discourse,* VII.vi (p. 159); cf. Fesko, 'Lapsarian Diversity,' 119-20.

32. Maccovius, *Scholastic Discourse,* VII.iv (pp. 156-57).

within the decree. To say the least, Barth's misunderstanding of Reformed Orthodoxy leads him to set up a straw man and then posit a christological doctrine of predestination as if it was an earth-shattering insight. Pierre Maury was not the first theologian to posit an indissoluble link between christology and predestination. Reformed theologians had been doing so for hundreds of years before Maury's 1936 lecture.

Election and the pactum salutis

Given the close coordination between predestination and the *pactum* for early Reformed theologians, which was especially evident in Part I of this study, how should we conceive of the relationship between these two doctrines? John Owen (1616-83), for example, places the trinitarian *consilium Dei* logically prior to the *pactum*.[33] Geerhardus Vos (1862-1949) takes a similar approach:

> The so-called 'counsel of peace' does not precede election but follows it in order. The former must be viewed as the first step in the implementation of the idea of election. The counsel of peace comprises the eternal suretyship of Christ, on which all God's gracious treatment of sinners in time depends. If now that surety is particular, that is, is not entered into for the human race in general but very specifically for the elect and for the elect only, then it follows that there must already have been a determining of the elect, an establishing of their persons, before the undertaking between the Father and the Son concerning suretyship began (this 'before' and this 'began' are not to be understood temporally).[34]

---

33. Laurence O'Donnell, III, 'The Holy Spirit's Role in John Owen's "Covenant of the Mediator" Formulation: A Case Study in Reformed Orthodox Formulations of the *Pactum Salutis*,' *PRJ* 4/1 (2012): 91-134.

34. Geerhardus Vos, *Reformed Dogmatics*, 5 vols., trans. Annemie Godbehere, et al., ed. Richard B. Gaffin, Jr. (Bellingham: Logos Bible Software, 2012-), vol. 1, V.55.

Vos contends that if the *pactum* appears logically prior to election a doctrine of universal atonement is the outcome. While Vos has in mind the views of Moises Amyraut (1596-1664), who posited the decree of Christ's universal satisfaction to be prior to the decree of election, his comments also fit Barth's position of the universal elected and rejected man, a position that produces universalism.[35]

Jan van Genderen (1923-2004) and Willem Hendrik Velema (1929-) have recognized other formulas such as Bert Loonstra's.[36] Loonstra contends that the decree of election and reprobation occurs within the *pactum salutis* between the Father and the Son. Van Genderen and Velema see a problem with such a construction because reprobation cannot be a part of the *pactum*, a covenant intended to save, not condemn. Consequently, van Genderen and Velema leave the question open regarding the sequence between election and the *pactum* because they believe the Bible is silent on the matter. Moreover, they claim that since the concepts of time and sequence are inapplicable to God's eternal counsel, the relationship between the *pactum* and predestination should be considered from a single perspective.[37]

On the one hand, one has to wonder whether Vos's supralapsarianism motivates his ordering of the *pactum* and

---

In subsequent citations of Vos's *Dogmatics* I cite only the volume and section number, since the digital edition does not have page numbers.

35. Vos, *Reformed Dogmatics*, vol. 1, V.55; cf. Moyse Amyraut, *Bref Traite de la Predestination* (Saumur: Isaac Desbordes, 1634).

36. Cf. Bertus Loonstra, *Verkiezing – Verzoening – Verbond: Beschrijving en Beoordeling van de Leer van het* Pactum Salutis *in de Gereformeerde Theologie* (Gravenhage: Uitgeverij Boeken Centrum B. V., 1990).

37. Jan van Genderen and Willem Hendrik Velema, *Concise Reformed Dogmatics*, trans. Gerrit Bilkes, Ed M. van der Maas (1992; Phillipsburg: P & R, 2008), 15.2 (p. 207); cf. 16.7 (pp. 231-35).

predestination. As desirous as he was to minimize the differences between infra- and supralapsarianism, his pursuit of the upper way (*supra lapsum*), likely drives his understanding of the relationship between election and the *pactum*.[38] Vos's supralapsarianism comes out in his separation of the decree from the mediator, as he contends that the decree of election only connects logically to the mediator after the consideration of sin: 'As Mediator He is surety. A surety presupposes a debt that must be paid. Debt presupposes sin. Christ as Mediator can only appear where sin is present.' In this respect, Vos separates the decree from all other considerations because, in his mind, 'A logical connection (*nexus causalis*) cannot exist between supralapsarianism and other doctrines, already simply because all other parts of the doctrine of salvation presuppose sin.'[39] Van Genderen and Velema take a different approach and arrive, in my judgment, at a correct conclusion but for the wrong reasons. They argue that predestination and the *pactum* should be considered from a single perspective because of the unity of God's eternal counsel and because Scripture is silent on the question of priority. True, the two should be taken together, but the simplicity of God and the supposed silence of Scripture are not reasons to pursue this path.

On the contrary, divine simplicity implies that the decree of the triune God is one and has no parts. But since we do not attempt archetypal but ectypal theology, the only option we have is to discuss the logical priorities present in the singular decree of God and therefore to speak of multiple decrees. Hence, recognizing the priority of different elements of the decree is not speculative. Rather, one must ask whether the ectypal prioritization of the singular triune decree follows the priorities

38. Vos, *Reformed Dogmatics*, vol. 1, V.65.

39. Vos, *Reformed Dogmatics*, V.73.

set forth in Scripture. In this respect, one must turn to a number of statements in Scripture to see that the Bible does address the question of relationship between the *pactum* and predestination.

In contrast to the opinions of Vos and van Genderen and Velema, the Scriptures are not silent about the relationship between the *pactum* and predestination nor do they present an abstract election, disconnected from the mediator. Ephesians 1:4 presents the elect as being chosen in Christ. As discussed above, Ephesians 1:1-14 is a chief *locus classicus* for the covenant of redemption. To be chosen in *Christ,* the Messiah, entails the presupposition of sin, which requires the logical necessity of a presupposed creation and fall. Such a pattern follows a common infralapsarian order of the decrees, but such a conclusion offers a better explanation of Ephesians 1:4 than Vos's assumption that election is separated from consideration of the covenant surety and mediator, Christ.[40]

To consider election divorced from the mediator runs counter to Paul's statements in Ephesians 1:4 and posits a collection of individuals that do not constitute a body, namely, the church. They can only be constituted the body of Christ after consideration of creation, the fall, and the necessity of the covenant surety. As is evident from Ephesians 1:4, Scripture is not silent regarding the relationship between the *pactum* and predestination. If the *pactum* establishes the *logos asarkos* as the *logos incarnandus* and the elect are chosen in Christ as such, then one must ask which takes precedence, the *pactum* or election. Vos's construction runs against the grain of Ephesians 1:4, but to posit a mediator apart from the need to save anyone also runs into problems. Why would the Trinity constitute the Son as the *logos incarnandus*

40. Cf. Francis Turretin, *Institutes of Elenctic Theology*, 3 vols., trans. George Musgrave Giger, ed. James T. Dennison, Jr. (Phillipsburg: P & R, 1992-97), IV.ix.1-31.

if there is no one who requires a covenant surety?[41] Vos boxes himself into a corner because he lacks the more nuanced approach of Maccovius, who viewed the object of election from several different perspectives.

A superior path to Vos's supralapsarianism, I believe, comes in the correct idea that van Genderen and Velema offer, namely, considering predestination and the *pactum* from a single perspective. The triune God logically determines predestination and the *pactum* in tandem. Like the carpenter who lays hold of the hammer and nails together, the triune God considers the head and the body conjointly. There is no election in Christ apart from the need for a covenant surety (*pace* Vos), and there is no consideration of the *logos incarnandus* apart from His body, the church. Indeed, as Paul writes: 'He predestined us for adoption as sons through Jesus Christ, according to the purpose of his will' (Eph. 1:5; cf. Rom. 8:29). If election is of *homo creatus et lapsus*, this addresses concerns raised by van Genderen and Velema. Both theologians were concerned with how to account for reprobation if it is drawn into a coordinate relationship with the *pactum*. How does constituting the Son as covenant surety account for the rejection of the reprobate? If one tries to wed supralapsarianism with the *pactum*, then such questions should be addressed. This is one of the likely factors that motivates Vos to separate the decree of election and reprobation from any consideration of Christ's office as covenant surety.

However, if one pursues an infralapsarian understanding of the object of election, as Ephesians 1:4 suggests, then the

---

41. Some have recently re-opened the question of the so-called supralapsarian christology. That is, the Son would have become incarnate irrespective of the fall. Such a question goes beyond the scope of this chapter. See Edwin Chr. van Driel, *Incarnation Anyway: Arguments for Supralapsarian Christology* (Oxford: Oxford University Press, 2008).

apparent problem evaporates. Nowhere do we find the Scriptures placing election and reprobation on equal footing. There are not, for example, Books of Life and Death (cf. Rev. 3:5; 13:8; 17:8; 20:12; 20:15; 21:27). The repeated refrain in John's apocalypse is that the non-elect did not have their names written in the Book of Life. In older dogmatics, the non-elect were discussed in terms of divine preterition.[42] The Westminster Confession of Faith, for example, states: 'The rest of mankind God was pleased, according to the unsearchable counsel of his own will, whereby he extendeth and withholdeth mercy, as he pleaseth, for the glory of his sovereign power over his creatures, to pass by; and to ordain them to dishonor and wrath for their sin, to the praise of his glorious justice' (III.vii).[43] In Augustinian terms, God chooses the elect from the *massa corrupta*, the *massa perditionis*: He chooses them out of the fallen mass of Adamic humanity.[44]

Chosen by the Father

Now at this point, Barth and his fellow Barthians would undoubtedly say, 'A pox on both your houses!' In other words, Barth would reject both infra- and supralapsarian constructions of the relationship between the *pactum* and predestination. Both suffer from all that Barth finds problematic with the traditional Reformed view. Such a construction posits a metaphysical, abstract, and particular doctrine of election that fails to account for the preferable actualist christology and purified supralapsarianism that recognizes Christ as the electing God and the one elected

---

42. See, e.g., John Arrowsmith, *Armilla Catechetica: A Chain of Principles* (Cambridge: John Field, 1659), V.ii (pp. 310-15).

43. For analysis of WCF III.vii, see J. V. Fesko, *The Theology of the Westminster Standards: Historical Context and Theological Insights* (Wheaton: Crossway, 2014), 119-22.

44. See Augustine, *To Simplician*, I.xx, *Augustine: Earlier Writings*, eds. John Baillie, et al., LCC, vol. 6, trans. John H. S. Burleigh (London: SCM Press, 1953), 402.

and rejected man. We must begin, therefore, with a question of who, within the Godhead, is responsible for election.

Barth claims that Christ is the electing God. The question we must ask is whether this aligns with what we find in Scripture. Barth, after all, repeatedly argues in volume II/2 of his dogmatics that revelation, not reason, must be the arbiter in all things theological.[45] The New Testament Scriptures mention election by the Father a number of times. For example, Paul identifies the subject as 'God and Father of our Lord Jesus Christ, who has blessed us in Christ with every spiritual blessing in the heavenly places even as he [the Father] chose us in him [Christ] ... he [the Father] predestined us for adoption as sons through Jesus Christ, according to the purpose of his [the Father's] will' (Eph. 1:3-5).[46] Likewise, the elect exiles were chosen 'according to the foreknowledge of God the Father' (1 Pet. 1:2; cf. 2:6). These texts counter Barth's claim that Christ is the electing God. Moreover, we must also consider the fact that the Father not only chooses the elect but also elects the Messiah: 'This is my Son, my Chosen One; listen to him!' (Luke 9:35; cf. 23:35). 'Behold, my servant whom I have chosen, my beloved with whom my soul is well pleased. I will put my Spirit upon him, and he will proclaim justice to the Gentiles' (Matt. 12:18). Some might aver that there are several passages in the Scriptures that attribute election to the Son (e.g., John 6:70; 13:18; 15:16, 19; Acts 1:2, 24). Yet, these passages do not refer to the doctrine of predestination but rather the redemptive historical mission of the *logos incarnatus* ('the incarnated word').[47] This is especially evident

45. Barth, CD, II/2: 3-4, 38-39.

46. Peter T. O'Brien, *The Letter to the Ephesians*, PNTC (Grand Rapids: Eerdmans, 1999), 98-102, esp. 99 n. 53.

47. D. A. Carson, *The Gospel According to John*, PNTC (Grand Rapids: Eerdmans, 1991), 304, 470, 523-25.

in Christ's designation of Judas as one of His chosen ones in spite of his status as 'the devil' (John 6:70*).[48] In this respect we can comment that nowhere does Scripture ascribe election to the Son or to the Holy Spirit.[49]

This once again provokes a potential objection that the covenant of redemption entails tritheism: if God the Father covenants with God the Son, there are necessarily two different competing wills within the Trinity, for how else can the Father and the Son enter into an agreement?[50] The answer to this question is that the unified will of the triune God is manifest in each person of the Trinity. The Father wills to send the Son and the Son wills to obey the command of the Father. This is one will that accounts for the individual persons within the Trinity. That is, the unity of the Trinity must be pressed but only insofar as the relational opposition within the Godhead allows.[51] As Vos rightly notes:

> In predestination the divine persons act communally, while economically it is attributed to the Father. In the covenant of redemption they are related to one another judicially. In predestination there is the one, undivided, divine will. In the counsel of peace this will appears as having its own mode of existence in each person. One cannot object to this on the basis of the unity of God's being. To

---

48. Carson, *John*, 304.

49. Vos, *Reformed Dogmatics*, vol. 1, V.54.

50. See, e.g., Robert Letham, 'John Owen's Doctrine of the Trinity in Its Catholic Context,' in *The Ashgate Research Companion to John Owen's Theology*, eds. Kelly M. Kapic and Mark Jones (Farnham: Ashgate, 2012), 196; idem, *The Westminster Assembly: Reading Its Theology in Historical Context* (Phillipsburg: P & R, 2009), 235-37.

51. St Anselm, *On the Procession of the Holy Spirit*, §I, in *Anselm of Canterbury: The Major Works*, eds. Brian Davies and G. R. Evans (Oxford: Oxford University Press, 1998), 393; Thomas Aquinas, *Summa Theologica* (rep.; Allen: Classic Reprints, 1948), Ia q. 34 art. 1.

> push unity so strongly that the persons can no longer be related to one another judicially would lead to Sabellianism and would undermine the reality of the entire economy of redemption with its person to person relationships.[52]

To say that the Father elects does not mean that He must be separated from the Godhead or that His will is separate from the Son and the Spirit. Rather, it recognizes the scriptural pattern that the Father elects, the Son acts as covenant surety of the elect, and the Spirit applies the work of Christ to the elect. In this manner the triune God executes the unified triune will in a manner respective of the triune missions and processions.

Particular in nature

Barth objected to the concept of particularity in election, dividing humanity into two categories of elect and reprobate. Barth has accused the Reformed tradition of devolving into unbiblical speculative metaphysics because it posits such a division of humanity. Yet, if we descend into the middle of God's initial covenantal dealings with Israel, the one thing that confronts us is the particularity of election: 'For you are a people holy to the LORD your God. The LORD your God has chosen you to be a people for his treasured possession, out of all the peoples who are on the face of the earth' (Deut. 7:6). The particularity of Yahweh's choice of Israel stands out in this statement. Israel alone out of all the nations on the earth was chosen – Israel and no other. Moreover, in the heart of this passage on Israel's election particularity stands out quite prominently, as their election is given alongside of the ban, or *herem*. When Yahweh brought

52. Geerhardus Vos, 'The Doctrine of the Covenant in Reformed Theology,' in *Redemptive History and Biblical Interpretation: The Shorter Writings of Geerhardus Vos*, ed. Richard B. Gaffin, Jr. (Phillipsburg: P & R, 1980), 246.

Israel into the land he was going to eject its Gentile inhabitants: 'And when the LORD your God gives them over to you, and you defeat them, then you must devote them to complete destruction [החרם תחרים]' (Deut. 7:2). Israel's election was not abstract but was concretized in the requirement to place the former inhabitants of the land under the ban.

Some have recognized the potential difficulties associated with *herem* warfare, namely, God's command that Israel destroy her Gentile enemies. How can a loving God order the destruction of the non-elect inhabitants of the land? Some Old Testament scholars, therefore, largely ignore the subject (e.g., Eichrodt, von Rad, Childs, Brueggemann, Goldingay, Waltke, et al.).[53] Some scholars try to mitigate the connection between the ban and election by use of the Documentary Source Hypothesis: *herem* warfare was a later addition to the text and not originally associated with election. Others argue that *herem* warfare was simply part of the culture of the period, and though removed from modern Western culture, this is how ancient Near Eastern culture operated.[54] And still others argue that *herem* warfare is simply metaphorical language to impress the need for sanctity upon Israel. That is, they were supposed to maintain their unique identity as the elect people of Yahweh.[55] 'The practice of *herem*,' writes R. W. L. Moberly, 'apparently originally a battlefield practice involving killing, has been retained, and indeed highlighted in Deuteronomy only because it was seen to be amenable to metaphorical reconstrual

53. R. W. L. Moberly, *Old Testament Theology: Reading the Hebrew Bible as Christian Scripture* (Grand Rapids: Baker, 2013), 41, 56; cf. Patrick Miller, *Deuteronomy* (Louisville: Westminster John Knox, 1990), 110-14.

54. Moberly, *Old Testament Theology*, 57.

55. Moberly, *Old Testament Theology*, 58-62, 67-71.

in terms of practices that enhance Israel's covenant faithfulness to YHWH in everyday life.'[56]

The rest of the Pentateuch mitigates Moberly's interpretation. True, there is undoubtedly a preservation element associated with the ban – Yahweh did not want the former inhabitants of the land leading Israel astray into idolatry and false worship (e.g., Deut. 20:16-18). But in Deuteronomy 7:1-2 the ban is specifically associated with the destruction of the inhabitants of the land.[57] As Moshe Weinfeld notes; '*Herem* in the context of war denotes dedication to God: if it is man or animal, it should be sacrificed to God, and if it is property, it should be devoted to him (Exod. 22:19; Lev. 27:29; Deut. 13:16; 1 Sam. 15:3, 33).'[58] Some have maintained that *herem* warfare passages such as Deuteronomy 7:1-2 were the Deuteronomist's wishful rewriting of Israel's history – what should have been. But such a reading fails to account for numerous accounts of *herem* warfare, such as Israel's siege and destruction of Jericho: 'Then they devoted all in the city to destruction [ויחרימו], both men and women, young and old, oxen, sheep, and donkeys, with the edge of the sword' (Josh. 6:21; cf. 1 Sam. 15:3; 22:19).[59] A similar pattern unfolds in Judges when the tribes of Judah and Simeon devoted Zephath to destruction (Judg. 1:17-18).[60]

---

56. Moberly, *Old Testament Theology*, 72.

57. Moshe Weinfeld, 'The Ban on the Canaanites in the Biblical Codes and Its Historical Development,' in *History and Traditions of Early Israel*, eds. André Lemaire and Benedikt Otzen (Leiden: Brill, 1993), 150. My thanks to my pastor, Zach Keele, for alerting me to this source. See also, J. A. Thompson, *Deuteronomy*, TOTC (Downers Grove: InterVarsity Press, 1974), 128-29.

58. Weinfeld, 'The Ban,' 150 n. 23.

59. Richard S. Hess, *Joshua*, TOTC (Downers Grove: InterVarsity Press, 1996), 42-46; 132-33.

60. Weinfeld, 'The Ban,' 152; Robert G. Boling, *Judges*, AB (Garden City: Doubleday, 1975), 58.

Some might counter that the purported destruction of some of the inhabitants of the land originated with Feuerbach rather than Yahweh. That is, they were simply the sinful and violent actions of Israel, and not truly a correlate of Israel's election. Such a contention conflicts with statements that attribute the destruction of the Canaanites ultimately to Yahweh: 'I sent the hornet before you, which drove them out before you, the two kings of the Amorites; it was not by your sword or by your bow' (Josh. 24:12; Exod. 23:28; Deut. 6:10-11). The psalmist is also quite clear on this point: 'In the days of old you with your own hand drove out the nations … for not by their own sword did they win the land, nor did their own arm save them, but your right hand and your arm, and the light of your face, for you delighted in them' (Ps. 44:1-3).[61] And while the Old Testament does not classify the exodus as *herem* warfare, particularity still appears. Egypt fell under God's judgment with the plagues, which culminated in the destruction of the firstborn, while God preserved Israel's firstborn (Exod. 14).

If subsequent New Testament interpretation is any indication, the exodus from Egypt was a work of Christ. Jude speaks of 'Jesus, who saved a people out of the land of Egypt' (Jude 5; cf. 1 Cor. 10:1-11).[62] Scripture clearly testifies that election is particular, whether in the salvation of Noah and his family (Gen. 6-9), God's election of Abraham, Isaac, and Jacob (Gen. 12:1-2), His preterition of Esau and Ishmael, the deliverance of Israel from Egypt, the judgment against Pharaoh, the Egyptians, and their firstborn, or the *herem* warfare against

---

61. Weinfeld, 'The Ban,' 143; Hans-Joachim Kraus, *Psalms 1-59* (Minneapolis: Fortress, 1993), 446-47.

62. Cf. Richard J. Bauckham, *Jude, 2 Peter*, WBC, vol. 50 (Waco: Word, 1983), 49-50.

the Canaanites. The particularity of election continues in the New Testament, whether in the testimony of Christ or in the apostle Paul's famous statements in Romans 9. Particularity is not a postulate of metaphysical ontology but a brute fact of divine revelation.

Predestination and covenant

Does this defense of the particularity of election suggest a speculative Christ-less and non-covenantal doctrine of divine election? Predestination does involve election and preterition, but this divine choice is not abstract as Barth and others maintain. Rather, as stated above, election, christology, and the *pactum* are coordinate elements within the divine decree. The Father elects people *creatus et lapsus* in Christ, their covenant head and surety within the broader context of the covenant of redemption, which in turn produces the covenant of grace. The covenantal context of election is especially evident in the *locus classicus* of Israel's election in Deuteronomy 7:5-7, but covenantal nomenclature appears in other texts too.

In Paul's famous statement, 'Jacob I loved, but Esau I hated' (Rom. 9:13), we find language sometimes interpreted in emotional or affective terms.[63] In the broader canon, however, love and hate reflect covenantal language, and in this context have secondary affective implications.[64] Again, within Deuteronomy 7, Yahweh's love for Israel is evident: 'It was not because you were more in number than any other people that the LORD set his love on you and chose you, for you were the fewest of all peoples, but it is because the LORD loves you and

63. See, e.g., John Murray, *The Epistle to the Romans*, NICNT (Grand Rapids: Eerdmans, 1968), 21-24.

64. Cf. Douglas Moo, *The Epistle to the Romans*, NICNT (Grand Rapids: Eerdmans, 1996), 587.

is keeping the oath that he swore to your fathers, that the LORD has brought you out with a mighty hand and redeemed you from the house of slavery, from the hand of Pharaoh king of Egypt' (Deut. 7:7-8). By way of contrast, the psalmist writes: 'The LORD tests the righteous, but his soul hates the wicked and the one who loves violence' (Ps. 11:5; cf. 5:5).[65] This pattern applies not only to God's love for those who are in covenant with Him, but also finds expression in His covenant people. God's covenanted people love Him; conversely, those who disobey God hate Him (Exod. 20:6; Deut. 5:10; 7:9; 10:12; 11:1, 13, 22; 13:3; 19:9; 30:16, 20; Deut. 7:10).[66]

In God's election, He sets His love upon those whom He chooses. This is the nature of Paul's opening statement in his epistle to Ephesus, 'In love he predestined us for adoption as sons through Jesus Christ, according to the purpose of his will' (Eph. 1:4-5). Only those who are outside of Christ, beyond the pale of the decree of election, receive the holy hatred of God. The outcome of predestination is also quite evident on the pages of Scripture. The typical shadows of the Old Testament with Israel's unique elect status among the surrounding non-elect nations comes to fruition in the antitypical reality of heaven and hell. Elect Israel lives in the presence of Yahweh, whereas the non-elect dwell away from Him. Old Testament shadows give way to the concrete realities of heaven and hell. In terms reminiscent of the architecture and geography of Israel's place in the holy land, the elect reside within the gates of Zion while the non-elect, 'the dogs and sorcerers and the sexually immoral and murderers and

65. Kraus, *Psalms 1-59*, 155.

66. Rekha M. Chennattu, *Johannine Discipleship as Covenant Relationship* (Peabody: Hendrikson, 2006), 65; Steven L. McKenzie, *Covenant* (St. Louis: Chalice Press, 2000), 37-39; cf. James D. G. Dunn, *Romans 9-16*, WBC, vol. 38b (Dallas: Word, 1988), 549-50.

idolaters, and everyone who loves and practices falsehood' dwell outside the gates (Rev. 22:15).[67]

Noteworthy is Christ's statement that precedes the description of Zion's architecture and inhabitants: 'Behold, I am coming soon, bringing my recompense with me, to repay each one for what he has done. I am the Alpha and the Omega, the first and the last, the beginning and the end' (Rev. 22:12-13). John does not present Christ as the elected and rejected man, but as the coming judge, who executes His righteous judgment upon the wicked, those who ultimately dwell beyond the gates of Zion. Moreover, the following statement precedes Christ's warning: 'Let the evildoer still do evil, and the filthy still be filthy, and the righteous still do right, and the holy still be holy' (Rev. 22:11; cf. Dan. 12:10). The outcome at the consummation, that which determines whether one lives within or without Zion's gates, has its roots in the particular decree of predestination that elects Christ as covenant surety and specific individuals.[68] Christ is not Barth's elected and rejected man. He is the elect, the chosen of the Lord, and the head of His holy bride, the church; He is the object of election. He has suffered outside the gates on behalf of His elect (Heb. 13:12); those who reject Christ must themselves suffer outside the gates as Revelation makes abundantly clear.

The question of metaphysics

Immediately evident is the great disparity between Barth's doctrine of predestination and the traditional Reformed doctrine presented here in this chapter. The traditional view supposedly

---

67. G. K. Beale, *The Book of Revelation*, NIGTC (Grand Rapids: Eerdmans, 1999), 1140-43.

68. Beale, *Revelation*, 1131-34.

embodies an alien metaphysical and speculative view of God and Barth's represents a post-metaphysical understanding of predestination. According to Barthian norms and commitments, the traditional Reformed view should be rejected because of its faulty metaphysical foundation. But the closer one approaches the two competing views, two questions arise: (1) is the traditional view metaphysical and speculative and (2) does Barth truly present a post-metaphysical doctrine of predestination?

The Reformed tradition and metaphysics

Closer engagement with the tradition's doctrine and its supporting scriptural texts defies all claims of metaphysical speculation. Do Reformed theologians make metaphysical claims about God's nature and attributes as they relate to predestination? Yes, they do. To say that the God of Scripture displays all of His attributes in election and reprobation is a metaphysical statement based upon divine revelation. When Paul expounds the doctrine of election in Romans 9, he quotes the Old Testament to demonstrate the divine rationale for election and reprobation: 'For the Scripture says to Pharaoh, "For this very purpose I have raised you up, that I might show my power in you, and that my name might be proclaimed in all the earth." So then he has mercy on whomever he wills, and he hardens whomever he wills' (Rom. 9:17-18). In his explanation of election Paul alludes to Exodus 33:19b, 'I will be gracious to whom I will be gracious, and will show mercy on whom I will show mercy.' The original context for Yahweh's statement appears on the heels of Moses' asking to see His glory, 'Please show me your glory,' to which Yahweh responds, 'I will make all my goodness pass before you and will proclaim before you my name, the Lord' (Exod. 33:18-19a). These statements reveal who God is ontologically and metaphysically – they reveal the nature of God's being.

Within this original context, when Yahweh declares His name to Moses, God utters His name: 'I will be gracious to whom I will be gracious, and will show mercy on whom I will show mercy.'[69] Yahweh reveals His mercy and justice in His actions of election and reprobation. This is Paul's precise point when he writes: 'What if God, desiring to show his wrath and to make known his power, has endured with much patience vessels of wrath prepared for destruction, in order to make known the riches of his glory for vessels of mercy, which he has prepared beforehand for glory?' (Rom. 9:22-23). The preparation of the vessels of destruction reveals the glory of Yahweh's just judgment against the wicked and highlights the depths of the grace He shows to the vessels of mercy. Election, therefore, reveals who God is – this is evident in the correlation of the divine name, Yahweh, with His proclamation of the name to Moses, 'I will be gracious to whom I will be gracious, and will show mercy on whom I will show mercy.' In metaphysical terms, God's being is logically prior to the decree of predestination. Otherwise, why would Paul state that God's purpose in election was to 'make known his power' to His vessels of mercy by demonstrating His longsuffering to the vessels of wrath prepared for destruction?[70]

Barth and metaphysics

This brings us to the second of two points, namely, does Barth genuinely present a post-metaphysical doctrine of predestination?[71] In Barth's understanding, election and revelation are synonymous

69. John Piper, *The Justification of God: An Exegetical and Theological Study of Romans 9:1-23*, 2nd ed. (Grand Rapids: Baker, 1993), 121-22, 219-20.

70. Moo, *Romans*, 605-06. The same particularly appears in Psalms 1 and 2 with judgment falling upon the wicked and salvation only for those who kiss the son (Robert L. Cole, *Psalms 1-2: Gateway to the Psalter* [Sheffield: Sheffield Phoenix Press, 2013], 136-41).

71. Cf. Jones, *Humanity of Christ*, 90.

since they center upon Jesus Christ: 'It is the name of Jesus Christ, which according to the divine self-revelation, forms the focus at which the two decisive beams of the truth forced upon us converge and unite: on the one hand the electing God and the on the other elected man.'[72] Barth's understanding of John's text – 'In the beginning was the Word, and the Word was with God, and the Word was God. He was in the beginning with God' – requires us to affirm the full deity of Christ but also to identify the word with Jesus. Barth coordinates John 1:1-2 with Colossians 1:17, 'And he is before all things, and in him all things hold together.' Barth contends that Colossians 1:17 refers to the Son of God *in concreto* and not *in abstracto*, namely, Jesus Christ.[73] To be sure, Barth cites a cluster of other texts (2 Cor. 4:4; Col. 1:15; Heb. 1:3) but understands them in the light of his correlation of John 1:1-2 and Colossians 1:17, to the effect that,

> If it is true, then in the name and person of Jesus Christ we are called upon to recognize the Word of God, the decree of God and the election of God at the beginning of all things, at the beginning of our own being and thinking, at the basis of our faith and the ways and works of God. Or, to put it the other way, in this person we are called upon the recognize the beginning of the Word and decree and election of God, the conclusive and absolute authority in respect of the aim and origin of all things.[74]

One cannot accuse Barth of failing to engage in exegesis, as he seeks to base his doctrine in revelation. But the same applies to the traditional Reformed view.

---

72. Barth, CD, II/2:59; cf. David Gibson, *Reading the Decree: Exegesis, Election and Christology in Calvin and Barth* (London: T & T Clark, 2009), 42.

73. Barth, CD, II/2:96-98.

74. Barth, CD, II/2: 99.

The specific question at hand, then, is whether the transition from exegesis to dogmatic formulation produces warranted or unwarranted conclusions. Since the Son of God is fully God, and since other passages identify the Son of God as the Christ, is Christ the elected and rejected man and at the same time the electing God? In my judgment this is an unwarranted conclusion and is more speculatively metaphysical rather than exegetical. In response to Barth's doctrine of election, Emil Brunner (1889-1966), who was sympathetic to Barth's cause and critical of the traditional Reformed view, writes:

> No special proof is required to show that the Bible contains no such doctrine, nor that no theory of this kind has ever been formulated by any theologian. If the eternal pre-existence of the God-Man were a fact, then the Incarnation would no longer be an *Event* at all; no longer would it be the great miracle of Christmas. In the New Testament the new element is the fact that the eternal Son of God *became* Man, and that hence forth through His Resurrection and Ascension, in Him humanity has *received* a share in the heavenly glory; yet in this view of Barth's, all this is now anticipated, as it were, torn out of the sphere of history, and set within the pre-temporal sphere, in the pre-existence of the Logos.[75]

In brief, Brunner rejects Barth's presupposition that the *logos* is always the *logos incarnandus*. To make such a move, in Brunner's view, makes eternity swallow time. Moreover, how does Barth reach the conclusion that because the *logos* is always *incarnandus* that He is therefore the one elected and rejected man? What of all the passages in Scripture that speak about particularity?

---

75. Emil Brunner, *The Christian Doctrine of God,* Dogmatics vol. 1, trans. Olive Wyon (Philadelphia: Westminster Press, 1949), 347; cf. Jones, *Humanity of Christ,* 90-91; McCormack, 'Grace and Being,' 92.

True, in a sense, the *logos* is eternally *incarnandus* prior to the incarnation – such is the nature of the eternality of the decree.[76] However, in traditional Reformed dogmatics the relationship between eternity and time (or history) is not the primary purpose of the distinction between the *logos asarkos* and *incarnatus*. The point of the distinction is to highlight the contingency of the decree – the triune God's freedom to create or not to create, to redeem or not to redeem.[77] More specifically, the distinction highlights Christ's voluntary willingness to enter into the covenant with the Father and to serve as covenant surety. The apostle Paul captures the freedom of God and contingency of the creation in his famous statement to the Athenian philosophers at Mars Hill: 'The God who made the world and everything in it, being Lord of heaven and earth, does not live in temples made by man, nor is he served by human hands, as though he needed anything, since he himself gives to all mankind life and breath and everything' (Acts 17:24-25; cf. 1 Kings 8:27; Isa. 66:1-2).[78] Such seems to be the import and rationale as to why John begins not with Jesus Christ but with the *logos*, which invokes Genesis 1:1.[79] Only when John contemplates the incarnation does he then introduce the Christ: 'And the Word became flesh and tabernacled among us ...' (John 1:14*; cf. v. 17).

---

76. Douglas A. Felch, 'From Here to Eternity: A Biblical, Theological, and Analogical Defense of Divine Eternity in the Light of Recent Challenges Within Analytic Philosophy' (Ph.D. diss., Calvin Theological Seminary, 2005).

77. Richard A. Muller, 'God as Absolute and Relative, Necessary, Free, and Contingent: The *Ad Intra – Ad Extra* Movement of Seventeenth-Century Reformed Language About God,' in *Always Reformed: Essays in Honor of W. Robert Godfrey*, ed. R. Scott Clark and Joel E. Kim (Escondido: Westminster Seminary California, 2010), 59.

78. Darrell C. Bock, *Acts*, BECNT (Grand Rapids: Baker, 2007), 565-66; cf. Barth, CD, II/1: 280-81.

79. G. K. Beale and D. A. Carson, eds., *Commentary on the New Testament Use of the Old Testament* (Grand Rapids: Baker, 2007), 421.

The illegitimacy of Barth's dogmatic conclusions becomes more evident in his exegesis of Romans 9, a text that he does not incorporate into the exegetical foundation of his doctrine of election. That is, Romans 9 does not feature in support of his claim that Christ is the electing God and the elected and rejected man. Barth nevertheless explains that the contrast of Moses and Pharaoh displays the mystery of election: 'When we contrast Moses and Pharaoh, we are not concerned with some nice differentiation of soul, or with the distinction between two "personalities" but with the unobservable paradox of election and rejection.' Barth claims that Moses and Pharaoh have different purposes: one manifests the divine Yes and the other his No.[80] Moses and Pharaoh point to election and rejection but this does not necessarily indicate their own personal status. Barth offers a similar explanation for the statement, 'Jacob I loved, but Esau I hated' (Rom. 9:13). Jacob and Esau do not reveal their personal status but the divine 'paradox that eternity becomes time, and yet not time ... the riddle of the beloved Jacob and the hated Esau, that is to say, in the secret of eternal, twofold predestination. Now, this secret concerns not this or that man, but all men. By it men are not divided, but united. In its presence they all stand on one line—for Jacob is always Esau also, and in the eternal "Moment" of revelation Esau is also Jacob.'[81] In other words, all the apparent particular texts lead back to John 1:1-2 and Christ – the electing God and the elected and rejected man.

The significant question to ask is whether Barth's dogmatic conclusions comport with the text. Do Jacob and Esau reveal the divine Yes and No of Christ's election? Does election actually unite all humanity rather than divide it into the elect and reprobate? Barth's conclusions run into a number of exegetical obstacles

80. Barth, *Romans*, 352-53.

81. Barth, *Romans*, 347.

especially as it pertains to Esau. Esau was the firstborn, yet God chose Jacob over him (cf. Gen. 25:25-26; Rom. 9:12). Esau, not Jacob, sold his birthright and interest in the covenant to his younger brother; in fact, 'Esau despised his birthright' (Gen. 25:32-34).[82] The pre-incarnate Christ wrestled with Jacob, not Esau (Gen. 32:24-25; cf. Hosea 12:4-5).[83] God gave the Promised Land to the descendants of Jacob, not Esau. The prophets record the judgment that was to fall upon Esau and his descendants, indeed the destruction of his children and neighbors, even his annihilation (Jer. 49:10; Oba. 18). Yahweh declared His love for Jacob and hatred for Esau to convey Esau's cursed condition and Jacob's blessed estate (Mal. 1:2-3).[84] Perhaps the strongest indictment against Esau appears in the book of Hebrews, which characterizes him as 'sexually immoral or unholy, who sold his birthright for a single meal' (Heb. 12:16). Significant is the fact that the author of Hebrews characterizes Esau as *unholy* (βέβηλος), that is, one who is profane (cf. 1 Tim. 1:9; 4:7; Gen. 25:32; Lev. 10:10; Ezek. 22:26; 44:23 LXX).[85] In other words, Esau stands outside of the covenant – he stands outside of Christ.

In this respect, the sympathetic but nonetheless critical Brunner opines: 'Barth is in absolute opposition, not only to the whole ecclesiastical tradition, but—and this alone is the final objection to it—to the clear teaching of the New Testament.'[86] What drives Barth's flawed exegesis? In short, Barth employs

82. Nahum Sarna, *Genesis*, JPSTC (Philadelphia: Jewish Publication Society, 1989), 180-82.

83. Geerhardus Vos, *Biblical Theology: Old and New Testaments* (Edinburgh: Banner of Truth, 1948), 72-76.

84. Beale and Carson, *New Testament Commentary*, 641.

85. William L. Lane, *Hebrews 9-13*, WBC, vol. 47b (Dallas: Word, 1991), 455-56.

86. Brunner, *Doctrine of God*, 349.

Hegelian metaphysics to undergird his doctrine of predestination. Ironically, Barth's doctrine of election is just as metaphysical as that of Reformed Orthodoxy. The use of metaphysics, whether from Aristotle or Hegel, does not automatically disqualify a theologian's conclusions. All theology to some extent must employ metaphysics.[87] The pertinent question is whether the metaphysics creates onto-theology or theo-ontology. That is, does the tail wag the dog, or the dog the tail? Do metaphysical principles drive and shape exegesis, or does exegesis regulate the metaphysics? In this case, Barth's Hegelianism is evident, especially in his characterization of the nature of predestination.

But one should not automatically rule out Barth's doctrine of predestination based upon mere association with Hegel. Some have noted that, unlike Hegel, Barth never sought to resolve the tension of the dialectic; he never sought a synthesis from the thesis + antithesis.[88] He never sought to explain the dialectic of predestination, that Jacob is Esau, and Esau is Jacob. Nevertheless, his doctrine should be evaluated on the basis of whether his view is driven more by Hegelian metaphysics rather than scriptural exegesis. On this count, Barth himself recognized that he should be free to entertain elements of various schools of thought without embracing the ideas *in toto*: 'I can entertain elements of Marxism without becoming a Marxist ... Today we are offered existentialism, and it too doubtless has important elements ... I myself have a certain weakness for Hegel and am always fond of doing a bit of "Hegeling".'[89] In fact, McCormack has criticized his detractors for failing to employ

87. Matthew Levering, *Scripture and Metaphysics: Aquinas and the Renewal of Trinitarian Theology* (Oxford: Oxford University Press, 2004), 21, 63-64, 83, 87.

88. D. Stephen Long, *Saving Karl Barth: Hans Urs von Balthasar's Preoccupation* (Minneapolis: Fortress, 2014), 43.

89. Barth as cited in Eberhard Busch, *Karl Barth: His Life from Letters and Autobiographical Texts* (Philadelphia: Fortress, 1975), 387.

Hegelian dialectics in their understanding of predestination and its relation to God's being.[90] Barth himself wondered why Hegel never became as influential as Thomas Aquinas, though he thought that Hegel's influence might eventually rise to Thomist levels. In fact, Barth believed Hegel's thought could not be ignored.[91]

The million dollar question is, Does Barth's Hegelian dialectic of Christ as the elected and rejected man best explain those texts associated with predestination? It does not. Barth's Hegelian sleight of hand cannot explain the persistent presence of particularity in the text, in terms of the concrete reality of redemptive history, whether in Israel's *herem* warfare against the Canaanites, Esau's bowl of lentils traded for his covenantal birthright, Christ's refusal to pursue those disciples that left Him, or Paul's angst for his fellow countrymen in the flesh (Rom. 9:1-5). The particularity of election is inescapable. In his effort to flee from speculative ontology and metaphysics, Barth runs headlong into the arms of Hegel and his speculative dialectical metaphysics. Moreover, Barth's Hegelian metaphysical dialectics damages the value and meaning of history.[92] Barth's Hegelian sleight of hand negates the blood, sweat, and tears of real historical people. If Jacob is Esau, and Esau is Jacob, their historical existence is utterly meaningless.[93] And such a view of history imperils not merely the humanity of God's creatures, but ultimately the humanity of Christ, the incarnation. Barth's reliance upon Hegel is problematic, not because he employs metaphysics, but because his metaphysical dialectics applied to predestination contradict

---

90. McCormack, *Orthodox and Modern*, 277; cf. Berkouwer, *Triumph of Grace*, 9.

91. Barth, *Protestant Theology*, 370, 376, 382-83.

92. Cf. Barth, *Protestant Theology*, 395, 401, 405.

93. Cornelius Van Til, *The New Modernism: An Appraisal of the Theology of Barth and Brunner* (Philadelphia: P & R, 1947), 76-79.

Scripture. Barth's Hegelian metaphysics and actualist ontology ultimately fall short because they have no exegetical foundation.

Theological implications

The remaining issues concern the implications of the correlation of the *pactum* and predestination. Why is it necessary to affirm the logical priority of being over act, and conversely why does an actualist christology miss the mark? At one level, Barth's actualist christology falls short because it fails adequately to deal with numerous texts of Scripture, especially those of the Old Testament. Barth locks on to John 1:1-2 as the exegetical focal point of his actualist ontology and doctrine of election without considering the word–act–word pattern of revelation. The anticipatory Old Testament revelation shows the particularity of election, which Christ confirms by His own actions during His bread of life discourse, and established by the subsequent interpretive revelation, whether in Paul's famous ninth chapter of Romans or the architecture of Zion in the closing chapters of the Bible.

The *herem* warfare of Deuteronomy, for example, is not an anomaly, an embarrassing cultural artifact from a backwards and bygone era or a sinful grotesque aberration marring God's otherwise admirable revelation. Rather, it is a typological intrusion of God's eschatological judgment against the wicked, the non-elect, that becomes manifest in the antitypical second advent of Christ.[94] This pattern reveals both the particularity of election and the character of the triune God – as Christ will sit upon the throne to judge the nations. The typical destruction of the Canaanites anticipates the antitypical work of the Messiah,

94. Meredith G. Kline, *The Structure of Biblical Authority*, 2nd ed. (1989; Eugene: Wipf & Stock, 1997), 154-71, esp. 162-64.

the one who breaks the unrepentant with a rod of iron and dashes them like a potter's vessel (Ps. 2:8-9). He has the sharp two-edged sword in His mouth by which He wages war against the wicked (Rev. 1:16; 2:16). He strikes down the nations and rules them with a rod of iron, and treads the winepress of the fury of God's wrath (Rev. 19:15). *Herem* warfare, therefore, is linked to election. But predestination is not merely about particularity, or God's sovereign election of some unto salvation and the rejection of others. There are a host of issues that relate to history, the incarnation, the doctrine of the covenant, the active obedience of Christ, and ultimately eschatology. These connections should be briefly explored, since the *pactum* embraces them all.

Genuine history and the humanity of Christ

For all of the talk about the abstract nature of the decree, when considered in connection with the *pactum*, the election of the Son involves His incarnation and anointing with the Spirit. As mentioned above, the Son's election necessitates His incarnation; the distinction between the *logos asarkos* and *incarnandus* simply highlights the freedom of the Trinity. The triune God was free to create and not create, to redeem or not redeem. The decree is contingent, not necessary to God's being. Correlatively, the Father could have sent or not sent His only begotten Son, and the Son could have consented or not consented to redeem the elect. The triune God freely chose to redeem the elect by means of the Father's election, the Son's redemption, and the Spirit's sanctification. Predestination envelopes the Trinity's love for fallen sinners, and it commits the eternal God to enter into time as a human being.

If, on the other hand, we assume an actualist christology in which the Son is always logically the *logos incarnandus*, where is the Son's freedom to enter into the human condition? It seems that eternity swallows history, and as such, the Son is no longer fully divine and fully human.[95] In this case His humanity is necessary because He is always the *logos incarnandus*. McCormack has responded to this issue by explaining that God chooses to be triune, and this preserves God's freedom. But if God chooses to be triune, then in light of His antecedent decision, the Son and the Spirit are not free – they are determined, not by their being, but by the antecedent will of God. Who is this God prior (logically) to the decision to constitute the Trinity? Apparently He (or she or it) is the *deus ignotus*, the unknown God. He is not merely the *Deus absconditus* who also is the *Deus revelatus*. We ultimately never know who God truly is. Revelation only

95. E.g., Barth, CD II/1:623; cf. Jones, *Humanity of Christ*, 100-01, 190, 192-93; George Hunsinger, *Disruptive Grace: Studies in the Theology of Karl Barth* (Grand Rapids: Eerdmans, 2000), 197-209; idem, *How To Read Karl Barth: The Shape of His Theology* (New York: Oxford University Press, 1991), 238-42. Part of the issue with his view of the relationship between eternity and time, as Hunsinger notes, is that Barth employs a dialectic between the two ideas: 'For not only are God and the world thought of as being dialectically included in the Mediator, but in and through the Mediator they are thought of as being dialectically included in one another as well' (*How To Read Barth*, 238). Once again, as with the doctrine of election, does Barth's commitment to Hegelian metaphysics break through the exegetical guardrails? In my judgment the answer to this question is, yes. To say that God and the world are dialectically included in the mediator rests upon the false presupposition that God and the world (and hence time) are antithetical and contradictory ideas. If there is an antithesis between God and the world, it is an ethical one – human beings are covenant-breakers and hence ethically antithetical to God's holiness, but they are not metaphysically antithetical – they are different and distinct, not antithetical. Humans are an analog to God, not His ontological antithesis – they are ectypes of the archetype. Case in point, when the Son becomes man, He does not become the antithesis of God – the archetype becomes the ectype. Christ, for example, becomes sin (e.g., 2 Cor. 5:20-21) by imputation, not by committing sin and thus becoming ethically and antithetically opposed to God. In His incarnation, therefore, the Son assumes human nature, which is different and distinct from Him, but not antithetical. The same dynamic, I believe, applies to God's relationship to time. Eternity and time are distinct, but not antithetical. Hence, a dialectical metaphysical presupposition does not best explain God's relationship to the world and time.

discloses what God has decided to be rather than who He truly is. Christ merely reveals God's decision, not God Himself.

On this count, to call Barth's view an actualist ontology is misleading. Reformed Orthodoxy has maintained that God is pure being.[96] To put it in simpler and exegetical terms, God is a verb, not a noun, He is the great I AM (Exod. 3:14), the God who was, is, and is to come (Rev. 1:8). God is pure actuality apart from His decree to create and redeem. A more accurate description is to say that the tradition maintains an actualist ontology and Barth holds to a voluntarist ontology.[97] In the latter, God is only what He decides to be, rather than the God who reveals who He truly is. In this respect, Barth's invoking the categories of *in abstracto* and *in concreto* concerning God's being reveals an inclination towards panentheism, at least as it pertains to the incarnation. Additionally, Barth's reversing the order between Adam and Christ, making Christ the only true Adam, allows the panentheist impulse to spread into his broader system, something that will be explored below. Nevertheless, to say that we can only know God *in concreto*, i.e., the *logos incarnandus*, means that the incarnation is not contingent but necessary. And hence God is never free from history, since it is necessary for His existence vis-à-vis the incarnation.

We must instead recognize that there is no such thing as God *in abstracto* – He is His own context – eternal Father, Son, and

---

96. Richard A. Muller, *Post-Reformation Reformed Dogmatics*, vol. 3 (Grand Rapids: Baker, 2003), 308-20; Sebastian Rehnman, 'The Doctrine of God in Reformed Orthodoxy,' in *A Companion to Reformed Orthodoxy*, ed. Herman Selderhuis (Leiden: Brill, 2013), 384-85; Christopher Cleveland, *Thomism in John Owen* (Farnham: Ashgate, 2013), 27-68.

97. Cf. Jones, *Humanity of Christ*, 26; Eberhard Jüngel, *God's Being Is in Becoming: The Trinitarian Being of God in the Theology of Karl Barth* (Grand Rapids: Eerdmans, 2001), 81; Robert W. Jenson, *Systematic Theology*, vol. 1 (Oxford: Oxford University Press, 1997), 140.

Holy Spirit. He is always *Deus in concreto*. When theologians have historically employed the distinction between God as *absolute* and *relative*, they did so to guard the freedom of the Trinity and the contingency (contra pantheism and panentheism) of the creation.[98] This equally applies to the incarnation. The incarnation is contingent, not necessary to God's being. The Son's election, therefore, lies at the heart of a Nicene and Chalcedonian christology, that affirms the full divinity and humanity of Christ. The logical distinction between the *logos asarkos* and *logos incarnandus* highlights God's freedom and His love for fallen sinners: 'What is man that you are mindful of him, and the son of man that you care for him?' (Ps. 8:4).

But it seems that with his construction of election, Barth slights the humanity of Christ because he eternalizes it prior to the creation – there is no place for a genuine historical natural order. Christ's humanity is bound with Adam's historical and real existence. By making the creation merely the external aspect of the covenant of grace, Barth reduces Adam to non-being.[99] Adam only functions as a literary a-historical precursor to Christ and as a mythic type of humanity in Barth's exegesis of Romans 5:12-19.[100] As John Murray notes, 'It cannot be too plainly said that if we adopt this construction of Romans 5:12-19 we must abandon exegesis.'[101] In other words, if Adam is merely mythological, then Romans

---

98. Cf. Jones, *Humanity of Christ*, 72-73.

99. Barth, CD III/1: 42-228; Horton, 'Covenant, Election, and Incarnation,' 117; Berkouwer, *Triumph of Grace*, 85-86.

100. Barth, CD III/1: 81, 92, 252-53; idem, *Christ and Adam: Man and Humanity in Romans 5*, trans. T. A. Smail (1956; Eugene: Wipf & Stock, 2004), 17, 23, 34-35, 46; cf. John Webster, *Barth's Moral Theology: Human Action in Barth's Thought* (1998; London: T & T Clark, 2004), 73.

101. John Murray, 'Appendix D: Karl Barth on Romans 5,' in *The Epistle to the Romans*, NICNT (Grand Rapids: Eerdmans, 1968), 386.

5:12-19 is meaningless. By denying the historicity of Adam, Barth ultimately undercuts the genuine humanity of Christ. According to Reformed Orthodoxy, one of the purposes of positing the natural realm first is to demonstrate that Adam, representative of all humanity, was genuinely capable of offering his covenant faithfulness (*hesed*), his love to the Father. Humanity's failure to love must be real so that Christ's obedience stands out all the more. The decree was no hindrance to Adam's failure to love and obey.

The Westminster Confession, for example, maintains that, by the decree 'God is not the author of sin, nor is violence offered to the will of creatures; nor is the liberty or contingency of second causes taken away, but rather established' (III.i). Correlatively, the Confession affirms: 'Man in his state of innocency, had freedom, and power to will and to do that which was good and well pleasing to God' (IX.ii).[102] The implications of Adam's genuine freedom and ability are not, as Barth accuses, to carve out a natural Christ-less platform by which humanity might lay hold of eternal life. Rather, it establishes the inherent goodness of the creation and maintains the genuine humanity of the incarnate Son. Jesus Christ, the last Adam, offered His voluntary, free, and contingent *hesed* to His heavenly Father, whether in His commitment to be covenant surety in the *pactum salutis*, or as the God-man in its execution in redemptive history in the covenant of grace.

Barth's doctrine of election, therefore, undercuts the humanity of Christ – he leaves no room for Paul's structure for history: 'But it is not the spiritual that is first but the natural, and then the spiritual' (1 Cor. 15:46). Stated more simply, the path to heaven runs through the earth.[103] By eliminating the natural order and

---

102. Cf. Willem J. van Asselt, et al., eds., *Reformed Thought on Freedom: The Concept of Free Choice in Early Modern Reformed Theology* (Grand Rapids: Baker, 2010).

103. This statement comes from my colleague, Bryan Estelle.

Adam with it, Barth collapses history into eternity and veers into the arms of Eutyches (ca. 375-454) and monophysitism. As Mike Higton notes, regarding his christology in volume II/2, Barth does not provide 'the resources we need if we are to say that Jesus of Nazareth's complex, contingent, particular, creaturely humanity, which is utterly and entirely not-God, is nevertheless united with God so as to become God's humanity.'[104]

Christ as covenant surety

The correlate of the Son's election is that He is chosen by the Father to serve as covenant surety. As covenant surety the Son pledges to stand in the gap for sinners who have broken God's covenant. The tendency might be, however, to prioritize the passive obedience of Christ because He repairs the breach between God and fallen sinners. As important as it is that Christ offers satisfaction for sins, the Son's appointment must take into account the priority of eschatology to soteriology. This appears prominently in the covenant of works. According to the terms of the covenant of works Adam was supposed to obey his covenant Lord and pass probation, at which point he would have been permitted to eat from the tree of life, thus securing eternal life

---

104. Mike Higton, *Christ, Providence and History: Hans W. Frei's Public Theology* (London: T & T Clark, 2004), 60, also 5-6, 39-64, esp. 54-59; cf. Bertrand Russell, *The Problems of Philosophy* (Radford: Wilder Publications, 2008), 89-90; Wolfhart Pannenberg, *Systematic Theology*, vol. 2, trans. G. W. Bromiley (Grand Rapids: Eerdmans, 1994), 368 n. 127; Kuo-An Wu, 'The Concept of History in the Theology of Karl Barth,' (Ph. D. Diss., University of Edinburgh, 2011), 190-229, esp. 192-93, 196, 213, 217-19, 221-23; Jones, *Humanity of Christ*, 3. Once again, the question of Hegelian metaphysics raises its head regarding Barth's christology. Hunsinger notes that Barth maintains a Chalcedonian christology, but the reason he has been accused of compromising this creedal line is 'rooted mainly in a failure to appreciate that he employs a dialectical strategy of juxtaposition' (George Hunsinger, 'Karl Barth's Christology: Its basic Chalcedonian Character,' in *The Cambridge Companion to Karl Barth*, ed. John Webster [Cambridge: Cambridge University Press, 2000], 132).

for himself and his progeny. Adam was, to use older theological nomenclature, a 'public person.'[105] That is, he was the federal head for all of humanity. Moreover, there was no mediator between God and man – Adam stood alone. He should have relied upon the Spirit of God to obey and pass the probation. Adam failed, but prior to the entrance of sin into the world, there was an eschatological goal. Eschatology is the exponent of protology, not soteriology. Eschatology is older than soteriology, as it was on the scene of pre-redemptive history prior to it.[106] In fact, eschatology is 'the mother soil out of which the tree of the whole redemptive organism has sprung.'[107]

The Son, the last Adam, enters into history to redeem fallen sinners, but given the priority of eschatology to soteriology, this means that His active obedience takes priority to His passive obedience. Adam had to offer his active obedience to reach the eschatological goal but failed, hence Christ's active obedience takes priority over His passive obedience. To recognize the priority of His active obedience does not mean the passive is superfluous. Both are necessary but the active has priority. In terms of Vos's sphere of being versus the sphere of knowing, we encounter the need for Christ's passive obedience first because of the albatross of God's wrath, sin, guilt, and condemnation.[108] But in terms of the sphere of being, the active obedience takes priority, a point evident not only in the *pactum* but also in Christ's ministry. He

105. See, e.g., Edward Fisher, *The Marrow of Modern Divinity* (London: G. Calvert, 1645), 14, 60-61; Samuel Rutherford, *The Covenant of Life Opened; or, A Treatise on the Covenant of Grace* (Edinburgh: Robert Broun, 1655), II.ii (p. 234).

106. Geerhardus Vos, *The Pauline Eschatology* (1930; Phillipsburg: P & R, 1996), 325 n. 1; idem, *Biblical Theology*, 140.

107. Geerhardus Vos, *The Self-Disclosure of Jesus: The Modern Debate about the Messianic Consciousness* (1953; Phillipsburg: P & R, 1978), 21-22.

108. Vos, *Self-Disclosure*, 189-92.

had to be the sinless sacrifice, which means the culmination of His lifelong passive obedience in His crucifixion was predicated upon His active obedience, His perfect law-keeping. But His active obedience was not merely to qualify or establish His passive obedience, but was the Edenic prerequisite for attaining eschatological life before the entrance of sin and death into the world. As Paul writes, 'But it is not the spiritual that is first but the natural, and then the spiritual' (1 Cor. 15:46). The Father does not rewrite Adam's vocation but rather sends His Son to fulfill what Adam failed to do.[109] As Vos observes:

> That the Son, who as a divine Person stood above the law, placed Himself in His assumed nature under the law, that is to say, not only under the natural relationship under which man stands toward God, but under the relationship of the covenant of works, so that by active obedience He might merit eternal life. Considered in this light, the work of Christ was a fulfillment of what Adam had not fulfilled, a carrying out of the demand of the covenant of works. [110]

The *pactum* is the anchor or eternal foundation of the covenant of grace, that which establishes the Son's voluntary obedience to secure eternal life for those who are united to Him by the Father's divine election – to obey the Father's will in the power of the Spirit, to fulfill the law, and thereby to secure both eternal life and the forgiveness of sins. It is here in the decree of election where the *pactum*, covenant of grace, christology, and the active obedience meet.

---

109. N. T. Wright, *The New Testament and the People of God* (Philadelphia: Fortress, 1992), 262-64; idem, *The Resurrection of the Son of God* (Philadelphia: Fortress, 2004), 334, 336, 440.

110. Vos, *Dogmatics*, vol. 2, III.5.

Indeed, predestination unites the elect in the decree to Christ as covenant surety. If one denies election, then he must also deny the merit of Christ in both His active and passive obedience.[111] Christ's appointment as covenant surety and the imputation of His active and passive obedience, therefore, means that Christ's legal–forensic work takes precedence to its transformative aspects of the application of redemption.[112] The covenant of grace admits no other basis or foundation because no one else but the Son was appointed and elected as covenant surety. The question of when, precisely, the elect lay hold of the imputed righteousness of Christ is a matter to be addressed in the following chapter. This subject must be addressed because, as Part I revealed, it was a matter of debate among proponents of the *pactum*.

The root of eschatology

The last related doctrine is eschatology. As important as it is to distinguish the eternal decree from the consummation, we must nevertheless acknowledge their intimate connection. Christology is inherently eschatological. The kingdom and the last days arrive with the king. Hence, the Son's election and appointment as covenant surety contain the blueprint for the rest of redemptive history. The Son's election is the seed of the eschaton – a seed that grows into a massive tree.[113] Consequently, God ordains all of history to anticipate the advent of the Son. History is linear, not cyclical, in that it leans forward in eager anticipation of the revelation of the eschatological Son, the *last* Adam, the 'life-giving

---

111. Vos, *Dogmatics*, vol. 1, V.4c-d

112. Geerhardus Vos, 'The Alleged Legalism in Paul's Doctrine of Justification,' in *Redemptive History and Biblical Interpretation: The Shorter Writings of Geerhardus Vos*, ed. Richard B. Gaffin, Jr. (Phillipsburg: P & R, 1980), 384; Louis Berkhof, *Systematic Theology: New Combined Edition* (1932-38; Grand Rapids: Eerdmans, 1996), 452.

113. Vos, *Pauline Eschatology*, 1-41.

Spirit' (1 Cor. 15:45*). This means that all of history (pre- or post-fall) either anticipates (or typifies) the person and work of the last Adam and the eschaton or reveals the antitypical reality. Adam, God's son (Luke 3:38), therefore, is a type of Him who was to come (Rom. 5:14), and God placed Israel, His son (Exod. 4:22; Hosea 11:1), under the law. But both sons were unfaithful – they failed to obey, to love, and to demonstrate covenant faithfulness (*ḥesed*).

But Adam's and Israel's failure was not unforeseen. Rather, they were typically anticipatory of the elect Son, Jesus the Messiah, the one anointed by the Spirit who would offer His *ḥesed* to His heavenly Father and thus usher in the eschaton. The upshot of the election of the Son as covenant surety is that, *pace* Aquinas, predestination is not a subset of providence.[114] Rather, the inverse is true – providence is a subset of predestination, the election of the covenant surety and His confederated bride, the church. Divine providence moves at the impulse and heartbeat of the covenantally embedded decree of election.

Conclusion

The doctrine of predestination is one of the key elements of the *pactum salutis*, since it entails the election of the Son as covenant surety and His particular bride. The Lion of the Tribe of Judah cannot be tamed – as much as Barth wants to eliminate the particularity of election, this element cannot be sidelined by a metaphysical sleight of hand. The theme of particular election is simply too pervasive to dismiss. To say that Jacob is Esau

---

114. Aquinas, *Summa Theologica*, Ia q. 22 art. 1, Ia q. 23 art. 1; cf. W. J. Hankey, *God In Himself: Aquinas' Doctrine of God as Expounded in the Summa Theologiae* (Oxford: Oxford University Press, 1987), 19-36; Lee H. Yearly, 'St. Thomas Aquinas on Providence and Predestination,' *ATR* 49 (1967): 409.

and Esau is Jacob all but eliminates the specificity of the decree – it renders it meaningless. While all theologians engage in metaphysics, not all metaphysical statements are equal or valid. Metaphysical claims must be judged at the bar of Scripture. In this case, Barth's use of Hegelian dialectics is found wanting.

~:4:~

Imputation

Introduction

In historic iterations of the *pactum salutis* the doctrine of imputation lies close at hand. The Father appoints the Son as covenant surety, and as such, His representative obedience and substitutionary suffering remedy the fractured covenant of works. God imputes the Son's obedience to the elect. Such convictions and formulations were common within the sixteenth and seventeenth centuries. But with the onset of the Enlightenment and the rejection of the foundational pillars of theology, the obedience of the Son took on a quite different role within the scope of redemption. Friedrich Schleiermacher (1768-1834) once opined that just because Christ's opponents sought His life did not automatically mean that His death was required. Schleiermacher makes the case that when certain Greeks sought to speak with Him, Jesus delivered a discourse about His impending death (John 12:23-28), but: 'This is combined with a consciousness of a greater success of his work, but not with any idea that his death was necessary as an essential part of redemption in and for itself.'[1] Schleiermacher deemed Christ's obedience unto death superfluous. In more recent theology, however, Christ's obedience has taken on a renewed emphasis. For example, recent research has demonstrated that the theme of Christ's obedience is central to Hans Urs von Balthasar's (1905-88) entire theological project.[2] But contemporary theologians often do not attach the same significance to Christ's obedience that earlier generations did.

As central as Christ's obedience was to various versions of the *pactum salutis*, many of the common assumptions that underpinned the doctrine of imputation have been rejected. Theologians have doubted once commonly held presuppositions, such as federal representation and imputed guilt and righteousness.[3] Scholars have questioned whether texts once assumed to be about Jesus, such as Isaiah 53, are better explained by appealing to the nation of Israel or to the prophet (Deutero-) Isaiah as the suffering servant.[4] Biblical scholars go round and round chasing their tails trying to determine whether the suffering servant is corporate or individual. New Testament scholars also doubt whether Paul's use of the term λογίζομαι entails all that Reformed theologians have claimed. For example, concerning Romans 4:4-5, where one's 'faith is counted [λογίζεται] as righteousness,' N. T. Wright contends: 'Paul develops the bookkeeping metaphor in the direction of employment and wage-earning. This is the only time he uses this metaphorical field in all his discussions of justification, and we

1. Friedrich Schleiermacher, *The Life of Jesus*, ed. Jack C. Verheyden (1864; Philadelphia: Fortress, 1975), 384-85.

2. Daniel Paul Burns, 'So That Love May Be Safeguarded: The Nature, Form, and Function of Obedience as a Heuristic Device for the Theology of Hans Urs Von Balthasar' (Ph.D. Diss., Loyola University Chicago, 2011).

3. E.g., Dorothee Sölle, *Christ the Representative: An Essay in Theology After the 'Death of God'* (London: SCM Press Ltd., 1967).

4. R. N. Whybray, *Thanksgiving for a Liberated Prophet* (Sheffield: JSOT, 1978).

should not allow this unique and brief sidelight to become the dominant note, as it has in much post-Reformation discussion.'[5]

In contrast to recent treatments of Christ's obedience and the doctrine of imputation, this chapter presents a case for the basic soundness of the early modern Reformed doctrine of the imputation of Christ's active and passive obedience to fallen sinners. In particular, this chapter defends the thesis that Christ was elected and appointed as covenant surety, which means that He offers His representative obedience and is the sacrificial substitute for the elect, His bride. The *pactum salutis* is the all-important covenantal context in which these categories originate. As with the doctrine of predestination, the *pactum* connects the seemingly disparate elements of the Son's representative relationship to His confederated bride with His role as covenant surety. The Son pledges to secure the blessings of the covenant through His loving obedience to His Father, and He promises to be a substitute and to suffer the penalty of the broken covenant of works, the consequences of Adam's first sin.

This chapter defends this thesis by first surveying the state of the question, including the rejection of Christ's representative role, hyper-individualism, corporate readings of key New Testament texts, and excising legal–forensic categories in favor of ideas of deification and participation. Second, it presents evidence for the connections between the *pactum* and imputation primarily through the idea of the Son's appointment, role, and function as covenant surety, or ἔγγυος (Heb. 7:22). Though the term ἔγγυος occurs once, the idea of the one representing the many appears in numerous biblical narratives, such as Achan's sin at the battle of Ai (Josh. 7), David's sinful census of Israel (2 Sam. 24), and

5. N. T. Wright, *The Letter to the Romans: Introduction, Commentary, and Reflections*, NIB, vol. 10 (Nashville: Abingdon, 2002), 491.

the discussion of the Son of Man (Dan. 7). Third, the chapter explores the themes of covenant, representation, and obedience through an examination of Isaiah 53 and its use in the New Testament. Fourth, it addresses theological issues related to the rejection of imputation and why the doctrine must be maintained. Fifth, and finally, the chapter concludes with a few observations regarding the relationship between the *pactum* and the Son's imputed obedience.

State of the question

Traditional Reformed view

From the outset of the sixteenth century, Reformed theologians advocated a forensic doctrine of justification in contrast to the dispositional view formalized at the Council of Trent (1546).[6] By and large, the Reformed tradition adhered to the idea that Christ's active and passive obedience was imputed in the sinner's justification, though there were certainly exceptions to this rule.[7] By the time of High Orthodoxy (1630/40–1700), the idea was not only codified in the Westminster Confession of Faith but also coordinated with the *pactum salutis* in its Congregational version, the Savoy Declaration (1658). The Declaration states: 'It pleased God, in his eternal purpose, to choose and ordain the Lord Jesus his only-begotten Son, according to a covenant

---

6. E.g., Council of Trent, 'Decree on Justification,' Session 6, 13 January 1547, in *Creeds and Confessions of Faith in the Christian Tradition*, vol. 2, ed. Jaroslav Pelikan and Valerie Hotchkiss (New Haven: Yale University Press, 2003), 826-39; cf. Carl E. Maxcey, 'Double Justice, Diego Laynez, and the Council of Trent,' *CH* 48/3 (1979): 269-78; Jesus Olazarán, 'En el IV Centenario de un Voto Tridentio del Jesuita Alfonso Salmeron sobre la doble justitia,' *Estudios Eclesiasticos* 20 (1946): 211-40.

7. E.g., Heber Carlos De Campos, Jr., 'Johannes Piscator (1526-1625) and the Consequent Development of the Doctrine of the Imputation of Christ's Active Obedience' (Ph.D. Diss., Calvin Theological Seminary, 2011).

made between them both, to be the Mediator between God and man ... unto whom he did from all eternity give a people to be his seed, and to be by him in time redeemed, called, justified, sanctified, and glorified' (VIII.i). Savoy also declares that the elect are eventually justified in time through the imputation of 'Christ's active obedience to the whole law, and passive obedience in his death for their whole and sole righteousness' (XI.i).

The Declaration carefully balances the *pactum* and its relationship with history, by recognizing that though the triune God decrees to justify the elect, they are nevertheless 'not justified personally, until the Holy Spirit doth in due time actually apply Christ unto them' (XI.iv). Congregational theologians inserted the word *personally* to the statement as it originally appeared in the Westminster Confession, 'not justified, until the Holy Spirit doth in due time actually apply Christ unto them' (XI.i). Congregational theologians wanted to distinguish between the decree to justify, Christ's own personal justification, and the personal justification of the individual sinner. As evident in Part I, however, not all Reformed orthodox theologians were content to express the relationship between the *pactum* and justification in this manner. A number employed the distinction between *active justification*, the imputation of the Son's obedience in the *pactum*, and *passive justification*, the reception of the imputed obedience by faith in time.[8] Versions of this distinction also appear in the

8. E.g., Francis Turretin, *Institutes of Elenctic Theology*, ed. James T. Dennison, Jr., trans. Geroge Musgrave Giger (Phillipsburg: P & R, 1992-97), XVI.ix.11; Leonard Rijssen, *Compendium Theologiae Didactico-Elencticae* (Amsterdam: 1695), XIV (pp. 145-46); Johannes Marckius, *Compendium Theologiae Christianae Didactico-Elencticum* (1716; Amsterdam: 1749), XXII.xxiii, XXIV.iii; Bartholomäus Keckerman, *Systema S. S. Theologiae* (Hanau: 1602), III.vii.3; Johannes Heidegger, *Corpus Theologiae Christianae* (Tiguri: ex Officina Heideggeriana, 1732), XXII.lxxviii; cf. Heinrich Heppe, *Reformed Dogmatics: Set Out and Illustrated from the Sources*, trans. G. T. Thomson, ed. Ernst Bizer (London: George Allen & Unwin Ltd, 1950), 555-59.

formulations of Herman Bavinck (1854-1921), Geerhardus Vos (1862-1949), and Louis Berkhof (1873-1957).[9]

Kant, Schleiermacher, and Bultmann

With the onset of the Enlightenment, theologians placed unprecedented emphasis upon the individual in contrast to sixteenth- and seventeenth-century formulations. Reformed theologians bound individual and corporate categories together with their doctrines of election, covenant, and ecclesiology. And in early modern Reformed doctrine individuals based their epistemological convictions upon the *Deus dixit* of Scripture and the *regula fidei*, the historic teaching of Scripture as taught by the church, and through confessional documents individuals were part of larger corporate readings of Scripture. In the Enlightenment these pillars were razed and the *ego*, divorced from this corporate context, became supreme. This *Zeitgeist* is best captured in René Descartes's (1596-1650) famous aphorism, *Cogito ergo sum*, 'I think therefore I am.' No longer did the individual know God and the world around him because of the *Deus dixit* but because of a foundation built upon *ego*.

This radical Enlightenment individualization appears quite prominently in Immanuel Kant's (1724-1804) rejection of representation and, hence, imputation. Concerning the idea of original sin, what Kant terms *radical evil*, he opines:

> For this is no *transmissible* liability which can be made over to another like a financial indebtedness (where it is all one to the creditor whether the debtor himself pays the debt or whether some one else pays it for him); rather is it *the most personal of all debts*,

9. Herman Bavinck, *Reformed Dogmatics*, 4 vols., ed. John Bolt, trans. John Vriend (Grand Rapids: Baker, 2003-08), III:590; Louis Berkhof, *Systematic Theology: New Combined Edition* (Grand Rapids: Eerdmans, 1996), 517; Geerhardus Vos, *Dogmatiek*, 5 vols. (Grand Rapids: n. p., 1900), V.12 (vol. IV, pp. 22-23).

> namely a debt of sins, which only the culprit can bear and which no innocent person can assume even though he be magnanimous enough to wish to take it upon himself for the sake of another.[10]

Kant stripped any notion of representative obedience or suffering and, though he does not acknowledge it, removed the idea of covenant from the equation of redemption. The bud of Kant's radical individualism arguably flowered in the nineteenth century in the existential theology of Schleiermacher, who claimed that salvation was an acknowledgement of *das Gefühl*, or the feeling of absolute dependence upon God.[11] And as noted in the introduction, Schleiermacher believed Christ's obedience was superfluous.

In the twentieth century, Rudolf Bultmann (1884-1976) maintained that salvation was the individual's existential encounter with God, which is reflected in his understanding of Romans 5:12-21. Bultmann argues that Adam only opened the possibility of sin and death and that Christ only opens the possibility of life. A person can only become guilty by his own particular actions, not those of Adam.[12] From Kant, Schleiermacher, and Bultmann, the lone individual takes center stage. In such theological constructions there is little, if any, place for concepts of covenant and imputation, which are inherently corporate ideas. One must be bound to the covenant community and federal head in order to benefit from Christ's representative obedience.

---

10. Immanuel Kant, *Religion Within the Limits of Reason Alone*, trans. Theodore M. Greene and Hoyt H. Hudson (New York: Harper & Row, 1960), II.i (p. 66).

11. Friedrich Schleiermacher, *The Christian Faith*, ed. H. R. Mackintosh and J. S. Stewart (1830; London: T & T Clark, 1999), 1-12.

12. Rudolf Bultmann, *Theology of the New Testament*, 2 vols., trans. Kendrick Grobel (New York: Charles Scribner's Sons, 1951-55), I:252.

New Perspective on Paul

In the twentieth century there has been a backlash against this rampant individualism. Karl Barth (1886-1968) rejected Schleiermacher's and Bultmann's emphasis upon the individual and offered his own corporate emphasis by election in Christ as well as through participation, or union with Christ.[13] Within the New Testament guild, N. T. Wright has leveled critiques of Bultmann and the perceived connections between individualism and classic Reformation formulas of justification.[14] In this vein Wright rejects the idea of imputation and argues that it is a minor sidelight within the Pauline corpus, and receives undue attention in the hands of Reformed theologians. Rather than advocate what Martin Luther (1483-1546) and John Calvin (1509-64) once called the 'glorious exchange,' where God imputes the sins of the elect to Christ and His obedience to the elect by faith alone, Wright makes the case that union with Christ is the true Pauline category.[15] Other New Testament scholars such as James D. G. Dunn have argued that justification, and hence imputation, is but one of the many multifaceted but nevertheless interchangeable metaphors that Paul employs. Consequently, justification should not be given too much influence in the formulation of a biblical soteriology, which should instead center upon union with Christ.[16] Other New Testament

13. Adam Neder, *Participation in Christ: An Entry into Karl Barth's Church Dogmatics* (Louisville: Westminster John Knox, 2009).

14. E.g., N. T. Wright, *What Saint Paul Really Said: Was Paul of Tarsus the Real Founder of Christianity?* (Grand Rapids: Eerdmans, 1997), 14-15,113-34.

15. N. T. Wright, *Justification: God's Plan and Paul's Vision* (Downers Grove: InterVarsity Press, 2009), 135-36, 157-58, 232-33; cf., e.g., Martin Luther, *Lectures on Galatians*, in LW 26:132-33, 167-68; John Calvin, *Institutes of the Christian Religion*, trans. John Allen (Grand Rapids: Eerdmans, 1949), IV.xvii.2.

16. James D. G. Dunn, *The Theology of Paul the Apostle* (Grand Rapids: Eerdmans, 1998), 231.

scholars sympathetic to Wright and Dunn argue similarly for 'incorporated righteousness' rather than imputed righteousness.[17]

Hans Urs von Balthasar

Von Balthasar places heavy emphasis upon the obedience of Christ as an aspect of His procession as manifest in His temporal mission.[18] Obedience to the Father's will constitutes a chief element in both von Balthasar's christology and soteriology. Von Balthasar rejects Anselm's (1033-1109) satisfaction theory of the atonement, where Christ's action on behalf of sinners is governed by a concept of superabundant merit that He communicates to believers.[19] Von Balthasar rejects this theory because he believes that Christ's obedience must not be interpreted as the Father imposing a required act of penance upon the Son. Rather, in a fashion similar to arguments for the *pactum salutis*, von Balthasar contends that the Son's obedience finds its origin in the salvific decision made by the Trinity.[20] He explains the nature of the decision as follows:

> As for this eternal decision, however, it is not made by the Son in lonely isolation; it is always a triune decision in which the hierarchy

17. Michael F. Bird, 'Incorporated Righteousness: A Response to Recent Evangelical Discussion Concerning the Imputation of Christ's Righteousness in Justification,' *JETS* 47/2 (2004): 253-75; idem, 'Justification as Forensic Declaration and Covenant Membership: A *Via Media* Between Reformed and Revisionist Readings of Paul,' *TynB* 57/1 (2006): 109-30; idem, *The Saving Righteousness of God: Studies on Paul, Justification, and the New Perspective* (Milton Keynes: Paternoster, 2007), 60-87, 113-54; idem, 'Progressive Reformed View,' in *Justification: Five Views*, ed. James K. Beilby and Paul Rhodes Eddy (Downers Grove: InterVarsity Press, 2011), 145-52.

18. Hans Urs von Balthasar, *Theo-Drama: Theological Dramatic Theory*, 5 vols. (San Francisco: Ignatius Press, 1994), III:165-73.

19. St Anselm, *Why God Became Man*, in *Anselm of Canterbury: The Major Works*, ed. Brian Davies and G. R. Evans (Oxford: Oxford University Press, 1998), 260-356, esp. 268-69, 276-77, 283.

20. Von Balthasar, *Theo-Drama*, III:240-42.

> of the hypostatic processions is preserved, notwithstanding the consubstantiality and coeternity of the Persons. It is always in the Holy Spirit that the Son takes up the mission that comes from the Father. Thus the incarnate Son, in his freedom (which is now a human freedom too), does not embrace his own will as God primarily the Father's will, to which he has always consented.[21]

But unlike *pactum* formulations that recognize the Son's appointment as covenant surety, von Balthasar finds the concept of representation a biblical one but in need of recovery from mystical and juridical associations.[22]

Rather than conceive of Christ's mission in terms of representative obedience, the actions of the one on behalf of the many, von Balthasar argues that Christ's mission opens the 'acting area' (invoking his theme of dramatic theology) through His obedience and death.[23] In this way,

> As an earthly man, he is obedient to the Spirit; exalted, he breathes the Spirit into the world. So he can cause believers to share in both obeying the Spirit and communicating the Spirit, essential roles for members of the Church of Jesus. In this way the divine life, which is manifested to the world through the humanity of the Son, is also imparted to this world, in the community of believers called the 'Body of Christ,' to be lived and shared by it.[24]

Christ, therefore, is not the federal head of His body, though He does have a representative function. Rather, Christ trailblazes a path upon the stage of redemptive history, a path that allows others to follow, recapitulate, and re-enact Christ's obedience to

21. Von Balthasar, *Theo-Drama*, III:199.

22. Von Balthasar, *Theo-Drama*, III:245.

23. Von Balthasar, *Theo-Drama*, III:249.

24. Von Balthasar, *Theo-Drama*, III:258-59.

the Father. Christ 'is not only the main character but the model for all other actors and the one who gives them their own identity as characters.' Christ's representative role as the last Adam gives meaning to the entire drama and embodies humanity's dramatic context and relationship to itself and to God.[25]

In contrast to juridical or federal conceptions of Christ's representative work, based upon passages such as 2 Corinthians 5:21, *inter alia*, von Balthasar argues that Christ ontologically transfers us so that we might be reconciled to God. Von Balthasar invokes the doctrine of the covenant at this point because he recognizes that redemption has something to do with God's covenant righteousness.[26] But in a covenant, there is a twofold or bilateral relationship, give and take. Von Balthasar consequently rejects Luther's understanding of the 'glorious exchange' where the redeemed sinner looks to Christ by faith alone (*sola fide*) to lay hold of His representative obedience. Von Balthasar's chief critique is that this makes love involved only in the sanctification of the sinner, not in his justification. 'Artificially,' writes von Balthasar, 'but very deliberately, the unity of grace—which justifies *and* sanctifies—is torn asunder.'[27] Instead, we must understand that Christ has 'changed places' with sinners to free fallen humanity to be initiated into the divine life.[28]

Brief analysis

With the onset of the Enlightenment and the rise of the supremacy of the individual, theologians scuttled an important biblical category, namely, that of covenant. The category must be

25. Von Balthasar, *Theo-Drama*, III:201.

26. Von Balthasar, *Theo-Drama*, IV:242-43.

27. Von Balthasar, *Theo-Drama*, IV:290.

28. Von Balthasar, *Theo-Drama*, IV:317.

maintained and employed, if for no other reason than because we find it in the Bible. Theologically, the covenant situates the individual within the broader context of a corporate body. And although New Perspective scholars have given attention to the doctrine of the covenant, many have failed to see how it functions in terms of uniting the concepts of the one and the many.[29] With Enlightenment presuppositions of the autonomous individual, there is of course no category for representative obedience. But within the context of the covenant, one can act on behalf of the many. Moreover, in contrast to recent efforts to pit legal against relational categories, the previous chapters have demonstrated the close coordination between seemingly disparate concepts, such as father and son, and obedience and love, evident throughout the book of Deuteronomy. In other words, one need not pit legal against relational categories or somehow view imputation as a redundancy in light of the believer's union with Christ. Rather, there are legal relationships and legal aspects to our union with Christ. Not only does the doctrine of the covenant hold these different elements together, but this is especially the case when we coordinate covenant and the decree within the *pactum salutis*.

Covenant and imputation

The covenant concept is vital to understanding the nature of imputation. In the relationship between these two concepts, Christ's role as covenant surety is central. The one covenant surety acts on behalf of His confederated people. Hence, this section explores the idea of Christ's role as covenant surety and three key Old Testament texts that constitute some of the soil from which the concept arises: Achan's sin (Josh. 7), David's

---

29. E.g., N. T. Wright, *Climax of the Covenant: Christ and the Law in Pauline Theology* (Minneapolis: Fortress, 1991).

census (2 Sam. 24), and Daniel's son of man (Dan. 7). Imbedded throughout the Old Testament is the dynamic between the one and the many, the covenantally bound individual and the corporate body.

Covenant surety

A problem with much of the recent literature critical of the doctrine of imputation is that it focuses, almost exclusively, upon a few isolated Pauline texts. This trend also appears in literature that defends the doctrine.[30] As important as the Pauline corpus is to the New Testament and the whole of Scripture, such a narrow field of analysis undoubtedly leads to a myopic and thin understanding of the concept. A broader canonical approach is required, one that pays close attention to a number of key Old Testament texts and themes. In this respect, the apostle Paul is not innovating when he writes of imputed righteousness, but rather his statements are merely the tip of an exegetical iceberg. His brief but nevertheless theologically dense statements in Romans 4–5, 8, and 2 Corinthians 5 tap into massive subterranean Old Testament streams of revelation found chiefly in the Pentateuch and the prophets. To that end, the survey and

30. Ben C. Dunson, 'Do Bible Words Have Bible Meaning? Distinguishing Between Imputation as Word and Doctrine,' *WTJ* 75 (2013): 254-56. Critics of the doctrine include, e.g., Robert H. Gundry, 'The Nonimputation of Christ's Righteousness,' in *Justification: What's at Stake in the Current Debates*, ed. Mark Husbands and Daniel J. Treier (Downers Grove: InterVarsity Press, 2004), 17-45; N. T. Wright, 'On Becoming the Righteousness of God,' in N. T. Wright, *Pauline Perspectives: Essays on Paul, 1978-2013* (Minneapolis: Fortress, 2013), 68-76; Bird, 'Progressive Reformed View,' 145-52. Proponents of the doctrine include, e.g., D. A. Carson, 'The Vindication of Imputation: On Fields of Discourse and Semantic Fields,' in *Justification: What's at Stake in the Current Debates*, ed. Mark Husbands and Daniel J. Treier (Downers Grove: InterVarsity Press, 2004), 46-80; John Piper, *Counted Righteous in Christ: Should We Abandon the Imputation of Christ's Righteousness?* (Wheaton: Crossway, 2002); Brian Vickers, *Jesus' Blood and Righteousness: Paul's Theology of Imputation* (Wheaton: Crossway, 2006).

defense of imputation and its connections to the *pactum salutis* should begin with the Son's appointment as covenant surety, a concept mentioned in the New Testament that has roots in the Old Testament.

The primary text where the concept of the Son's surety appears is Hebrews 7:22, 'This makes Jesus the guarantor [ἔγγυος] of a better covenant.' Within the broader context of Hebrews, the author explains the superiority of Christ's priesthood to the Levitical order (Heb. 7:1-21). What, specifically, is an ἔγγυος, guarantor, or covenant surety? The term means to offer surety and guarantee that the legal terms of a covenant will be carried out. The term only appears in the New Testament in Hebrews 7:22, but its usage in extra-biblical literature confirms this definition.[31] We find that one can be surety for another person's life: 'Do not forget the kindness of your guarantor, for he has given his life for you' (Sirach 29:15). In another context, God's pledge, his ἔγγυος, brings victory in a battle (2 Maccabees 10:28).[32] Within the book of Hebrews, Christ offers Himself up (Heb. 7:27) and has fulfilled the typical priestly work through His own sacrifice and has entered the heavenly holy of holies to fulfill the covenant obligations on behalf of those whom He represents (Heb. 9:12).[33]

As demonstrated in Part II, the author of Hebrews explains that the Son was appointed covenant surety in eternity, which is

---

31. Herman Witsius argues the Old Testament counterpart to the ἔγγυος is the kinsman-redeemer, or גאל (Herman Witsius, *Economy of the Covenants Between God and Man*, 2 vols., trans. William Crookshank [1822; Escondido: Den Dulk Foundation, 1990], II.iv.4).

32. O. Becker, ἔγγυος, in *Dictionary of New Testament Theology*, vol. 1, ed. Colin Brown (Grand Rapids: Baker, 1971), 372; Herbert Preisker, ἔγγυος, in *Theological Dictionary of the New Testament*, vol. 2, ed. Gerhard Kittel (Grand Rapids: Eerdmans, 1964), 329.

33. Becker, ἔγγυος, 372.

evident in his citation of Psalm 110, one of several key texts for the *pactum salutis* (Heb. 1:13; 7:17, 21). In fact, the author links the concepts of the divine oath (Heb. 7:20) with the Son's role as covenant surety (Heb. 7:22) through comparative expressions, καθ' ὅσον ... κατὰ τοσοῦτο ('in so far as ... just so far ...').[34] Hence, the NAS, for example, renders Hebrews 7:20-22 in the following manner: '*And inasmuch* it was not without an oath (for they indeed became priests without an oath, but He with an oath through the One who said to Him, "The Lord has sworn and will not change His mind, 'You are a priest forever'"); *so much the more* also Jesus has become the guarantee of a better covenant' (emphasis).[35] The Son is the covenant surety because of this oath, because of this covenant between the Father and the Son. And if Deuteronomy is any indication, the surety must be a faithful son and obey the law – he must love the father. But in this particular instance, the covenant surety must not only fulfill the legal obligations of the covenant but also bear the consequences of its violation.

At this juncture the covenant concept is vital because apart from it the relationship between the individual and the group, or the one and the many, collapses for lack of ligaments to hold the disparate parts of the body together. The author of Hebrews does not introduce a new concept but employs categories long present in Israel's covenant past, evident by his engagement with the Levitical priesthood, Psalm 110 and the Davidic priest-king, and the category of covenant. The individual and the group do not exist in antithesis, since the individual could not exist apart from the group and the group cannot exist apart from individuals. In fact, throughout Scripture we find the individual–corporate

34. William L. Lane, *Hebrews 1-8*, WBC, vol. 47a (Dallas: Word, 1991), 175.

35. Cf. KJV, NKJ, NLT-SE, NIV.

dynamic scattered throughout.[36] Each of the three forthcoming examples deserves significant exposition but for the sake of space I simply draw the reader's attention to the principle.

Achan's sin

When Israel entered the Promised Land the conquest was brought to a screeching halt due to the sin of one individual. The individual–corporate dynamic appears in the opening verse of the narrative account: 'But the people of Israel broke faith in regard to the devoted things, for Achan the son of Carmi, the son of Zabdi, the son of Zerah, of the tribe of Judah, took some of the devoted things. And the anger of the LORD burned against the people of Israel' (Josh. 7:1). The text states that the people (lit. *sons*) of Israel committed a breach of that which was holy – they committed a מעל (*maal*; cf. Lev. 5:15) by taking what had been placed under the ban חרם (*herem*; cf. Josh. 6:17-19). The verse opens with the sons of Israel, focuses upon the act of one person, and then concludes with all of Israel suffering as a result of the actions of this one person. Moreover, the fact that the narrative provides Achan's genealogy also suggests corporate guilt despite the actions of a lone individual.[37] This

36. H. Wheeler Robinson, *Corporate Personality in Ancient Israel* (Philadelphia: Fortress, 1964), 21-22. Though Robinson introduces the concept of'corporate personality,' a weakness in his overall thesis, his observations concerning the dynamic between the individual and corporate categories are valid (cf. J. W. Rogerson,'The Hebrew Conception of Corporate Personality,' *JTS* 21 [1970]: 1-16; Aubrey R. Johnson, *The One and the Many in the Israelite Conception of God* [Cardiff: University of Wales Press, 1961]; E. Earle Ellis, *Pauline Theology: Ministry and Society* [Grand Rapids: Eerdmans, 1989], 8-10; Russell Phillip Shedd, *Man in Community: A Study of St. Paul's Application of Old Testament and Early Jewish Conceptions of Human Solidarity* [Grand Rapids: Eerdmans, 1964], 3-41). Another important recent study is, Joel K. Kaminsky, *Corporate Responsibility in the Hebrew Bible* (Sheffield: Sheffield Academic Press, 1995), 1-66.

37. Richard S. Hess, *Joshua: An Introduction and Commentary*, TOTC (Downers Grove: InterVarsity Press, 1996), 143-44.

text pulsates with the individual–corporate dynamic, evident in Israel's corporate solidarity, and hence its corporate guilt, as well as specifically naming Achan as the one who perpetrated the *maal*.[38] Achan as an individual was covenantally bound to Israel and, in this particular case, his breach of covenant fidelity became representative disobedience for all of Israel – all of Israel was covenantally, and hence legally, bound to Achan.[39]

David's census

Another occurrence of the individual–corporate dynamic occurs in David's sinful census of Israel (2 Sam. 24; cf. 1 Chron. 21). Against the advice of Joab, the commander of his armies, David proceeded with a census of Israel's armies in an effort to measure the nation's might (2 Sam. 24:3; cf. 1 Sam. 8:11-19; 14:6).[40] David was subsequently conscience-stricken, repented of his sin, and sought forgiveness from the Lord (2 Sam. 24:10). When David received a response to his entreaty, he discovered that God would give him one of three options: three months of famine, three months of fleeing from his enemies, or three days of plague in the land (2 Sam. 24:12). David chose the third option and 70,000 Israelites perished. When David saw the messenger of the Lord striking down the people, he responded: 'I have sinned; I, the shepherd, have done wrong. These are but sheep. What have they done? Let your hand fall on me and my family' (2 Sam. 24:17).

38. Marten H. Woudstra, *The Book of Joshua*, NICOT (Grand Rapids: Eerdmans, 1981), 120-21.

39. Important to note is that the individual–corporate dynamic at this point is earthly, typically illustrative, and not eternal. Only Adam and Christ are federal heads with eternal consequences (cf. Jer. 31:29-30; Ezek. 18:2-3, 20). I am grateful to Mike Allen for encouraging me to point this out.

40. Cf. Kyle R. Greenwood, 'Labor Pains: The Relationship between David's Census and Corvée Labor,' *BBR* 20/4 (2010): 467-78; Shimon Bakon, 'David's Sin: Counting the People,' *Jewish Bible Quarterly* 41/1 (2013): 53-54.

The text is clear – David the lone individual ordered the census and the nation as a whole suffered the consequences of his representative disobedience. In this particular case, David, unlike Achan, was the king, the earthly covenantal head of the nation. His individual actions had corporate implications. This is true not only in his disobedience but also in his quest for corporate forgiveness. David was told to build an altar to the Lord 'that the plague on the people may be stopped' (2 Sam. 24:21). After David paid fifty shekels for the oxen and altar site, he sacrificed burnt and fellowship offerings, at which point 'the LORD answered his prayer in behalf of the land, and the plague on Israel was stopped' (2 Sam. 24:25). We find, then, the corporate solidarity of Israel with her king – his sin brings their punishment and his repentance yields their healing.[41] A parting observation regarding David's census and sacrifice is in order – the location of his sacrifice became the future site of the Solomonic temple. In other words, David's action, seeking forgiveness, blankets David and the corporate body, and this all occurs at the site of the typical temple, which points forward to the antitypical reality of Christ.[42]

Daniel's son of man

Of the many titles that the Scriptures ascribe to Jesus, the most common is 'son of man,' an ascription that has roots in Daniel 7, among other texts (cf., e.g., Ps. 8; Gen. 1:26-28). Within the heart of Daniel's angst-inducing vision the prophet inquires about its meaning and is told: 'The saints of the Most High shall receive

41. Bruce Waltke, *An Old Testament Theology: An Exegetical, Canonical, and Thematic Approach* (Grand Rapids: Zondervan, 2007), 677-78; cf. Joshua J. Adler, 'David's Last Sin: Was it the Census?' *Jewish Bible Quarterly* 23/2 (1995): 91-95; Raymond Dillard, 'David's Census,' in *Through Christ's Word: A Festschrift for Dr. Philip E. Hughes* (Phillipsburg: P & R, 1985), 104-06.

42. Dillard, 'David's Census,' 106-07.

the kingdom and possess the kingdom forever, forever and ever' (Dan. 7:18). The immediate reference is clearly to multiple people, the 'saints' (cf. Dan 7:22, 27). Some have therefore concluded that references to the Son of Man are corporate.[43] The individual beasts in Daniel's vision, for example, refer to nations, not individuals. Thus, they claim, the Son of Man title is a designation for Israel, for the people of God. But within the context of this vision, these beasts, first and foremost, represent kings, who in turn represent nations. In other words, efforts to swing the pendulum too hard in one direction or the other, individual versus corporate, fail to deal adequately with the particulars of the text. In Daniel's vision the references to the Son of Man have in view an individual who is the representative for the corporate group.[44]

In this case, that the Son of Man refers to one individual is evident in the fact that He enters the scene with the clouds of heaven. In the Old Testament the only one who rides on the clouds is Yahweh. Hence, the Son of Man cannot be a reference to a community of people but to a divine figure, who receives kingly authority to rule over the creation.[45] Jesus confirms this connection during His interrogation before the religious leaders – Jesus is the Son of Man that the prophet saw in his vision (cf. Matt. 24:30; 26:64; Mark 13:26; 14:62; Luke 21:27; Rev. 14:14). Hence, within the broader scope of Daniel 7, the Son of Man is the Messiah, the one to whom Yahweh gave a kingdom, authority, and power, and who reigns and represents the saints,

---

43. See, e.g., C. H. Dodd, *According to the Scriptures: The Sub-Structure of New Testament Theology* (London: Nisbet & Co, Ltd., 1952), 117-19.

44. G. K. Beale, *A New Testament Biblical Theology: The Unfolding of the Old Testament in the New* (Grand Rapids: Baker, 2011), 394-95; R. T. France, *Jesus and the Old Testament: His Application of Old Testament Passages to Himself and His Mission* (Vancouver: Regent College Publishing, 1998), 169-71.

45. Beale, *Biblical Theology*, 396.

those who 'receive the kingdom and possess the kingdom forever' (Dan. 7:18). The kingdom of God, of course, is a covenantal reality, evident in numerous places throughout the Old and New Testaments, and once again the covenant is the context that binds the king, the Son of Man, to His people, the saints.

One element not disclosed in Daniel's vision, however, is the precise manner by which the Son of Man accomplishes His mission. In particular, Mark's Gospel provides the link between the Son of Man's rule and the means by which He accomplishes His mission: 'For even the Son of Man came not to be served but to serve, and to give his life as a ransom for many' (10:45). This text links the Son of Man with elements that arise from Isaiah 53 and the suffering servant, the one who intervenes on behalf of the many.[46]

Isaiah 53 and the suffering servant

Background

Isaiah 53 is one of the most famous passages in the Old Testament, and over the centuries the church has asked many questions about this text and its significance. Who, for example, is the suffering servant, and what specifically does he accomplish by his suffering?[47] In addition to these questions there has been

---

46. On the connections between Mark 10:45 and Isaiah 53, see France, *Jesus and the Old Testament*, 116-23; Seyoon Kim, *The Son of Man as the Son of God* (Grand Rapids: Eerdmans, 1983), 38-60.

47. Within the New Testament guild, specifically within German circles, there is debate regarding the differences between place taking (*Stellvertretung*) and exclusive-place taking (*exkludierende Stellvertretung*). The former idea argues that Jesus is representative for His people, but not a substitute. The latter idea is that Christ is the representative and substitute, i.e., vicarious representative. For a survey of the literature and adherents to the two positions, see David P. Bailey, 'Concepts of *Stellvertretung* in the Interpretation of Isaiah 53,' and idem, 'The Suffering Servant: Recent Tübingen Scholarship on Isaiah 53,' in *Jesus and the Suffering Servant: Isaiah 53 and Christian*

significant debate over the authorship of the book of Isaiah. Are there one, two, or three different authors, or perhaps different prophetic schools? Was the book written over a protracted period of time well past the lifetime of the so-called proto-Isaiah? Critical scholars typically posit breaks between Isaiah 1–39, 40–55, and 56–66, labeling these sections as Isaiah, deutero-Isaiah, and trito-Isaiah respectively.[48] Space prohibits a thorough examination of these issues, nevertheless there is good reason to take the book of Isaiah as a whole, written by one author. There is no indication from the many New Testament references to Isaiah that it was written by multiple authors, and the oldest copies of Isaiah present one continuous undivided book. There is no manuscript evidence to suggest multiple authors.[49] The unity of Isaiah has implications, not merely for authorship, but also for the intra-textual connections between the various sections of the book.

In the opening of the book, the prophet portrays the coming glory of Zion in Davidic terms (Isa. 1:26), a theme that emerges in chapters 7–11 (e.g., 7:14, 9:1-7; 11:1-9). The coming king will rule over a universal empire (Isa. 14–16) that he creates in the

---

Origins, ed. William H. Bellinger, Jr., and William R. Farmer (Eugene: Wipf & Stock, 1998), 223-50, 251-59.

48. On the history of the interpretation of Isaiah, cf. Christopher R. North, *The Suffering Servant in Deutero-Isaiah: An Historical Critical Study*, 2nd ed. (Oxford: Oxford University Press, 1969), 1-119; H. H. Rowley, 'The Servant of the Lord in the Light of Three Decades of Criticism,' in *The Servant of the Lord and other Essays on the Old Testament*, 2nd ed. (Oxford: Basil Blackwell, 1965), 1-60; Antti Laato, *Who Is the Servant of the Lord? Jewish and Christian Interpretations on Isaiah 53: From Antiquity to the Middle Ages* (Winona Lake: Eisenbrauns, 2012), 1-48, 259-80, 307-82.

49. J. Alec Motyer, *Isaiah: An Introduction and Commentary*, TOTC (Downers Grove: InterVarsity Press, 1999), 27-35; idem, *The Prophecy of Isaiah: An Introduction and Commentary* (Downers Grove: InterVarsity Press, 1993), 25-32; Oswald T. Allis, *The Unity of Isaiah: A Study in Prophecy* (Eugene: Wipf & Stock, 2000); Rachel Margalioth, *The Indivisible Isaiah: Evidence for the Single Authorship of the Prophetic Book* (New York: Sura Institute for Research, 1964).

midst of the unbelieving world. This conflict comes to a climax in the world's efforts to exist without God (Isa. 24:10) and the city of the king, the city of salvation (Isa. 26:1). These broader themes echo elements that appear in earlier portions of the Scriptures, such as the conflict between the rulers of the earth and the Lord's Anointed (Ps. 2). In chapters 28–37 the prophet deals with issues pertaining to his own immediate historical context, specifically as it relates to the then world superpowers of Egypt and Assyria. Would the southern kingdom of Judah and King Hezekiah seek shelter in Yahweh or in the fleeting blanket of protection from Merodach-Baladan (Isa. 39:1-4)? God would use earthly forces to chastise His people (Isa. 39:5-7; 42:18-25) and send them into exile, but in the end His mercy would prevail. Cyrus, a foreshadow of the Messiah, would restore them to Jerusalem (44:28; 45:1-3; 48:20-22). But most importantly, Isaiah prophesies of the Servant of the Lord, the redeemer who would restore the people back to God and bear their sins (Isa. 49:5-6; 53:8-12).[50] Within the broader scope of the prophecy, we must connect the coming Davidic king with the suffering servant – they are not two different figures but different images of the one Messiah.[51]

The unity of the book, therefore, links the two concepts (the kingly and priestly figures), and provides the broader context for Isaiah 53.[52] The links between the kingly and priestly figures are especially evident within the context of the four servant songs,

50. Motyer, *Isaiah*, 15-17.

51. R. E. Clements, 'Isaiah 53 and the Restoration of Israel,' in *Jesus and the Suffering Servant: Isaiah 53 and Christian Origins*, ed. William H. Bellinger, Jr. and William H. Farmer (Eugene: Wipf & Stock, 1998), 44-47, 54.

52. Richard Schultz, 'The King in the Book of Isaiah,' in *The Lord's Anointed: Interpretation of Old Testament Messianic Texts*, ed. Philip E. Satterthwaite, Richard S. Hess, and Gordon J. Wenham (Eugene: Wipf & Stock, 1995), 155-64.

where we find Isaiah 53 (Isa. 42:1-4; 49:1-6; 50:4-9; 52:13–53:12).[53] In the first song, Yahweh indicates that the servant is His chosen Spirit-anointed individual who would 'bring forth justice to the nations' (Isa. 42:1), which is kingly imagery. The second song identifies the servant as the one who would make Israel a light to the nations and return Israel to the Lord (Isa. 49:6). In terms of the prophesied exile, Isaiah indicates that the servant will break the grip of the Deuteronomic law, the impelling cause and legal ground of Israel's exile from the Promised Land. The third song describes the rejection and persecution of the servant and, in terms that echo Psalm 40:7-9 (cf. Heb. 10:7-10) and the 'opened ear' (Isa. 50:5), the servant nevertheless renders his obedience to Yahweh.[54] These themes all culminate in the fourth song, which presents the servant as the one who permanently breaks the claim of Deuteronomic law and ends the exile. Within the broader scope of the book, the servant not only ends the exile but he also ushers in the eschaton, the new heavens and earth. Recognizing the unity of the book of Isaiah, therefore, contextualizes the fourth servant song. But what, specifically, does the fourth song state and how does it relate to the *pactum salutis* and imputation?

The fourth servant song

Space does not permit a verse-by-verse exegesis of the fourth servant song. Instead, we will focus on chief elements within the song that highlight connections between the *pactum* and imputation. For centuries scholars have noted the suffering that the servant endures in the fourth song: 'He was oppressed, and he was afflicted, yet he

---

53. Note, though the fourth servant song covers Isaiah 52:13–53:12, I refer to this passage as Isaiah 53.

54. Derek Kidner, *Psalms 1-72: An Introduction and Commentary*, TOTC (Downers Grove: InterVarsity Press, 1973), 159; William Lane, *Hebrews 9-13*, WBC, vol. 47b (Dallas: Word, 1997), 262-63.

opened not his mouth; like a lamb that is led to the slaughter, and like a sheep that before its shearers is silent, so he opened not his mouth' (Isa. 53:7). But opinions are divided regarding a number of statements in Isaiah 53:10, chiefly, 'Yet it was the will of the LORD to crush him.' The impression one gets is that Yahweh delightfully submits His servant to suffering apart from His consent (e.g., KJV, NKJ, 'It pleased the LORD to bruise him,' cf. NAS). But a number of key factors in verse 10 point to the *pactum salutis*.

First, some English translations render the Hebrew term חפץ as 'will' (so ESV, NIV, TNIV, RSV, NRSV), which begins to approach what the term denotes but does not entirely reflect its meaning. The term חפץ is better translated as 'plan.' The NLT-SE reflects this meaning of the term when it offers the following translation: 'But it was the LORD's good plan to crush him and cause him grief' (cf. Eph. 1:4, 11). But this plan was not something that was arbitrarily foisted upon the servant, for the servant willingly carried out Yahweh's plan. Commentators note that Isaiah 53:12 emphasizes the servant's consent to Yahweh's 'good plan' by its repeated use of the third person personal pronoun, הוא, 'Because *he* poured out *his* soul to death and was numbered with the transgressors; yet *he* bore the sin of many and makes intercession for the transgressors.' The servant willingly carried out Yahweh's plan.[55] From Isaiah's point of view, these events had not yet transpired, yet he reports them as accomplished facts.[56]

55. Hermann Spieckermann, 'The Conception and Prehistory of the Idea of Vicarious Suffering in the Old Testament,' in *The Suffering Servant: Isaiah 53 in Jewish and Christian Sources*, ed. Bernd Janowski and Peter Stuhlmacher, trans. Daniel P. Bailey (1996; Grand Rapids: Eerdmans, 2004), 6; Bernd Janowski, 'He Bore Our Sins: Isaiah 53 and the Drama of Taking Another's Place,' in *Suffering Servant*, 64-65; Otfried Hoffius, 'The Fourth Servant Song in the New Testament Letters,' in *Suffering Servant*, 167.

56. Contra Whybray, *Thanksgiving*, 59, 61; cf. Rowley, 'Servant of the Lord,' 54-55.

The question naturally arises: When did Yahweh and the servant enter upon this agreement?

My contention is that the *pactum salutis* best explains this agreement, this covenant. Within the *pactum* the Father appoints the Son as covenant surety, who fulfills the legal requirements of the covenant. Confirmation of this conclusion comes not only from the interconnected web of texts that constitute the exegetical foundation of the *pactum* (e.g., Ps. 2:7; 89; 110:1; 2 Sam. 7:14; Zech 6:13; Eph. 1:1-11; 2 Tim. 1:8-9) but also from Christ's invocation of the covenant concept in the Lucan account of the Last Supper. Christ tells His gathered disciples: 'I covenant to you, as my Father covenanted to me, a kingdom' (Luke 22:29*). Within this context Christ invokes the words of Isaiah 53:12, 'For I tell you that this Scripture must be fulfilled in me: "And he was numbered with the transgressors." For what is written about me has its fulfillment' (Luke 22:37).[57] That Christ connects His own ministry with the fulfillment of Isaiah 53 and with the Father covenanting a kingdom to Him indicates that the *pactum* as a doctrine has sufficient exegetical warrant. This covenant is distinct from the one that Christ initiates with His disciples. Within the *pactum* the Father appoints the Son as covenant surety, but what specifically does the Son accomplish in this role and how does it relate to imputation?

Isaiah states that the servant would be an 'offering for guilt' (אשם). This is a somewhat unique category of offering within Israel's sacrificial system. The term occurs in several places in the Levitical code, but most notably in Leviticus 5:17-19, which treats unconscious violations against Yahweh's commands, and

57. Darrell L. Bock, *Luke 9:51-24:53*, BECNT (Grand Rapids: Baker, 1996), 1747-49; G. K. Beale and D. A. Carson, eds., *Commentary on the New Testament Use of the Old Testament* (Grand Rapids: Baker, 2007), 384-89.

in 6:1-7 (MT 5:20-26), instructions to make amends for violated oaths. At first glance such sins may not seem immediately relevant to Isaiah's context and the servant's mission – to break the claim of the law, offer an אשם, and somehow end the exile. How does this concept connect to imputation, the *pactum*, and Christ's role as covenant surety? Briefly, an אשם was a multifaceted remedy for breaches of the covenant that were committed specifically against Yahweh. The אשם was a remedy for a *maal*, or for violating the sanctity of anything that Yahweh designated as holy (Lev. 5:15; 6:2; Num. 5:6; Ezra 10:10, 19).[58] In fact, this was the nature of Achan's sin – he committed a *maal* by taking booty that was placed under the ban (Josh. 7:1ff; 22:20; 1 Chron. 2:7).[59]

A *maal* was a significant breach of the covenant that required exile from the community, or from that which was holy. It is a sin specifically against God (cf. Num. 5:6).[60] In Achan's case, his *maal* required the death of him and his family because he broke the covenant.[61] When Miriam challenged Moses' leadership, she committed a *maal* and was therefore struck with leprosy and exiled from the camp (cf. Num. 5:5-7; 12:1-16; Lev. 14:12, 21).[62] Isaiah invokes the term אשם to convey the idea that Israel had breached the covenant and desecrated the sanctity of the land and Yahweh's holiness. This required their expulsion from the land, which contained God's dwelling place, the temple (cf.

58. Jacob Milgrom, *Cult and Conscience: the ASHAM and the Priestly Doctrine of Repentance* (Leiden: Brill, 1976), 7, 13, 16, 20-21, 125; cf. idem, *Leviticus 1-16: A New Translation with Introduction and Commentary* (New York: Doubleday, 1991), 339-45.

59. Milgrom, *Cult and Conscience*, 18; idem, *Leviticus 1-16*, 345-56.

60. Milgrom, *Leviticus 1-16*, 345.

61. Kaminsky, *Corporate Responsibility*, 92.

62. Milgrom, *Cult and Conscience*, 80.

2 Chron. 36:14-21).[63] But in this case, the nation's *maal* is repaired, not by a vicarious animal substitute (e.g., Lev. 5:15-17), but by the servant. That Isaiah invokes the category of אשם means that Israel has breached the covenant, they have committed a *maal*. And now, the servant brings reconciliation as covenant surety. The servant stands in the gap and reconciles Yahweh to the covenantally unfaithful Israelites. The one servant acts as covenant surety for the many confederated individuals.

In this respect the individual–corporate dynamic appears. The individual servant suffers, as 'he poured out his soul to death and was numbered with the transgressors; yet he bore the sin of many, and makes intercession for the transgressors' (Isa. 53:12). The servant alone poured out his soul unto death, and he alone bore the sin of the רבים ('many'), for the פשעים ('transgressors'). The one and the many dynamic is operative in the fourth song, a point confirmed by Christ's own invocation of this language. Arguably alluding to the third and fourth servant songs, Christ tells His disciples: 'For even the Son of Man came not to be served but to serve, and to give his life as a ransom for many' (Mark 10:45). Here Christ, the one, offers His life as a ransom for the many. Moreover, He characterizes His sacrificial activity in Isaianic servant-terms. Jesus serves, He does not come to be served (cf. Luke 22:27).[64] Furthermore, as noted above,

---

63. Richard E. Averbeck, 'Christian Interpretations of Isaiah 53,' in *The Gospel According to Isaiah 53: Encountering the Suffering Servant in Jewish and Christian Theology*, ed. Darrell L. Bock and Mitch Glaser (Grand Rapids: Kregel, 2012), 48-58; Milgrom, *Leviticus 1-16*, 346, 356; William Johnstone, 'Guilt and Atonement: The Theme of 1 and 2 Chronicles,' in *A Word In Season: Essays in Honor of William McKane*, ed. James D. Martin and Philip R. Davies (Sheffield: JSOT, 1986), 113-38, esp. 117, 119, 121, 124-25; idem, 'The Use of Leviticus in Chronicles,' in *Reading Leviticus: A Conversation with Mary Douglas*, ed. John F. A. Sawyer (Sheffield: Sheffield Academic Press, 1996), 243-55.

64. Scholars are divided as to whether Jesus consciously invoked the fourth servant song in Mark 10:45. For those against the idea, see Morna Hooker, *Jesus and the Servant:*

Christ invokes the title of the Son of Man, which alludes to Daniel 7 and the corporate solidarity that exists between the Messiah and His people. This individual–corporate dynamic is simply an extension of God's election of His chosen servant, His appointment of the Son as covenant surety, and the election of His body, all of which is bound within the concept of the covenant – one intra-trinitarian covenant that establishes the Son's role as mediator and surety, and a connected but nevertheless distinct covenant that constitutes the context for the redemption of the elect. In traditional dogmatic categories, we find the link between the covenants of redemption and grace.

But what of imputation? The first important element of exegetical data appears in the latter half of Isaiah 53:12, 'He bore [נשא] the sin of many, and makes intercession for the transgressors.' This language hearkens back to the protocols from the Day of Atonement in Leviticus 16 where the high priest placed his hands upon the scapegoat and transferred Israel's sins to the sacrificial animal (Lev. 16:22).[65] The

---

The Influence of the Servant Concept of Deutero-Isaiah in the New Testament (London: SPCK, 1959), 74-79; idem, 'Did the Use of Isaiah 53 to Interpret His Mission Begin with Jesus?' in *Jesus and the Suffering Servant*, 88-103; Whybray, *Thanksgiving*, 72-75; Laato, *Servant of the Lord*, 192. Scholars who recognize Christ's self-conscious appeal to Isaiah 53 in Mark 10:45 include, Otto Betz, 'Jesus and Isaiah 53,' in *Jesus and the Suffering Servant*, 83-87; Mikeal C. Parsons, 'Isaiah 53 in Acts 8: A Reply to Professor Morna Hooker,' in *Jesus and the Suffering Servant*, 104-19; Rikki E. Watts, 'Jesus' Death, Isaiah 53, and Mark 10:45: A Crux Revisited,' in *Jesus and the Suffering Servant*, 125-51; N. T. Wright, 'The Servant and Jesus: The Relevance of the Colloquy for the Current Quest for Jesus,' in *Jesus and the Suffering Servant*, 281-98; Peter Stuhlmacher, 'Isaiah 53 in the Gospels and Acts,' in *The Suffering Servant: Isaiah 53 in Jewish and Christian Sources*, ed. Bernd Janowski and Peter Stuhlmacher (Grand Rapids: Eerdmans, 2004), 153-53; France, *Jesus and the Old Testament*, 116-23; Kim, *Son of Man*, 38-60.

65. John Goldingay, *The Message of Isaiah 40-55: A Literary-Theological Commentary* (London: T & T Clark, 2005), 510-11; Gordon J. Wenham, *The Book of Leviticus*, NICOT (Grand Rapids: Eerdmans, 1979), 235; Milgrom, *Leviticus 1-16*, 1041.

imposition of the hands upon another, depending upon the context, symbolized the transfer of something from one person to another, such as with the transfer of authority from Moses to Joshua (Num. 27:18).[66] But in this particular case, the text clearly states that the 'goat shall bear [נשׂא] all their iniquities on itself' (Lev. 16:22). Isaiah's use of the term נשׂא has roots in the Day of Atonement with its transfer of sin from Israel, through the high priest, to the goat, which would then bear the sin and carry it into the wilderness never to be seen again.[67] In Isaiah 53, the sins of the many are transferred to the servant, to the one.[68] Of specific interest is how the LXX translates this phrase: καὶ ἐν τοῖς ἀνόμοις ἐλογίσθη ('and was numbered,' or 'reckoned,' 'with the lawless ones'*). The LXX employs λογίζομαι, the same term Paul later uses in key texts about imputation (e.g., Rom. 4:1-8, 22-24; 2 Cor. 5:19; cf. Luke 22:37).

---

66. Milgrom, *Leviticus 1-16*, 1043; cf. David P. Wright, 'The Gesture of Hand Placement in the Hebrew Bible and Hittite Literature,' *Journal of the American Oriental Society* 106/3 (1986): 432-46; René Peter, 'L'Imposition des Mains dans L'Ancien Testament,' *VT* 27/1 (1977): 48-55.

67. J. Alan Groves, 'Atonement in Isaiah 53,' in *The Glory of the Atonement*, ed. Charles E. Hill and Frank A. James, III (Downers Grove: InterVarsity, 2004), 78, 86; J. Alec Motyer, 'Stricken for the Transgression of My People,' in *From Heaven He Came and Sought Her: Definite Atonement in Historical, Biblical, Theological, and Pastoral Perspective*, ed. David Gibson and Jonathan Gibson (Wheaton: Crossway, 2013), 258; Laato, *Servant of the Lord*, 31; Shedd, *Man in Community*, 38; Baruch J. Schwartz, 'The Bearing of Sin in the Priestly Literature,' in *Pomegranates and Golden Bells: Studies in Biblical, Jewish, and Near Eastern Ritual, Law, and Literature in Honor of Jacob Milgrom*, ed. David P. Wright, David Noel Freedman, and Avi Hurvitz (Winona Lake: Eisenbrauns, 1995), 3-21; Mary Douglas, *Jacob's Tears: The Priestly Work of Reconciliation* (Oxford: Oxford University Press, 2004), 49-52.

68. David L. Allen, 'Substitutionary Atonement and Cultic Terminology in Isaiah 53,' in *The Gospel According to Isaiah 53: Encountering the Suffering Servant in Jewish and Christian Theology*, ed. Darrell L. Bock and Mitch Glaser (Grand Rapids: Kregel, 2012), 175-76.

Isaiah 53:11 states: 'By his knowledge shall the righteous one, my servant, make many to be accounted righteous, and he shall bear their iniquities.' Once again the Day of Atonement language appears, with the servant bearing the iniquities of the many, but the prophet also states that the servant is righteous (צדיק). The servant is not merely innocent of wrongdoing but is positively righteous (cf. Deut. 6:25). That is, he has positively fulfilled the law.[69] His perfect law-keeping is evident given the servant's reward. The servant bore the iniquities of the many, that is, he was obedient to Yahweh's plan (חפץ), and therefore (לכן) Yahweh will divide the servant's portion and spoil with the many. The inferential particle (לכן) establishes the cause and effect relationship between the servant's obedience unto death and his reception of his reward. This connection between obedience and reward appears in earlier Old Testament Scripture, particularly in Deuteronomy 17:14-20, where the king's representative (dis) obedience either resulted in curse or blessing for the people, the many (cf. Ps. 2:7).[70] And this interconnected web of texts provides

69. John Oswalt notes the debate surrounding whether 'by his knowledge' should be joined with the second or third colon, e.g., 'he shall see and be satisfied by his knowledge,' vs. 'by his knowledge shall the righteous one, my servant, make many to be accounted righteous' (Isa. 53:11). Oswalt chooses the former, while others argue that 'knowledge' (תעד) refers to obedience (John N. Oswalt, *The Book of Isaiah: Chapters 40-66*, NICOT [Grand Rapids: Eerdmans, 1998], 403-04). Whether the phrase belongs with the second or third colon does not mitigate that the servant is righteous vis-à-vis the law – he is obedient. Nevertheless the placement of the phrase with the third colon does (so ESV, KJV, NAS, NIV, RSV, TNIV) make sense against the broader backdrop of Isaiah's use of the term. Lack of knowledge is the impelling cause behind Israel's exile (47:10). Idolaters lack knowledge (44:19, 25). Yahweh possesses it whereas His people, Israel, do not (40:14; 48:4). The servant is anointed with the Spirit of knowledge and fear of the Lord, the proper disposition to produce obedience (11:2; 33:6) (Goldingay, *Message of Isaiah*, 514).

70. Peter C. Craigie, *Psalms 1-50*, WBC, vol. 19 (Nashville: Thomas Nelson, 1983), 59-60; W. H. Brownlee, 'Psalms 1-2 as Coronation Liturgy, *Bib* 52 (1971): 321-26; J. A. Thompson, *Deuteronomy*, TOTC (Downers Grove: InterVarsity Press, 2008), 206;

the likely subtext for Paul's famous statement from his epistle to the Philippians: 'And being found in human form, he humbled himself by becoming obedient to the point of death, even death on a cross. Therefore God has highly exalted him and bestowed on him the name that is above every name' (Phil. 2:8-9).[71]

The manner by which the servant, therefore, makes 'many to be accounted righteous' (יצדיק) is by his representative obedience. The fact that the prophet employs the hiphil imperfect form of the verb צדק ('to be righteous'), reflects the causative of the Qal verb stem form and is unique in the Old Testament and is usually followed by a direct object: 'If there is a dispute between men and they come into court and the judges decide between them, justifying the righteous [והצדיקו את הצדיק] and condemning the guilty' (Deut. 25:1*; cf. 2 Sam. 15:4). But in this case, the verb is followed by an indirect object governed by a prepositional *lamed* (ל), which conveys the meaning of bringing or providing righteousness *to* or *for* the many (לרבים).[72] The many 'transgressors' (פשעים) receive the servant's righteous law-keeping status – they are no longer transgressors but righteous. The

---

M. G. Kline, *Treaty of the Great King* (Grand Rapids: Eerdmans, 1963), 98; Peter C. Craigie, *Deuteronomy*, NICOT (Grand Rapids: Eerdmans, 1976), 256; J. G. McConville, *Deuteronomy*, AOTC (Downers Grove: InterVarsity Press, 2002), 296; Aubrey R. Johnson, *Sacral Kingship in Ancient Israel* (1955; Eugene: Wipf & Stock, 2006), 11, 22.

71. Peter T. O'Brien, *The Epistle to the Philippians*, NIGTC (Grand Rapids: Eerdmans, 1991), 232-33; Ralph P. Martin, *A Hymn of Christ: Philippians 2:5-11 in Recent Interpretation & In the Setting of Early Christian Worship* (Downers Grove: InterVarsity Press, 1997), 231-35; Beale and Carson, *New Testament Commentary*, 836-37; cf. Moisés Silva, *Philippians*, 2nd ed., BECNT (Grand Rapids: Baker, 2005), 108-09; Gordon D. Fee, *Paul's Letter to the Philippians*, NICNT (Grand Rapids: Eerdmans, 1995), 220-21; John Calvin, *Galatians, Ephesians, Philippians, & Colossians*, CNTC (Grand Rapids: Eerdmans, 1996), 25.

72. Motyer, *Prophecy of Isaiah*, 442; also E. J. Young, *The Book of Isaiah*, 3 vols. (Grand Rapids: Eerdmans, 1972), 356-58; cf. Oswalt, *Isaiah*, 404-05; Goldingay, *Message of Isaiah*, 515. Brevard Childs notes that the verb can be both declarative and causative (Brevard Childs, *Isaiah*, OTL [Louisville: Westminster John Knox, 2001], 419).

many receive the legal status and righteousness of the one. In a word, the imputation of the servant's righteousness to transgressors was part of the eternal plan of the Father, and Isaiah had the privilege of eavesdropping on this amazing conversation. Indeed, the prophet himself was stunned and surprised, indicated by his own statement, 'Who has believed what he has heard from us?' (Isa. 53:1).

New Testament connections

Against this Isaianic Old Testament background, which involves the covenantal agreement between the Father and the Son, we can adequately reflect upon several key New Testament texts that have the fourth servant song as their subtext. A number of New Testament texts draw upon the subterranean prophetic wellspring of Isaiah 53 and directly quote it (e.g., Matt. 8:17; Luke 22:37; John 12:38; Acts 8:32-33; Rom. 10:16; 15:21; 1 Pet. 2:4, 22, 24; Rev. 14:5). In fact, the fourth servant song is one of the most frequently cited Old Testament texts.[73] Beyond this, a number of other texts allude to Isaiah 53.[74] Five key texts warrant brief examination: Matthew 3:15, Romans 4:25, 5:12-19, 8:1-4, and 2 Corinthians 5:19-21.

Matthew 3:15

As recent scholarship has demonstrated, the Gospels have numerous quotations and allusions to the book of Isaiah.[75] Nevertheless, we can focus our attention specifically upon the Matthean account of

---

73. Laato, *Servant of the Lord*, 165.

74. Michael J. Wilkins, 'Isaiah 53 and the Message of Salvation in the Gospels,' in *The Gospel According to Isaiah 53*, ed. Darrell L. Bock and Mitch Glaser (Grand Rapids: Kregel, 2012), 109-32; Craig A. Evans, 'Isaiah 53 in the Letters of Peter, Paul, Hebrews, and John,' in *Gospel According to Isaiah*, 145-70.

75. See, e.g., essays by Morna Hooker, Richard Beaton, Bart Koet, and Catrin Williams, in *Isaiah in the New Testament*, ed. Steve Moyise and Maarten J. J. Menken (London: T & T Clark, 2007), 35-50, 63-78, 79-100, 101-16.

the baptism of Christ. Within the gospel narrative John conducts his ministry in the wilderness entreating his fellow countrymen to repent, flee the coming wrath, and be baptized. John invokes the words of Isaiah, 'Prepare the way for the Lord, make straight paths for him' (Matt. 3:3; Isa. 40:3). In the midst of his cries, Jesus, a lone and solitary figure, emerges and seeks to be baptized by John. The prophet was shocked, and objected; but Jesus replied: 'Let it be so now; it is proper for us to do this to fulfill all righteousness' (Matt. 3:15). Jesus, of course, did not have to repent of His sin, which is evident because John sought to be baptized by Jesus (Matt. 3:14). That Jesus refers to His need of baptism 'to fulfill all righteousness' is another Isaianic allusion: 'Here is my servant, whom I uphold, my chosen one in whom I delight; I will put my Spirit on him, and he will bring justice to the nations' (Isa. 42:1). Matthew places us within the realm of Isaiah 40–66. Moreover, Christ's subsequent baptism, anointing with the Spirit, and the approbation by the heavenly voice echo concepts present in Isaiah 42:1 (Matt. 3:16-17).[76]

Jesus' invocation of the phrase 'fulfill righteousness' is a likely allusion to Isaiah 53:11. These words refer to His willingness to carry out His Father's plan, His covenantally appointed role as surety, and to offer His loving obedience to His heavenly Father. The phrase, therefore, does not refer merely to the act of His baptism but also to the 'good plan' (חפץ) and Jesus' willingness to carry it out. Parallel accounts of Christ's baptism confirm this connection, particularly when John's gospel alludes to Isaiah 53:7, 'Behold, the Lamb of God who takes away the sin of the world' (John 1:29). In fact, Jesus later tells His audience, 'John came to show you the way of righteousness, and you did not believe him, but the tax collectors and the prostitutes did' (Matt. 21:32).[77]

76. Wilkins, 'Isaiah 53,' 119-20.

77. Wilkins, 'Isaiah 53,' 120; R. T. France, 'Servant of Yahweh,' *Dictionary of Jesus and*

Hence, Isaiah's 'by his knowledge shall the righteous one, my servant, make many to be accounted righteous, and he shall bear their iniquities' (53:11) finds its counterpart in Jesus' willingness to undergo a baptism of repentance, though He Himself was sinless, in order that He might fulfill all righteousness.

Jesus demonstrates His solidarity with His people by obediently executing His role as covenant surety. Christ's representative obedience is manifest not only in His willing submission to baptism, but also in His subsequent obedient, forty-day, Spirit-led, wilderness wanderings, which evokes Israel's disobedient, forty-year, wilderness wanderings (Matt. 4:1-11).[78] Among other connections that warrant mention, scholars place both Isaiah 42:1 and Psalm 2:7 behind the heavenly voice, 'This is my beloved Son, with whom I am well pleased' (Matt. 3:17). Jesus is the suffering servant who executes Yahweh's covenant, 'You are my son; today I have begotten you' (Ps. 2:7).[79] As argued, Psalm 2:7 is one of the key texts for the *pactum*.

Romans 4:25

In the second text Paul states the following: 'It will be counted to us who believe in him who raised from the dead Jesus our Lord, who was delivered up for our trespasses and raised for our justification' (Rom. 4.24b-25). Several key features connect

---

the Gospels, ed. Joel B. Green, Scot McKnight, and I. Howard Marshall (Downers Grove: InterVarsity, 1992), 746; D. A. Carson, *Matthew: 1-12*, EBC (Grand Rapids: Zondervan, 1995), 107-08; Oscar Cullmann, *Baptism in the New Testament* (Philadelphia: Westminster, 1950), 18; Donald A. Hagner, *Matthew 1-13*, WBC, vol. 33a (Dallas: Word, 1993), 57; cf. W. D. Davies and D. C. Allison, *Matthew 1-7*, ICC (London: T & T Clark, 2006), 325-27.

78. William L. Kynes, *A Christology of Solidarity: Jesus as the Representative of His People in Matthew* (Lanham: University Press of America, 1991), 26-28, 36, 51-52, 169-70; Joel Kennedy, *The Recapitulation of Israel: Use of Israel's History in Matthew 1:1-4:11* (Tübingen: Mohr Siebeck, 2008), 172-87, 193-94.

79. Beale and Carson, *New Testament Commentary*, 14.

Romans 4:25 to Isaiah 53, such that we can say that this one verse concisely summarizes the fourth servant song.[80] The first connection appears when we compare Romans 4:25 with the LXX text of Isaiah 53:

Romans 4:25a	**Isaiah 53:12 LXX**
παρεδόθη διὰ τὰ παραπτώματα ἡμῶν ('delivered up for our trespasses')	διὰ τὰς ἁμαρτίας αὐτῶν παρεδόθη ('delivered because of their iniquities')

In both cases, Paul, echoing the LXX, states that the Christ was παρεδόθη ('handed over,' or 'delivered up') for the sins of the many. The second line of Romans 4:25 continues to reflect the LXX text of Isaiah 53:11:

Romans 4:25b	**Isaiah 53:11 LXX**
ἠγέρθη διὰ τὴν δικαίωσιν ἡμῶν ('raised for our justification')	ἀπὸ τοῦ πόνου τῆς ψυχῆς αὐτοῦ, δεῖξαι αὐτῷ φῶς ('from the travail of his soul, to show him light')

The idea is that, after the servant's death, he will see light, or be raised from the dead, hence Paul's phrase, 'raised for our justification.'[81] The LXX's insertion of φῶς ('light') to the MT's phrase, 'Out of the anguish of his soul he shall see [נפשו יראה מעמל],' is an amplification of the idea of resurrection. In a number of Old Testament texts the expression 'to see light' is

80. Otfried Hofius, 'The Fourth Servant Son in the New Testament Letters,' in *The Suffering Servant: Isaiah 53 in Jewish and Christian Sources*, ed. Bernd Janowski and Peter Stuhlmacher (Grand Rapids: Eerdmans, 2004), 180; Morna Hooker, 'Did the Use of Isaiah 53 to Interpret His Mission Begin with Jesus?' in *Jesus and the Suffering Servant: Isaiah 53 and Christian Origins* (Eugene: Wipf & Stock, 1998), 101-02.

81. Hofius, 'Fourth Servant Song,' 180-81.

a metaphor for 'to live' (Pss. 36:9; 49:19; Job 3:16; 33:28-30; cf. Ps. 56:13).[82]

Paul's use of these Isaianic phrases shows that Christ substitutionally bore the sins of the many in His death – He is their vicarious representative. Taking the two texts combined (Rom. 4:25 and Isa. 53:11-12), the causative force of the prepositional διὰ indicates the cause of Christ being handed over, and in the second line the purpose and end goal in view: '[He was] delivered up for [*because of*] our trespasses, and raised for [*the purpose of*] our justification.'[83] Within the broader context of Romans 4, Paul echoes the themes of the fourth servant song, that Isaiah's 'transgressors' are 'accounted righteous' (Isa. 53:11) and the justification of the 'ungodly' (Rom. 4:5).[84] Noteworthy is the fact that both Paul and Isaiah employ λογίζομαι in their respective passages. Isaiah states that the suffering servant was τοῖς ἀνόμοις ἐλογίσθη ('numbered with the transgressors') and Paul explains in Romans 4:24b, ἀλλὰ καὶ δι' ἡμᾶς, οἷς μέλλει λογίζεσθαι ('it will be counted to us who believe'). Both employ imputation language.

Romans 5:12-21

These themes continue, with a fuller explanation, in Romans 5:12-21, as well as in Romans 6 and 8.[85] Romans 4:25 states that Christ bears sins and by His resurrection justifies sinners, but

---

82. Hofius, 'Fourth Servant Song,' 181 n. 68; cf. Hans-Joachim Kraus, *Psalms 1-59* (Minneapolis: Fortress, 1993), 399-400, 483-84, 527; David J. A. Clines, *Job 1-20*, WBC, vol. 17 (Dallas: Word, 1989), 95; idem, *Job 21-37*, WBC 18a (Nashville: Thomas Nelson, 2006), 740.

83. Hofius, 'Fourth Servant Song,' 181; cf. Douglas Moo, *The Epistle to the Romans*, NICNT (Grand Rapids: Eerdmans, 1996), 289.

84. Hofius, 'Fourth Servant Song,' 182.

85. Hooker, 'Use of Isaiah 53,' 102.

Romans 5:12-21 offers a fuller explanation of the mechanisms by which this exchange occurs. A broad observation is that this text exhibits the one and the many pattern in both negative and positive directions. Through one (ἑνὸς) man, Adam, sin entered the world and 'death spread to all men because all sinned' (Rom. 5:12). Paul labels those affected by Adam's sin as τοὺς πολλοὺς ('the many'). Conversely, echoing Isaianic themes, Paul explains: 'For the judgment following one trespass brought condemnation, but the free gift following many trespasses brought justification' (Rom. 5:16). In contrast to Adam's disobedience, Christ, the last Adam, offers His representative righteousness, or obedience, which brings justification. Paul oscillates back and forth between the actions of one and the effect upon the many, whether unto condemnation or justification. The fact that Paul mentions that the οἱ πολλοί 'will be constituted righteous' (δίκαιοι κατασταθήσονται οἱ πολλοί, Rom. 5:19*) likely arises directly from Isaiah 53:11b (LXX).[86]

Romans 8:1-4

Related to Paul's invocation of the contrast between the (dis) obedience of the two Adams is the direct connection that Paul draws between Jesus, His obedience, and the law. At the beginning of Romans 8 Paul invokes the concept of justification: 'There is therefore now no condemnation for those who are in Christ Jesus' (Rom. 8:1). Condemnation is the antonym of justification, which means that Paul's statement can be glossed as, 'There is therefore

---

86. Hofius, 'Fourth Servant Song,' 182; cf. Vickers, *Jesus' Blood*, 122; Moo, *Romans*, 345-46; Albrecht Oepke, καθίστημι, in *Theological Dictionary of the New Testament*, vol. 3, ed. Gerhard Kittel (Grand Rapids: Eerdmans, 1965), 445; Charles Hodge, *Romans* (1835; Edinburgh: Banner of Truth, 1989), 173-74; Ben C. Dunson, *Individual and Community in Paul's Letter to the Romans* (Tübingen: Mohr Siebeck, 2012), 148-54; Sang-Won (Aaron) Son, *Corporate Elements in Pauline Anthropology: A Study of Selected Terms, Idioms, and Concepts in the Light of Paul's Usage and Background* (Rome: Pontifico Instituto Biblico, 2001), 61, 77.

now justification for those who are in Christ Jesus.' Paul then states the following:

> For the law of the Spirit of life has set you free in Christ Jesus from the law of sin and death. For God has done what the law, weakened by the flesh, could not do. By sending his own Son in the likeness of sinful flesh and for sin, he condemned sin in the flesh, in order that the righteous requirement of the law might be fulfilled in us, who walk not according to the flesh but according to the Spirit. (Rom. 8:2-4)

Common explanations of these verses run along the following lines: Jesus has justified us and freed fallen but redeemed sinners to be able to fulfill the law and produce Spirit-motivated obedience, that which fulfills the law.[87] In technical terms, commentators argue that verses 2-4 deal with the doctrine of sanctification. The grammar of the text, however, suggests a different interpretation.

Some contend that Paul transitions from discussing justification in verse 1, evident by his use of judicial language (i.e., κατάκριμα), to matters pertaining to sanctification in the following verses. There is a sense in which Paul descends from redemptive history (*historia salutis*) to matters pertaining to the *ordo salutis*. Yet, when Paul writes that the law of the Spirit has set sinners free in Christ from the law of sin and death, sanctification is not primarily in view but he rather speaks of realm transfer. That is, those who are in Christ are under the

87. John Murray, *The Epistle to the Romans*, NICNT (Grand Rapids: Eerdmans, 1968), 283-84; N. T. Wright, *Romans*, NIB, vol. 10 (Nashville: Abingdon, 2002), 577-81; idem, *Climax of the Covenant*, 203, 11; Herman Ridderbos, *Paul: An Outline of His Theology* (1975; Grand Rapids: Eerdmans, 1992), 280-88; similarly Thomas Aquinas, *Commentary on the Letter of Saint Paul to the Romans* (Lander: Aquinas Institute for the Study of Sacred Doctrine, 2012), §613 (p. 207).

aegis of the last Adam, not the first. In terms of Romans 5:12-21, believers are not under the representative disobedience of Adam with all its negative consequences but rather the representative obedience of Christ with all its positive effects. The Spirit's liberating work only takes place within the redemptive space opened by Christ (cf. e.g., Gal. 3:13-14).[88]

Paul explains in the next step of his argument how Christ has created this context in which the Spirit works to free sinners from death and the condemnation of the law. There are challenges regarding the proper translation of verse 3, Τὸ γὰρ ἀδύνατον τοῦ νόμου ἐν ᾧ ἠσθένει διὰ τῆς σαρκός ('For what the law, weakened by the flesh, could not do'*). Among the various alternatives, the best solution appears in most English translations. That is, the verse highlights what *God* has done, and this stands in contrast to what the law could not do.[89] Verses 3-4, therefore, are not about what redeemed man might do, but about what God has done in Christ to fulfill the requirements of the law: 'God has done what the law ... could not do. By sending his own Son in the likeness of sinful flesh and for sin, he condemned sin in the flesh, in order that the righteous requirement of the law might be fulfilled in us,' that is, in humanity. God sent His Son, which places us within the conceptual realm of the *pactum* as well as Isaiah 53 and Yahweh's 'good plan' (חפץ), and He came in the likeness of sinful flesh. Christ did not Himself sin but rather entered into the sin-fallen human condition, hence Paul's use of ὁμοιώματι ('likeness') to qualify 'flesh.'[90] When Christ entered this condition, God then condemned sin in the flesh, which parallels the substitutionary and vicarious suffering categories

88. Moo, *Romans*, 477.

89. Moo, *Romans*, 477-78 n. 37.

90. Moo, *Romans*, 479.

that appear in Isaiah 53. In this sense, to borrow words from another place, Christ 'was made to be sin' (2 Cor. 5:21).

There are further connections to Isaiah 53 when Paul writes that God sent His Son in the likeness of sinful flesh καὶ περὶ ἁμαρτίας ('and for sin,' or 'and concerning sin'). There is the possibility that Paul simply means to say that Christ's mission dealt with sin.[91] On the other hand, the phrase frequently means 'sin offering' in the LXX. Forty-four of fifty-four occurrences of the phrase περὶ ἁμαρτίας refer to sacrifice, and it translates אשם in Isaiah 53:10 (cf. Lev. 7:37).[92] At a minimum, Paul has in view the idea that Christ was sent to be a sin offering, and he indicates this by the common LXX phrase περὶ ἁμαρτίας. But a maximal reading, warranted by Paul's engagement with Isaiah throughout his epistle, but especially in Romans 4:25 and 5:12-21, is that Paul still has his copy of Isaiah's scroll sitting before him as he reflects upon Isaiah 53 and employs these categories in his explanation of Christ's work.

To what end did Christ enter into the fallen human estate? Paul answers this question with a purpose clause (ἵνα) in verse 4: 'that the righteous requirement [δικαίωμα] of the law might be fulfilled in us.' What does Paul mean by the term δικαίωμα? Space prohibits a thorough examination of the different interpretive options. Nevertheless, the term δικαίωμα has the suffix -μα, which suggests that it refers to the consequences of 'establishing right.' This meaning frequently appears in the LXX where the plural form occurs numerous times to refer to statutes and

---

91. So, e.g., Murray, *Romans*, 280.

92. Moo, *Romans*, 480; so also James D. G. Dunn, 'Paul's Understanding of the Death of Jesus as Sacrifice,' in *The Christ and the Spirit: Christology*, vol. 1, *Collected Essays of James D. G. Dunn* (Grand Rapids: Eerdmans, 1998), 198-99; N. T. Wright, 'The Meaning of περὶ ἁμαρτίας in Romans 8:3,' in *The Climax of the Covenant: Christ and the Law in Pauline Theology* (Minneapolis: Fortress, 1991), 220-25.

ordinances of God's law: 'And now, O Israel, listen to the statutes and the rules [אל החקים ואל המשפטים / τῶν δικαιωμάτων καὶ τῶν κριμάτων] that I am teaching you' (Deut. 4:1; cf. 5:1). Notable is that Deuteronomy 4:1 and 5:1 both employ the plural of חק, the same term employed in Psalm 2:7, 'I will tell of the decree [חק] ...,' a term synonymous with ברית ('covenant') (cf. Ps. 105:8-10). Paul therefore states that the purpose of Christ coming in the likeness of sinful flesh was 'in order that the righteous requirement of the law might be fulfilled.' Paul has in view covenantal-legal categories. In other words, Christ's role as covenant surety, to which He was appointed in the *pactum*, is in view. Paul connects δικαιώμα to Christ (Rom. 5:18-19) and His obedience, not to the obedience of those whom He redeems.

But some might object to this imputation reading because of what follows in Paul's statement: 'In order that the righteous requirement of the law might be fulfilled *in us* [ἐν ἡμῖν], who walk not according to the flesh but according to the Spirit' (Rom. 8:4). Based upon the concluding portion of the statement, some have argued that Paul has in view matters related to sanctification and the law as it has been written upon believers' hearts, which enables them to fulfill the requirements of the law.[93] But two

---

93. E. g., Wright, *Romans*, 577-81; idem, *Climax of the Covenant*, 203, 11. Note that Romans 8:1-4 was a key text in debates over the imputed active obedience of Christ in the late sixteenth century. Theodore Beza (1519-1605) argued that Romans 8:1-4 was about justification and Christ's habitual holiness, that is, His own obedience, and Johannes Piscator (1546-1625), who denied the imputation of the active obedience of Christ, argued that the pericope dealt with justification and sanctification (Campos, 'Piscator,' 150-54). Among the Reformed, Franciscus Gomarus (1563-1641), Giovanni Diodati (1576-1649), and Thomas Manton (1620-77) argued that Romans 8:4 referred to sanctification. By contrast, Johannes Heidegger (1633-98), the Leiden Synopsis, John Davenant (1572-1641), Thomas Goodwin (1600-80), Anthony Burgess (d. 1664), the Westminster Assembly's annotations on the Bible, John Owen (1616-83), Herman Witsius (1636-1708), Francis Turretin (1623-87), and others held that Romans 8:4 is about justification and the obedience of Christ (Campos, 'Piscator,' 214 n. 68). See,

considerations point away from this sanctification reading. First, the verb 'might be fulfilled' (πληρωθῇ) is an aorist passive, which indicates that it is not something that believers do but something that is done for them. The main thrust of Paul's argument is to contrast what the law could not do versus what God has done. Second, given the demands of the law, how can Christians fulfill the law in any sense? How can their imperfect obedience constitute a δικαίωμα?

Instead, Paul's point pertains primarily to the *historia salutis*, what Christ has done as covenant surety through His substitutionary suffering and representative obedience, which transfers elect but fallen sinners into the realm of the new creation.[94] Paul does go on in the verses that follow (Rom. 8:5ff) to discuss the Spirit-empowered obedience of those who are united to Christ, but his primary point in verses 1-4 is christological. As Francis Turretin (1623-87) explains:

> Being made like to sinful flesh (yet without sin), he offered himself for us as a victim for sin and having made a most full satisfaction condemned sin (i.e., perfectly expiated it) in the flesh for this end – that the condemnation of sin might give place to our

---

e.g., Johannes Heidegger, *Commentarius In Epistolam St. Pauli ad Romanos* (Tiguri: Davidis Gessneri, 1699), 58; Johannes Polyander, et al., *Synopsis Purioris Theologiae*, ed. Herman Bavinck (Lugduni Batavorum: apud Didericum Donner, 1881), XXXIII. viii (p. 332); John Davenant, *A Treatise on Justification*, vol. 1, trans. Josiah Allport (London: Hamilton, Adams, & Co., 1844), 240; Thomas Goodwin, *Of Christ the Mediator*, V.xx, in *The Works of Thomas Goodwin*, vol. 5 (Eureka: Tanski, 1996), 350-52; Anthony Burgess, *The True Doctrine of Justification* (London: Thomas Underhill, 1654), serm. XXXV (pp. 358-59); *Annotations Upon All the Books of the Old and New Testament* (London: Evan Tylers, 1657), comm. Rom. 8:3-4; John Owen, *The Doctrine of Justification by Faith*, in *The Works of John Owen*, vol. 5, ed. Thomas Russell (1862; Edinburgh: Banner of Truth, 1996), 35; Herman Witsius, *Economy of the Covenants Between God and Man* (Escondido: Den Dulk Foundation, 1990), II.v.6.

94. Moo, *Romans*, 482-83.

> justification and the righteousness of the law (*to dikaoma nomou*) (i.e., the right which it has) whether as to obedience or as to punishment is fulfilled in us (not inherently, but imputatively); while what Christ did and suffered in our place is ascribed to us as if we had done that very thing. Thus we are considered in Christ to have fulfilled the whole righteousness of the law because in our name he most perfectly fulfilled the righteousness of the law as to obedience as well as to punishment.[95]

This passage is, therefore, about Christ's representative and vicarious suffering and obedience, which propels those who are in Him into the new creation, where they then produce the fruit of holiness and obedience.

2 Corinthians 5:21

A fifth and final text for consideration is 2 Corinthians 5:21, and Paul's famous statement: 'For our sake he made him to be sin who knew no sin, that in him we might become the righteousness of God.' One of the most recent challenges to citing this text in support of the doctrine of imputation comes from N. T. Wright.[96] Wright contends that Paul's statement should not be treated as an isolated bit of soteriology that purports to disclose the imputation of sin to Christ and the imputation of Christ's righteousness to sinners. Instead, Paul's statement comes within the context of a defense of his ministry, and that Paul has in view, not soteriology, but God's covenant faithfulness, His righteousness. Wright argues that, when Paul says that Christ became sin so that 'we might become the righteousness of God,' it should be understood

---

95. Francis Turretin, *Institutes of Elenctic Theology*, ed. James T. Dennison, Jr., trans. George Musgrave Giger (Phillipsburg: P & R, 1992-97), XVI.iii.19.

96. Wright, 'On Becoming the Righteousness of God,' 68-76; idem, *Paul and the Faithfulness of God*, 2 vols. (Minneapolis: Fortress, 2013), 881-85.

that he and the other apostles have become a manifestation of God's covenantal faithfulness, which they carry out in their apostolic ministry. Another recent challenge to employing this verse in the service of imputation comes from Michael Bird, who claims that if forensic realities are in view, such as imputation, then Paul's word-choice is odd, since he states that in Christ 'we become' (γενώμεθα) the righteousness of God.[97] This, in Bird's assessment, is not legal–forensic nomenclature (e.g., λογίζομαι).[98] Rather than treating the subject of imputation, Bird believes the statement addresses the fact that believers 'experience the status of "righteousness."'[99] In dogmatic terms, the contested verse is not about imputation but a broader statement about soteriology.

Once again, the Old Testament background to this text is vital to determining Paul's meaning. As with the aforementioned Pauline passages (Rom. 4:25, 5:12-21, 8:1-4), this text also has the literary complex of Isaiah 40–66 as its subtext.[100] That Paul operates within the orbit of Isaiah 40–66 is evident from 2 Corinthians 5:17*, with his invocation of the concept of new creation: 'Therefore, if anyone is in Christ, he is new creation. The old has passed away; behold, the new has come.' Paul not only talks of the new creation, but he uses a phrase that is evocative of two different passages in Isaiah, evident by the following terminological parallels:[101]

---

97. Bird, 'Progressive Reformed View,' 149.

98. Cf. Murray J. Harris, *The Second Epistle to the Corinthians*, NIGTC (Grand Rapids: Eerdmans, 2005), 451, 454-55.

99. Bird, 'Progressive Reformed View,' 149.

100. Mark Gignilliat, *Paul and Isaiah's Servants: Paul's Theological Reading of Isaiah 40-66 in 2 Corinthians 5:14-6:10* (London: T & T Clark, 2007), 45-50, 57.

101. G. K. Beale, 'The Old Testament Background of Reconciliation in 2 Corinthians 5-7 and Its Bearing on the Literary problem of 2 Corinthians 6:14-7:1,' in *The Right Doctrine from the Wrong Texts: Essays on the Use of the Old Testament in the New*, ed. G. K. Beale (Grand Rapids: Baker, 1994), 219-20.

<table>
<tr><td>Isaiah 43:18-19
Μὴ μνημονεύετε τὰ πρῶτα καὶ τὰ ἀρχαῖα μὴ συλλογίζεσθε. ἰδοὺ ποιῶ καινὰ
('Remember not the former things, and do not consider the ancient things. Behold, I do new things'*)</td><td rowspan="2">2 Corinthians 5:17
εἴ τις ἐν Χριστῷ, καινὴ κτίσις· τὰ ἀρχαῖα παρῆλθεν, ἰδοὺ γέγονεν καινά
('If anyone is in Christ, he is new creation. The old has passed away, behold, the new has come')</td></tr>
<tr><td>Isaiah 65:17
ἔσται γὰρ ὁ οὐρανὸς καινὸς καὶ ἡ γῆ καινή, καὶ οὐ μὴ μνησθῶσιν τῶν προτέρων
('For there will be a new heaven and a new earth, and they will not remember the former'*)</td></tr>
</table>

Paul echoes the Isaianic ideas of new creation contrasted with the old, evident in the repetition of the terms τὰ ἀρχαῖα ('the old') and καινὰ ('new') and even does so with the same emphatic ἰδοὺ ('behold') as Isaiah. Yet, how does this statement fit within Paul's overall argument? Wright is correct to claim that the chief function of 2 Corinthians is Paul's apology for his ministry.[102] But contra Wright, Paul does not merely state that God's covenant faithfulness is manifest in Paul's ministry (note Wright's much controverted definition of δικαιοσύνη θεοῦ).[103] There is another covenantal concept to describe God's fidelity, namely, His *hesed*. God keeps His covenant promises, and in this vein He is covenantally faithful (e.g., Deut. 7:9; cf. 1 Cor. 1:9, 10:13; 2 Cor. 1:18-20).

As much as God's covenant faithfulness undergirds Paul's ministry, this is not the specific subject under consideration.

102. Wright, 'On Becoming the Righteousness of God,' 72.

103. For a critique of Wright's definition of God's righteousness as covenant faithfulness, see C. Lee Irons, 'Dikaiosyne Theou: A Lexical Examination of the Covenant-Faithfulness Interpretation' (Ph.D. Diss., Fuller Theological Seminary, 2011). One thing to note is that the LXX employs the term δικαιοσύνη to translate the Hebrew term *hesed* (חסד) in nine different places, which some might believe mitigates my argument. On these nine texts, see Irons, 'Dikaiosyne Theou,' 208-23.

Rather, Paul invokes the concept of God's righteousness. In this particular case, Paul urges the Corinthians to be reconciled to him, and not to evaluate his ministry κατὰ σάρκα ('according to the flesh') (2 Cor. 5:16), that is, the standards of this present evil age. They must instead evaluate Paul and the other apostles according to the standards of the new creation – 'the old has passed away; behold the new has come' (2 Cor. 5:17). If they understand this tectonic shift in redemptive history, the in-breaking of the eschaton and new creation, then they will evaluate Paul's ministry in the proper light.[104] Paul appeals and alludes to the literary complex of Isaiah 40–66 not only to announce that the new creation has burst onto the scene of history with the ministry of Christ, but also because the Isaianic text originally dealt with the reconciliation and restoration of Israel.[105] Paul desires that the Corinthians would be reconciled to him. Reconciliation in the church is not simply a matter of conflict resolution but is based upon the reconciliation wrought by God in Christ. Hence Paul appeals to this Isaianic passage that deals with reconciliation.

How precisely did God accomplish this reconciliation? He accomplished it through the obedience and intercession of His servant. His servant ushered in the new creation by breaking the grip of sin and death through His vicarious representative obedience and suffering. Hence Paul states: 'For our sake he made him to be sin who knew no sin, so that in him we might become the righteousness of God' (2 Cor. 5:19). Paul appealed to the Corinthians to embrace this reconciliation, which meant embracing Paul and his ministry because he was God's ambassador – to reject Paul and his message

---

104. Beale, 'Background of 2 Corinthians 5-7,' 219; Scott J. Haffemann, 2 *Corinthians*, NIVAC (Grand Rapids: Zondervan, 2000), 243.

105. Beale, 'Background of 2 Corinthians 5-7,' 222; Gignilliat, *Paul and Isaiah*, 54, 60.

was to reject God's reconciliation (2 Cor. 5:20).[106] In this instance, Paul's description of the exchange, Christ becoming sin and those who are united to Him becoming righteousness, reflects the categories that lie at the heart of Isaiah 53 – the one and the many and the vicarious and representative work of the servant. Isaiah 53 stands in the background not only because of these elements but also because of Paul's phrase, 'he made him to be sin' (ἁμαρτίαν ἐποίησεν), which echoes Isaiah 53:9*, 'although he had committed no sin [ἀνομίαν οὐκ ἐποίησεν]' (LXX).[107]

Due to the absence of legal–forensic language in 2 Corinthians 5:20-21, questions undoubtedly arise as to whether Paul had in mind representative obedience and suffering, let alone the doctrine of imputation. As noted above, Bird objects to appealing to this text as a basis for the doctrine of imputation because Paul uses the verb γίνομαι, 'so that we might *become* the righteousness of God' (2 Cor. 5:21; emphasis).[108] Hence, Paul has something other than forensic categories in mind. But as others have observed, Paul's allusion to Isaiah 53 is general and free, and at verse 21 he adheres neither to the language of the MT or LXX.[109] The general nature of Paul's statement applies in the terminology he uses to discuss not only Isaiah's justification of the many ('so that in him we might become the righteousness of God'), but also the manner by which Christ bore the sins of the many ('he made him to be sin') (cf. Rom. 8:3).[110]

---

106. Beale, 'Background of 2 Corinthians 5-7,' 223-25.

107. Victor Paul Furnish, *II Corinthians*, AB, vol. 32a (New York: Doubleday, 1984), 340; Haffeman, *2 Corinthians*, 247.

108. Bird, 'Progressive Reformed View,' 149.

109. John Hoad, 'Some New Testament References to Isaiah 53,' *ExpT* 67 (1957): 254-55.

110. Murray Harris suggests the possibility that when Paul invokes the term *sin*

Bird offers an unsatisfactory explanation: 'So Paul does not say that "God imputed our sin to the sinless one, and imputed God's righteousness to us." We can say what the text says, no more and no less: Christ was made sin probably in the sense of carrying, bearing and taking sins upon himself, and those who are in Christ share in the "righteousness of God."'[111] Ironically, Bird does not follow his own rule, namely, saying only what the text states. Paul says God *made* Christ to be sin. On the ground of Bird's objections, Paul's use of the verb ποιέω becomes equally problematic. The verb, like γίνομαι, is not strict legal nomenclature. In fact, the LXX employs the term ποιέω to translate the Hebrew ברא, to create or make. On Bird's analysis, we would have to conclude that God actually made Christ to be sin – it was not a legal imputation but an ontological transformation. Yet Bird invokes imputational categories, 'carrying, bearing and taking sins' (terms used in Leviticus 16 and Isaiah 53 and associated with imputation), which are not reflected by the word ποιέω. But as others have noted, exegesis does not merely involve repeating the language of the biblical text but interpreting what it means.[112]

How to interpret Paul's statement, consequently, should not be decided merely by a lexical appeal and definition of individual words or one lone statement. Rather, how does Paul's statement in 2 Corinthians 5:21 fit within the broader context of his argument, and how does it sit within the bigger canonical context? In this case, the immediate surrounding context presents strong evidence to suggest that Isaiah 40–66 is the subtext of Paul's

---

(ἁμαρτία), that he does not intend the category, but the LXX rendering of sin- and guilt-offering, hence Paul has Isaiah's אשם in view (Harris, *Second Corinthians*, 452).

111. Bird, 'Progressive Reformed View,' 149.

112. Dunson, 'Imputation as Word and Doctrine,' 256.

argument, and that he focuses on Isaiah 53 in 2 Corinthians 5:21. We can safely conclude these connections not only because of the similarities between the two passages mentioned above (Christ's impeccability, the one and the many) but also because of the exchange of sin and righteousness, key subjects in the fourth servant song. Regarding the issue of Paul's terminology (ποιέω and γίνομαι), the answer appears in the nature of his appeal to Isaiah 53.[113] Paul clearly does not quote Isaiah 53; he alludes to it. An allusion is when an author offers a brief expression and is consciously dependent upon an Old Testament passage without reproducing its exact wording of the text. The text need only present parallel wording, syntax, or concepts to qualify as an allusion.[114] In this instance, therefore, Paul's terminology is inconsequential against the broader Isaianic backdrop. He alludes to the fourth servant song and the reader should understand that they receive Christ's righteousness in the same manner as Christ receives their sin, namely, through imputation.[115]

There is one further possible objection to consider: Paul specifically states that we become the δικαιοσύνη θεοῦ ('righteousness of God'), thus how can we speak of *Christ's* imputed righteousness if Paul states that it is *God's*?[116] Two simple points sufficiently answer this query. First, within the Isaianic subtext, the suffering figure is Yahweh's chosen servant (Isa. 43:10; 44:1-2; 44:21; 45:4; 49:3, 6). This point especially comes to the forefront at the beginning of the fourth servant

---

113. Oepke, καθίστημι, 445

114. G. K. Beale, *Handbook on the New Testament Use of the Old Testament: Exegesis and Interpretation* (Grand Rapids: Baker, 2012), 31.

115. Gignilliat, *Paul and Isaiah*, 104-05; Harris, *Second Corinthians*, 455.

116. Bird, 'Progressive Reformed View,' 149; also, Gundry, 'Nonimputation of Christ's Righteousness,' 41-42.

song: 'Behold, my servant shall act wisely' (Isa. 52:13).[117] Second, Paul states that we become the righteousness of God ἐν αὐτῷ ('in him'), in Christ, the servant. Paul repeats this: 'God, who through Christ reconciled us to himself …' and, 'In Christ God was reconciling the world to himself …' (2 Cor. 5:18-19). God's righteousness does not come immediately to sinners apart from Christ. In this sense, sinners receive the imputed righteousness of Christ, which ultimately comes from God because God was in Christ reconciling the world to Himself.

What, however, does Paul specifically mean when he writes that ἐν αὐτῷ ('in him') we become the righteousness of God? Paul's use of the preposition with the dative has three different possible readings.[118] It could refer to realm transfer, as it does in 2 Corinthians 5:17, anyone who is 'in Christ' is part of the new creation. But Paul's use of the verb γίνομαι mitigates this possibility because Paul does not describe believers as entering into a realm of righteousness but becoming the righteousness of God. The 'in him' could be instead instrumental, which means that Paul intends to convey the idea that God accomplishes redemption by the agency of Christ. This idea is certainly in view in verses 18-19, as Paul states that God reconciled διὰ Χριστοῦ ('through Christ').

The third and most likely reading, however, is that the 'in him' refers to union with Christ. Believers are justified by the representative obedience and vicarious suffering of Christ, benefits they enjoy through union with Christ. This is the most likely reading given the symmetry between Christ being made sin and sinners becoming the righteousness of God. This symmetry

---

117. Harris, *Second Corinthians*, 455 n. 207.

118. For what follows, see Constantine R. Campbell, *Paul and Union with Christ: An Exegetical and Theological Study* (Grand Rapids: Zondervan, 2012), 185-88.

weakens the instrumental reading because if believers became righteous instrumentally through Christ, it is not clear how this parallel would work with Christ being made sin. Christ's sharing in the condemnation of sinners means that sinners are made righteous by sharing in His right standing – this occurs through imputation. On this point, note Paul's similar use of the ἐν αὐτῷ construction: 'I have suffered the loss of all things and count them as rubbish, in order that I may gain Christ and be found in him [ἐν αὐτῷ], not having a righteousness of my own that comes from the law, but that which comes through faith in Christ, the righteousness from God that depends on faith' (Phil. 3:8-9).[119] Once again, Paul does not rest in his own law-keeping, but in the representative law-keeping of the *pactum*-appointed covenant surety, the servant of Yahweh. The *pactum* accounts for the imputed righteousness of God through Christ.

Theological reflection

Imputation and contemporary criticism

As we take a closer look at the biblical text and matters related to imputation, it becomes apparent how vital covenantal categories are for understanding the relationship between Christ and those whom He redeems. Both sides of the contemporary rejection of imputation, whether in Bultmann or Wright, excise vital covenantal elements. Bultmann embraces the post-Enlightenment category of the autonomous individual, who is abstracted from covenantal bonds of any sort. Yet the Bible presents only two alternatives – covenantal solidarity with either the first or last Adam. No one stands alone.[120] Enlightenment individualism

119. Silva, *Philippians*, 159-63; cf. O'Brien, *Philippians*, 391-400.

120. Dietrich Bonhoeffer, *Sanctorum Communio: A Theological Study of the Sociology of the Church*, Dietrich Bonhoeffer Works, vol. 1 (Minneapolis: Fortress, 1998), 120-21.

fails to connect the individual to his corporate context and hence rejects the concept of corporate responsibility – i.e., that the actions of one can affect the many, whether positively or negatively. While individualism may be theoretically possible, the isolated individual does not actually exist – it is an abstraction, suspended in mid-air and divorced from history.

Wright and others are correct to highlight the corporate dimension of Christ's relationship with those whom He redeems, but they do so at the expense of crucial covenantal-legal categories. Wright and Bird contend imputation is either a minor sidelight in Paul's explanation of justification or that it is a redundant concept in view of union with Christ.[121] Yet, neither states what he means by union with Christ. A simple survey of the different uses of the common phrases denoting the concept reveals that it is quite expansive and does not always have the same meaning. Paul states that believers were chosen 'in him,' in Christ, before the foundation of the world (Eph. 1:4). Paul cannot refer to the personal indwelling of the believer by the Holy Spirit, since the elect person does not yet exist. As the previous chapter on predestination and the *pactum* demonstrates, election of individuals and their union to Christ occurs within the context of the covenant of redemption. Moreover, as their covenant surety, the Son voluntarily undertakes the *legal* obligations of the covenant. His pledge of obedience fulfills the requirements of the covenant.

Christ's pre-temporal covenantal appointment to this role, however, requires the concept of imputation to preserve His exclusive place as covenant surety. We can sharpen the focus of this specific aspect of Christ's suretyship by asking, What is the legal ground of the sinner's justification before the divine bar?

---

121. Wright, *Paul*, 135-36, 157-58, 232-33, idem, *Romans*, 491; Bird, 'Incorporated Righteousness,' 267, 273-74.

What is the basis for the sinner being declared righteous with regard to the law? The basis for the verdict does not lie within the person, hence categories of divine indwelling as the judicial basis must be excluded. The stipulations of the covenant are extrinsic to the individual – he must perform the law. If he performs the law, then he will be declared righteous vis-à-vis this external covenantal obligation; conversely, if he does not perform the law, he will be condemned. The extrinsic nature of the law and justification is quite evident, for example, with Achan's and David's sins. Both violated the covenant and the nation suffered. The extrinsic nature of corporate responsibility is especially evident in Adam's sin. No one, whether Israelite or member of the human race, was indwelt by Adam, Achan, or David, but in these instances corporate communities were held accountable for the actions of individuals. The covenant provides the legal context and means by which the extrinsic actions of one are accredited to the rest of the covenant community. Personal indwelling, therefore, is not the basis for either justification or condemnation.

This does not mean, however, that personal indwelling is unnecessary. We must believe in Christ – we must have faith in Him, and this only occurs through the personal indwelling of the Holy Spirit. Christ through the Spirit must personally indwell the elect to bring about their justification. Only those who believe in Christ can receive the imputed righteousness of the covenant surety, and only those who have been effectually called by the Holy Spirit can exercise faith. But as the Protestant Reformers insisted in contrast to Roman Catholic formulations, faith is the instrumental cause of a person's justification. The means (or instrument) by which a person lays hold of Christ's representative obedience is faith alone, but this faith is not the material cause of his justification. The sole meritorious or material cause of justification is Christ's obedience. Faith is required but is not the legal basis for the verdict. In Roman Catholic formulations, personal indwelling becomes the basis for the verdict because faith is defined as the exercise of virtue, that is, faith working through love.[122] The material cause is no longer exclusively the obedience of the covenant surety but also includes the believer's obedience.[123]

This is the problem with von Balthasar's formulation, which has great affinities with classic Tridentine categories but also has Eastern Orthodox participatory accents. Von Balthasar invokes covenantal categories, but never accounts for Christ's role as covenant surety.[124] By rejecting juridical conceptions from Christ's representative obedience, only ontological categories remain. Apart from the covenantal ligatures that bind the one and the many, indwelling is the only option. This means that sinners can only know of redemption by sharing in Christ's essential righteousness, such as in the views of Andreas Osiander (1498-1552), or by providing their own obedience. In the case of the former, with the ontological assumption of the believer into Christ, the covenant as a legal binding context becomes irrelevant. The one and the many lose their identities as they become a *tertium quid*, and history becomes superfluous, as no fulfillment of the extrinsic historically administered covenantal law is necessary. What the sinner lacks becomes his by merging with Christ through union with Him and sharing in His essential righteousness, not in His perfect law-keeping. In the case of the

122. See, e.g., Council of Trent, Session 6 (13 January 1547), 'Decree on Justification,' §§5-7.

123. Cf. Council of Trent, 'Decree on Justification,' §7; Calvin, III.xiv.17; idem, *Canons and Decrees of the Council of Trent, with the Antidote* (1547), in *John Calvin: Tracts and Letters*, vol. 3, ed. Henry Beveridge (1851; Edinburgh: Banner of Truth, 2009), 114-21.

124. Von Balthasar, *Theo-Drama*, IV.242-43.

latter, Christ is not covenantal surety but merely an enabler – the whole office of surety shifts from Christ to the believer. The surety no longer fulfills the obligations of the covenant but only transfers them back to the believer. There is no rest for the weary and heavy-laden – the law once again stands before them like Everest jutting out of the landscape requiring obedience.[125]

To say, then, that union with Christ is the basis for a person's justification lacks specificity and is misleading.[126] If *basis* means that one cannot be justified apart from union with Christ, then such a statement is true. Justification requires faith in Christ, and only one who is in union with Him can exercise faith. But if by *basis* the legal ground for justification is intended, then, no, union with Christ, the personal indwelling, is not the legal basis of justification. As Louis Berkhof observes:

> The mystical union in the sense in which we are now speaking of it is not the judicial ground, on the basis of which we become partakers of the riches that are in Christ. It is sometimes said that the merits

---

125. Cf. Calvin, *Institutes*, III.xi.5-12; Andreas Osiander, *Disputatio de Iustifcatione* (Konigsberg: Hans Lufft, 1550); Alister McGrath, *Iustitia Dei: A History of the Christian Doctrine of Justification*, 3rd ed. (Cambridge: Cambridge University Press, 2005), 241-43; Timothy J. Wengert, 'Philip Melanchthon and John Calvin Against Andreas Osiander: Coming to Terms with Forensic Justification,' in *Calvin and Luther: The Continuing Relationship*, ed. R. Ward Holder (Göttingen: Vandenhoeck & Ruprecht, 2013), 63-87.

126. Wright, Vanhoozer, and Johnson employ 'union as basis of justification' language. See, e.g., N. T. Wright, 'Justification,' in *New Dictionary of Theology*, ed. David F. Wright, Sinclair Ferguson, and J. I. Packer (Downers Grove: InterVarsity, 1988), 359-61; idem, *Justification*, 232-33; idem, 'Justification: Yesterday, Today, Forever,' *JETS* 54/1 (2001): 62-63; Kevin Vanhoozer, 'Wrighting the Wrongs of the Reformation? The State of the Union with Christ in St. Paul and Protestant Theology,' in *Jesus, Paul and the People of God: A Theological Dialogue with N. T. Wright*, ed. Nichales Perrin and Richard B. Hays (Downers Grove: InterVarsity, 2011), 235-58, esp. 246-57; Marcus Peter Johnson, *One with Christ: An Evangelical Theology of Salvation* (Wheaton: Crossway, 2013), 87-98, 111-14, 161.

> of Christ cannot be imputed to us as long as we are not in Christ, since it is only on the basis of our oneness with Him that such an imputation could be reasonable. But this view fails to distinguish between our legal unity with Christ and our spiritual oneness with Him, and is a falsification of the fundamental element in the doctrine of redemption, namely, of the doctrine of justification. Justification is always a declaration of God, not on the basis of an existing condition, but on that of a gracious imputation,—a declaration which is not in harmony with the existing condition of the sinner. The judicial ground for all the special grace which we receive lies in the fact that the righteousness of Christ is freely imputed to us.[127]

Rather, the legal aspect of a believer's union with Christ, the covenant surety's representative obedience, is the legal basis of the sinner's justification.

Even though Geerhardus Vos's comments were written more than a century ago, they are still relevant against the attempts to gut imputation from union and rest solely on participatory categories. Vos writes:

> In our opinion Paul consciously and consistently subordinated the mystical aspect of the relation to Christ to the forensic one. Paul's mind was to such an extent forensically oriented that he regarded the entire complex of subjective spiritual changes that take place in the believer and of subjective spiritual blessings enjoyed by the believer as the direct outcome of the forensic work of Christ applied in justification. The mystical is based on the forensic, not the forensic on the mystical.[128]

---

127. Berkhof, *Systematic Theology*, 452.

128. Geerhardus Vos, 'The Alleged Legalism in Paul's Doctrine of Justification,' in *Redemptive History and Biblical Interpretation: The Shorter Writings of Geerhardus Vos*, ed. By Richard B. Gaffin, Jr. (Philipsburg: P & R, 1980), 384.

Vos made such claims because he presupposed the categories of the covenant, and in particular, the imputation of the obedience of Christ within the *pactum salutis*. Vos and Berkhof both assumed these categories and recognized that if these legal-covenantal categories are ignored, the *extra nos* of Christ's unique work as covenant surety becomes either obscured or entirely lost.[129] Imputation recognizes the extrinsic reality, the *extra nos*, of Christ's work *pro nobis*.[130] In this respect, Christ's work and role as covenant surety *pro nobis* is the legal ground of His work through the Spirit *in nobis*. Imputation guards the utterly gratuitous and free nature of justification.[131]

In the consideration of Christ's obedience, we must not forget the affective dimension of Christ's willingness to undertake the role as covenant surety. Critics have been quick to claim that imputation is a cold piece of business, like reconciling the columns in an accounting ledger, an action devoid of love.[132] But such criticisms fail to see the unbreakable covenantal bond between love and obedience. When Christ was asked which of the commandments was most important, He responded with the heart of the Deuteronomic covenantal *law*: 'Love the Lord your God with all your heart and with all

---

129. This is the case with two recent books. Michael Gorman argues for a participatory justification where, through union with Christ and co-crucifixion, believers are justified (Michael J. Gorman, *Inhabiting the Cruciform God: Kenosis, Justification, and Theosis in Paul's Narrative Soteriology* [Grand Rapids: Eerdmans, 2009], 63-86). Similar views appear in Douglas A. Campbell, *The Deliverance of God: An Apocalyptic Rereading of Justification in Paul* (Grand Rapids: Eerdmans, 2009).

130. R. Michael Allen, *Justification and the Gospel: Understanding the Contexts and Controversies* (Grand Rapids: Baker, 2013), 50.

131. Allen, *Justification*, 14.

132. Wright, *What St. Paul Really Said*, 110. Others, such as Michael Williams offer no exegesis and simply propose psychological categories that pit legal against relational categories (Michael Williams, 'Adam and Merit,' *Presbyterion* 35/2 [2009]: 87-94).

your soul and with all your strength and with all your mind' (Luke 10:27 // Mark 12:30 // Matt. 22:37; cf. Deut. 6:4). Imputation is not a cold piece of business or merely balancing the ledger, although the Bible itself employs this accounting nomenclature at a number of points (Matt. 6:12; 18:21-35; Rom. 4:4; Col. 2:14; cf. Lev. 25; Matt. 6:19-20). Rather, the covenant surety agrees to the Father's good plan and pledges His love to His Father and for His confederated bride – to obey perfectly His Father's will and to do so in the place of His bride – to love her first so that she can love and obey the bridegroom and the Father.

In love, the triune God chose the elect in Christ (Eph. 1:4). The Father so loved the world that He sent His only begotten Son (John 3:16). Christ demonstrated His love for His Father by obeying His commands (John 14:31). In love, Christ offered His obedience and laid down His life for His bride (John 15:9; Rom. 5:8; 2 Cor. 5:14). All of these expressions of love occur within the context of a covenant, whether in the *pactum salutis* or in its historical execution in the covenant of grace. Just as a watch does not function apart from its gears, union with Christ does not function apart from the gears of imputation. And just as the housing of the timepiece holds the watch face and gears together, imputation and union with Christ cannot function apart from the context of covenant, that which binds the one and the many.

Some still might object on the grounds that imputation relies upon unbiblical medieval notions of merit. Christ's obedience is banked and stored for distribution in an *ad hoc* fashion.[133]

---

133. Michael Bird, *Evangelical Theology: A Biblical and Systematic Introduction* (Grand Rapids: Zondervan, 2013), 227, 562-63; Wright, *Justification*, 228, 231; also Norman Shepherd, *The Call of Grace: How the Covenant Illuminates Salvation and Evangelism* (Phillipsburg: P & R, 2000), 61-62.

First, we must demythologize a term. As much as some might consider *merit* a theological slur, it simply denotes the concept of equity – the idea that if someone meets stated obligations of an agreement then he is entitled to the consequent goal or reward.[134] A number of Reformed confessions employ the term in this manner.[135] Simply invoking the term *merit* does not automatically commit one to a specific theological position, evident by the fact that Roman Catholic and Protestant theologians have historically both spoken of merit within their respective theological systems. Where a theologian places merit, who specifically earns it, and how it is defined, on the other hand, is another matter entirely.

Second, medieval discussions of merit typically center upon the ability of redeemed sinners to merit their final justification. God grants the first grace of initial justification by His grace, but then, by faith working through love, those who are in union with Christ cooperate with the grace of God to increase in their righteous standing.[136] Often devoid of the doctrine of the covenant, medieval theologians resorted to the category of *condign* (full) and *congruent* (half) merit. Only Christ is capable of condign merit, whereas God looks upon the merit of believers and grades it on a curve.[137] Beyond this, the Roman Catholic Church maintains that when saints perform works of supererogation, obedience above and beyond what the law requires, their earned merit is

134. Contra Williams, 'Adam and Merit,' 88-89.

135. WCF XVI.v, XVII.ii, WLC qq. 55, 174, 193; Belgic Conf., §XXII-XXIV, XXXV.

136. Council of Trent, 'Decree on Justification,' §7; cf. C. Stephen Sullivan, *The Formulation of the Tridentine Doctrine on Merit* (Washington, DC: Catholic University of America Press, 1959); McGrath, *Iustitia Dei*, 138-50.

137. Joseph P. Wawrykow, *God's Grace and Human Action: 'Merit' in the Theology of Thomas Aquinas* (Notre Dame: University of Notre Dame Press, 1995), 177-259.

placed within the treasury of merits to be dispensed by the Pope through indulgences.[138]

True, in the Roman Catholic understanding we find representative obedience and merit transferred from one party to another. But there are significant dissimilarities in comparison to traditional Reformed formulations of imputation. In a covenantal context, there is no need for the categories of condign or congruent merit. Rather, God, as covenant lord, sets the terms of the covenant – if one obeys the law perfectly he receives the reward of eternal life, but if he disobeys he receives eternal death.[139] Concepts of merit that introduce the condign–congruent distinction often do so apart from the context of the covenant, and thereby excise the office of covenant surety.[140] Apart from a covenant surety, they must somehow account for how redeemed but nonetheless sinful creatures can merit eternal life. A number of medieval theologians saw the deficiencies in the failure to account for the covenant and therefore incorporated it into their understanding of how

138. See, e.g., *The Manual of Indulgences Being a Collection of Prayers and Good Works, to which the Sovereign Pontiffs Have Attached Holy Indulgences* (London: Burns & Oates, 1878), xii-xxviii; cf. Robert W. Shaffern, 'The Medieval Theology of Indulgences,' in *Promissory Notes on the Treasury of Merits*, ed. R. N. Swanson (Leiden: Brill, 2006), 11-36, esp. 25-27. Note, the concept of a treasury of merits does not originate with Roman Catholic theology but in Rabbinic theology (see Arthur Marmorstein, *The Doctrine of Merits in Old Rabbinical Literature* [London: Jews' College, 1920], 20-21, 91).

139. Cf., e.g., Johannes Cocceius, *Summa Theologiae ex Scripturis Repetita*, XXII.27, in *Operum Johannis Coccei* (Amsterdam: Johannis à Someren, 1673), 90; Turretin, *Institutes*, VIII.iv.16-17; Daniel Wyttenbach, *Tentamen Theologiae Dogmaticae Methodo Scientifico Pertractatae*, vol. 2 (Frankfurt: Andreae et Hort, 1747), §739 (p. 569); cf. Heinrich Heppe, *Reformed Dogmatics: Set Out and Illustrated from the Sources*, trans. G. T. Thomson, ed. Ernst Bizer (London: George Allen & Unwin Ltd., 1950), 288, 296.

140. See McGrath, *Iustitia Dei*, 145-46; Stephen Strehle, *Calvinism, Federalism, and Scholasticism: A Study of the Reformed Doctrine of Covenant* (New York: Peter Lang, 1988), 24-82.

God accepts human merit, but they still failed to account for the necessity of the covenant surety.

Within the *pactum* the Father establishes the requirement of perfect obedience by His Son, which entirely precludes any category of congruent merit. Whether in the fourth servant song, Matthew 3–4, Romans 4:25, 5:12-21, 8:1-4, or 2 Corinthians 5:20-21, one thing is clear – Christ has no companions in His covenantal work as surety. Christ alone was baptized to fulfill all righteousness, and when Jesus went to the cross in fulfillment of Isaiah 53, He went alone while His disciples remained behind. Christ alone breaks the death-grip of the law and alone ushers in the eschaton, the new heavens and earth. Like Atlas bearing the weight of the world upon his shoulders, Christ alone bears the weight of the sin of the world (John 1:29). Contrary to the claims of von Balthasar, Jesus does not merely open up acting space for others to recapitulate His obedience.[141] Christ stands in the place of His elect and offers the obedience they never offered in Adam, and subsequently could not offer in a sin-fallen state, and then because of that obedience He ushers them into the new creation where they offer their obedience to the Father. As surety Christ provides an indefectible standing before the divine bar for His elect bride, which frees her to love and obey.[142]

The timing of imputation

Two more related issues require comment, namely, the nature and timing of the imputation of Christ's righteousness. The first issue relates to the seventeenth-century debate over whether Christ was a conditional (*fideiussor*) or absolute (*expromissor*) surety. Briefly, Turretin's critique of Cocceius's position rings true – the Scriptures

---

141. Von Balthasar, *Theo-Drama*, III:201, 249.

142. R. Michael Allen, *The Christ's Faith: A Dogmatic Account* (London: T & T Clark, 2009), 155-57.

do not admit any distinction in the nature of the forgiveness of sins.[143] Isaiah 53 does not indicate that Old Testament saints would receive anything less than full reconciliation. Abraham, in fact, is *the* model recipient of the imputed righteousness of Christ for New Testament saints (Rom. 4:1-5). Paul nowhere indicates that Abraham experienced anything less than the full forgiveness of his sins and the imputation of Christ's righteousness. Although Christ had yet to become incarnate and complete His earthly ministry, the very existence of the *pactum salutis* alone was inherently sufficient to provide for the redemption of Old Testament saints. The promise that Christ would execute the office of covenant surety was sufficient, not because the execution of the promise (incarnation, life, death, and resurrection) was unnecessary, but because God always keeps His word. Old Testament believers could be united to Christ and experience the provisional outpouring of the Spirit. The effectual calling and regeneration of Old Testament saints were the initial sparks of the same fire that was eventually fully ignited at Pentecost through the outpouring of the Spirit. Turretin is also correct – the concept of a conditional surety should be rejected because it represents the foreign imposition of the categories of Roman law upon the biblical text.

The second issue involves the timing of the imputation of Christ's righteousness. When do the elect receive His righteousness, in the *pactum* or in the historical execution of the covenant of grace? As Part I demonstrated, a number of Reformed theologians have advocated the idea that Christ's righteousness is imputed in the *pactum*. The fact that they place the imputation in the *pactum* produced the distinction between active and passive justification – the objective imputation and its subjective reception by faith. Herman Bavinck, for example, contends that though the

143. Turretin, *Institutes*, XII.ix.

covenant of grace occurs in history, its roots lie in eternity with the *pactum*. Bavinck writes, 'Hence in eternity an imputation of Christ to his own and of the church to Christ took place. Between them an exchange took place, and a mystical union was formed that underlies their realization in history, indeed produces and leads them.'[144] Bavinck comments that these ideas lead some to advocate that the elect were therefore justified from eternity, but that this position met with stiff resistance.

Rather, theologians who advocated 'a kind of eternal justification' believed that this exchange never constituted a full justification: 'They considered it its first component and expressly stated that this justification had to be repeated, continued, and completed in the resurrection of Christ, in the gospel, in the calling, in the testimony of the Holy Spirit by faith and from its works, and finally at the last judgment.'[145] To this end Bavinck points out that the advocates of *pactum*-imputation never treated the doctrine of justification under theology proper but rather under applied soteriology.[146] Bavinck follows this path and therefore contends:

> Atonement, forgiveness, justification, the mystical union, sanctification, glorification, and so on—they do not come into being after and as a result of faith but are objectively, actively present in Christ. They are the fruits solely of his suffering and dying, and they are appropriated on our part by faith. God grants them and imputes them to the church in the decree of election, the resurrection of Christ, in his calling by the gospel. In God's own time they will also become the subjective possession of believers.[147]

144. Bavinck, *Reformed Dogmatics*, III:590.

145. Bavinck, *Reformed Dogmatics*, III:591.

146. Bavinck, *Reformed Dogmatics*, III:591.

147. Bavinck, *Reformed Dogmatics*, III:523.

Elsewhere Bavinck succinctly states: 'The imputation of Christ precedes the gift of the Spirit, and regeneration, faith, and conversion do not first lead us to Christ but are taken from Christ by the Holy Spirit and imparted to his own.'[148]

Bavinck's case is logically strong but exegetically weak. He starts from biblical premises, namely, the *pactum*, the appointment of Christ as covenant surety, election, and the imputation of Christ's righteousness. But he never makes an exegetical case for the timing of the imputation of Christ's righteousness. He never exegetically proves that election and imputation are coordinate events. Moreover, his construction runs against the grain of a number of biblical statements about the corporate identity of the elect prior to their union with Christ. Three points determine the question of the timing of imputation.

First, Isaiah 53 serves as a window into the *pactum* and the plan to impute Christ's righteousness to the elect. As common as it is for Old Testament prophets to speak or write in the prophetic-past, speaking about future events in the past tense to convey the idea that the events will with all certainty come to pass, Isaiah sees the whole complex surrounding the double-imputation as a future event.[149] Isaiah peered into the *pactum* and saw that the servant would justify many and bear their iniquities, not that his righteousness had already been imputed or that the sins of the elect had already been imputed to Him. Isaiah 53 leaves no room for a distinction between the so-called active and passive justification. Yes, we can distinguish between the objective character of Christ's imputed righteousness and its subjective reception by faith, but we must not conflate the decree to impute with the actual imputation by faith.

---

148. Bavinck, *Reformed Dogmatics*, III:525.

149. Allis, *Unity of Isaiah*, 30-31.

Second, though the elect are united to Christ in the decree of election, this does not mean, *pace* Bavinck, that they are already mystically united to Him. All fallen sinners are united to Adam and under a state of condemnation – they are, by nature, children of wrath (Eph. 2:1-3). It seems like an irreconcilable and contradictory assertion to say that the elect are at the same time in possession of the imputed righteousness of Christ and under divine condemnation, dead in their trespasses and sins, and still legally united to Adam.

Third, when Paul speaks of the justification of elect sinners, he always conjoins justification and faith (e.g., Rom. 1:17; 3:22, 25-26, 28; 4:5, 9, 13, 16, 22; 5:1-2; 9:30, 32). While it is possible to employ biblical words (e.g., justification) in a dogmatic sense that goes beyond biblical usage, it seems undesirable to attach the biblical term *justification* to Christ's appointment as covenant surety. There does not appear to be exegetical warrant to support the claim that His righteousness is imputed in eternity. Granted, Bavinck and other theologians qualify its usage with the term *active* and explain that this is not a full justification, and it requires other steps in the process, namely, its application in time. But nevertheless, apart from exegetical warrant, it seems unhelpful to employ the common distinction between active and passive justification. Occurrences of the term *justification* appear to be related to historical instances when people place their faith in Christ, not simply to the imputation of Christ's righteousness. Imputation is necessary for justification but does not constitute the entirety of the judicial act. Hence, the term *justification*, even if qualified, should not be used for the imputation of Christ's righteousness. It should be reserved for the historical soteriological judicial act when God declares a person righteous by faith alone in Christ alone.

How, then, should we account for Christ's role as covenant surety and the timing of imputation? As common as the active–passive justification distinction may be, it appears that the equally common distinction between the *decree* and its *execution* is a better way to account for the timing of imputation. In the *pactum salutis* the triune God decrees to impute the righteousness of Christ to the elect, but the actual dispensation and reception of that imputed righteousness do not occur until the person receives it by a Spirit-wrought faith. The statements in the Westminster Confession, and subsequent modifications made by congregational theologians at Savoy, aptly capture the decree–execution distinction. The Westminster Confession states: 'God did, from all eternity, decree to justify all the elect, and Christ did, in the fullness of time, die for their sins, and rise again for their justification: nevertheless, they are not justified, until the Holy Spirit doth, in due time, actually apply Christ unto them' (XI.iv).

Apart from faith, there is no instrumental means by which a person might receive the imputed righteousness of Christ. This decree–execution formulation not only better explains the relationship between Isaiah 53 and Paul's statements about justification but also elucidates how one might at the same time be elect but still under condemnation, a child of wrath, and in Adam. One might still be in prison but nevertheless designated as the recipient of a pardon. It is one thing to designate that one should be pardoned and another thing to possess it, which is manifest in freedom from imprisonment. In other words, there is a difference between the *right* and *title* to imputation and the possession of it by faith. An heir has right and title to an inheritance but does not have possession of it until the will is executed. The winner of a presidential election is the president-elect, but he does not actually assume office and possess authority until he takes the oath.

Bavinck might reply to this construction that, yes, the decree–execution distinction is common, but it nevertheless creates a problem because it means that 'regeneration, faith, and conversion' might become 'preparations that occur apart from Christ and the covenant of grace ... conditions that a person has to meet in toto or in part in his or her own strength to be incorporated into that covenant.'[150] This is where the distinction between the *pactum salutis* and the covenant of grace is important and necessary to maintain. The elect are part of the *pactum salutis* by virtue of their election in Christ, the covenant surety, but they are not participants in the covenant of grace until they are indwelled by the Spirit and united to Christ by faith. The older distinction between the *legal* (or federal) union and *mystical* (personal indwelling) union to delineate between these aspects of redemption proves to be quite helpful at this juncture.[151] Union with Christ as a theological category has several different facets for which one must account, and to confuse or fail to distinguish them can lead to significant problems.

Another consideration is that, while faith is a necessary pre-condition for the reception of Christ's righteousness, this does not necessitate the idea that the elect person must somehow prepare himself to receive Christ. Effectual calling and faith are sovereign works of the Holy Spirit predicated upon Christ's role as covenant surety and the decree to impute His righteousness to the elect sinner. Just as Old Testament believers enjoyed the benefits of union with Christ prior to His incarnation, so too elect sinners receive Christ's imputed righteousness on the same legal basis. The covenant of redemption is absolutely binding. Christ's imputed righteousness is the sole legal basis for the elect sinner's

150. Bavinck, *Reformed Dogmatics*, III:525.

151. So, e.g., Charles Hodge, *Ephesians* (1856; Edinburgh: Banner of Truth, 1991), 9.

mystical union with Christ. The sinner is effectually called and given faith, through which he receives the imputed righteousness of Christ because of the legal union and the decreed imputation in the *pactum salutis*.

Conclusion

A Jewish rabbi tells the story about several men sitting in a boat upon the ocean. One of them began to drill a hole in the bottom of the boat and was immediately asked, 'What do you think you're doing?' The man responded, 'Whatever I'm doing is none of your concern,' to which his companion retorted, 'On the contrary, if you sink the boat we will all die!' This amusing story illustrates that all human beings live within a corporate context. The cliché is true, no man is an island unto himself. We all live on one of two islands, that of the first or last Adam. There are no other places in the cosmos where one might stand. The covenantal relationship between the Son and His bride, however, has an eternal source in the covenant of redemption.

There in the intra-trinitarian council, the Father creates a plan to lay the sins of the elect upon His Son, and the Son willingly submits to His Father's will and offers His loving obedience in their stead. In dogmatic terms, the Son's appointment and role as covenant surety establishes the loving legal–forensic foundation upon which all of the other benefits of redemption rest. Apart from the imputation of the obedience of the covenant surety, there is no firm foundation upon which to build salvation. But as this chapter has noted, Christ's appointment as covenant surety does not comprise the whole of our redemption. The decree to redeem requires the execution of the decree. The work of the covenant surety involves both His own work as well as the consequential outpouring of the Spirit to apply the work to the elect. The

Son not only agreed to be sent, but so did the Spirit. Hence, in the next chapter we turn to matters related to the *pactum*, the Spirit, and the application of redemption, or the nature of the *ordo salutis*. The work of the Spirit and the *ordo salutis* receives its origins and structure from the *pactum*. In other words, the order of the trinitarian missions within the *pactum* and its subsequent execution determine the sequence of the *ordo salutis*.

~:5:~

Ordo Salutis

Introduction

The *ordo salutis* (order of salvation) was once common and unquestioned within the Reformed tradition but recently it has come under significant criticism from a wide range of theologians and scholars.[1] Debate over the legitimacy of the *ordo* typically centers upon the exegesis of one particular text, Romans 8:28-30, the apostle Paul's famous golden chain of salvation. A common Reformed order of salvation is as follows: election, effectual calling, faith, justification, adoption, sanctification,

1. See critical remarks by G. C. Berkouwer, *Faith and Justification* (Grand Rapids: Eerdmans, 1954), 30-31; Otto Weber, *Foundations for Dogmatics*, 2 vols., trans. Darrell L. Guder (Grand Rapids: Eerdmans, 1983), II:337-39; Wolfhart Pannenberg, *Systematic Theology*, 3 vols. (Grand Rapids: Eerdmans, 1993), III:228-31; William B. Evans, *Imputation and Impartation: Union with Christ in American Reformed Theology* (Eugene: Wipf & Stock, 2008), 265; Karl Barth, *The Theology of the Reformed Confessions*, trans. Darrell L. Guder and Judith J. Guder (Louisville: Westminster John Knox, 2002), 139; Richard B. Gaffin, Jr., *Resurrection and Redemption: A Study in Paul's Soteriology* (1978; Phillipsburg: P & R, 1987), 135-43; cf. idem, *By Faith, Not by Sight: Paul and the Order of Salvation*, 2nd ed. (Phillipsburg: P & R, 2013), 49-50 n. 22.

perseverance, and glorification.[2] Is the application of redemption accomplished in one single act where the various facets do not have any particular order, or is there a logical (not chronological or temporal) and in some sense causal sequence present? Historic iterations of the *ordo* maintain that there is a logical sequence between its various elements. This is evident from Paul's use of a cause and effect argument in Romans 8:28-30, a *sorites*.[3] But as important as the proper exegesis of Romans 8:28-30 is, the *ordo* does not rest upon this lone text. We must take a large step back from this debate and ask, How does the *pactum salutis* relate to the question and viability of the *ordo salutis*?

At first glance, given the paucity of theologians who correlate the *pactum* and *ordo*, some might think that the two doctrines have no connection. But even though few make the connection, some theologians have recognized the relationship between Christ's appointment as covenant surety within the covenant of redemption and the *ordo salutis*, as Part I demonstrates. Thomas Aquinas (1225-74) makes the connection between the ontology of the Trinity and redemption, though he does not discuss it in the specific terms of the *pactum* and *ordo salutis*. Aquinas argues that the trinitarian processions determine the nature and manner by which fallen humanity returns to God.[4] Karl Rahner echoes this idea to a certain extent: 'Each one of the three

2. Cf. Louis Berkhof, *Systematic Theology: New Combined Edition* (1932-36; Grand Rapids: Eerdmans, 1996), 415-22.

3. For a treatment of the history, criticism, and exegetical and theological defense of the *ordo salutis* see J. V. Fesko, 'Romans 8:29-30 and the Question of the *Ordo Salutis*,' *Journal of Reformed Theology* 8 (2014): 35-60.

4. Thomas Aquinas, *Commentum in Lib. I Sententiarum*, bk. I, d. 14, q. 2, art. 2, in *Doctoris Angelici divi Thomae Aquinatis: Opera Omnia*, vol. 7 (Paris: apud Ludovicum Vives, 1871), 170-71; cf. Gilles Emery, *The Trinitarian Theology of St. Thomas Aquinas* (Oxford: Oxford University Press, 2010), 362-63, 375-76. My thanks to Brian Hecker for reminding me of these passages.

divine persons communicates himself to man in gratuitous grace in his own personal particularity and diversity. This trinitarian communication is the ontological ground of man's life of grace and eventually of the direct vision of the divine persons in eternity.'[5]

Along these lines, two theologians from different traditions have made similar observations about the connections between the intra-trinitarian missions and the *ordo*, Geerhardus Vos (1862-1949) and Thomas Weinandy (b. 1946-). In a nutshell, both Vos and Weindandy argue that the intra-trinitarian processions and missions shape the *ordo salutis*. Vos, a Reformed theologian, holds to the doctrine of the *pactum* and argues for the priority of the forensic over the transformative aspects of redemption based upon Christ's foundational appointment as covenant surety. Weinandy, a Roman Catholic theologian, argues for a different understanding of the trinitarian processions. He contends that because both the Father and the Spirit participate in the Son's procession, we must reconfigure our understanding of the divine missions. The consequence of reconfiguring the trinitarian missions means that we must rethink the *ordo salutis*. Both Vos and Weinandy come from different theological traditions and arrive at very different conclusions, but they have this in common: they recognize the connection between the processions, missions, and the *ordo salutis*. The order of the trinitarian missions determines the order of salvation.

This chapter is not merely concerned with a comparison between Vos and Weinandy, however, as interesting as this might be. Rather, I employ Vos and Weinandy as comparative foils to showcase one chief idea: the processions, missions, and *ordo* are interconnected. If the *pactum–ordo* connection is viable, and

---

5. Karl Rahner, *The Trinity*, trans. Joseph Donceel (New York: Herder & Herder, 2005), 34-35.

even necessary, we must first explore the relationship between the *pactum* and the mission of the Holy Spirit. Even those theologians who opt for a christological *pactum* must nevertheless relate the work of Christ to the Holy Spirit. As I have argued at the beginning of Part III, I believe that a trinitarian formulation of the *pactum* offers a thicker account of the pre-temporal intra-trinitarian activity.

Hence, this chapter first explores the Spirit's connections to and role within the *pactum salutis*. Although the Son alone is covenant surety, He is not alone in His work. Redemption is an act of the triune God – the Father sends the Son, the Son executes His mission as covenant surety, and the Father and the Son send the Spirit to apply the Son's work of Christ to the elect. The Son's work as surety, however, is pneumatically charged – Christ executes His mission in the power of the Holy Spirit. The Spirit is integral to the Son's work as covenant surety. Second, the chapter examines the Spirit's mission in connection with the *pactum*. The covenant of redemption entails the appointment of the covenant surety as well as the Spirit's mission to apply the surety's work to the elect. The Spirit, therefore, not only applies the work of Christ to the elect in terms of the imputation of His righteousness, but is also the agent of sanctification. The *pactum* has both legal–forensic and transformative realities and blessings in view. The triune God planned both the justification and sanctification of the Son's bride. Third, the chapter examines the different positions of Vos and Weinandy to show how the trinitarian processions and covenantal missions determine the *ordo salutis*. Specifically, this chapter defends the idea that the *pactum salutis* provides the original context to recognize the trinitarian character of redemption, the foundation of the *ordo salutis*, and the relationship between the forensic and transformative aspects of redemption. In this particular case, the *pactum salutis* necessitates the logical priority of the forensic to the transformative aspects of redemption. The chapter then addresses two possible objections to the idea that the forensic takes priority over the transformative. Last, the chapter concludes with a few summary observations.

The pactum salutis and the Holy Spirit

The role of the Holy Spirit in the *pactum salutis* originates in eternity but we find hints of His function within the historical unfolding drama of redemption. In particular, it is important to note the pneumatological character of the Son's mission so that we continue to recognize the fully trinitarian character of His appointment as covenant surety. Therefore we will first survey the pneumatic nature of Christ's mission and then turn to explore the Spirit's unique mission.

Pneumatic christology

The pneumatic character of the Messiah's mission first unfolds in the shadow lands of the Old Testament in a number of passages where various figures have the Spirit descend or 'rush' upon them. Joshua was 'full of the spirit of wisdom' (Deut. 34:9; cf. Num. 27:18; Isa. 11:2), and the Spirit fell upon a number of the judges and empowered them to carry out their divinely ordained missions (Judg. 3:10; 11:29). The Spirit of Yahweh rushed upon Samson and empowered him to strike down thirty men from Ashkelon (Judg. 14:19). The Spirit of God similarly rushed upon Saul and inspired him to prophesy (1 Sam. 10:10). The Spirit rushed upon David when Samuel anointed him king of Israel (1 Sam. 16:13). At one level, the Spirit empowered these different Old Testament individuals to carry out various tasks. The Spirit rushed upon Saul as he had rested on other Old Testament savior-judges, such as Othniel, Gideon, Jephthah, and Samson. Saul prophesied in his anointed state, and the Spirit also equipped him for holy war (1 Sam. 10:7; 11:1-11).[6] But there is more to the Spirit's activity with these Old Testament figures. The Spirit endowed individuals with pneumatic gifts to foreshadow the pinnacle of His work, the anointing of the Messiah. Unlike His fallible and flawed typical predecessors, Christ would offer His perfect loving obedience in the power of the Holy Spirit.[7]

The prophecy of Isaiah has a number of key elements that reveal the pneumatic character of Messiah's work, which stands in contrast to the sinful typical predecessors. The Spirit of Yahweh would rest upon Him, the Spirit of wisdom, understanding, counsel, might, knowledge, and especially the 'fear of the Lord' (Isa. 11:2). Wisdom (חכמה) and understanding (בינה) are governmental attributes necessary for righteous rule (Deut. 1:13; 1 Kings 3:9). Counsel (עצה) and might (גבורה) are military attributes necessary to execute a wise course of action. Knowledge (דעת) and a fear of the Lord (יראת יהוה) are necessary to apply truth to life.[8] These three couplets of attributes that come from Yahweh's Spirit are the standard qualities of a righteous king (cf. Isa. 10:13; 2 Sam. 14:17; 1 Kings 3:5-6).[9] These attributes also ensured that the servant would be marked by ethical purity.[10] In this vein, the fear of the Lord is the beginning of wisdom and knowledge (Ps. 111:10; Prov. 1:7; 9:10), a fountain of life (Prov. 14:26-27), and the motivating factor behind obedience, *hesed* (Prov. 16:6;

---

6. Christopher J. H. Wright, *Knowing the Holy Spirit* (Downers Grove: InterVarsity Press, 2006), 40-41; Ralph W. Klein, *1 Samuel*, WBC, vol. 10 (Waco: Word, 1983), 107.

7. Wright, *Holy Spirit*, 92-93.

8. J. Alec Motyer, *The Prophecy of Isaiah: An Introduction and Commentary* (Downers Grove: InterVarsity, 1993), 122.

9. John D. W. Watts, *Isaiah*, WBC, 2 vols. (Waco: Word, 1987), I:171.

10. John C. Oswalt, *The Book of Isaiah*, 2 vols., NICOT (Grand Rapids: Eerdmans, 1986), I:279-80; Brevard S. Childs, *Isaiah*, OTL (Louisville: Westminster John Knox, 2001), 102-03.

Exod. 20:20), the reward for which is 'riches and honor and life' (Prov. 22:4; cf. 19:23; 3:16; 15:33; 18:12; 1 Kings 3:12-14).[11] Noteworthy is the fact that the Spirit-anointed servant would possess the fear of *Yahweh*. Isaiah invokes the tetragrammaton, the covenant name of God, which has connections to God's law (Exod. 3:14).[12] The servant's anointing with the Spirit means that He would, with all certainty, yield His life in loving obedience to the will of His heavenly Father.

The Spirit's presence upon and with the Messiah is by design within the framework of the *pactum salutis*. The prophet reveals that Yahweh's 'chosen,' the one in whom Yahweh delighted, would have the Spirit rest upon Him, and through Him would 'bring forth justice to the nations' (Isa. 42:1).[13] The *pactum* is the context in which Christ's election as covenant surety takes place, but it is also the realm where the Spirit's role in support of the Son's mission finds its genesis. These Isaianic texts reveal that the Father promised to equip the Son with the necessary pneumatic gifts to carry out His mission as covenant surety. The Spirit empowered the Son's mission to herald the gospel, and through His life, death, resurrection, and ascension to unleash the eschatological exodus out from under the bondage of Satan, sin, and death (Isa. 61:1). In fact, Christ read this very passage from the scroll of Isaiah, 'The Spirit of the Lord GOD is upon me, because the LORD has anointed me to bring good news to the poor,' and told the gathered people that this prophecy had been

---

11. Bruce K. Waltke, *The Book of Proverbs*, 2 vols., NICOT (Grand Rapids: Eerdmans, 2005), I:202-03; cf. Edward J. Young, *The Book of Isaiah*, 3 vols., NICOT (Grand Rapids: Eerdmans, 1965), I:383.

12. Tremper Longman, *Proverbs*, BCOTWS (Grand Rapids: Baker, 2006), 101.

13. Some argue that Isaiah 42:1 speaks of Yahweh placing His 'breath' upon the servant, not the Holy Spirit (John Goldingay, *The Message of Isaiah 40-55* [London: T & T Clark, 2005], 154-58.

fulfilled in their hearing (Luke 4:18-21).[14] That Christ read this passage and claimed to fulfill it meant He was conscious of His messianic identity, mission, and pneumatic anointing.[15]

Further confirmation of the Spirit's role in the Son's mission appears in numerous places throughout the New Testament. From the very outset, the Spirit brings about the incarnation of Christ (Matt. 1:18-20; Luke 1:35). Christ was anointed with the Spirit from on high. In imagery evocative of the initial creation and Israel's own baptism at the Red Sea, Christ emerged from the waters of His baptism and, in the language of Psalm 2:7 and Isaiah 42:1, the Father declared His approbation: 'This is my beloved Son, with whom I am well pleased' (Matt. 3:17).[16] The Spirit descended like a dove and rested upon Him (Matt. 3:16). Then, like Israel of old, who was led by the pillar of cloud by day and fire by night, the Spirit led Christ into the wilderness (Matt. 4:1; cf. Ps. 143:10; Isa. 63; Hag. 2:5). Where Israel failed her probation wandering in the wilderness, Jesus the true Israel of God succeeded. He offered Spirit-empowered obedience to His heavenly Father in accord with the terms of the *pactum*.[17] Following the opening of Christ's ministry, the Spirit's work in support of His mission appears in several key places. Christ

---

14. David W. Pao, *Acts and the Isaianic New Exodus* (Grand Rapids: Baker, 2000), 70-84.

15. Geerhardus Vos, *The Self-Disclosure of Jesus: The Modern Debate about the Messianic Consciousness* (Phillipsburg: P & R, 1953), 114.

16. G. K. Beale and D. A. Carson, eds., *Commentary on the New Testament Use of the Old Testament* (Grand Rapids: Baker, 2007), 14.

17. On these themes, see Brandon D. Crowe, *The Obedient Son: Deuteronomy and Christology in the Gospel of Matthew* (Berlin: De Grutyer, 2012); Joel Kennedy, *The Recapitulation of Israel: Use of Israel's History in Matthew 1:1–4:11* (Tübingen: Mohr Siebeck, 2008), 153-215; Thomas Schreiner, *New Testament Theology: Magnifying God in Christ* (Grand Rapids: Baker, 2008), 441.

wields the Spirit to cast out demons (Matt. 12:28). According to the author of Hebrews, Jesus offered Himself up on the cross 'through the eternal Spirit' (Heb. 9:14).[18] Hebrews connects Christ's sacrificial offering to Isaiah's Spirit-anointed servant, the suffering servant who bears the sins and justifies the many (Isa. 53).[19] And Christ was raised from the dead by the power of the Spirit (Rom. 1:4; 8:11), which constituted His justification (1 Tim. 3:16).[20]

The Son, therefore, does not carry out His work apart from the Spirit. The Son carries out His work and mission as covenant surety in the power of the Spirit. The Reformed tradition has historically acknowledged this but has not emphasized it in recent years.[21] In fact, the pneumatic nature of Christ's work is embedded in a number of Reformed confessions and catechisms.[22] For example, question 35 of the Heidelberg Catechism (1563) states that the Spirit's work of the incarnation insured that original sin did not infect Christ. Heidelberg Catechism q. 31 acknowledges

---

18. William L. Lane, *Hebrews*, 2 vols., WBC (Dallas: Word, 1991), II:240.

19. F. F. Bruce, *Hebrews*, NICNT (Grand Rapids: Eerdmans, 1964), 205; David Coffey, 'The Holy Spirit as the Mutual Love of the Father and the Son,' *Theological Studies* 51 (1990): 209-11.

20. Schreiner, *New Testament Theology*, 477.

21. Some either fail to address the subject or give it slight attention, e.g., John Frame, *Systematic Theology: An Introduction to Christian Belief* (Phillipsburg: P & R, 2013), 401, 926; J. van Genderen and W. H. Velema, *Concise Reformed Dogmatics* (Phillipsburg: P & R, 1992), 463-510; Robert L. Reymond, *A New Systematic Theology of the Christian Faith*, 2nd ed. (Nashville: Thomas Nelson, 1998), 545-82, 623-69. Two notable exceptions to this trend are Abraham Kuyper, *The Work of the Holy Spirit* (1900; Chattanooga: AMG Publishers, 1995), 85-120; and Sinclair B. Ferguson, *The Holy Spirit* (Downers Grove: InterVarsity, 1996), 35-56.

22. See Yuzo Adhinarta, *The Doctrine of the Holy Spirit in the Major Reformed Confessions and Catechisms of the Sixteenth and Seventeenth Centuries* (Carlisle: Langham Monographs, 2012), 56-66.

that God ordained Christ to be the chief prophet and teacher and, as such, was anointed with the Holy Spirit. The Westminster Confession (1647) teaches that the Spirit-wrought incarnation brought about the hypostatic union of the two distinct yet inseparable natures, the divinity and the humanity.[23]

In fact, according to the Westminster Standards, Christ did no work in His earthly ministry apart from the anointing and empowering of the Holy Spirit.[24] To this end the Westminster Confession states:

> The Lord Jesus, in his human nature thus united to the divine, was sanctified, and anointed with the Holy Spirit, above measure, having in him all the treasures of wisdom and knowledge; in whom it pleased the Father that all fullness should dwell; to the end that, being holy, harmless, undefiled, and full of grace and truth, he might be thoroughly furnished to execute the office of a mediator, and surety (WCF VIII.iii).

Echoing Hebrews 9:14, the Confession also states: 'The Lord Jesus, by his perfect obedience, and sacrifice of himself, which he, through the eternal Spirit, once offered up unto God, hath fully satisfied the justice of his Father; and purchased, not only reconciliation, but an everlasting inheritance in the kingdom of heaven, for all those whom the Father hath given unto him' (WCF VIII.v). Through His anointing, the Spirit bathes the entire ministry of Christ.

John Owen (1616-83) provides an example of ten different ways the Spirit is involved in the Son's mission.[25] The Spirit:

---

23. WCF VIII.ii; cf. WLC q. 37; WSC q. 22.

24. O. Palmer Robertson, 'The Holy Spirit and the Westminster Confession of Faith,' in *The Westminster Confession into the 21st Century*, vol. 1, ed. J. Ligon Duncan (Fearn: Christian Focus, 2003), 57-100, esp. 78-79.

25. For other similar treatments and statements, see, e.g., Francis Turretin, *Institutes of Elenctic Theology*, 3 vols., ed. James T. Dennison, Jr., trans. George Musgrave Giger

1. Framed, formed, and miraculously conceived of the body of Christ.

2. Sanctified Christ's human nature and filled it with grace according to the measure of its receptivity.

3. Carried on His work and was the immediate principle in all of Christ's moral operations.

4. Anointed Christ with all of the extraordinary powers and gifts that were necessary for the exercise of His office.

5. Wrought the miraculous works by which Christ's ministry was attested and confirmed.

6. Guided, comforted, and supported Christ throughout His ministry in temptation, obedience, and suffering.

7. Undergirded Christ as He offered Himself up.

8. Continued Christ's hypostatic union of the divine and human natures even in His state of death.

9. Was a co-agent in Christ's resurrection with the Father and Son, whereby Christ was '"justified in the Spirit," by a declaration of his acquitment from the sentence of death and all the evils which he underwent ... through the mighty and effectual working of the Spirit of God.'

(Phillipsburg: P & R, 1992-97), XIII.xii.1-8; David Dickson, *An Exposition of All St. Pauls Epistles* (London: Francis Eglesfield, 1659), 221; James Ussher, *A Body of Divinity* (London: Jonathan Robinson, 1702), 74; Patrick Gillespie, *The Ark of the Covenant Opened* (London: Tho. Parkhurst, 1677), 173-74, 226-29; Thomas Goodwin, *An Exposition of Various Passages of the Epistle to the Ephesians*, in *The Works of Thomas Goodwin*, 12 vols. (1861-66; Eureka: Tanski Publications, 1996), II:399-406; idem, *The Work of the Holy Ghost in Our Salvation*, in *Works*, I.iii (vol. VI, pp. 10-13); Thomas Watson, *A Body of Practical Divinity* (London: Thomas Parkhurst, 1692), 99, 204; John Brown, *The Life of Justification Opened* (Utrecht: 1695), 394.

10. Glorified Christ's human nature and made it suitable for its eternal session at the right hand of the Father.[26]

Owen was a proponent of the *pactum salutis*, which means that he coordinated the Spirit's supporting work with the Son's covenantal mission.[27] The pneumatic character of the Son's covenantal mission originates within the *pactum salutis* and further evidences the fully trinitarian character of both the intra-trinitarian covenant as well as its consequential redemption. That the Father anoints His Son with the Spirit does not undermine the fact that He alone is the covenant surety. Christ did not cheat by relying upon the Spirit, like an athlete resorting to banned substances to enhance his performance.[28] When God first placed humans in the garden of Eden, Adam was supposed to rely upon the power of the Spirit and offer his obedience to secure eternal life. The Son's role in redemption, therefore, is no different from Adam's relationship to the Spirit vis-à-vis his Spirit-empowered obedience. According to the terms of the *pactum salutis*, this means that the Father promised to give to His Son the anointing of the Spirit to carry out His mission. The Son offered His obedience in the power of the Spirit, in accordance with the terms of the covenant. And the Spirit willingly consented to support the Son's mission.

---

26. John Owen, ΠΝΕΥΜΑΤΟΛΟΓΙΑ, or, *A Discourse Concerning the Holy Spirit*, in *The Works of John Owen*, vol. 3, ed. William H. Goold (1850-53; Edinburgh: Banner of Truth, 1994), 162-83.

27. John Owen, 'Exercitation XXVIII: Federal Transactions Between the Father and the Son,' in *Works of John Owen*, vol. 19, ed. W. H. Goold (Edinburgh: T & T Clark, 1862), 77-97; Laurence R. O'Donnell, III, 'The Holy Spirit's Role in John Owen's "Covenant of the Mediator" Formulation: A Case Study in Reformed Orthodox Formulations of the *Pactum Salutis*,' *PRJ* 4/1 (2012): 91-115.

28. Kuyper, *Holy Spirit*, 113.

The Spirit's mission

Once the Son completed His Spirit-empowered work, His earthly ministry would be complete. His resurrection and ascension would signal the next phase of the execution of the *pactum* with the outpouring of the Spirit, the power of the age to come (Heb. 6:5). As with the first creation where the Son and Spirit acted as the hands of God, Christ and the Spirit inaugurate the new creation (cf. Gen. 1:2; John 1:1-3, 9; Col. 1:16).[29] There are a number of Old Testament texts that prophesy of a future outpouring of the Spirit (e.g., Isa. 44:3; Joel 2:28; Ezek. 36:26-27; 37:14; 39:29). Within the context of Isaiah's prophecy, the Spirit-anointed servant of Yahweh (Isa. 42:1) would bring forth justice to the nations, and do so through His work as covenant surety. The Father would first anoint the Son, who would then in turn anoint the elect with the Spirit. This Christ–Spirit connection appears quite prominently in several key passages in the New Testament.

Paul succinctly spells out the nexus between the relative missions of the Son and the Spirit: 'Christ redeemed us from the curse of the law by becoming a curse for us – for it is written, "Cursed is everyone who is hanged on a tree" – so that in Christ Jesus the blessing of Abraham might come to the Gentiles, so that we might receive the promised Spirit through faith' (Gal. 3:13-14; cf. Isa. 44:3). Here Paul presents a link between righteousness that comes by faith and the gift of the Spirit.[30] The last Adam offers His righteous obedience to the Father's will, which thereby unleashes the gift of the Spirit.[31] The Spirit both grants believers

29. Irenaeus, *Against Heresies*, IV, preface, in ANF, I:463.

30. A. Andrew Das, *Galatians*, Concordia Commentary (St. Louis: Concordia Publishing, 2014), 334; Douglas J. Moo, *Galatians*, BECNT (Grand Rapids: Baker, 2013), 216.

31. Thomas R. Schreiner, *Galatians*, ZECNT (Grand Rapids: Zondervan, 2010), 218-19.

a justifying faith that looks extraspectively to Christ, and He also sanctifies them. In sanctification, the Spirit transforms and conforms the elect to the image of Christ. A similar link appears in Paul's letter to Rome: 'The Spirit is life because of righteousness' (Rom. 8:10b). In other words, because of Christ's work as covenant surety, His imputed righteousness, anyone united to Him receives life through the Spirit (cf. Rom. 5:19-21).[32]

Christ's curse-bearing suffering and crucifixion are not the sole triggers for the outpouring of the Spirit. The promise of the eschaton stood before Adam in the garden prior to the entrance of sin and need for salvation.[33] Hence, pneumatically conditioned existence in the eschaton was supposed to be the fruit and effects of the first Adam's Spirit-empowered obedience: 'But it is not the spiritual that is first but the natural, and then the spiritual' (1 Cor. 15:46). Adam's state in the garden was preparatory for a heavenly one.[34] And Paul's contrast between the spiritual (πνευματικὸν) and natural (ψυχικόν) bodies extends to the two world-orders connected with the first and last Adam.[35] With the entrance of sin into the world, the last Adam both had to offer His loving obedience to His Father's will in order to usher in the eschaton, and had to deal with making satisfaction for sin given its

32. Douglas Moo, *Romans*, NICNT (Grand Rapids: Eerdmans, 1996), 492; Gordon D. Fee, *God's Empowering Presence: The Holy Spirit in the Letters of Paul* (Peabody: Hendrickson, 1994), 551-52; Joseph A. Fitzmyer, *Romans*, AB (New York: Doubleday, 1992), 491; cf. NIV; RSV; NAS; Charles Hodge, *Romans* (1835; Edinburgh: Banner of Truth, 1989), 259-60.

33. E.g., Geerhardus Vos, *The Pauline Eschatology* (1930; Phillipsburg: P & R, 1996), 325 n. 1.

34. Charles Hodge, *1 & 2 Corinthians* (1857; Edinburgh: Banner of Truth, 1994), 351.

35. Andrew T. Lincoln, *Paradise Now and Not Yet: Studies in the role of the heavenly dimension in Paul's thought with special reference to his eschatology* (Cambridge: Cambridge University Press, 1981), 44.

presence in the world. Hence, Christ had to fulfill the requirements of the law first, by loving His Father with all His heart, soul, mind, and strength, and then suffer the curse of the law in order to unleash the outpouring of the Spirit.[36] In this manner He becomes a life-giving Spirit (πνεῦμα ζῳοποιοῦν) (1 Cor. 15:45).[37]

Important to note at this juncture, then, is that justification and glorification are not exclusively soteriological realities. Rather, they are first and foremost eschatological. If the first Adam in his protological probation had succeeded, he would have been justified, declared righteous, and then glorified. That is, he would have permanently and indefectibly entered the pneumatic eternal Sabbath-rest of Yahweh. Paul's maxim is key: first the natural and then the spiritual. God promised Adam that he would be glorified – the Spirit would transform Adam's natural body to a spiritual body. God gave Adam this promise prior to the entrance of sin and death. In terms of the traditional *ordo salutis*, Adam's justification would have opened the way to a pneumatic eschatological existence – glorification. In a sin-fallen world, however, justification and glorification now operate in the context of sin and the tension between the two ages, this present evil age and the age to come. Or, in biblical-theological terminology, justification and glorification operate in the midst of the already but not-yet. Sinners receive the already

36. Kuyper, *Holy Spirit*, 112-13.

37. Geerhardus Vos, 'Paul's Eschatological Concept of the Spirit,' in *Redemptive History and Biblical Interpretation: The Shorter Writings of Geerhardus Vos*, ed. Richard B. Gaffin, Jr. (Phillipsburg: P & R, 1980), 107-08; G. K. Beale, *A New Testament Biblical Theology: The Upholding of the Old Testament in the New* (Grand Rapids: Baker, 2011), 43-45; Schreiner, *New Testament Theology*, 477. Others, such as John Levison, who argues for a panentheistic anthropology, contend that Paul has departed from the Old Testament idea of the Spirit indwelling all people. According to Levison, there is no contrast between the ages, no proton or eschaton (John R. Levison, *Filled with the Spirit* [Grand Rapids: Eerdmans, 2009], 311-16).

declaration of their eschatological status in their justification, but the Spirit does not immediately glorify sinners, as He would have in a successful adamic probation.[38] Rather, pneumatic eschatological life progresses in terms of our sanctification – the gradual transformation of the justified sinner unto glorification.

In the midst of the sin-fallen world, one goal of Christ's earthly ministry was once again to open the gates to the eschaton, which had been closed due to Adam's sin. Christ would baptize the

---

38. There are some, such as G. K. Beale and Richard Gaffin, who argue for a two-stage justification. Beale and Gaffin contend that the already-not-yet characterizes every aspect of redemption, hence there are already and not-yet aspects of justification (G. K. Beale, 'The Eschatological Conception of New Testament Theology,' in *Eschatology in Bible and Theology: Evangelical Essays at the Dawn of a New Millennium*, eds. Kent E. Brower and Mark W. Elliott [Downers Grove: InterVarsity, 1997], 32-34; idem, *Biblical Theology*, 497-526; Gaffin, *By Faith*, 95-122). *Pace* Beale and Gaffin, to posit a not-yet of justification that hinges upon the evaluation of the believer's works supplants the sole place of Christ's obedience as covenant surety within the *pactum salutis*. Note the following from Beale: 'Justification and final judgment have their foundation in the believer's union with Christ. Justification occurs by faith alone, and judgment happens on the basis of an examination of works, which are the fruit of the genuine faith-union with Christ and are empowered by the Spirit' (Beale, *Biblical Theology*, 517). He makes a similar statement elsewhere: 'Initial justification and final justification (or twofold justification) are grounded in believers' union with Christ, the former coming by faith and the later through the threefold demonstration of (1) the bodily resurrection, (2) God's public announcement to the cosmos, and (3) evaluation by works' (Beale, *Biblical Theology*, 515). Beale expands justification, which historically in the Reformed tradition rests exclusively upon the work of Christ, the covenant surety, to include an evaluation of the believer's works. Compare Beale's statements with the WCF: 'Those whom God effectually calleth, he also freely justifieth: not by infusing righteousness into them, but by pardoning their sins, and by accounting and accepting their persons as righteous; *not for anything wrought in them, or done by them, but for Christ's sake alone*' (XI.i, emphasis added; cf. WLC qq. 70-71, 97). In fact, WLC q. 71 specifically states that God requires 'nothing of them for their justification but faith.' At face value, Beale's formulation contradicts the statements in the Westminster Standards. I contend that the Standards are correct because justification is entirely an already aspect of redemption because it rests exclusively upon the completed work of the covenant surety. Christ has already irreversibly secured eschatological life for His bride.

creation in the Spirit, which would give birth to the new heavens and earth. John the Baptist recognized this from the outset: 'I baptize you with water for repentance, but he who is coming after me is mightier than I, whose sandals I am not worthy to carry. He will baptize you with the Holy Spirit and fire' (Matt. 3:11).[39] Throughout Christ's earthly ministry the disciples would later reflect upon the fact that their theological ignorance was due, in part, to the Spirit's relative absence: 'Now this he said about the Spirit, whom those who believed in him were to receive, for as yet the Spirit had not been given, because Jesus was not yet glorified' (John 7:39). The implication from John's statement is that the Spirit's presence was predicated upon the completion of Christ's work – His obedience and suffering.[40] But the outpouring of the Spirit was not accomplished through an inanimate mechanism, like a vending machine that produces a candy bar when the proper amount of currency is inserted. Rather, the Spirit would be sent, which echoes the *pactum*-originated sending of Christ. At several points Christ instructed His disciples that the Father would send the Spirit: 'But the Helper, the Holy Spirit, whom the Father will send in my name, he will teach you all things and bring to your remembrance all that I have said to you' (John 14:26). Here Christ states that the Father would send the Spirit, but He later indicates that He too would send Him: 'But when the Helper comes, whom I will send to you from the Father, the Spirit of truth, who proceeds from the Father, he will bear witness about me' (John 15:26).

As with the sending of the Son, the intra-trinitarian processions determine the order of their *pactum*-framed missions.

39. James D. G. Dunn, *Baptism in the Holy Spirit: A Re-examination of the New Testament Teaching on the Gift of the Spirit in relation to Pentecostalism Today* (Philadelphia: Westminster Press, 1970), 38-54.

40. D. A. Carson, *The Gospel According to John* (Grand Rapids: Eerdmans, 1991), 329.

The Father eternally generates the Son, hence the Son's mission precedes the Spirit's mission. The Spirit proceeds from the Father and the Son, therefore, the Spirit's mission follows the Son's mission. The Spirit's mission could not precede the Son's mission. Moreover, the order of the missions is not simply a function of the divine will. That is, the Trinity could not have merely decided that the Father or Spirit would have become incarnate and executed the office of covenant surety. The work of redemption and, consequently, the relative order of the Son's and Spirit's missions is based upon their intra-trinitarian processions. This conclusion is sound given that the Father and Son send the Spirit. As with the Father's sending of the Son, the fact that one is sent means that someone else sends him. A person cannot send himself. The decisions to send and the voluntary agreement to go originate, as I have argued, in the *pactum salutis*. The Spirit was no mere bystander, nor simply a secretary to witness and record the covenantal agreement between the Father and Son.[41] Rather, the Spirit was a full participant in the *pactum salutis*. The Father promised the Son to equip Him with the Spirit, and the Spirit agreed to undergird the Son's mission. And the Father and the Son agreed to send the Spirit, and the Spirit agreed to go. But the trinitarian missions were not solely the product of the intra-trinitarian agreement, but rather a covenant made in accordance with the trinitarian processions.[42] The ontology of

---

41. Cf. Thomas Goodwin, *Of Christ the Mediator*, in *The Works of Thomas Goodwin*, 12 vols. (1861-66; Eureka: Tanski Publications, 1996), I.vii (vol. V, p. 23); idem, *Work of the Holy Ghost*, IX.iii (vol. VI, p. 419).

42. I do not have the space to defend the claim in detail, but I do want to acknowledge its debated nature. Namely, some have argued that the processions do not dictate the missions. Aquinas, for example, claimed that the missions were fitting (*convenientia*) but not restricted to each member of the Trinity. In an absolute sense, the Father could have become incarnate rather than the Son, but it was fitting that the Son would assume human nature. For literature on the debated question, see Jeremy Daniel Wilkins,

the Trinity determines the shape of the freely willed ensuing covenantal missions and subsequent application of redemption.

As a result of the intra-trinitarian processions, the Son's mission precedes the Spirit's mission, which is evident by the Spirit's relative absence until His outpouring at Pentecost. The Spirit was not totally absent prior to His outpouring at Pentecost, but His presence was geared towards preparing the way for the Son's mission. Once the Son accomplished His mission, the Spirit's mission would formally begin. In His post-resurrection activity, Christ instructed His disciples to wait in Jerusalem for the 'promise of the Father,' Christ's baptizing them in the Holy Spirit (Acts 1:4-5). Then at Pentecost, Peter invoked Joel's (2:28-32) end-time prophecy of the outpouring of the Spirit as the explanation for the wonders and signs that the people witnessed (Acts 2:17-21). Peter draws attention to the complex of texts surrounding the *pactum salutis*:

> Being therefore exalted at the right hand of God, and having received from the Father the promise of the Holy Spirit, he has poured out this that you yourselves are seeing and hearing. For David did not ascend into the heavens, but he himself says, 'The Lord said to my Lord, "Sit at my right had until I make your enemies your footstool."' Let all the house of Israel therefore know for certain that God has

---

'Emanatio Intelligibilis in Deo: A Study of the Horizon and Development of Thomas Aquinas's Trinitarian Theology,' (Ph.D. Dissertation, Boston College, 2004), 23-33; cf. Rahner, *Trinity*, 28-33; John Milbank, *Being Reconciled: Ontology and Pardon* (London: Routledge, 2003), 64-66; idem and Catherine Pickstock, *Truth in Aquinas* (London: Routledge, 2001), 61-64; Richard Cross, *The Metaphysics of the Incarnation* (Oxford: Oxford University Press, 2005), 178-79. On the idea of *convenientia*, see Bernard Lonergan, 'The Notion of Fittingness: The Application of Theological Method to the Question of the Purpose of the Incarnation,' in *Collected Works of Bernard Lonergan*, vol. 19, *Early Latin Theology*, eds. Robert M. Doran and H. Daniel Monsour, trans. Michael G. Shields (Toronto: University of Toronto Press, 2011), 483-533. I am grateful to Brian Hecker for alerting me to this literature.

made him both Lord and Christ, this Jesus whom you crucified (Acts 2:33-36).

These statements warrant several observations.

First, Peter explains that the Son has been 'exalted at the right hand of God,' and he invokes Psalm 110:1, which is a key text for the *pactum salutis*. Psalm 110 reveals the pre-temporal oath, the Father's binding covenantal promise to His Son, to appoint Him to the priestly line of Melchizedek (Ps. 110:4; cf. 2 Kings 11:4; Ezek. 16:59; 17:13, 16, 18-19; Hosea 10:4; Ps. 132:11; 89:3-4). Second, Peter identifies the Son as 'Lord and Christ,' which invokes connections to Psalm 2:7, another key *pactum* text. The Christ, the Lord's anointed, was now installed on Zion, God's holy hill, by virtue of His accomplished obedience, suffering, and resurrection (cf. Pss. 1-2; Acts 4:23-28).[43] Third, the Father promised He would anoint His Son with the Spirit and that, upon the accomplishment of His work as surety, the Son would in turn pour out the Spirit and baptize the creation to produce the new heavens and earth.[44] The centerpiece of the new creation, would be the eternal dwelling place of the triune God, the living stones, the elect from every tribe, tongue, and nation, those who had been chosen in Christ before the foundation of the world (Eph. 1:4).[45]

The pactum and the ordo salutis

Given the broad contours of what has been outlined above, some theologians have observed the connection between the

---

43. Robert L. Cole, *Psalms 1–2: Gateway to the Psalter* (Sheffield: Sheffield Academic Press, 2013), 140-41.

44. Boris Bobrinskoy, *The Mystery of the Trinity: Trinitarian Experience and Vision in the Biblical and Patristic Tradition* (Crestwood: St. Vladimir's Seminary Press, 1999), 102-03.

45. Beale, *Biblical Theology*, 559-650.

pactum salutis and the *ordo salutis*, or more generally the nexus between the processions, missions, and nature of redemption. As noted above, Vos, a Reformed theologian, and Weinandy, a Roman Catholic theologian, have drawn these connections but offer different formulations, which naturally produce different outcomes. This section, therefore, surveys the two theologians and their respective views, and then offers analysis and critique of Weinandy's position. Vos's observations about the *pactum–ordo* connection are valid, though they require minor modification as noted in the previous chapter regarding the distinction between active and passive justification.

Vos on the ordo salutis

In his essay on the history of the Reformed doctrine of the covenant, Vos offers one of the few historical surveys of the *pactum salutis*, however brief, in addition to his own dogmatic observations about the doctrine. Vos contends that if God's work of salvation has a covenantal cast at its root, i.e., the *pactum salutis*, then the entire economy of redemption must unfold in a covenantal manner. From the very beginning God determined to give His love and faithfulness as with a man to his friend, and thus He covenantally committed Himself to the restoration of the violated faithfulness. The covenant of grace, therefore, is the historical execution of the eternal *pactum salutis*: 'By virtue of His official appointment, His being anointed as Mediator in the covenant of redemption, the Son rules throughout the ages in the house of grace, gathers unto Himself a church through Word and Spirit, and lays claim on all those who desire to live according to His ordinances.'[46] According to Vos, the Son became covenant

46. Geerhardus Vos, 'The Doctrine of the Covenant in Reformed Theology,' in *Redemptive History and Biblical Interpretation: The Selected Shorter Writings of Geerhardus Vos*, ed. Richard B. Gaffin, Jr. (Phillipsburg: P & R, 1980), 252.

surety so that the elect could become parties to the covenant of grace and behave in a covenantally faithful manner. There is no imputation of Christ's merits, argues Vos, apart from re-creation in God's image.[47] But for Vos, the *pactum* provides the structure and foundation for two realities: (1) the covenant of grace and (2) the *ordo salutis*.[48]

Vos illustrates his point by comparing Reformed and Lutheran soteriologies, though his analysis is problematic at points on historical-theological grounds given his exclusive reliance upon secondary sources.[49] Vos nevertheless offers a valid observation regarding some principal differences between Lutheran and Reformed conceptions of salvation.[50] Vos points to the fact that, unlike the Lutherans, the Reformed contend that the covenant of grace presupposes the electing grace of God, that is, elements of the *pactum salutis*.[51] Vos draws the strongest connections between the *ordo* and *pactum* in the priority he assigns to forensic elements of redemption. Vos argues that Paul consistently subordinated the mystical aspect of the believer's relationship to Christ to the forensic aspect: 'Paul's mind was to such an extent forensically oriented that he regarded the entire complex of subjective spiritual changes that take place in the believer and of subjective spiritual blessings enjoyed by the believer as the direct outcome of the forensic work of Christ applied in justification. The mystical is based on the forensic, not the forensic on the mystical.'[52] In his

47. Vos, 'Covenant,' 253.

48. Vos, 'Covenant,' 253.

49. Cf. J. V. Fesko, *Beyond Calvin: Union with Christ and Justification in Early Modern Reformed Theology (1517-1700)* (Göttingen: Vandenhoeck & Ruprecht, 2012), 124-26.

50. Vos, 'Covenant,' 256-58, also 257 n. 10.

51. Vos, 'Covenant,' 258.

52. Geerhardus Vos, 'The Alleged Legalism in Paul's Doctrine of Justification,' in

Compendium Vos explains the relationship between the forensic and transformative in the following manner: 'We must distinguish between the judicial acts of God and the regenerational acts of God.'[53] Vos further stipulates: 'The justifying acts serve as the foundation upon which the regenerational acts of God rest. Although (for instance) justification follows the new birth in time, nevertheless, the former is the foundation of the latter.'[54] Vos came to these conclusions based upon his exegesis of Paul's corpus but also because of his understanding of the *pactum salutis*.

Vos, like Louis Berkhof and Herman Bavinck, employed the Reformed Orthodox distinction between active and passive justification.[55] Active justification is the imputation of Christ's righteousness in the *pactum salutis*, whereas passive justification is the subjective reception of Christ's imputed righteousness. In the context of the pre-temporal *pactum*, the active justification of the elect is the ground for the subjective and transformative changes that occur in the *applicatio salutis* in history within the temporal execution of the covenant of grace. As noted in the previous chapter, one need not embrace the active–passive justification distinction that Vos, Bavinck, and Berkhof maintain. The common distinction between the decree and its execution preserves the same point

---

Redemptive History and Biblical Interpretation: The Shorter Writings of Geerhardus Vos, ed. Richard B. Gaffin, Jr. (Phillipsburg: P & R, 1980), 384.

53. Geerhardus Vos, *Systematische Theologie: Compendium* (Grand Rapids: 1900), 132: 'Welke onderscheiding moeten we op de trappen der heilsorde toepassen?... Tusschen de rechterlijke daden Gods en de herscheppende daden Gods.' I am grateful to my colleague, Derk Bergsma, who translated this portion of Vos's *Compendium* for me.

54. Vos, *Systematische Theologie*, 133: 'De rechterlijke daden sijn de grond waarop de herscheppende daden berusten. Al volgt b.v. de Rechtvaardigmaking in tijd op de wadergeboorte, toch is sij de rechtsgrond voor den laatste.'

55. Herman Bavinck, *Reformed Dogmatics*, 4 vols., ed. John Bolt, trans. John Vriend (Grand Rapids: Baker, 2005-09), III:523; Berkhof, *Systematic Theology*, 517; Geerhardus Vos, *Dogmatiek*, 5 vols. (Grand Rapids: 1900), V.12 (vol. IV, pp. 22-23).

that the active–passive distinction entails without potentially confusing historical acts (justification) with the decree. The point is that Christ's appointment and mission as covenant surety take logical priority over the Spirit's mission as the one who applies His legal–forensic work through mystical union with Christ. Or in terms of the *ordo salutis*, justification takes logical priority over sanctification. The Son's procession and mission logically and temporally precede the procession and mission of the Spirit, hence the *ordo salutis* reflects this order, whether in the intra-trinitarian processions or the *pactum*-framed missions.

Weinandy on processions, missions, and the ordo salutis

Thomas Weinandy offers his own reconfigured doctrine of the Trinity from within the broader context of what has been called a 'Spirit-christology' among a largely Roman Catholic body of theologians.[56] These Roman Catholic theologians contrast a Spirit-christology with a Logos-christology that isolates the doctrine of Christ from pneumatology, and argue to different degrees that the Spirit must be factored into christology. This theological movement, however, seems to be unaware of historic Reformed treatments of the Spirit's role in Christ's mission as covenant surety. Nevertheless, Weinandy makes observations similar to Vos's regarding the link

56. See, e.g., Ralph Del Colle, *Christ and the Spirit: Spirit Christology in Trinitarian Perspective* (Oxford: Oxford University Press, 1994); Roger Haight, 'The Case for Spirit Christology,' *Theological Studies* 52 (1992): 257-87; Harold Hunter, 'Spirit Christology: Dilemma and Promise,' *The Heythrop Journal* 24/2 (1983): 127-40; Philip Rosato, 'Spirit Christology: Ambiguity and Promise,' *Theological Studies* 38 (1977): 423-49. An exception to this largely Roman Catholic trend is James D. G. Dunn, *Jesus and the Spirit: A Study of the Religious and Charismatic Experience of Jesus and the First Christians as Reflected in the New Testament* (1975; Grand Rapids: Eerdmans, 1997), 11-67, 301-44. Critics of Spirit-christology include Wolfhart Pannenberg, who contends that to accord the Spirit a chief role in the ministry of Christ leads to an adoptionistic christology (Wolfhart Pannenberg, *Jesus – God and Man* [Philadelphia: Westminster Press, 1975], 115-21).

between the processions, missions, and order of salvation, though he does so apart from invoking the technical term, *ordo salutis*.

Weinandy begins his book, *The Father's Spirit of Sonship*, with the following thesis: 'Within the Trinity the Father begets the Son in or by the Holy Spirit, who proceeds then from the Father as the one in whom the Son is begotten.'[57] Weinandy is well aware of the fact that his understanding of the trinitarian processions is different from the traditional Western view in which the Father generates the Son, and the Father and Son together generate the Spirit.[58] Supplementing this common formula, Weinandy argues that the Father generates the Son through the Spirit. Weinandy bases his conclusion of this different processional order on Rahner's rule, namely, that the ontological Trinity is the economic Trinity.[59] In this particular case, 'The immanent Trinity is identical to the economic Trinity.'[60] Given this presupposition, Weinandy examines redemptive history and notes that the Spirit, not the Son, appears first. There are a number of different texts to which he appeals, but Weinandy argues that the Spirit's conception of the God-man reveals the intra-trinitarian processions: 'The depiction of the Father begetting the Son in the womb of Mary by the Holy Spirit becomes, I believe, a temporal icon of his eternally begetting the Son by the Holy Spirit.'[61]

Weinandy elaborates this point by surveying a number of biblical texts that he believes support his conclusions. He appeals to the creation account where the Spirit hovered over the creation

57. Thomas Weinandy, *The Father's Spirit of Sonship: Reconceiving the Trinity* (Eugene: Wipf & Stock, 1995), ix.

58. Weinandy, *Spirit of Sonship*, 6.

59. Rahner, *Trinity*, 22.

60. Weinandy, *Spirit of Sonship*, 22.

61. Weinandy, *Spirit of Sonship*, 42.

and gave birth to it (Gen 1:2). Similarly, God first inspired the prophets of old to speak, but the Spirit's inspiration preceded the verbal utterances of their words. The prophet Ezekiel, for example, was first inspired and then spoke to the valley of dry bones to animate them and bring them to life (Ezek. 37).[62] The same pattern unfolds, argues Weinandy, with respect to Christ's ministry. Christ's work begins with His baptism by the Spirit, which confirms the priority of the Spirit's procession and mission to Christ's. Weinandy comments: 'Thus the Father's testimony to Jesus' Sonship, in affiliation with the descent of the Holy Spirit, intimates that he eternally authenticates (begets) the Son in the Spirit.'[63] The pattern emerges once again in Christ's resurrection. According to Paul, the Spirit raised Jesus from the dead (Rom. 8:11; 1:4). Weinandy is aware of other texts that attribute the resurrection to the Father, but he nevertheless claims: 'While it is the Father who raises Jesus from the dead, he does so by the Spirit, and in that act, the Son, who was in the flesh, is now, through the resurrection of that flesh, once again designated Son of God in power.'[64] These redemptive historical events reveal the economic activity of the triune God, and also reveal the ontology of the Trinity – the Father begets the Son through the Spirit.

Weinandy's reconfigured trinitarian processions and missions lead him to the conclusion that soteriology conforms to this trinitarian activity. It is inconceivable, argues Weinandy, that we would become sons and daughters of God in a different manner from Christ's, whether in His ontological or economic Spirit-begetting.[65] Weinandy writes:

62. Weinandy, *Spirit of Sonship*, 26-27.

63. Weinandy, *Spirit of Sonship*, 28.

64. Weinandy, *Spirit of Sonship*, 32.

65. Weinandy, *Spirit of Sonship*, 36.

> Our resurrection in the Spirit then becomes an icon of Jesus' resurrection in the Spirit, but because of this we see more clearly that his own resurrection is then the supreme icon of the inner trinitarian life. If our sonship is established in the Holy Spirit and finds its resurrection completion in the Holy Spirit, mirroring the work of the Spirit in Jesus' own resurrection, we have a transparent window into the work of the Spirit within the Trinity. Reversing the argument, if the Father raises both Jesus and us to glory by the Holy Spirit, and our resurrection is founded on our being adopted as sons by the Holy Spirit, then Jesus' resurrection not only establishes him as Son in power in the Spirit, but equally manifests (in a manner analogous to our own adopted sonship) his being son by nature in the Spirit.[66]

Weinandy's broader observation is that the processions and missions determine the nature of soteriology. If the Spirit constitutes the active agent of Christ's sonship, then the same occurs with respect to believers. In his view, 'New life that we live with the Father in Christ is founded exclusively on the work of the Spirit.' This new life, which includes justification, occurs through faith and baptism.[67]

Weinandy makes the procession–mission–salvation connection explicit: 'The ontology of grace is analogous to the ontology of the Trinity and inseparably connected with it.' Through faith and baptism, argues Weinandy, the Spirit indwells people and transforms them into adopted sons and daughters of the Father. At this point, Weinandy's soteriology takes a decidedly traditional Roman Catholic cast, evident both by his appeal to faith and baptism as the means by which people receive the Spirit, and his reliance upon the categories of uncreated and created grace.[68]

---

66. Weinandy, *Spirit of Sonship*, 38.

67. Weinandy, *Spirit of Sonship*, 35.

68. Cf. Thomas Aquinas, *Summa Theologica* (Allen: Christian Classics, 1948), IaIIae

The uncreated life and presence of the Spirit within recipients of baptism produces the effect of created grace, or habitual grace, which enables people to live in relationship with the Father and the Son.[69] Through the Spirit's indwelling, we share in God's divine nature (2 Pet. 1:4) and we existentially know of the Father's love for us.[70]

Analysis

When we compare the views of Vos and Weinandy, two things are clear: (1) they both link the processions, missions, and order of salvation; and (2) they come to very different conclusions. Both theologians correctly connect the trinitarian processions to redemption. The intra-trinitarian relations determine the nature of the *ordo salutis*. Stated more simply, redemption reflects the nature of our triune God. God does not redeem in a manner alien or contrary to His nature. The question remains, however, as to whether Vos or Weinandy has a proper understanding of the *ordo salutis*. As stated above, Vos's understanding is closer to an accurate view of the God–redemption connection for a number of reasons.

First, Weinandy makes some valid and important observations regarding the Spirit's relationship to the work of Christ. As noted above, the Spirit plays an important role with regard to the Son's mission, a role that perhaps some have forgotten or overlooked. Nevertheless, Weinandy's reconstruction of the

---

q. 110 art. 2; Thomas Dubay, *God Dwells Within Us* (New York: Dimension Books, 1971), 112-15; *Catechism of the Catholic Church* (Ligouri: Ligouri Publications, 1992), §§ 1999-2000; Richard A. Muller, *Dictionary of Latin and Greek Theological Terms: Drawn Principally from Protestant Scholastic Theology* (Grand Rapids: Baker, 1986), s.v. *habitus gratiae, gratia infusa*.

69. Weinandy, *Spirit of Sonship*, 103.

70. Weinandy, *Spirit of Sonship*, 104-05.

intra-trinitarian missions appears unwarranted. The Spirit undoubtedly undergirds the mission of the Son, but just because the Spirit is the agent of the Son's incarnation as the God-man does not necessarily mean that the Spirit generates the Son with the Father. At this point Weinandy recognizes that he advocates a unique view never promoted by any ecumenical council or creed.[71] Church tradition alone should never dictate whether a theological view is heterodox or orthodox. Nevertheless, we should question it if we believe that the church arrived at its creedal conclusions through responsible exegesis of Scripture. In this case, as common as challenges to the *filioque* clause of the Nicene Creed are, the Scriptures clearly state that the Father sends the Son, and the Father and the Son both send the Spirit.[72] The Scriptures nowhere state that the Spirit sends the Son. If Weinandy is correct, that the economic Trinity is precisely the ontological Trinity, then this is a significant piece of evidence that does not fit his thesis.

Second, Weinandy believes that the traditional Western understanding of the trinitarian processions, specifically the *filioque*, has led to christomonism. He argues that this in turn has subordinated the gift of the Spirit to law and institution, with legalism and power as the negative consequences. The *filioque* has fostered a tendency to view the Spirit as inferior to

---

71. Weinandy, *Spirit of Sonship*, 100.

72. Critics of the *filioque* include Wolfhart Pannenberg, *Systematic Theology*, 3 vols. (Grand Rapids: Eerdmans, 1988), I:317-19; Yves Congar, *I Believe in the Holy Spirit*, 3 vols. (1983; New York: Herder & Herder, 2013), III:72-78; Jürgen Moltmann, *The Trinity and the Kingdom* (Minneapolis: Fortress, 1993), 185-90. Defenders of the *filioque* include Karl Barth, *Church Dogmatics*, 14 vols., ed. Geoffrey Bromiley (Edinburgh: T & T Clark, 1936-75), I/1:477-89. For a mediating view, see Robert Letham, *The Holy Trinity: In Scripture, History, Theology, and Worship* (Phillipsburg: P & R, 2004), 201-20. For a history of the controversy, see A. Edward Siecienski, *The Filioque: History of a Doctrinal Controversy* (Oxford: Oxford University Press, 2010).

the Son.[73] Without doubt, christomonism is undesirable, since it represents a deflection from a fully trinitarian theology. But the danger of christomonism should not prompt rejection of a biblical understanding of the trinitarian processions and missions. A trinitarian understanding of the *pactum* preserves the Spirit's role both in the planning and execution of the impetration and application of redemption. According to the terms of the *pactum*, the Father sends the Son, and then the Father and Son send the Spirit. This is why the biblical text refers to the 'Spirit of Christ' on a number of occasions and never the 'Spirit's Christ' (Rom. 8:9; Phil. 1:19; 1 Pet. 1:11). Moreover, as noted above, Paul designates Christ as a 'life-giving Spirit' (1 Cor. 15:45). Christ gives the Spirit, not vice versa.

Related to the issue of the *filioque* and the charge of christomonism is whether Weinandy has gone to the opposite extreme by positing a pneumatic monism. Weinandy's defense of his thesis mentions little to nothing about legal–forensic categories, whether about sin, condemnation, righteousness, or justification. His soteriology virtually bypasses all questions of sin and righteousness, and goes straight to the Spirit's indwelling and transformation of people apart from any questions about satisfying the demands of the law. At this point Weinandy's views look similar to those of Hans Urs von Balthasar (1905-88), and to a certain extent echo Eastern Orthodox views in which salvation is about overcoming ontological estrangement rather than repairing the breach of the law and covenant.[74]

---

73. Weinandy, *Spirit of Sonship*, 98-99.

74. E.g., Hans Urs von Balthasar, *Theo-Drama: Theological Dramatic Theory*, 5 vols. (San Francisco: Ignatius Press, 1994), IV:242-43; cf., e.g., Veli-Matti Kärkkäinen, 'Deification View,' in *Justification: Five Views*, eds. James K. Keilby & Paul Rhodes Eddy (Downers Grove: InterVarsity Press, 2011), 219-43; John Meyendorff, *Byzantine Theology: Historical Trends and Doctrinal Themes* (New York: Fordham University

This raises an important question: Why does Paul draw a comparison between the first and last Adams? Paul argues that Adam's probation in the garden is revelatory of Christ's work because he is a 'type of the one who was to come' (Rom. 5:14).[75] Moreover Christ was 'born under the law to redeem those who were under the law' (Gal. 4:4-5), and He came to fulfill every jot and tittle of the law and prophets (Matt. 5:17). And according to Galatians 3:13-14, Christ does not pour out the Spirit apart from satisfying the demands of the law by becoming a curse for us. Contrary to Weinandy's view, the possession of the Spirit is the natural correlate, crown, and infallible exponent of the state of righteousness, or obedience.[76] As important as it is to recognize the pneumatic character of the Son's mission, we cannot invert the missions of the Son and the Spirit and neither can we invert their processions. Apart from the antecedent work of the *pactum*-appointed covenant surety, there is no outpouring of the Spirit. The covenant of works is a mirror image of the *pactum salutis* – it reflects the pre-temporal covenant but also reveals and projects into history a rough sketch of the work of the last Adam and the effects of His obedience – pneumatic life through the outpouring of the Spirit.

Potential objections

Priority

At this point, some object to the idea that the mystical aspects of salvation are subordinated to the forensic. If effectual calling,

---

Press, 1983), 143, 145; Vladimir Lossky, *The Mystical Theology of the Eastern Church* (Crestwood: St Vladimir's Seminary Press, 1973), 87-90.

75. Moo, *Romans*, 333-34; Richard M. Davidson, *Typology in Scripture: A Study of Hermeneutical* τύπος *Structures* (Berrien Springs: Andrews University Press, 1981), 297-316.

76. Vos, 'Paul's Eschatological Concept of the Spirit,' 109.

for example, precedes justification logically and perhaps even temporally, and this work of the Spirit mystically unites the elect sinner to Christ, then is it not preferable to say that union with Christ is the ground of justification and sanctification? And if the *duplex gratia* of justification and sanctification comes through union with Christ, then how can justification take priority to sanctification if both benefits come simultaneously in union? Should we therefore say that union with Christ, not justification, is the more fundamental soteric category and hence takes priority over both justification and sanctification?[77] As common as these questions are, they fail to grasp several important points.

First, these questions approach the subject of priority from the vantage point of the covenant of grace and the application of redemption. Seldom, if ever, have those who raise such questions invoked the category of the *pactum salutis*. Questions about priority must not begin with the application of redemption but with its pre-temporal design. Questions of priority can only be answered from the vantage point of the processions and *pactum*-framed missions. The elect are indeed 'in Christ' (Eph 1:4) before the foundation of the world, and this warrants the conclusion that they are united to Him in some sense. But they are not yet mystically united to Christ. This observation led Reformed theologians to distinguish between the *federal* and *mystical* unions – not that there are multiple unions, but that there are different aspects of this one union.

77. E.g., Gaffin, *Resurrection and Redemption*, 138-39; idem, 'Union with Christ: Some Biblical and Theological Reflections,' in *Always Reforming: Explorations in Systematic Theology*, ed. A. T. B. McGowan (Downers Grove: InterVarsity Press, 2006), 280; A. A. Hodge, 'The *Ordo Salutis*; or Relation in the Order of Nature of Holy Character and Divine Favor,' *PTR* 54 (1878): 305-21; Marcus Peter Johnson, *One with Christ: An Evangelical Theology of Salvation* (Wheaton: Crossway, 2013), 75-77, 95, 164-67.

Second, the *duplex gratia* undeniably comes to believers through union with Christ, union is the ground of this twofold grace in some sense. But such a statement lacks specificity and fails to acknowledge that there is something that stands behind the application of redemption through mystical union with Christ, namely, election. As previously argued, this election comes wrapped in the context of the *pactum,* with the undergirding work of the covenant surety. The surety swears a covenantal oath to meet all of the legal obligations on behalf of His confederated bride. In love, He fulfills the law, which opens the gateway to eschatological life. The reason that believers enter into mystical union with Christ in the temporal covenant of grace is because of Christ's antecedent sworn oath in the *pactum* to fulfill the law and impute His righteousness to His bride. Old Testament believers enjoyed the benefits of union with Christ and His imputed righteousness prior to His earthly ministry. The covenantal-legal agreement of the *pactum* was sufficient in and of itself due to the Trinity's utter trustworthiness to carry out its covenant-oaths. In other words, the stipulations of the *pactum,* an inherently legal arrangement, are the foundation for the application of redemption in covenant of grace.

In this sense justification is foundational for the transformative aspects of redemption because it is the means through which the elect lay hold of the righteousness of the covenant surety. Even faith as a subjective and transformative aspect of redemption, and which is necessary to be justified, is not foundational but instrumental to the reception of the imputed righteousness of Christ. Hence, justification does not rest upon the subjective changes brought about by the Spirit but upon the legal–forensic work of Christ. Moreover, one need not maintain, with Vos, Bavinck, and Berkhof, the imputation of Christ's righteousness in the *pactum* to guard the priority of the forensic over the transformative elements of redemption. The decree to impute the righteousness of the surety is sufficient in and of itself to support the priority of the forensic to the transformative. In simpler words, Christ's promise to the Father to obey the law on behalf of His bride is sufficient unto itself.

Third, recognizing the priority of the forensic over the transformative does not somehow sideline or minimalize the doctrine of sanctification. To prioritize the forensic simply means that the work of the covenant surety provides the legal context for the ensuing transformative work of the Spirit.[78] Additionally, the bond that the persons of the triune God share ensures the inseparability of justification and sanctification. But the inseparability of the processions and missions does not mean they should be conflated or confused. Correlatively, this means that efforts either to conflate justification and sanctification, as in traditional Tridentine Roman Catholic soteriology, or to bypass the work of Christ and argue that the Spirit's work is foundational in salvation, as does Weinandy, fail to recognize the relationship among the processions, missions, and order of salvation.[79] Such efforts fail to recognize the exclusive place of the covenant surety and that the reception of the Spirit and entrance into the eschaton occurs only through Him. In other words, the logical relationship between justification and sanctification cannot be reversed.

Legalism

Some might object to the prioritization of the legal to transformative aspects because it supposedly fosters or even creates

78. Cf. *pace* Johnson, *One with Christ*, 54, 76-77 n. 45, 96-98 n. 20; 112-13; Mark Jones, *Antinomianism: Reformed Theology's Unwelcome Guest?* (Phillipsburg: P & R, 2013), 58-59.

79. E.g., a similar pattern unfolds in Frank D. Macchia, *Justified in the Spirit: Creation, Redemption, and the Triune God* (Grand Rapids: Eerdmans, 2010), 3-14.

an atmosphere where love is boxed out from the equation of salvation. Weinandy expresses this concern, as did Karl Barth (1886-1968).[80] Barth inverted the Reformed category distinction of law and gospel to gospel and law to register his dissatisfaction with the traditional order.[81] But as I have argued in earlier chapters, theologians who pit obedience against love posit a false dichotomy. The second giving of the law in Deuteronomy is, according to some Old Testament scholars, chiefly a book about filial love between Israel and Yahweh. When Jesus explains the greatest commandment, legal and affective categories are inextricably intertwined: 'You shall love the Lord your God with all your heart and with all your soul and with all your mind. This is the great and first commandment' (Matt. 22:37-39). Where God's sons, Adam and Israel, failed, Jesus succeeded and offered His loving obedience to His heavenly Father, which secured redemption for His bride.

But if this chapter has demonstrated anything, it is that Christ offered this obedience in the power of the Spirit. At a minimum, Christ's obedient love is a pneumatic expression of love. But a seemingly forgotten concept that theologians should reconsider and employ is that the Spirit is the bond of love between the Father and Son. This idea goes back to Augustine (354-430) and was promoted by Aquinas in his *Summa Theologica*. Based upon 1 John 4:8, 'God is love,' Augustine argues that this verse characterizes the entire Trinity, but especially the Holy Spirit; Aquinas makes similar arguments.[82] God is love and thus love

---

80. Weinandy, *Spirit of Sonship*, 98-99.

81. E.g., Karl Barth, 'Gospel and Law,' in *Community, State and Church: Three Essays* (1960; Eugene: Wipf & Stock, 2004), 71-100.

82. Augustine, *On the Trinity*, VI.v, in NPNF[1] III:100; Aquinas, *Summa Theologica*, Ia q. 37 art. 2. See also, Coffey, 'Holy Spirit as the Mutual,' 193-229; Dumitru Staniloae,

characterizes the intra-trinitarian relationships as well as His decreed and executed redemption. The Father predestines the elect in love (Eph. 1:4-5); He sent His Son in love (John 3:16; Rom. 5:8). And Christ's outpouring of the Spirit at Pentecost was equally an outpouring of love: 'God's love has been poured into our hearts through the Holy Spirit who has been given to us' (Rom. 5:5; cf. Titus 3:5-6; Acts 2:17).[83]

It stands to reason, then, that the Father's promise to give His Son the Spirit to carry out His mission as covenant surety was a promise to anoint Him with love. The Father poured out the Spirit and anointed Him in love that Christ might render His obedience in love, and this loving obedience gave Him right to unleash the outpouring of the Spirit, another manifestation of trinitarian love. John Owen makes an observation of this nature in an extended statement that is worth quoting in full:

> The Father Loves us, and 'chose us before the Foundation of the world;' but in the pursuit of that love, he blesseth us with all spiritual blessings in heavenly places in Christ,' Eph. 1. 3, 4. From his love, he sheds, or pours out the Holy Spirit richly upon us, through Jesus Christ our Saviour, Titus 3.6. In the pouring out of his love, there is not one drop that falls besides the Lord Christ. The holy anointing oil, was all poured on the head of Aaron: Ps. 133.2. and thence went down to the skirts of his clothing. Love is first poured out on Christ; and from him, it drops as the dew of Hermon upon the souls of his saints. The Father will have him to have 'in all things the pre-eminence,' Col. 1.18; 'it pleased him that in him all fulness should dwell,' verse 19; that 'of his fulness we might receive, and grace for

---

Theology and the Church (Crestwood: St. Vladimir's Seminary Press, 1980), 96; Boris Bobrinskoy, 'The Filioque Yesterday and Today,' in *Spirit of God, Spirit of Christ: Ecumenical Reflections on the Filioque Controversy*, ed., Lukas Vischer (London: SPCK, 1981), 142-43.

83. Moo, *Romans*, 305.

> grace,' John 1.16. Though the love of the Father's purpose and good pleasure have its rise and foundation in his mere grace and will, yet the design of its accomplishment is only in Christ. All the fruits of it are first given to him; and it is in him only that they are dispensed to us. So that though the saints may, nay, do, see an infinite ocean of love unto them in the bosom of the Father, yet they are not to look for one drop from him but what comes through Christ. He is the only means of communication. Love in the Father, is like *honey in the flower*; it must be in the comb, before it be for our use. Christ must extract and prepare this honey for us. He draws this water from the fountain through union and dispensation of fullness;—we by faith, from the wells of salvation that are in him.[84]

The Father, then, pours out His love through the Spirit upon the Son, and then the Son in turn pours out the love of the triune God through the Spirit upon His body, the elect.

Christ, therefore, poured out the love of the triune God through the baptism of the Spirit, and because of His perfect obedience the law can never arise to condemn those who are united to Him (Rom. 8:33-39). Indeed, the Spirit empowered Christ to render His obedience in fulfillment of the law, to offer himself in sacrifice upon the cross, and raised Him from the dead to declare Him righteous and herald His eschatological sonship to the world (Matt. 3:13-4:11; Heb. 9:14; Rom. 1:4; 1 Tim. 3:16). The Spirit performs the same work in those united to Christ with one major difference: Christ offered His obedience to secure the outpouring of the Spirit on behalf of the elect, whereas we offer our obedience because Christ has already irreversibly secured our pneumatic life and laid a foundation for our sanctification in His own obedience (Rom. 5:12-21). We offer our obedience,

84. John Owen, *Communion with God*, in *The Works of John Owen*, 24 vols., ed. William H. Goold (1851-62; Edinburgh: Banner of Truth, 1966), II:27.

therefore, not to secure eternal life but in love and thanksgiving to the triune God (Col. 3:16; 1 John 3:10; 4:7-10, 16, 20; 5:1, 3; Rev. 7:12).[85] The blessing of the Spirit comes exclusively through Christ, not through adherence to the law (Gal. 4:4-6; cf. 3:2-5).[86] Far from legalism, the triune God covers redemption in His love, from the *pactum* through to the eschaton, from beginning to end, and it finds a loving response in the power of the Spirit from those who have been redeemed: 'We love because he first loved us' (1 John 4:19). We obey because we love our triune Lord (cf. Exod. 20:6; Deut. 5:10; 11:1, 13; 30:16, 20; John 13:34; 14:15, 21; 15:10; 1 John 3:23; 4:21; 5:2). The prioritization of the forensic over transformative aspects of our union with Christ is anything but legalistic. Properly understood, to prioritize justification to sanctification recognizes that God first loved us before we loved Him, whether in the *pactum salutis* or in its execution in the covenant of grace through the *ordo salutis*.

Conclusion

This chapter set out to prove the thesis that the intra-trinitarian processions, missions, and *ordo salutis* are interconnected. While few theologians explicitly draw the connection between these three realities, some, such as Vos and Weinandy, have made the connections explicit. In simple terms, redemption reflects the nature of the triune God. To deny a logical inter-related sequence between the different aspects of redemption in the *ordo salutis* fails to recognize that *ordo* derives its sequence from the trinitarian processions and missions. This clearly emerged in Vos' and Weinandy's formulations. The Son's mission comes

85. Cf. Heidelberg Cat. q. 86; Belgic Conf. § XXIV; WCF XVI.ii-iii, v.

86. Das, *Galatians*, 315.

first in Vos's formulation and the Spirit comes first for Weinandy, which naturally grants priority to legal–forensic categories in the former and transformative in the latter. It is worth noting that, though many theologians do not advocate the *ordo salutis,* all theologians implicitly embrace the category. There is an order to the application of redemption.

This chapter has also challenged those who maintain that union with Christ is the all-determinative category in soteriology, which then eliminates questions about the priority of legal to transformative categories, or justification to sanctification in the *ordo salutis*. Those who question the idea of priority almost invariably approach the question from the perspective of the application of redemption and the covenant of grace. Few ask what stands behind mystical union with Christ. Election undoubtedly comes first in the *ordo salutis,* but it is not an abstract point apart from a context.

The *pactum salutis* is where we find the connections between election, christology, pneumatology, soteriology, and the eternal covenantal roots of the historical covenant of grace. Questions of priority must rest, therefore, not upon the application of redemption but upon its design and trinitarian ontology in the *pactum salutis*. In this respect, once again, the *pactum salutis* offers a thick account of how the intra-trinitarian processions and missions frame redemption. The *ordo salutis* reflects the *pactum*-framed missions and shows the riches of the triune God's love for fallen sinners. The *ordo salutis* is not, therefore, the foreign and alien imposition of logic upon an ineffable redemption but is rather a reflection of the biblical idea that God first loved us so that we might love Him in return. Justification must logically precede sanctification in the *ordo salutis* because Christ's obedience as covenant surety is the sure foundation upon which the Spirit progressively conforms us to the image of Christ. To reverse the *duplex gratia* sidelines Christ's role as covenant surety and places redeemed humanity back in the protological garden rather than indefectibly in the eschaton, the age to come.

⁓ SUMMARY ⁓

THE third part of this study began with a basic statement of the doctrine, which offered a definition with supporting scriptural data. Then in each subsequent chapter Part III addressed the major issues connected to the doctrine of the *pactum salutis*: the doctrines of the Trinity, predestination, imputation, and the *ordo salutis*. Each of these chapters demonstrates both the viability of the *pactum*, but more importantly, how the doctrine constitutes the ligaments that hold the body of seemingly disparate doctrines together. The predestination of the elect, for example, is not a bald and abstract choice, but is rather the sovereign choice of God in concert with the election of the Son. In addition to this, the Son's election is not abstract and unto an indeterminate end but rather He is the Christ, the covenant surety of the elect. As surety, the triune God decrees to impute the righteousness of the Son to the elect and the sin of the elect to the Son. All of these different elements, christology, election, imputation, are held together in the intra-trinitarian covenant to design the nature and scope of redemption. The *pactum salutis* is, as many have argued, the root and impelling cause for the covenant of grace, the temporal execution of the eternal plan. With the completion of Part III, we can now conclude this study and reflect upon the importance of retrieving the doctrine of the *pactum salutis*.

Conclusion

THE *pactum salutis* offers the church an important scriptural rubric to understand how numerous theological doctrines intersect. I do not claim that those who do not employ the *pactum* cannot adequately account for the intra-trinitarian processions and missions and redemption. I do believe, however, that the *pactum* provides a thicker account of God's being and work and helps the church to understand a number of scriptural texts. What are we to make of Christ's statement that His Father covenanted a kingdom to Him (Luke 22:29), and others such as the covenant of Psalm 2:7, the Messiah's prophetic delight in doing His Father's will in Psalm 40:8, and Yahweh's covenantal oath to make His Son a priest according to the order of Melchizedek in Psalm 110? What are we to do with Zechariah 6:13 and the promise that the Branch and Yahweh would make a covenant of peace and that by Yahweh's good plan He would crush the suffering servant (Isa. 53:10)? When did Yahweh swear a covenantal oath to the Son? When did the Father covenant a kingdom to Him? When did the Son tell the Father that He delights to do His will? When did the Father determine in a decree, a covenant, that a Davidic scion would rule from Zion? When did Yahweh determine by His good plan that He would crush the suffering servant in order to make many righteous? The doctrine of the *pactum salutis* provides the answer to these questions.

The *pactum* offers the context and covenantal structure for how the trinitarian processions give way to the contingent missions, and it explains the covenantal love (*hesed*) of the triune God for His people, the need for their reciprocal response of obedient covenant love for their triune Lord, and even the intra-trinitarian love within the Godhead itself. In a word, the *pactum* helps us to understand what it means to say that God is love. The triune God enters into a covenant in which the Father appoints His Son in love as covenant surety of the elect, and the Son willingly agrees to offer His obedience, His love, to His heavenly Father on behalf of the elect. The Father and the Son agree to send the Spirit, both to support the Son in His work as covenant surety, and to apply the Son's work in the redemption of the elect. The triune God reveals this covenantal agreement when the Father declared, 'This is my beloved Son in whom I am well pleased,' and then poured out the Spirit upon Him. Upon the completion of the Son's work the Son poured out the Spirit of love upon the elect to unleash the power of the age to come, the eschaton, and to redeem the Son's bride. The love of the triune God is all over the whole process, from the beginning in the *pactum* to the end.

Far from speculation, the Scriptures reveal the covenant of redemption as the foundation of all of God's activity in time and history. The church can rest assured that salvation is secure because the covenant of grace, God's saving activity in history, rests upon the bedrock of the *pactum salutis*. The *pactum* therefore conveys the greatest assurance to the church in times of doubt. When a person trembles at the thought of standing before the divine bar, he can look to Christ, the Son who was appointed as covenant surety in the *pactum salutis*. The timorous saint can know that, because of the Son's pledged and fulfilled *hesed* to

His Father's will, the fallen but redeemed sinner has right and title to eternal life.

The *pactum* also proves immensely beneficial because it connects various doctrines – the sinews and ligatures that bind the body together. Election is not an abstract choice but rests in the cradle of the *pactum salutis,* as the Father chooses fallen sinners in Christ, their covenant head and surety. Eschatology is not merely an exclamation point at the end of the long narrative of redemptive history. Rather, within the grand architecture of the *pactum salutis,* before a single grain of sand dropped in the hourglass of history, the persons of the triune God covenanted together to ensure that the Son would unleash the age to come through His loving obedience to His Father with the consequential outpouring of the Spirit. Eschatology precedes soteriology because this was the design and fabric of the *pactum salutis*. Man's efforts to know God do not mean that he must try to leap Lessing's ugly ditch or somehow scale Kant's iron curtain to penetrate beyond the veil of the phenomenal realm. Rather, within the covenant of redemption the Son consented to enter the human condition and reveal the triune God. We can know God, therefore, because God became man and because the Spirit also covenanted to support and reveal the Son's mission. Human beings have been designed to receive revelation, to know and love the triune God. The *pactum* includes the reality and viability of divine revelation.

Taking the *pactum salutis* into account also eliminates the sometimes-perceived antithesis between systematic and biblical theology. The *pactum* provides the context to understand how the intra-trinitarian processions (ontology, a category of systematic theology) proceed to the covenantally framed missions. We are not left with two seemingly separate categories of the ontological Trinity (God unto Himself) and the economic Trinity (God in history), and hence two potentially different Gods, the God of eternity and the God of time. Rather, the *pactum* shows us that the God of eternity is the same God of time because the processions lead to the covenantal missions, which then unfold in time and history. Yet, the fact that the triune God makes a covenant reminds us that creation and redemption are contingent, not necessary, acts, and God therefore remains distinct from His creation. The *pactum*, an intra-trinitarian agreement, guards against the dangers of pantheism and panentheism. In all of these considerations, the *pactum* offers a thick account of how the triune God plans and fulfills His desire to redeem a people for Himself. The covenant of redemption guarantees that we can glorify God and enjoy Him forever.

Given the present state of the question regarding the *pactum salutis*, more work should be done to explore both the history and contemporary serviceability of this doctrine. The paucity of monographs, both dogmatic and historical, means there are undoubtedly many more treasures to be unearthed and employed to the edification of the church. Hopefully this exercise in theological retrieval has been one modest step forward in reviving interest in and the employment of the covenant of redemption, the doctrine that reveals the eternal love of God, a love shared and known among Father, Son, and Holy Spirit, and graciously poured out upon fallen but redeemed sinners.

Soli Deo Gloria

~: BIBLIOGRAPHY :~

À Brakel, Wilhelmus. *The Christian's Reasonable Service*. 4 volumes. Translated by Bartel Elshout. Morgan: Soli Deo Gloria, 1992.

A Confession of Faith, Put forth by the Elders and Brethren Of many Congregations of Christians, (Baptized upon Profession of their Faith) in London and the Country. With an Appendix concerning Baptism. London: John Harris, 1688.

A Declaration of the Faith and Order Owned and Practiced in the Congregational Churches in England. London: John Field, 1659.

Adhinarta, Yuzo. *The Doctrine of the Holy Spirit in the Major Reformed Confession and Catechisms of the Sixteenth and Seventeenth Centuries*. Carlisle: Langham Monographs, 2012.

Adler, Joshua J. 'David's Last Sin: Was it the Census?' *Jewish Bible Quarterly* 23/2 (1995): 91-95.

Alexander, Archibald. *A Treatise on Justification by Faith*. Philadelphia: Presbyterian Tract and Sunday School Society, 1837.

Allen, L. C. 'The Old Testament Background of (προ)'Οριζειν in the New Testament,' *NTS* 17 (1970-71): 104-08.

Allen, R. Michael. *The Christ's Faith: A Dogmatic Account*. London: T & T Clark, 2009.

__________. *Justification and the Gospel: Understanding the Contexts and Controversies*. Grand Rapids: Baker, 2013.

Allis, O. T. *The Unity of Isaiah: A Study in Prophecy*. Eugene: Wipf & Stock, 2000.

Amyraut, Moyse. *Bref Traite de la Predestination*. Saumur: Isaac Desbordes, 1634.

Anderson, A. A. 2 *Samuel*. WBC. Waco: Word Books, 1989.

Anselm. *Anselm of Canterbury: The Major Works*. Edited by G. R. Evans and Brian Davies. Oxford: Oxford University Press, 1998.

Aquinas, Thomas. *Summa Theologica*. Reprint; Christian Classics, 1948.

Ariew, Roger. *Descartes and the Last Scholastics*. Ithaca: Cornell University Press, 1999.

Arminius, Jacob. *The Works of James Arminius*. 3 volumes. Grand Rapids: Baker, 1996.

Arnold, Bill T. 'The Love-Fear Antinomy in Deuteronomy 5-11.' *VT* 61 (2011): 551-69.

Arnold, Bill and John H. Choi. *A Guide to Biblical Hebrew Syntax*. Cambridge: Cambridge University Press, 2003.

Arnold, Clinton E. *Ephesians*, ZECNT. Grand Rapids: Zondervan, 2010.

Arrowsmith, John. *Armilla Catechetica: A Chain of Principles*. Cambridge: John Field, 1659.

Bakon, Shimon. 'David's Sin: Counting the People,' *Jewish Bible Quarterly* 41/1 (2013): 53-54.

Baldwin, Joyce. *Haggai, Zechariah, Malachi: An Introduction and Commentary*. TOTC. London: IVP, 1972.

Baron, David. *The Visions and Prophecies of Zechariah*. 1918; Grand Rapids: Kregel, 1972.

Barrett, C. K. *Acts*. ICC. 2 volumes. Edinburgh: T & T Clark, 1998.

Barth, Karl. *Christ and Adam: Man and Humanity in Romans 5*. Translated by T. A. Smail. 1956; Eugene: Wipf & Stock, 2004.

________. *Church Dogmatics*, 14 volumes. Edited by G. W. Bromiley, T. F. Torrance. Edinburgh: T & T Clark, 1936-68.

________. *Credo*. New York: Charles Scribner's Sons, 1962.

________. *The Epistle to the Romans*. Sixth edition. Translated by Edwyn C. Hoskyns. 1933; Oxford: Oxford University Press, 1968.

________. *Karl Barth's Table Talk*. Edited by John D. Godsey. Edinburgh: Oliver and Boyd, 1963.

________. *Protestant Theology in the Nineteenth Century: Its Background and History*. 1947; Grand Rapids: Eerdmans, 2001.

________. *The Theology of the Reformed Confessions*. Translated by Darrell L. Guder and Judith J. Guder. Louisville: Westminster John Knox, 2002.

Batto, Bernard F. 'The Covenant of Peace: A Neglected Ancient Near Eastern Motif.' *CBQ* 49 (1987): 187-211.

________. *Slaying the Dragon: Mythmaking in the Biblical Tradition*. Louisville: WJK, 1992.

Bauckham, Richard J. *Jude, 2 Peter*. WBC. Volume 50. Waco: Word, 1983.

Bavinck, Herman. 'Foreword to the First Edition (Volume 1) of the *Gereformeerde Dogmatiek*.' Translated by John Bolt. *CTJ* 45 (2010): 9-10.

________. *Our Reasonable Faith*. Translated by Henry Zylstra. Grand Rapids: Eerdmans, 1956.

________. *Reformed Dogmatics*. 4 volumes. Edited by John Bolt. Translated by John Vriend. Grand Rapids: Baker, 2006.

Beach, J. Mark. 'The Doctrine of the *Pactum Salutis* in the Covenant Theology of Herman Witsius,' *MAJT* 13 (2002): 101-42.

Beale, G. K. *The Book of Revelation*. NIGTC. Grand Rapids: Eerdmans, 1999.

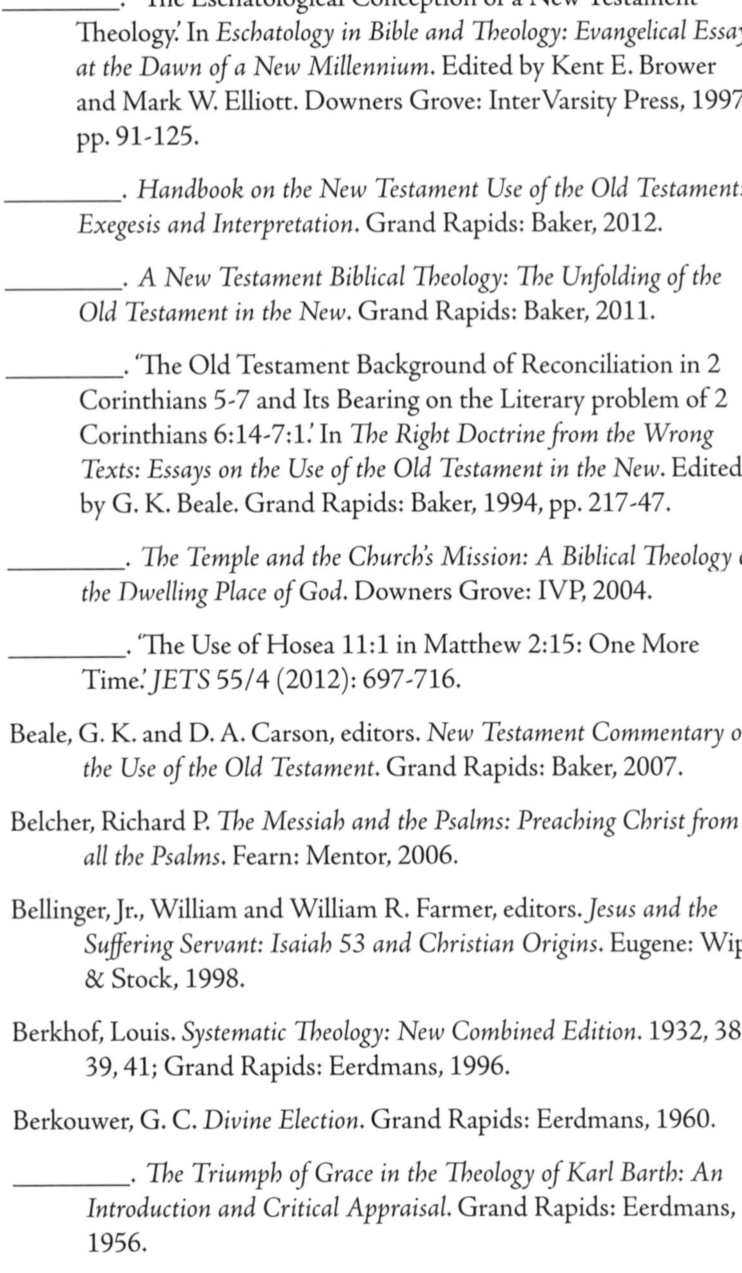

_________. 'The Eschatological Conception of a New Testament Theology.' In *Eschatology in Bible and Theology: Evangelical Essays at the Dawn of a New Millennium*. Edited by Kent E. Brower and Mark W. Elliott. Downers Grove: InterVarsity Press, 1997, pp. 91-125.

_________. *Handbook on the New Testament Use of the Old Testament: Exegesis and Interpretation*. Grand Rapids: Baker, 2012.

_________. *A New Testament Biblical Theology: The Unfolding of the Old Testament in the New*. Grand Rapids: Baker, 2011.

_________. 'The Old Testament Background of Reconciliation in 2 Corinthians 5-7 and Its Bearing on the Literary problem of 2 Corinthians 6:14-7:1.' In *The Right Doctrine from the Wrong Texts: Essays on the Use of the Old Testament in the New*. Edited by G. K. Beale. Grand Rapids: Baker, 1994, pp. 217-47.

_________. *The Temple and the Church's Mission: A Biblical Theology of the Dwelling Place of God*. Downers Grove: IVP, 2004.

_________. 'The Use of Hosea 11:1 in Matthew 2:15: One More Time.' *JETS* 55/4 (2012): 697-716.

Beale, G. K. and D. A. Carson, editors. *New Testament Commentary on the Use of the Old Testament*. Grand Rapids: Baker, 2007.

Belcher, Richard P. *The Messiah and the Psalms: Preaching Christ from all the Psalms*. Fearn: Mentor, 2006.

Bellinger, Jr., William and William R. Farmer, editors. *Jesus and the Suffering Servant: Isaiah 53 and Christian Origins*. Eugene: Wipf & Stock, 1998.

Berkhof, Louis. *Systematic Theology: New Combined Edition*. 1932, 38, 39, 41; Grand Rapids: Eerdmans, 1996.

Berkouwer, G. C. *Divine Election*. Grand Rapids: Eerdmans, 1960.

_________. *The Triumph of Grace in the Theology of Karl Barth: An Introduction and Critical Appraisal*. Grand Rapids: Eerdmans, 1956.

Best, Ernest. *A Critical and Exegetical Commentary on Ephesians*. ICC. Edinburgh: T & T Clark, 1998.

Beza, Theodore. *Iesu Christi D. N. Novum Testamentum, Graece & Latine Theodoro Beza Interprete*. [Geneva]: Henricus Stephanus, 1567.

Bierma, Lyle D. *German Calvinism in the Confessional Ages: The Covenant Theology of Caspar Olevianus*. Grand Rapids: Baker, 1996.

Bird, Michael F. *Evangelical Theology: A Biblical and Systematic Introduction*. Grand Rapids: Zondervan, 2013.

________. 'Incorporated Righteousness: A Response to Recent Evangelical Discussion Concerning the Imputation of Christ's Righteousness in Justification.' *JETS* 47/2 (2004): 253-75.

________. 'Justification as Forensic Declaration and Covenant Membership: A *Via Media* Between Reformed and Revisionist Readings of Paul.' *TynB* 57/1 (2006): 109-30.

________. *The Saving Righteousness of God: Studies on Paul, Justification, and the New Perspective*. Milton Keynes: Paternoster, 2007.

Bloesch, Donald G. *A Theology of Word and Spirit: Authority and Method in Theology*. Downers Grove: InterVarsity Press, 1992.

Bobrinskoy, Boris. 'The Filioque Yesterday and Today.' In *Spirit of God, Spirit of Christ: Ecumenical Reflections on the Filioque Controversy*. Edited by Lukas Vischer. London: SPCK, 1981, pp. 133-48.

________. *The Mystery of the Trinity: Trinitarian Experience and Vision in the Biblical and Patristic Tradition*. Crestwood: St. Vladimir's Seminary Press, 1999.

Bock, Darrell. *Acts*. BECNT. Grand Rapids: Baker, 2007.

________. *Luke 9:51-24:53*. BECNT. Grand Rapids: Baker, 1996.

Bock, Darrell and Mitch Glaser, editors. *The Gospel According to Isaiah 53: Encountering the Suffering Servant in Jewish and Christian Theology*. Grand Rapids: Kregel, 2012.

Boling, Robert G. *Judges*. AB. Garden City: Doubleday, 1975.

Bonhoeffer, Dietrich. *Sanctorum Communio: A Theological Study of the Sociology of the Church*, Dietrich Bonhoeffer Works. Volume 1. Minneapolis: Fortress, 1998.

Brown, Francis. *The New Brown – Driver – Briggs – Gesenius Hebrew and English Lexicon*. Reprint; Peabody: Hendrickson, 1979.

Brown, Sherri. *Gift Upon Gift: Covenant Through Word in the Gospel of John*. Eugene: Pickwick, 2010.

Brownlee, W. H. 'Psalms 1-2 as Coronation Liturgy.' *Bib* 52 (1971): 321-36.

Bruce, F. F. *The Book of Acts*. NICNT. Grand Rapids: Eerdmans, 1988.

_________. *The Epistle to the Hebrews*, NICNT. Grand Rapids: 1964.

_________. *The Epistles to the Colossians, to Philemon, and to the Ephesians*. NICNT. Grand Rapids: Eerdmans, 1984.

Brueggemann, Walter. *First and Second Samuel*. Louisville: John Knox Press, 1990.

_________. *The Theology of the Old Testament: Testimony, Dispute, Adovcacy*. Minneapolis: Fortress, 1997.

Brunner, Emil. *The Christian Doctrine of God*. Dogmatics. Volume 1. Translated by Olive Wyon. Philadelphia: Westminster Press, 1949.

Buchanan, J. M. 'The Only Begotten Son.' *CTJ* 16/1 (1981): 56-79.

Bultmann, Rudolf. *Theology of the New Testament*. 2 volumes. Translated by Kendrick Grobel. New York: Charles Scribner's Sons, 1951-55.

Burns, Daniel Paul. 'So That Love May Be Safeguarded: The Nature, Form, and Function of Obedience as a Heuristic Device for the Theology of Hans Urs Von Balthasar.' Ph.D. Diss., Loyola University Chicago, 2011.

Busch, Eberhard. *Karl Barth: His Life from Letters and Autobiographical Texts*. Philadelphia: Fortress, 1975.

Calvin, John. *Calvin's Commentaries*. 22 volumes. Reprint; Grand Rapids: Baker, 1993.

_________. *Institutes of the Christian Religion*. Translated by John Allen. Grand Rapids: Eerdmans, 1949.

Campbell, Constantine R. *Paul and Union with Christ: An Exegetical and Theological Study*. Grand Rapids: Zondervan, 2012.

Campbell, Douglas A. *The Deliverance of God: An Apocalyptic Rereading of Justification in Paul*. Grand Rapids: Eerdmans, 2009.

Carson, D. A. *The Gospel According to John*. Grand Rapids: Eerdmans, 1991.

_________. *Matthew: 1-12*. EBC. Grand Rapids: Zondervan, 1995.

_________. 'The Vindication of Imputation: On Fields of Discourse and Semantic Fields.' in *Justification: What's at Stake in the Current Debates*. Edited by Mark Husbands and Daniel J. Treier. Downers Grove: InterVarsity Press, 2004, pp. 46-80.

Charnock, Stephen. *Works of Stephen Charnock*. Volume 2. Edinburgh: James Nichol, 1864.

Chennattu, Rekha M. 'The Covenant Motif: A Key to the Interpretation of John 15-16.' In *Transcending Boundaries: Contemporary Readings of the New Testament. Essays In Honor of Francis J. Moloney*. Edited by Rekha M. Chennattu and Mary L. Coloe. Rome: Libreria Ateneo Salesiano, 2005, pp. 141-59.

_________. *Johannine Discipleship as a Covenant Relationship*. Peabody: Hendrickson, 2006.

Cherry, Conrad. *The Theology of Jonathan Edwards: A Reappraisal.* New York: Doubleday, 1966.

Chesterton, G. K. *Orthodoxy: The Romance of the Faith*. 1959; New York: Doubleday, 1990.

Childs, Brevard S. *Biblical Theology of the Old and New Testaments: Theological Reflection on the Christian Bible*. Minneapolis: Fortress, 1992.

_________. *Isaiah*. OTL. Louisville: Westminster John Knox, 2001.

Clark, Gordon R. *The Word Hesed in the Hebrew Bible*. Sheffield: JSOT Press, 1993.

Clark, R. Scott. *Caspar Olevian and the Substance of the Covenant: The Double Benefit of Christ*. Edinburgh: Rutherford House, 2005.

Clark, R. Scott and David VanDrunen. 'The Covenant Before the Covenants.' In *Covenant, Justification, and Pastoral Ministry*. Edited by R. Scott Clark. Phillipsburg: P & R, 2007, pp. 167-96.

Clarke, Adam. *The Holy Bible with A Commentary and Critical Notes.* Volume 4. London: Thomas Tegg and Son, 1836.

Cleveland, Christopher. *Thomism in John Owen*. Farnham: Ashgate, 2013.

Clines, David J. A. *Job 1-20*. WBC. Volume 17. Dallas: Word, 1989.

Cocceius, Johannes. *Opera Omnia theologica, exegetica, didactica, polemica, philologica*. 7 Volumes. Amsterdam: 1701.

_________. *To dodekapropheton sive Prophfetae Duodecim Minores.* Lugduni Batavorum, 1652.

Cockerill, Gareth Lee. 'The Melchizedek Christology in Hebrews 7:1-28.' Ph.D. Dissertation, Union Theological Seminary, 1976.

Coffey, David. 'The Holy Spirit as the Mutual Love of the Father and the Son.' *Theological Studies* 51 (1990): 193-229.

Cole, Robert L. *Psalms 1-2: Gateway to the Psalter*. Sheffield: Sheffield Phoenix Press, 2013.

Collins, C. John. 'Echoes of Aristotle in Romans 2:14-15: Or, Maybe Abimelech Was Not So Bad After All.' *Journal of Markets and Morality* 13/1 (2010): 123-74.

Congar, Yves. *I Believe in the Holy Spirit*. 3 volumes. 1983; New York: Herder & Herder, 2013.

Cooper, John W. *Panentheism: The Other God of the Philosophers: From Plato to the Present*. Grand Rapids: Baker, 2006.

Copleston, Frederick. *A History of Philosophy*, 9 volumes. New Jersey: Paulist Press, 1959.

Cowles, C. S., editor. *Show Them No Mercy: Four Views on God and Canaanite Genocide*. Grand Rapids: Zondervan, 2003.

Craigie, Peter C. *The Book of Deuteronomy*. NICOT. Grand Rapids: Eerdmans, 1976.

_________. *Psalms 1-50*. WBC. Volume 19. Nashville: Thomas Nelson, 1983.

Cross, Richard. *The Metaphysics of the Incarnation*. Oxford: Oxford University Press, 2005.

Crowe, Brandon C. *The Obedient Son: Deuteronomy and Christology in the Gospel of Matthew*. Berlin: De Grutyer, 2012.

Cullmann, Oscar. *Baptism in the New Testament*. Philadelphia: Westminster, 1950.

Curtis, Byron G. *Up the Steep and Stony Road: The Book of Zechariah in Social Location Trajectory Analysis*. Atlanta: Society of Biblical Literature, 2006.

Dahood, Mitchell. *Psalms I: 1-50*. AB. Volume 16. New York: Doubleday, 1965.

Das, A. Andrew. *Galatians*. Concordia Commentary. St. Louis: Concordia Publishing, 2014.

Davidson, Richard M. *Typology in Scripture: A Study of Hermeneutical τύπος Structures*. Berrien Springs: Andrews University Press, 1981.

Davies, W. D. and D. C. Allison. *Matthew*. ICC. 3 volumes. 1988; Edinburgh: T & T Clark, 2006.

De Campos, Jr., Heber Carlos. 'Johannes Piscator (1526-1625) and the Consequent Development of the Doctrine of the Imputation of Christ's Active Obedience.' Ph.D. Diss., Calvin Theological Seminary, 2011.

Del Colle, Ralph. *Christ and the Spirit: Spirit Christology in Trinitarian Perspective*. Oxford: Oxford University Press, 1994.

Dempsy, Michael T. *Trinity and Election in Contemporary Theology*. Grand Rapids: Eerdmans, 2011.

Dickson, David, 'Arminianism Discussed.' In *Records of the Kirk of Scotland, Containing the Acts and Proceedings of the General Assemblies, from the Year 1638 Downwards*. Edited by Alexander Peterkin. Edinburgh: Peter Brown, 1845.

Dickson, David and James Durham. *The Summe of Saving Knowledge, With the Practical use thereof*. Edinburgh: George Swintoun, and Thomas Brown, n. d.

Dillard, Raymond. 'David's Census.' In *Through Christ's Word: A Festschrift for Dr. Philip E. Hughes*. Phillipsburg: P & R, 1985, pp. 94-107.

Dodd, C. H. *According to the Scriptures: The Sub-Structure of New Testament Theology*. London: Nisbet & Co, Ltd., 1952.

Doran, Robert M. *The Trinity In History: A Theology of the Divine Missions*. Volume 1. *Missions and Processions*. Toronto: University of Toronto Press, n. d.

Douglas, Mary. *Jacob's Tears: The Priestly Work of Reconciliation*. Oxford: Oxford University Press, 2004.

Dubay, Thomas. *God Dwells Within Us*. New York: Dimension Books, 1971.

Dunn, James D. G. *Baptism in the Holy Spirit: A Re-examination of the New Testament Teaching on the Gift of the Spirit in relation to Pentecostalism Today*. Philadelphia: Westminster Press, 1970.

________. *Jesus and the Spirit: A Study in the Religious and Charismatic Experience of Jesus and the First Christians as Reflected in the New Testament*. 1975; Grand Rapids: Eerdmans, 1997.

________. 'Paul's Understanding of the Death of Jesus as Sacrifice.' In *The Christ and the Spirit: Christology*. Volume 1. *Collected Essays of James D. G. Dunn*. Grand Rapids: Eerdmans, 1998, pp. 190-211.

________. *Romans 9-16*. WBC. Volume 38b. Dallas: Word, 1988.

________. *The Theology of Paul the Apostle*. Grand Rapids: Eerdmans, 1998.

Dunson, Ben C. 'Do Bible Words Have Bible Meaning? Distinguishing Between Imputation as Word and Doctrine.' *WTJ* 75 (2013): 254-56.

________. *Individual and Community in Paul's Letter to the Romans*. Tübingen: Mohr Siebeck, 2012.

Durham, James. *Christ Crucified: or, The Marrow of the Gospel, Evidently holden forth in LXXII Sermons, on the whole 53 Chapter of Isaiah*. Edinburgh: Andrew Anderson, 1683.

Edwards, Jonathan. *The Works of Jonathan Edwards*. 26 volumes. New Haven: Yale University Press, 1957-2008.

Eichrodt, Walther. *Theology of the Old Testament*. 2 volumes. Translated by J. A. Baker. Philadelphia: Westminster, 1967.

Ellingworth, Paul. *The Epistle to the Hebrews*. NIGTC. Grand Rapids: Eerdmans, 1993.

Ellis, Brannon. 'The Eternal Decree in the Incarnate Son: Robert Rollock on the Relationship Between Christ and Election.' In *Reformed Orthodox in Scotland: Essays on Scottish Theology 1560-1775*. Edited by Aaron Denlinger. Edinburgh: T & T Clark, 2015, pp. 45-66.

Ellis, E. Earle. *Pauline Theology: Ministry and Society*. Grand Rapids: Eerdmans, 1989.

Emery, Gilles. Essentialism or Personalism in the Treatise on God in St. Thomas Aquinas.' *The Thomist* 64 (2000): 521-63.

_________. '*Theologia* and *Dispensatio*: the Centrality of the Divine Missions in St. Thomas's Trinitarian Theology.' *The Thomist* 74 (2010): 515-61.

_________. *The Trinitarian Theology of St. Thomas Aquinas*. Oxford: Oxford University Press, 2010.

_________. *The Trinity: An Introduction to Catholic Doctrine on the Triune God*, trans. Matthew Levering. Washington, DC: Catholic University of America Press, 2011.

Emery, Gilles and Matthew Levering, editors. *The Oxford Handbook of the Trinity*. Oxford: Oxford University Press, 2011.

Enns, Peter. חָק, in *New International Dictionary of Old Testament Theology & Exegesis*. Volume 2. Grand Rapids: Zondervan, 1997.

Estelle, Bryan D. 'Leviticus 18:5 and Deuteronomy 30:1-14 in Biblical Theological Development: Entitlement to Heaven Foreclosed and Proffered.' In *The Law is Not of Faith: Essays on Works and Grace in the Mosaic Covenant*. Edited by Bryan D. Estelle, J. V. Fesko, and David VanDrunen. Phillipsburg: P & R, 2009, pp. 109-46.

Evans, William B. *Imputation and Impartation: Union with Christ in American Reformed Theology*. Eugene: Paternoster, 2008.

Fee, Gordon D. *God's Empowering Presence: The Holy Spirit in the Letters of Paul*. Peabody: Hendrickson, 1994.

_________. *Paul's Letter to the Philippians*. NICNT. Grand Rapids: Eerdmans, 1995.

Felch, Douglas A. 'From Here to Eternity: A Biblical, Theological, and Analogical Defense of Divine Eternity in the Light of Recent Challenges Within Analytic Philosophy.' Ph.D. dissertation, Calvin Theological Seminary, 2005.

Ferguson, Sinclair. *The Holy Spirit*. Downers Grove: InterVarsity, 1996.

Fesko, J. V. 'Arminius on *Facientibus Quod In Se Est* and Likely Medieval Sources,' in *Church and School in Early Modern Protestantism: Studies in Honor of Richard A. Muller on the Maturation of a Theological Tradition*. Edited by Jordan Ballor, David Sytsma, Jason Zuidema. Leiden: Brill, 2013, pp. 347-60.

_________. *Beyond Calvin: Union with Christ and Justification in Early Modern Reformed Theology (1517-1700)*. Göttingen: Vandenhoeck & Ruprecht, 2012.

_________. *The Covenant of Redemption: Origins, Development, and Reception*. Göttingen: Vandenhoeck & Ruprecht, 2016.

_________. 'Lapsarian Diversity at the Synod of Dort,' in *Drawn Into Controversie: Reformed Theological Diversity and Debates Within Seventeenth-Century British Puritanism*. Edited by Michael A. G. Haykin and Mark Jones. Göttingen: Vandenhoeck & Ruprecht, 2011, pp. 99-123.

_________. 'Romans 8:29-30 and the Question of the *Ordo Salutis*.' *Journal of Reformed Theology* 8 (2014): 35-60.

_________. *The Theology of the Westminster Standards: Historical Context and Theological Insights*. Wheaton: Crossway, 2014.

_________. 'Vos and Berkhof on Union with Christ and Justification.' *CTJ* 47/1 (2012): 50-71.

Fisher, Edward. *The Marrow of Modern Divinity*. London: R. W. for G. Calvert, 1645.

Fitzmyer, Joseph. *The Dead Sea Scrolls and Christian Origins*. Grand Rapids: Eerdmans, 2000.

_________. *Romans*. AB. New York: Doubleday, 1992.

Flynn, Gabriel and Paul D. Murray, editors. *Ressourcement: A Movement for Renewal in Twentieth-Century Catholic Theology*. Oxford: Oxford University Press, 2012.

Frame, John. *Systematic Theology: An Introduction to Christian Belief*. Phillipsburg: P & R, 2013.

France, R. T. *Jesus and the Old Testament: His Application of Old Testament Passages to Himself and His Mission*. Vancouver: Regent College Publishing, 1998.

Franke, John R. *The Character of Theology: A Postconservative Approach*. Grand Rapids: Baker, 2005.

Frei, Hans. *The Eclipse of Biblical Narrative: A Study in Eighteenth and Nineteenth Century Hermeneutics*. New Haven: Yale University Press, 1974.

_________. *The Identity of Jesus Christ: The Hermeneutical Bases of Dogmatic Theology*. Philadelphia: Fortress Press, 1975.

Furnish, Victor Paul. *II Corinthians*. AB. Volume 32a. New York: Doubleday, 1984.

Gaffin, Jr., Richard B. *By Faith, Not By Sight: Paul and the Order of Salvation*. 2nd ed. Phillipsburg: P & R, 2013.

_________. *Resurrection and Redemption: A Study in Paul's Soteriology*. Phillipsburg: P & R, 1987.

_________. 'Union with Christ: Some Biblical and Theological Reflections.' In *Always Reforming: Explorations in Systematic Theology*. Edited by A. T. B. McGowan. Downers Grove: InterVarsity Press, 2006, pp. 271-88.

Gentry, Peter J. and Stephen J. Wellum. *Kingdom Through Covenant: A Biblical-Theological Understanding of the Covenants*. Wheaton: Crossway, 2012.

Gesenius, Wilhelm. *Gesenius's Hebrew Grammar*. Edited by Emil Kautzsch. Translated by Arthur Ernest Cowley. 1909; Mineola: Dover Publications, 2006.

Gibson, David. *Reading the Decree: Exegesis, Election and Christology in Calvin and Barth*. London: T & T Clark, 2009.

Gill, John. *A Complete Body of Doctrinal and Practical Divinity: or A System of Evangelical Truths*. 1809; Paris, AR: The Baptist Standard Bearer, Inc., 2007.

Gillespie, Patrick. *The Ark of the Covenant Opened: Or, a Treatise of the Covenant of Redemption Between God and Christ, as the Foundation of the Covenant of Grace*. The Second Part. London: Thomas Parkhurst, 1677.

Glomsrud, Ryan D. 'Engaging the Tradition: Karl Barth's Use of Reformed Orthodox Sources in *The Göttingen Dogmatics* (1924/25).' M. A. Thesis, Westminster Seminary California, 2004.

_________. 'Karl Barth: Between Pietism and Orthodoxy: A Post-Enlightenment Resourcement of Classical Protestantism.' D. Phil. Diss., Pembroke College, University of Oxford, 2009.

Glueck, Nelson. *Hesed in the Bible*. New York: Ktav Publishing House, 1975.

Gockel, Matthias. *Barth and Schleiermacher on the Doctrine of Election: A Systematic-Theological Comparison*. Oxford: Oxford University Press, 2006.

Goldingay, John. *The Message of Isaiah 40-55*. London: T & T Clark, 2005.

_________. *Psalms*. 3 volumes. Grand Rapids: Baker, 2008.

Gorman, Michael. *Inhabiting the Cruciform God: Kenosis, Justification, and Theosis in Paul's Narrative Soteriology*. Grand Rapids: Eerdmans, 2009.

Graves, J. R. *The Work of Christ in the Covenant of Redemption: Developed in Seven Dispensations*. Texarkana, TX: Baptist Sunday School Committee, 1928.

Greenwood, Kyle R. 'Labor Pains: The Relationship between David's Census and Corvée Labor.' *BBR* 20/4 (2010): 467-78.

Grenz, Stanley J. and John R. Franke. *Beyond Foundationalism: Shaping Theology in a Postmodern Context*. Louisville: Westminster John Knox, 2001.

Groves, J. Alan. 'Atonement in Isaiah 53.' In *The Glory of the Atonement*. Edited by Charles E. Hill and Frank A. James, III. Downers Grove: InterVarsity, 2004, pp. 61-89.

Grudem, Wayne. *Systematic Theology: An Introduction to Biblical Doctrine*. Grand Rapids: Zondervan, 1994.

Gundry, Robert H. 'The Nonimputation of Christ's Righteousness.' In *Justification: What's at Stake in the Current Debates*. Edited by Mark Husbands and Daniel J. Treier. Downers Grove: InterVarsity Press, 2004, pp. 17-45.

Haight, Roger. 'The Case for Spirit Christology.' *Theological Studies* 52 (1992): 257-87.

Haffemann, Scott J. *2 Corinthians*. NIVAC. Grand Rapids: Zondervan, 2000.

Hagner, Donald A. *Matthew 1-13*. WBC. Volume 33a. Dallas: Word, 1993.

Hahn, Scott W. *Kinship by Covenant: A Canonical Approach to the Fulfillment of God's Saving Promises*. New Haven: Yale University Press, 2009.

Hall, Basil. 'Calvin against the Calvinists.' In *John Calvin*. Edited by G. E. Duffield. Appleford: Sutton Courtenay Press, 1966, pp. 19-37.

Hankey, W. J. *God In Himself: Aquinas' Doctrine of God as Expounded in the Summa Theologiae*. Oxford: Oxford University Press, 1987.

Harris, Murray J. *The Second Epistle to the Corinthians*. NIGTC. Grand Rapids: Eerdmans, 2005.

Hay, David M. *Glory at the Right Hand: Psalm 110 in Early Christianity*. Nashville: Abingdon, 1973.

Healey, Jr., Nicholas J. 'Evangelical *Ressourcement*,' *First Things* 213 (May 2011): 56.

Hengstenberg, E. W. *Christology of the Old Testament and a Commentary on the Predictions of the Messiah by the Prophets*. Volume 2. Washington, DC: William M. Morrison, 1839.

Henry, Matthew. *An Exposition of the Old and New Testament*. Volume 4. Philadelphia: Ed. Barrington & Geo. D. Haswell, 1828.

Heppe, Heinrich. *Reformed Dogmatics: Set Out and Illustrated from the Sources*. Translated by G. T. Thomson. Edited by Ernst Bizer. London: George Allen & Unwin Ltd, 1950.

Hess, Richard S. *Joshua*. TOTC. Downers Grove: InterVarsity Press, 1996.

Higginson, R. E. *Zechariah*. In *The New Bible Commentary: Revised*. Edited by D. Guthrie and J. A. Motyer. Grand Rapids: Eerdmans, 1970.

Higton, Mike. *Christ, Providence and History: Hans W. Frei's Public Theology*. London: T & T Clark, 2004.

Hinckley, Mitchell G., et al. *Haggai, Zechariah, Malachi, and Jonah*. ICC. Edinburgh: T & T Clark, 1912.

Hoad, John. 'Some New Testament References to Isaiah 53.' *ExpT* 67 (1957): 254-55.

Hobbs, T. R. *2 Kings*. WBC. Waco: Word Books, 1985.

Hodge, A. A. *Outlines of Theology*. 1860; Edinburgh: Banner of Truth, 1991.

Hodge, Charles. 'Can God Be Known?' *Biblical Repertory and Princeton Review* 36/1 (1864): 122-52.

_________. *Ephesians*. 1856; Edinburgh: Banner of Truth, 1991.

_________. *Princeton Sermons: Outlines of Discourses Doctrinal and Practical*. 1879; Edinburgh: Banner of Truth, 2011.

_________. *Romans*. 1835; Edinburgh: Banner of Truth, 1989.

_________. *Systematic Theology*. 3 volumes. Reprint; Grand Rapids: Eerdmans, 1993.

Hoeksema, Herman. *Reformed Dogmatics*. 1963; Grand Rapids: Reformed Free Publishing Association, 1985.

Hog, James. *The Covenants of Redemption and Grace Displayed*. Edinburgh: John Morton, 1707.

Hooker, Morna. *Jesus and the Servant: The Influence of the Servant Concept of Deutero-Isaiah in the New Testament*. London: SPCK, 1959.

Horrell, J. Scott. 'Toward a Biblical Model of the Social Trinity: Avoiding Equivocation of Nature and Order,' *JETS* 47/3 (2004): 399-421.

Horton, Michael. *Covenant and Eschatology: The Divine Drama*. Louisville: WJK, 2002.

_________. *The Christian Faith: A Systematic Theology for Pilgrims on the Way*. Grand Rapids: Eerdmans, 2011.

_________. 'Covenant, Election, and Incarnation: Evaluating Barth's Actualist Christology.' In *Karl Barth and American Evangelicalism*. Edited by Bruce McCormack and Clifford B. Anderson. Grand Rapids: Eerdmans, 2011, pp. 112-47.

Hugenberger, Gordon P. *Marriage as Covenant: Biblical Law and Ethics as Developed from Malachi*. Grand Rapids: Baker, 1994.

Hunsinger, George. *Disruptive Grace: Studies in the Theology of Karl Barth*. Grand Rapids: Eerdmans, 2000.

_________. *How To Read Karl Barth: The Shape of His Theology*. New York: Oxford University Press, 1991.

Hunter, Harold. 'Spirit Christology: Dilemma and Promise.' *The Heythrop Journal* 24/2 (1983): 127-40.

Irons, C. Lee. 'Dikaiosyne Theou: A Lexical Examination of the Covenant-Faithfulness Interpretation.' Ph.D. Dissertation, Fuller Theological Seminary, 2011.

Janowski, Bernd and Peter Stuhlmacher, editors. *The Suffering Servant: Isaiah 53 in Jewish and Christian Sources*. Translated by Daniel P. Bailey. 1996; Grand Rapids: Eerdmans, 2004.

Jauhiainen, V. M. 'Turban and Crown Lost and Regained: Ezekiel 21:29-32 and Zechariah's Zemah.' *JBL* 127 (2008): 501-11.

Jenson, Robert W. 'Once More the *Logos asarkos*.' *IJST* 13 (2011): 130-33.

_________. *Systematic Theology*. Volume 1. Oxford: Oxford University Press, 1997.

_________. *The Triune Identity: God According to the Gospel*. Philadelphia: Fortress Press, 1982.

Jerome, *Commentarii in Zachariam*, in *Patrologia Latina*, ed. J. P. Migne, vol. 25. Paris: 1845.

Jewett, Robert. *Romans*, Hermenia. Minneapolis: Fortress, 2007.

Johnson, Aubrey. *The One and the Many in the Israelite Conception of God*. Cardiff: University of Wales Press, 1961.

_________. *Sacral Kingship in Ancient Israel*. 1955; Eugene: Wipf & Stock, 2006.

Johnson, Marcus Peter. *One with Christ: An Evangelical Theology of Salvation*. Wheaton: Crossway, 2013.

Johnstone, William. 'Guilt and Atonement: The Theme of 1 and 2 Chronicles,' In *A Word In Season: Essays in Honor of William McKane*. Edited by James D. Martin and Philip R. Davies. Sheffield: JSOT Press, 1986, pp. 113-38.

_________. 'The Use of Leviticus in Chronicles,' in *Reading Leviticus: A Conversation with Mary Douglas*. Edited by John F. A. Sawyer. Sheffield: Sheffield Academic Press, 1996, pp. 243-55.

Jones, Mark. *Antinomianism: Reformed Theology's Unwelcome Guest?* Phillipsburg: P & R, 2013.

_________. 'Covenant and Christology: Herman Bavinck and the *Pactum Salutis*.' In *Five Studies in the Thought of Herman Bavinck, A Creator of Modern Dutch Theology*. Edited by John Bolt. Lewiston: Edwin Mellen Press, 2011, pp. 129-52.

_________. *Why Heaven Kissed Earth: The Christology of the Puritan Reformed Orthodox Theologian, Thomas Goodwin (1600-80)*. Göttingen: Vandenhoeck & Ruprecht, 2010.

Jones, Paul Dafydd. *The Humanity of Christ: Christology in Karl Barth's Church Dogmatics*. London: T & T Clark, 2008.

Jüngel, Eberhard. *God's Being Is in Becoming: The Trinitarian Being of God in the Theology of Karl Barth*. Grand Rapids: Eerdmans, 2001.

Kalluveettil, Paul. *Declaration and Covenant: A Comprehensive Review of Covenant Formulae from the Old Testament and the Ancient Near East*. Rome: Biblical Institute Press, 1982.

Kaminsky, Joel K. *Corporate Responsibility in the Hebrew Bible*. Sheffield: Sheffield Academic Press, 1995.

Keckerman, Bartholomäus. *Systema S. S. Theologiae*. Hanau: 1602.

Keel, Othmar. *The Symbolism of the Biblical World: Ancient Near Eastern Inconography and the Book of Psalms*. Winona: Eisenbrauns, 1997.

Keil, C. F. and F. Delitzsch. *Commentary on the Old Testament*. 10 volumes. 1886-91; Peabody: Hendrickson, 1996.

Keilby, James. K. and Paul Rhodes Eddy, editors. *Justification: Five Views*. Downers Grove: InterVarsity Press, 2011.

Kelly, J. N. D. *The Pastoral Epistles*. BNTC. Peabody: Hendrickson, 1998.

Kennedy, Joel. *The Recapitulation of Israel: Use of Israel's History in Matthew 1:1-4:11*. Tübingen: Mohr Siebeck, 2008.

Kidner, Derek. *Psalms 1-72*. TOTC. Downers Grove: IVP, 1973.

_________. *Psalms 73-150*. TOTC. Downers Grove: IVP, 1973.

Kilby, Karen. 'Perichoresis and Projection: Problems with Social Doctrines of the Trinity.' *New Blackfriars* 81 (2000): 432-45.

Kim, Seyoon. *The Son of Man as the Son of God*. Grand Rapids: Eerdmans, 1983.

Kline, Meredith G. *Glory in Our Midst: A Biblical-Theological Reading of Zechariah's Night Visions*. Overland Park: Two Ages Press, 2001.

_________. *The Structure of Biblical Authority*. Eugene: Wipf & Stock, 1997.

_________. 'The Structure of the Book of Zechariah,' *JETS* 34/2 (1991): 179-93.

_________. *Treaty of the Great King*. Grand Rapids: Eerdmans, 1963.

Knight, George W. *The Pastoral Epistles: A Commentary on the Greek Text*. Grand Rapids: Eerdmans, 1992.

Koenker, Ernest B. *Great Dialecticians in Modern Christian Thought*. Minneapolis: Augsburg, 1971.

Kraus, Hans-Joachim. *Dictaten Dogmatiek: collegedictaat van een der studenten*. Volume 3. Locus de Providentia, Peccato, Foedere, Christo. 2nd edition Kampen: Stoomdrukkerij van J. H. Kok, n. d.

_________. *Psalms 1-59*. Minneapolis: Fortress, 1993.

_________. *Psalms 60-150*. Minneapolis: Fortress, 1993.

_________. *Theology of the Psalms*. 1986; Minneapolis: Fortress, 1992.

Kynes, William L. *A Christology of Solidarity: Jesus as the Representative of His People in Matthew*. Lanham: University Press of America, 1991.

Laato, Antti. *Who Is the Servant of the Lord? Jewish and Christian Interpretations on Isaiah 53: From Antiquity to the Middle Ages*. Winona Lake: Eisenbrauns, 2012.

LaCugna, Catherine Mowry. *God For Us: The Trinity and Christian Life*. San Francisco: Harper San Francisco, 1991.

Lane, William. *Hebrews*. 2 volumes. WBC. Waco: Word Books, 1991.

Lee, Brian J. 'The Covenant Terminology of Johannes Cocceius: the Use of *Foedus*, *Pactum*, and *Testamentum* in a Mature Federal Theologian,' *MAJT* 14 (2003): 11-36.

Leftow, Brian. 'Anti Social Trinitarianism.' In *The Trinity: An Interdisciplinary Symposium on the Trinity*. Edited by Stephen T. Davis, Daniel Kendall, and Gerald O'Collins. Oxford: Oxford University Press, 1999, pp. 203-49.

Legaspi, Michael C. *The Death of Scripture and the Rise of Biblical Studies*. Oxford: Oxford University Press, 2010.

Letham, Robert. *The Holy Trinity: In Scripture, History, Theology, and Worship*. Phillipsburg: P & R, 2004.

_________. 'John Owen's Doctrine of the Trinity in its Catholic Context.' In *The Ashgate Research Companion to John Owen's Theology*. Edited by Kelly M. Kapic and Mark Jones. Farnham: Ashgate, 2012, pp. 185-97.

_________. *Union with Christ: In Scripture, History, and Theology*. Phillipsburg: P & R, 2011.

_________. *The Westminster Assembly: Reading Its Theology in Historical Context*. Phillipsburg: P & R, 2009.

_________. *The Work of Christ*. Downers Grove: InterVarsity Press, 1993.

Levenson, Jon D. *Sinai & Zion: An Entry Into the Jewish Bible*. New York: Harper San Francisco, 1985.

Levering, Matthew. *Scripture and Metaphysics: Aquinas and the Renewal of Trinitarian Theology*. Oxford: Oxford University Press, 2004.

Levison, John R. *Filled with the Spirit*. Grand Rapids: Eerdmans, 2009.

Lewis, C. S. 'On the Reading of Old Books.' In *God in the Dock: Essays on Theology and Ethics*. Edited by Walter Hooper. Grand Rapids: Eerdmans, 1970, pp. 200-07.

Lim, Paul C. H. *Mystery Unveiled: The Crisis of the Trinity in Early Modern England*. Oxford: Oxford University Press, 2012.

Lincoln, Andrew T. *Ephesians*. WBC. Waco: Word, 1990.

_________. *Paradise Now and Not Yet: Studies in the role of the heavenly dimension in Paul's thought with special reference to his eschatology*. Cambridge: Cambridge University Press, 1981.

_________. 'The Use of the OT in Ephesians.' *JSNT* 14 (1982): 16-57.

Loader, W. R. G. 'Christ at the Right Hand—Psa. 110:1 in the New Testament,' *NTS* 24 (1978): 199-217.

Lonergan, Bernard. 'The Notion of Fittingness: The Application of Theological Method to the Question of the Purpose of the Incarnation.' In *Collected Works of Bernard Lonergan*. Volume 19. *Early Latin Theology*. Edited by Robert M. Doran and H. Daniel Monsour. Translated by Michael G. Shields. Toronto: University of Toronto Press, 2011, pp. 483-533.

_________. *The Triune God: Systematics, Collected Works of Bernard Lonergan*, Volume 12. Translated by Michael Shields. Edited by Robert M. Doran and H. Daniel Monsour. Toronto: University of Toronto Press, 2007.

Long, D. Stephen. *Saving Karl Barth: Hans Urs von Balthasar's Preoccupation*. Minneapolis: Fortress, 2014.

Longman, Tremper. *Proverbs*. BCOTWS. Grand Rapids: Baker, 2006.

Loonstra, Bertus. *Verkiezing – Verzoening – Verbond: Beschrijving en beoordeling van de leer van het pactum salutis in de gereformeerde theologie*. Gravenhage: Uitgeverij Boekencentrum, 1990.

Lossky, Vladimir. *The Mystical Theology of the Eastern Church*. Crestwood: St. Vladimir's Seminary Press, 1973.

Luther, Martin. *Luther's Works*. 55 volumes. Edited by Jaroslav Pelikan and Helmut T. Lehmann. Philadelphia: Muehlenberg and Fortress, and St. Louis Concordia, 1955-86.

Maccovius, Johannes. *Scholastic Discourse: Johannes Maccovius (1588-1644) on Theological and Philosophical Distinctions*. Translated by Willem J. van Asselt, et al. Apeldoorn: Instituut voor Reformatieonderzoek, 2009.

Machia, Frank D. *Justified in the Spirit: Creation, Redemption, and the Triune God*. Grand Rapids: Eerdmans, 2010.

Malatesta, Edward. *Interiority and Covenant: A Study of* εἶναι ἐν *and* μένει ἐν *In the First Letter of Saint John*. Rome: Biblical Institute Press, 1978.

Mann, C. S. *Mark*. AB. Volume 27. New York: Doubleday, 1986.

Marckius, Johannes. *Compendium Theologiae Christianae Didactico-Elencticum*. 1716; Amsterdam: 1749.

Margalioth, Rachel. *The Indivisible Isaiah: Evidence for the Single Authorship of the Prophetic Book*. New York: Sura Institute for Research, 1964.

Marmorstein, Arthur. *The Doctrine of Merits in Old Rabbinical Literature*. London: Jews' College, 1920.

Marshall, I. Howard. *The Pastoral Epistles*, ICC. Edinburgh: T & T Clark, 1999.

Martin, Ralph P. *A Hymn of Christ: Philippians 2:5-11 in Recent Interpretation & In the Setting of Early Christian Worship*. Downers Grove: IVP, 1997.

Martínez, Florentino García, editor. *The Dead Sea Scrolls Translated: The Qumran Texts in English*. Second edition. Grand Rapids: Eerdmans, 1996.

Mastin, B. A. 'A Note on Zechariah VI 13,' *VT* 26/1 (1976): 113-15.

Maury, Pierre. *Predestination and Other papers by Pierre Maury*. Translated by Edwin Hudson. Richmond: John Knox, 1960.

Maxcey, Carl E. 'Double Justice, Diego Laynez, and the Council of Trent.' *CH* 48/3 (1979): 269-78.

McCarthy, Dennis J. 'Notes on the Love of God in Deuteronomy and the Father-Son Relationship Between Yahweh and Israel.' *CBQ* 27 (1965): 144-47.

__________. *Treaty and Covenant: A Study in Form in the Ancient Oriental Documents and in the Old Testament*. Rome: Pontifical Biblical Institute, 1981.

McComiskey, Thomas Edward. *Zechariah*, in *The Minor Prophets: An Exegetical & Expository Commentary*. Edited by Thomas Edward McComiskey. Volume 3. Grand Rapids: Baker, 1998.

McConville, J. G. *Deuteronomy*, AOTC. Downers Grove: IVP, 2002.

McCormack, Bruce. *Karl Barth's Critically Realistic Dialectical Theology: Its Genesis and Development 1909-1936*. Oxford: Clarendon Press, 1995.

McGrath, Alister. *Iustitia Dei: A History of the Christian Doctrine of Justification*. third edition. Cambridge: Cambridge University Press, 2005.

McKenzie, John L. 'The Divine Sonship of Israel and the Covenant.' *CBQ* 8 (1946): 320-31.

McKenzie, Steven L. *Covenant*. St. Louis: Chalice Press, 2000.

Metzger, Bruce M. *A Textual Commentary on the Greek New Testament*. Second edition. 1971; Stuttgart: German Bible Society, 2002.

Meyendorff, John. *Byzantine Theology: Historical Trends and Doctrinal Themes*. New York: Fordham University Press, 1983.

Meyers, Carol L. and Eric M. Meyers. *Haggai, Zechariah 1-8*. AB. Volume 25B. New York: Doubleday, 1987.

Milbank, John. *Being Reconciled: Ontology and Pardon*. London: Routledge, 2003.

Milbank, John and Catherine Pickstock. *Truth in Aquinas*. London: Routledge, 2001.

Milgrom, Jacob. *Cult and Conscience: the ASHAM and the Priestly Doctrine of Repentance*. Leiden: Brill, 1976.

________. *Leviticus 1-16*. AB. New York: Doubleday, 1991.

Miller, Patrick D. 'The Beginning of the Psalter.' In *Shape and Shaping of the Psalter*. Edited by J. Clinton McCann, Jr. Sheffield: JSOT Press, 1993, pp. 83-92.

Moberly, R. W. L. *Old Testament Theology: Reading the Hebrew Bible as Christian Scripture*. Grand Rapids: Baker, 2013.

Molnar, Paul. *Divine Freedom and the Doctrine of the Immanent Trinity*. Edinburgh: T & T Clark, 2005.

Moltmann, Jürgen. *The Crucified God*. Philadelphia: Fortress Press, 1993.

________. *The Trinity and Kingdom: The Doctrine of God*. Minneapolis: Fortress, 1993.

Montgomery, J. Michael. 'The Covenant of Redemption in Dispensational Theology.' Th.M. Thesis, Dallas Theological Seminary, 1959.

Moo, Douglas. *The Epistle to the Romans*, NICNT. Grand Rapids: Eerdmans, 1996.

________. *Galatians*. BECNT. Grand Rapids: Baker, 2013.

Moody, Dale. 'The Translation of John 3:16 in the Revised Standard Version.' *JBL* 72 (1952): 213-19.

Moore, G. F. 'The Vulgate Chapter and Numbered Verses In the Hebrew Bible.' *JBL* 12/1 (1893): 73-78.

Moran, William L. 'The Ancient Near Eastern Background of the Love of God in Deuteronomy.' *CBQ* 25 (1963): 77-87.

Motyer, J. Alec. *Isaiah: An Introduction and Commentary*. TOTC. Downers Grove: InterVarsity Press, 1999.

________. *The Prophecy of Isaiah: An Introduction and Commentary*. Downers Grove: InterVarsity Press, 1993

________. 'Stricken for the Transgression of My People.' In *From Heaven He Came and Sought Her: Definite Atonement in Historical, Biblical, Theological, and Pastoral Perspective*. Edited by David Gibson and Jonathan Gibson. Wheaton: Crossway, 2013, pp. 247-66.

Mounce, William D. *Pastoral Epistles*, WBC. Nashville: Thomas Nelson, 2000.

Moyise, Steve and Maarten J. J. Mencken, editors. *Isaiah in the New Testament*. London: T & T Clark, 2007.

Muller, Richard A. *After Calvin: Studies in the Development of a Theological Tradition*. Oxford: Oxford University Press, 2003.

________. 'The Barth Legacy: New Athanasius or Origen Redivivus? A Response to T. F. Torrance.' *The Thomist* 54 (1990): 673-704.

________. *Dictionary of Latin and Greek Theological Terms: Drawn Principally from Protestant Scholastic Theology*. Grand Rapids: Baker, 1986.

________. 'God as Absolute and Relative, Necessary, Free, and Contingent: The *Ad Intra-Ad Extra* Movement of Seventeenth-Century Reformed Language about God.' In *Always Reformed: Essays in Honor of W. Robert Godfrey*. Edited by R. Scott Clark and Joel E. Kim. Escondido: Westminster Seminary California, 2010, pp. 56-73.

________. 'A Note on "Christocentrism" and the Imprudent Use of Such Terminology.' *WTJ* 68 (2006): 253-60.

________. *Post-Reformation Reformed Dogmatics*. 4 volumes. Grand Rapids: Baker, 2003.

________. 'Toward the *Pactum Salutis*: Locating the Origins of a Concept,' *MAJT* 18 (2007): 11-65.

________. *The Unaccommodated Calvin: Studies in the Foundation of a Theological Tradition*. Oxford: Oxford University Press, 2001.

Murphy, Francesca Aran. *God Is Not A Story: Realism Revisited*. Oxford: Oxford University Press, 2007.

Murray, John. *Collected Writings*. 4 volumes. Edinburgh: Banner of Truth, 1977.

Neder, Adam. *Participation in Christ: An Entry into Karl Barth's Church Dogmatics*. Louisville: Westminster John Knox, 2009.

Norcutt, William. *A Compendium of the Covenants*. London: Richard Hett, 1731.

North, Christopher R. *The Suffering Servant in Deutero-Isaiah: An Historical Critical Study*. Second edition. Oxford: Oxford University Press, 1969.

O'Brien, Peter T. *The Epistle to the Philippians*. NIGTC. Grand Rapids: Eerdmans, 1991.

O'Donnell, Laurence R. 'Categorical Rejection *and* Calculated Reformulation: A Demythologizing Reappraisal of Karl Barth's "Mythological" Polemic against the *pactum salutis*.' Unpublished paper, 3 January 2011.

________. 'The Holy Spirit's Role in John Owen's "Covenant of the Mediator" Formulation: A Case Study in Reformed Orthodox Formulations of the *Pactum Salutis*,' *PRJ* 4/1 (2012): 91-134.

________. *The Letter to the Ephesians*. PNTC. Grand Rapids: Eerdmans, 1999.

Olazarán, Jesus. 'En el IV Centenario de un Voto Tridention del Jesuita Alfonso Salmeron sobre la doble justitia.' *Estudios Eclesiasticos* 20 (1946): 211-40.

Oliphint, K. Scott. *God With Us: Divine Condescension and the Attributes of God*. Wheaton: Crossway, 2012.

Ollenburger, Ben C. *The Book of Zechariah: Introduction, Commentary, and Reflections*, NIB. Volume 7. Nashville: Abingdon, 1996.

Oswalt, John C. *The Book of Isaiah*. 2 volumes. NICOT. Grand Rapids: Eerdmans, 1986.

Owen, John. *The Works of John Owen*. Edited by William H. Goold. Edinburgh: T & T Cark, 1862.

Pannenberg, Wolfhart. *Jesus – God and Man*. Philadelphia: Westminster Press, 1975.

________. *Systematic Theology*. 3 volumes. Grand Rapids: Eerdmans, 1993.

Pao, David W. *Acts and the Isaianic New Exodus*. Grand Rapids: Baker, 2000.

Pelikan, Jaroslav. *The Christian Tradition*. Volume 1. Chicago: University of Chicago Press, 1971.

Peppard, M. 'Adopted and Begotten Sons of God: Paul and John on Divine Sonship.' *CBQ* 73/1 (2011): 92-110.

Peter, René. 'L'Imposition des Mains dans L'Ancien Testament.' *VT* 27/1 (1977): 48-55.

Petersen, David L. *Haggai and Zechariah*. OTL. Philadelphia: Westminster, 1984.

Petterson, Anthony R. *Behold Your King: The Hope for the House of David in the Book of Zechariah*. New York: T & T Clark, 2009.

Phan, Peter C., editor. *The Cambridge Companion to the Trinity*. Cambridge: Cambridge University Press, 2011.

Piper, John. *Counted Righteous in Christ: Should We Abandon the Imputation of Christ's Righteousness?* Wheaton: Crossway, 2002.

_________. *The Justification of God: An Exegetical and Theological Study of Romans 9:1-23*. Second edition. Grand Rapids: Baker, 1993.

Plantinga, Jr., Cornelius. 'Social Trinity and Tritheism.' In *Trinity, Incarnation, and Atonement: Philosophical and Theological Essays*. Edited by Ronald J. Feenstra and Cornelius Plantinga, Jr. Notre Dame: University of Notre Dame Press, 1989, pp. 21-47.

_________. 'The Threeness/Oneness Problem of the Trinity,' *CTJ* 23/1 (1988): 37-53.

Powell, Samuel M. *The Trinity in German Thought*. Cambridge: Cambridge University Press, 2001.

Pratt, Richard L. *1 and 2 Chronicles*. Fearn: Mentor, 1998.

Pusey, E. B. *The Minor Prophets: A Commentary*. Volume 2. 1950; Grand Rapids: Baker, 1976.

Rahner, Karl. *The Trinity*. Translated by Joseph Donceel. 1967; New York: Herder & Herder, 2005.

Reardon, Patrick Henry. *Christ in the Psalms*. Chesterton: Conciliar Press, 2000.

Rehnman, Sebastian. 'The Doctrine of God in Reformed Orthodoxy.' In *A Companion to Reformed Orthodoxy*. Edited by Herman Selderhuis. Leiden: Brill, 2013, pp. 384-85.

Reymond, Robert L. *A New Systematic Theology of the Christian Faith*. Second edition. Nashville: Thomas Nelson, 1998.

Ridderbos, Herman. *The Gospel of John*. Grand Rapids: Eerdmans, 1997.

Rijssen, Leonard. *Compendium Theologiae Didactico-Elencticae*. Amsterdam: 1695.

Robertson, O. Palmer. *The Christ of the Covenants*. Phillipsburg: P & R, 1980.

________. 'The Holy Spirit and the Westminster Confession of Faith.' In *The Westminster Confession into the 21st Century*. Volume 1. Edited by J. Ligon Duncan. Fearn: Christian Focus, 2003, pp. 57-100.

Robinson, H. Wheeler. *Corporate Personality in Ancient Israel*. Philadelphia: Fortress, 1964.

Rogerson, J. W. 'The Hebrew Conception of Corporate Personality.' *JTS* 21 (1970): 1-16.

Rosato, Philip. 'Spirit Christology: Ambiguity and Promise.' *Theological Studies* 38 (1977): 423-49.

Rowley, H. H. *The Servant of the Lord and other Essays on the Old Testament*. Second edition. Oxford: Basil Blackwell, 1965.

Russell, Bertrand. *The Problems of Philosophy*. Radford: Wilder Publications, 2008.

Rutherford, Samuel. *The Covenant of Life Opened: Or, a Treatise of the Covenant of Grace*. Edinburgh: Robert Brown, 1654.

Sakenfeld, Katherine Doob. *The Meaning of Hesed in the Hebrew Bible*. Missoula: Scholars Press, 1978.

Sarna, Nahum. *Genesis*, JPSTC. Philadelphia: Jewish Publication Society, 1989.

________. *On the Book of Psalms: Exploring the Prayers of Ancient Israel*. New York: Schocken Books, 1993.

Satterthwaite, Philip. E., Richard S. Hess and Gordon J. Wenham, editors. *The Lord's Anointed: Interpretation of Old Testament Messianic Texts*. Eugene: Wipf & Stock, 1995.

Schilder, Klaas. *Heidelbergsche Catechismus*. 3 volumes. Goes: Oosterbaan & Le Cointre, 1947-51.

Schleiermacher, Friedrich. *The Life of Jesus*. Edited by Jack C. Verheyden. 1864; Philadelphia: Fortress, 1975.

Schreiner, Thomas. *Galatians*. ZECNT. Grand Rapids: Zondervan, 2010.

________. *New Testament Theology: Magnifying God in Christ*. Grand Rapids: Baker, 2008.

________. *Romans*, BECNT. Grand Rapids: Baker, 1998.

Schwartz, Baruch J. 'The Bearing of Sin in the Priestly Literature.' In *Pomegranates and Golden Bells: Studies in Biblical, Jewish, and Near Eastern Ritual, Law, and Literature in Honor of Jacob Milgrom*. Edited by David P. Wright, David Noel Freedman, and Avi Hurvitz. Winona Lake: Eisenbrauns, 1995, pp. 3-21.

Scott, James M. *Adoption as Sons of God: An Exegetical Investigation into the Background of* υἱοθεσία *in the Pauline Corpus*. Tübingen: Mohr Siebeck, 1992.

Sedgwick, Obadiah. *The Bowels of Tender Mercy Sealed in the Everlasting Covenant*. London: Adoniram Byfield, 1661.

Seeburg, Reinhold. *Text-Book of the History of Doctrines*. 2 volumes. Grand Rapids: Baker, 1954.

Shaffern, Robert W. 'The Medieval Theology of Indulgences.' In *Promissory Notes on the Treasury of Merits*, ed. R. N. Swanson. Leiden: Brill, 2006, pp. 11-36.

Shaw, Robert. *An Exposition of the Westminster Confession of Faith*. 1845; Ross-shire: Christian Heritage, 1998.

Shedd, Russell Phillip. *Man in Community: A Study of St. Paul's Application of Old Testament and Early Jewish Conceptions of Human Solidarity*. Grand Rapids: Eerdmans, 1964.

Shepherd, Norman. *The Call of Grace: How the Covenant Illuminates Salvation and Evangelism*. Phillipsburg: P & R, 2000.

Siecienski, A. Edward. *The Filioque: History of a Doctrinal Controversy*. Oxford: Oxford University Press, 2010.

Silva, Moisés. *Philippians*. Second edition. BECNT. Grand Rapids: Baker, 2005.

Smith, Ralph L. *Zechariah*. WBC. Volume 32. Waco: Word, 1984.

Sölle, Dorothee. *Christ the Representative: An Essay in Theology After the 'Death of God.'* London: SCM Press Ltd., 1967.

Son, Sang-Won (Aaron). *Corporate Elements in Pauline Anthropology: A Study of Selected Terms, Idioms, and Concepts in the Light of Paul's Usage and Background.* Rome: Pontifico Instituto Biblico, 2001.

Staniloae, Dumitru. *Theology and Church.* Crestwood: St. Vladimir's Seminary Press, 1980.

Straus, S. A. 'Schilder on the Covenant,' in *Always Obedient: Essays on the Teachings of Dr. Klaas Schilder*, ed. J. Geertsema. Phillipsburg: P & R, 1995, pp. 19-33.

Strehle, Stephen. *Calvinism, Federalism, and Scholasticism: A Study of the Reformed Doctrine of Covenant.* New York: Peter Lang, 1988.

Sullivan, C. Stephen. *The Formulation of the Tridentine Doctrine on Merit.* Washington, DC: Catholic University of America Press, 1959.

Swain, Scott and Michael Allen. 'The Obedience of the Eternal Son.' *IJST* 15/2 (2013): 114-34.

Sweeney, Marvin A. *The Twelve Prophets.* Volume 2. Berit Olam. Collegeville: Liturgical Press, 2000.

Tanner, Kathryn. *Jesus, Humanity and the Trinity: A Brief Systematic Theology.* Minneapolis: Fortress Press, 2001.

Taylor, Mark C. *Erring: A Postmodern A/Theology.* Chicago: University of Chicago Press, 1981.

The Confession of Faith, Larger, and Shorter Catechisms, with the Scripture-proofs at large: Together with the Sum of Saving Knowledge ... Covenants, National and Solemn League; Acknowledgement of Sins, and Engagement to Duties; Directories for Publick and Family Worship; Form of Church Government ... Belfast: James Blow, 1729.

The Manual of Indulgences Being a Collection of Prayers and Good Works, to which the Sovereign Pontiffs Have Attached Holy Indulgences. London: Burns & Oates, 1878.

Thielman, Frank. *Ephesians*. BECNT. Grand Rapids: Baker, 2010.

Thompson, J. A. *Deuteronomy*, TOTC. Downers Grove: IVP, 2008.

Tillich, Paul. *Systematic Theology*. 3 volumes. Chicago: University of Chicago Press, 1951-63.

Torrance, Alan. 'The Trinity,' In *The Cambridge Companion to Karl Barth*. Edited by John Webster. Cambridge: Cambridge University Press, 2000, pp. 72-91.

Torrance, J. B. 'The Concept of Federal Theology—Was Calvin a Federal Theologian?' In *Calvinus Sacrae Scripturae Professor: Calvin as Confessor of Holy Scripture*. Edited by Wilehlm H. Neuser. Grand Rapids: Eerdmans, 1994.

________. 'Covenant or Contract? A Study of the Theological Background of Worship in Seventeenth-Century Scotland,' *SJT* 23 (1970): 51-76.

________. 'Strengths and Weaknesses of the Westminster Theology.' In *The Westminster Confession in the Church Today*. Edited by Alasdair I. C. Heron. Edinburgh: The Saint Andrews Press, 1982.

Torrance, T. F. *Scottish Theology: From John Knox to John McLeod Campbell*. Edinburgh: T & T Clark, 1996.

Toulmin, Joshua. *Memoirs of the Life, Character, Sentiments and Writings of Faustus Socinus*. London: J. Brown, 1777.

Trueman, Carl. 'The Harvest of Reformation Mythology? Patrick Gillespie and the Covenant of Redemption.' In *Scholasticism Reformed: Essays in Honour of Willem J. Van Asselt*. Edited by Maarten Wisse, Marcel Sarot, and Willemein Otten. Leiden: Brill, 2010, pp. 196-214.

Tseng, Shao Kai. 'God's Non-Capricious No: Karl Barth's "Purified Infralapsarianism" in Development 1920-23.' D. Phil. Dissertation, Wycliffe Hall, Oxford University, 2013.

Turretin, Francis. *Institutes of Elenctic Theology*. 3 volumes. Edited by James T. Dennison, Jr. Translated by George Musgrave Giger. Phillipsburg: P & R, 1992-97.

Van Asselt, Willem J. '*Expromissio* or *Fideiussio?* A Seventeenth-Century Theological Debate Between Voetians and Cocceians about the Nature of Christ's Suretyship in Salvation History.' *MAJT* 14 (2003): 37-57.

________. *The Federal Theology of Johannes Cocceius (1603-69).* Leiden: Brill, 2001.

________. 'The Fundamental Meaning of Theology: Archetypal and Ectypal Theology in Seventeenth-Century Reformed Thought,' *WTJ* 64 (2002): 319-35.

________., editor. *Reformed Thought on Freedom: The Concept of Free Choice in Early Modern Reformed Theology.* Grand Rapids: Baker, 2010.

Van Driel, Edwin Christian. *Incarnation Anyway: Arguments for Supralapsarian Christology.* Oxford: Oxford University Press, 2008.

________. 'Karl Barth on the Eternal Existence of Jesus Christ.' *SJT* 60/1 (2007): 45-61.

VanDrunen, David. *Divine Covenants and Moral Order: A Biblical Theology of Natural Law.* Grand Rapids: Eerdmans, 2014.

________. *Natural Law and the Two Kingdoms: A Study in the Development of Reformed Social Thought.* Grand Rapids: Eerdmans, 2010.

________. 'A System of Theology? The Centrality of Covenant for the Westminster Standards.' In *The Pattern of Sound Doctrine: Systematic Theology at the Westminster Seminaries. Essays in Honor of Robert B. Strimple.* Edited by David VanDrunen. Phillipsburg: P & R, 2004, pp. 195-222.

Van Genderen, J. and W. H. Velema. *Concise Reformed Dogmatics.* Phillipsburg: P & R, 1992.

Vanhoozer, Kevin. *Remythologizing Theology: Divine Action, Passion, and Authorship.* Cambridge: Cambridge University Press, 2010.

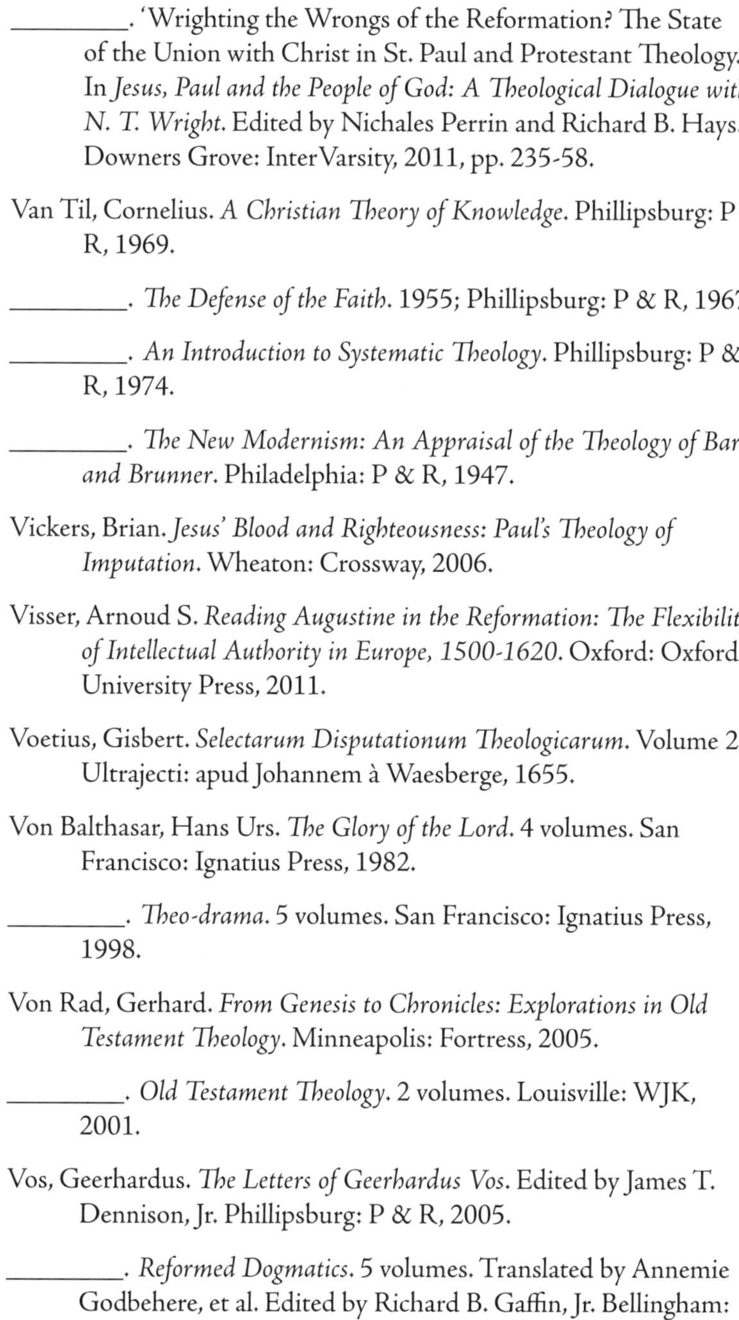

_________. 'Wrighting the Wrongs of the Reformation? The State of the Union with Christ in St. Paul and Protestant Theology.' In *Jesus, Paul and the People of God: A Theological Dialogue with N. T. Wright*. Edited by Nichales Perrin and Richard B. Hays. Downers Grove: InterVarsity, 2011, pp. 235-58.

Van Til, Cornelius. *A Christian Theory of Knowledge*. Phillipsburg: P & R, 1969.

_________. *The Defense of the Faith*. 1955; Phillipsburg: P & R, 1967.

_________. *An Introduction to Systematic Theology*. Phillipsburg: P & R, 1974.

_________. *The New Modernism: An Appraisal of the Theology of Barth and Brunner*. Philadelphia: P & R, 1947.

Vickers, Brian. *Jesus' Blood and Righteousness: Paul's Theology of Imputation*. Wheaton: Crossway, 2006.

Visser, Arnoud S. *Reading Augustine in the Reformation: The Flexibility of Intellectual Authority in Europe, 1500-1620*. Oxford: Oxford University Press, 2011.

Voetius, Gisbert. *Selectarum Disputationum Theologicarum*. Volume 2. Ultrajecti: apud Johannem à Waesberge, 1655.

Von Balthasar, Hans Urs. *The Glory of the Lord*. 4 volumes. San Francisco: Ignatius Press, 1982.

_________. *Theo-drama*. 5 volumes. San Francisco: Ignatius Press, 1998.

Von Rad, Gerhard. *From Genesis to Chronicles: Explorations in Old Testament Theology*. Minneapolis: Fortress, 2005.

_________. *Old Testament Theology*. 2 volumes. Louisville: WJK, 2001.

Vos, Geerhardus. *The Letters of Geerhardus Vos*. Edited by James T. Dennison, Jr. Phillipsburg: P & R, 2005.

_________. *Reformed Dogmatics*. 5 volumes. Translated by Annemie Godbehere, et al. Edited by Richard B. Gaffin, Jr. Bellingham: Logos Bible Software, 2012-.

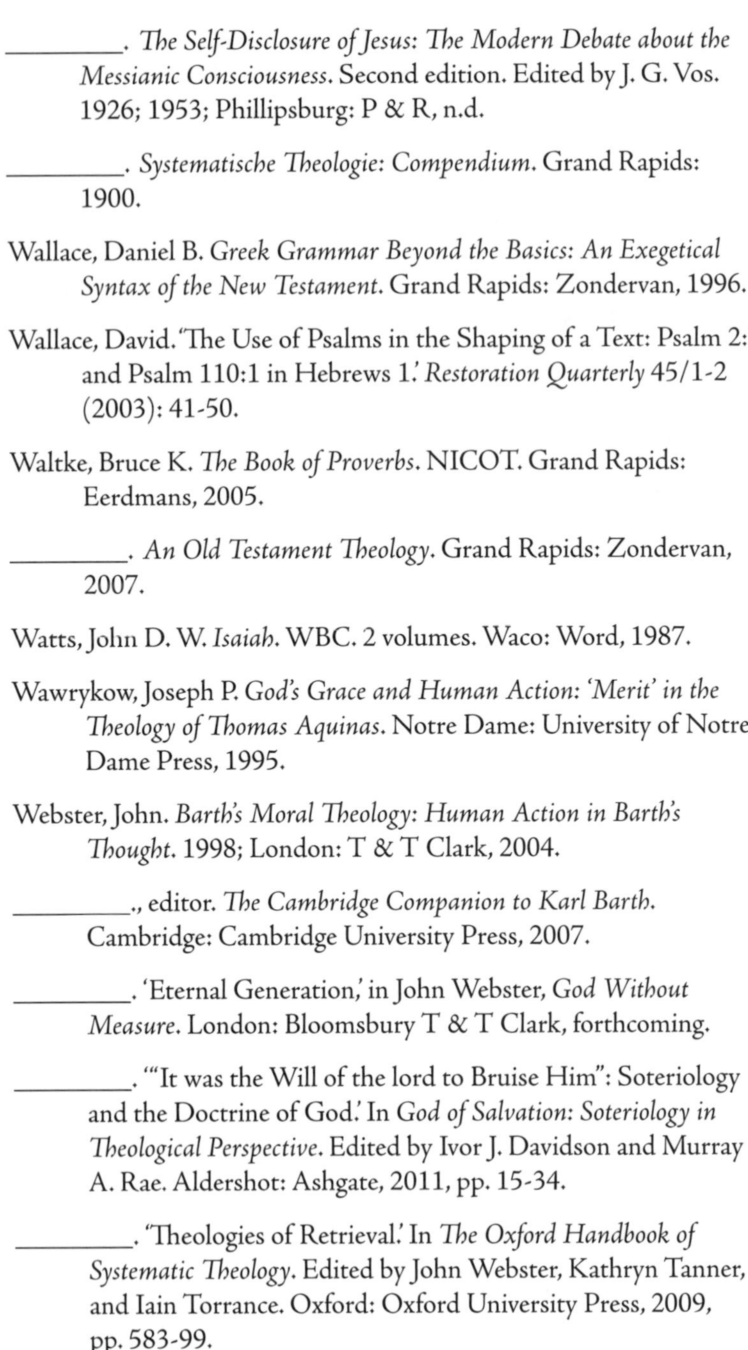

________. *The Self-Disclosure of Jesus: The Modern Debate about the Messianic Consciousness*. Second edition. Edited by J. G. Vos. 1926; 1953; Phillipsburg: P & R, n.d.

________. *Systematische Theologie: Compendium*. Grand Rapids: 1900.

Wallace, Daniel B. *Greek Grammar Beyond the Basics: An Exegetical Syntax of the New Testament*. Grand Rapids: Zondervan, 1996.

Wallace, David. 'The Use of Psalms in the Shaping of a Text: Psalm 2:7 and Psalm 110:1 in Hebrews 1.' *Restoration Quarterly* 45/1-2 (2003): 41-50.

Waltke, Bruce K. *The Book of Proverbs*. NICOT. Grand Rapids: Eerdmans, 2005.

________. *An Old Testament Theology*. Grand Rapids: Zondervan, 2007.

Watts, John D. W. *Isaiah*. WBC. 2 volumes. Waco: Word, 1987.

Wawrykow, Joseph P. *God's Grace and Human Action: 'Merit' in the Theology of Thomas Aquinas*. Notre Dame: University of Notre Dame Press, 1995.

Webster, John. *Barth's Moral Theology: Human Action in Barth's Thought*. 1998; London: T & T Clark, 2004.

________., editor. *The Cambridge Companion to Karl Barth*. Cambridge: Cambridge University Press, 2007.

________. 'Eternal Generation,' in John Webster, *God Without Measure*. London: Bloomsbury T & T Clark, forthcoming.

________. '"It was the Will of the lord to Bruise Him": Soteriology and the Doctrine of God.' In *God of Salvation: Soteriology in Theological Perspective*. Edited by Ivor J. Davidson and Murray A. Rae. Aldershot: Ashgate, 2011, pp. 15-34.

________. 'Theologies of Retrieval.' In *The Oxford Handbook of Systematic Theology*. Edited by John Webster, Kathryn Tanner, and Iain Torrance. Oxford: Oxford University Press, 2009, pp. 583-99.

Weinandy, Thomas. *The Father's Spirit of Sonship: Reconceiving the Trinity*. Eugene: Wipf & Stock, 1995.

Weinfeld, Moshe. 'The Ban on the Canaanites in the Biblical Codes and Its Historical Development.' In *History and Traditions of Early Israel*. Edited by André Lemaire and Benedikt Otzen. Leiden: Brill, 1993, pp. 142-60.

Wengert, Timothy J. 'Philip Melanchthon and John Calvin Against Andreas Osiander: Coming to Terms with Forensic Justification.' In *Calvin and Luther: The Continuing Relationship*. Edited by R. Ward Holder. Göttingen: Vandenhoeck & Ruprecht, 2013, pp. 63-87.

Wenham, Gordon J. *The Book of Leviticus*. NICOT. Grand Rapids: Eerdmans, 1979.

Westminster Confession of Faith. Glasgow: Free Presbyterian Publications, 1995.

Westphal, Merold. *Overcoming Onto-Theology: Toward a Postmodern Christian Faith*. New York: Fordham University Press, 2001.

White, Thomas Joseph. 'Intra-Trinitarian Obedience and Nicene-Chalcedonian Christology.' *Nova et Vera* 6/2 (2008): 377-402.

Whybray, R. N. *Thanksgiving for a Liberated Prophet*. Sheffield: JSOT Press, 1978.

Wilkins, Jeremy Daniel. 'Emanatio Intelligibilis in Deo: A Study of the Horizon of Development of Thomas Aquinas's Trinitarian Theology.' Ph.D. Dissertation, Boston College, 2004.

Willard, Samuel. *The Doctrine of the Covenant of Redemption*. Boston: Benjamin Harris, 1693.

Williams, Carol A. 'The Decree of Redemption is in Effect a Covenant: David Dickson and the Covenant of Redemption.' Ph. D. Dissertation, Calvin Theological Seminary, 2005.

Williams, Michael. 'Adam and Merit.' *Presbyterion* 35/2 (2009): 87-94.

Williamson, Paul R. *Sealed with an Oath: Covenant in God's Unfolding Purpose*. Downers Grove: IVP, 2007.

Wilson, Gerald Henry. *The Editing of the Hebrew Psalter*. Atlanta: SBL, 1985.

Witsius, Herman. *Animadversiones Irenicae*. Utrecht: 1696.

_________. *Conciliatory, or Irenical Animadversions on the Controversies agitated in Britain, under the Unhappy Names of Antinomians and Neonomians*. Translated by Thomas Bell. Glasgow: W. Lang, 1807.

_________. *Economy of the Covenants Between God and Man: Comprehending a Complete Body of Divinity*. Translated by William Crookshank. 1822; Escondido: Den Dulk Foundation, 1990.

_________. *Sacred Dissertations, on What is Commonly Called the Apostles' Creed*. 2 volumes. Translated by Donald Fraser. 1823; Escondido: Den Dulk Foundation, 1993.

Wolterstorff, Nicholas. *Art in Action: Toward a Christian Aesthetic*. Grand Rapids: Eerdmans, 1980.

Wong, David Wai-Sing. 'The Covenant Theology of John Owen.' Ph.D Dissertation, Westminster Theological Seminary, 1998.

Woo, Byunghoon. 'The *Pactum Salutis* in the Theologies of Witsius, Owen, Dickson, Goodwin, and Cocceius,' Ph.D. Dissertation, Calvin Theological Seminary, 2015.

Woudstra, Marten H. *The Book of Joshua*. NICOT. Grand Rapids: Eerdmans, 1981.

Wright, Christopher J. H. *Knowing the Holy Spirit*. Downers Grove: InterVarsity Press, 2006.

Wright, David P. 'The Gesture of Hand Placement in the Hebrew Bible and Hittite Literature.' *Journal of the American Oriental Society* 106/3 (1986): 432-46.

Wright, N. T. *Climax of the Covenant: Christ and the Law in Pauline Theology*. Minneapolis: Fortress, 1991.

_________. *Justification: God's Plan and Paul's Vision*. Downers Grove: InterVarsity Press, 2009.

_________. 'Justification: Yesterday, Today, Forever,' *JETS* 54/1 (2001): 49-63.

_________. *The Letter to the Romans: Introduction, Commentary, and Reflections*. NIB. Volume 10. Nashville: Abingdon, 2002.

_________. *The New Testament and the People of God*. Philadelphia: Fortress, 1992.

_________. 'On Becoming the Righteousness of God,' in N. T. Wright, *Pauline Perspectives: Essays on Paul, 1978-2013*. Minneapolis: Fortress, 2013, pp. 68-76.

_________. *Paul and the Faithfulness of God*. Parts III & IV. Minneapolis: Fortress, 2013.

_________. *The Resurrection of the Son of God*. Philadelphia: Fortress, 2004.

_________. *What Saint Paul Really Said: Was Paul of Tarsus the Real Founder of Christianity?* Grand Rapids: Eerdmans, 1997.

Wu, Kuo-An. 'The Concept of History in the Theology of Karl Barth.' Ph. D. Dissertation, University of Edinburgh, 2011.

Yazawa, Reita. 'Covenant of Redemption in the Theology of Jonathan Edwards: The Nexus Between the Immanent and the Economic Trinity,' Ph.D. Diss., Calvin Theological Seminary, 2013.

Yearly, Lee H. 'St. Thomas Aquinas on Providence and Predestination,' *ATR* 49 (1967): 409-27.

Young, E. J. *The Book of Isaiah*. 3 volumes. NICOT. Grand Rapids: Eerdmans, 1965.

Zanchi, Girolamo. *De Religione Fides – Confession of Christian Religion*. 2 volumes. Edited by Luca Baschera and Christian Moser. Leiden: Brill, 2007.

Zubiri, Xavier. *Nature, History, God*. Translated by Thomas B. Fowler, Jr. Washington, DC: University Press of America, 1981.

~: SUBJECT INDEX :~

K

L

M

~ SCRIPTURE INDEX ~